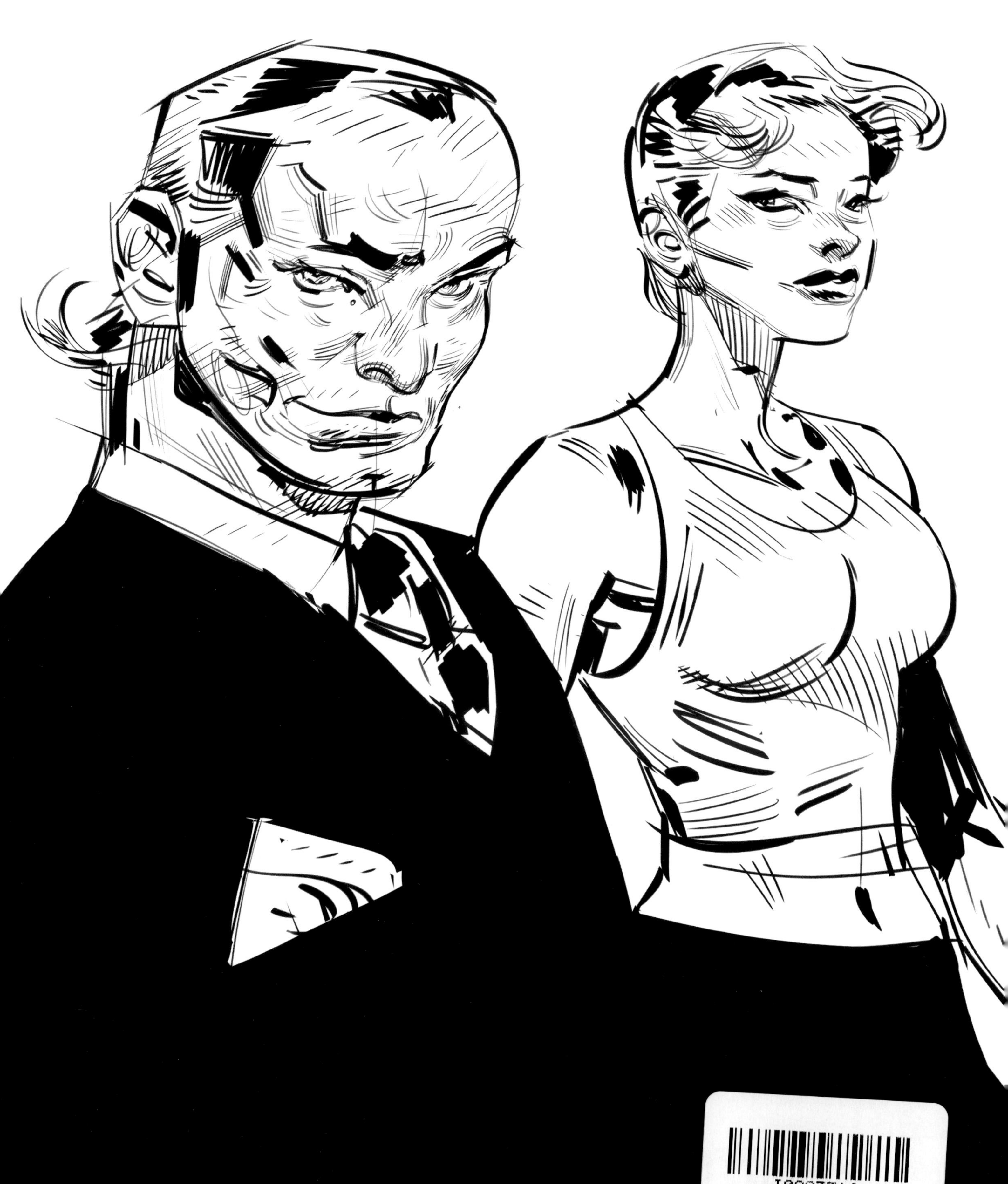

Framed Drawing Techniques:
Mastering Ballpoint Pen, Graphite Pencil, and Digital Techniques for Visual Storytelling

Book Design: Marcos Mateu-Mestre
Editor: Teena Apeles
Book Layout: Christopher J. De La Rosa

Published by
Design Studio Press
Website: www.designstudiopress.com
E-mail: info@designstudiopress.com

Printed in China
First edition, July 2019

10 9 8 7 6 5 4 3 2

ISBN: 9781624650406

Library of Congress Control Number: 2019936614

FSC
www.fsc.org
MIX
Paper from responsible sources
FSC® C012521

MARCOS MATEU-MESTRE

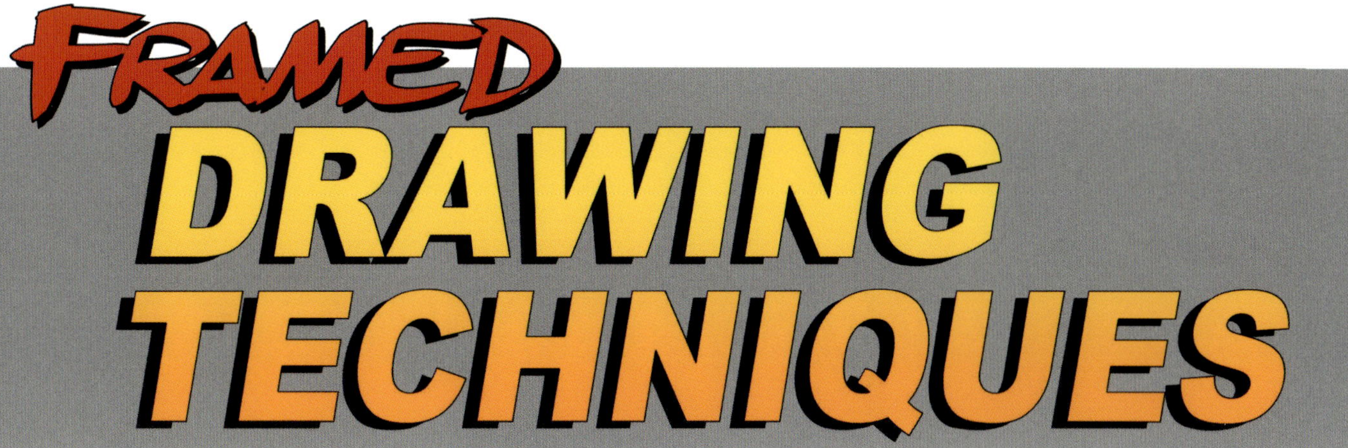

FRAMED DRAWING TECHNIQUES

MASTERING BALLPOINT PEN, GRAPHITE PENCIL, AND DIGITAL TECHNIQUES FOR VISUAL STORYTELLING

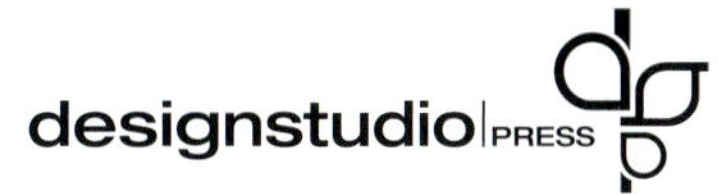

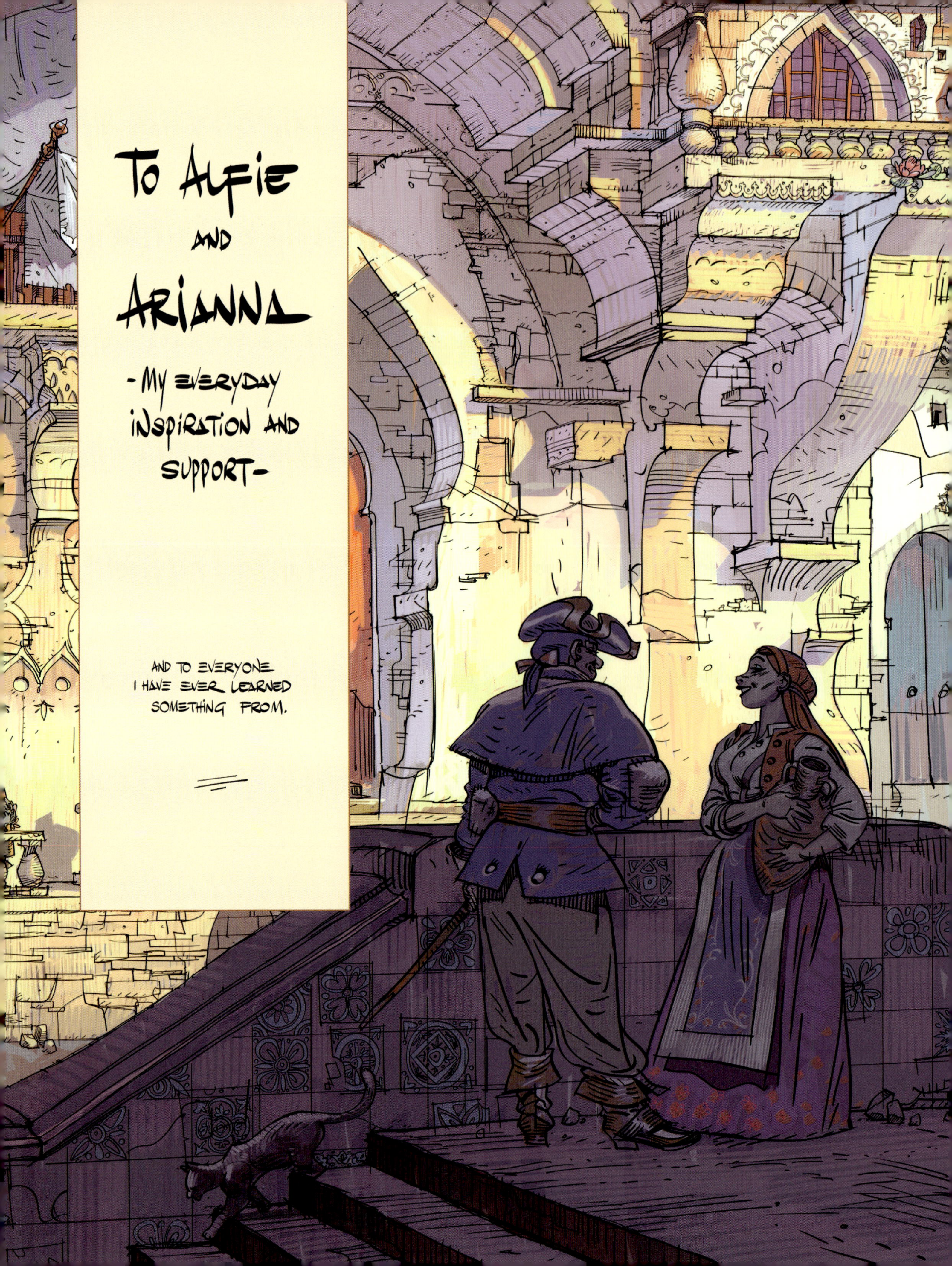
To Alfie
and
Arianna
- My everyday inspiration and support -
And to everyone I have ever learned something from.

TABLE OF CONTENTS

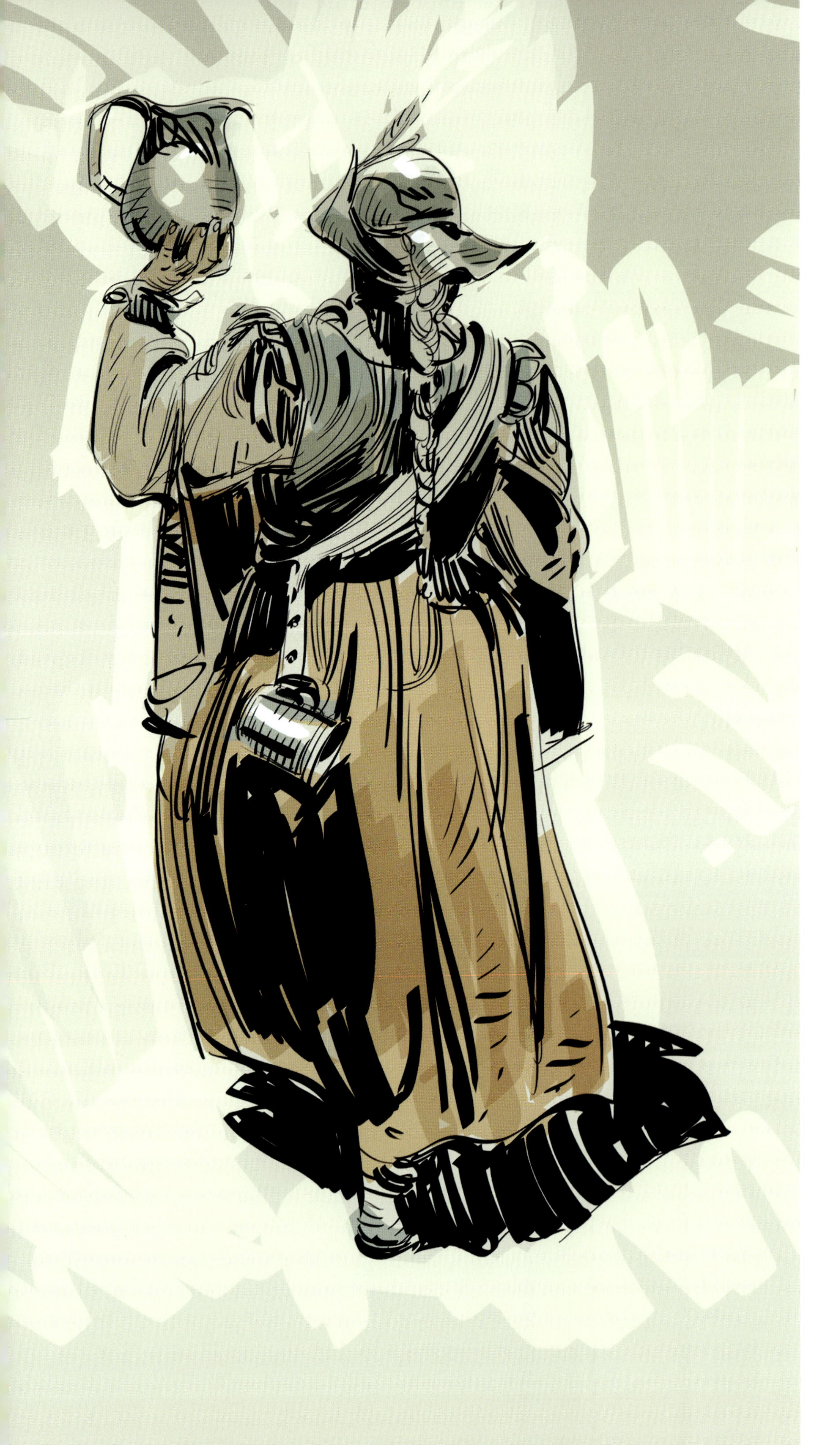

MY PARENTS AND MY SISTER

I owe them eternal gratitude. My mother, Margalida, who came from a long line of artists, loved and understood stories and characters, transferring to me her passion for the art of drawing, comics, and film. She always had a clear vision about anything she would take on, art-related or not; she would see the final result in her mind beforehand, and would find the way to get there either by traditional means or by coming up with alternative ways while thinking totally outside the box.

Most of what my sister, Carme, and I learned of perspective was through our father, Joan, a teacher of perspective himself amongst other talents. Beyond the practical knowledge, he also gave us sharp instincts and a sense of commitment through his creative example.

When drawing technical pieces, he sometimes would use rulers, yet a lot of the time he would work freehand. And I remember he worked those pencils in such a beautiful way that whether the line was curved, straight, or combined, they would just dance across the paper elegantly.

One of my earliest childhood memories was when my father brought some freelance work home, a perspective drawing of buildings. He had a long drawing board on which he laid out the roll of drawing paper and as usual he would give me some space at the end of the table so I could do my own drawings right beside him.

At some point that day I paused on my drawing to watch him work. I remember him drawing a line, freehand; he was holding his pencil in such a gracious, effortless, and weightless way. I thought, *If this is what you can do with a pencil, then drawing has got to be one of the most beautiful things a person can ever attempt to do.*

Growing up with my sister was also a very insightful experience, the extremely talented artist she is. We had many conversations and shared many points of view and opinions on visual art and art in general. Always a very generous person, through her art courses she helped to put many artistic careers in motion.

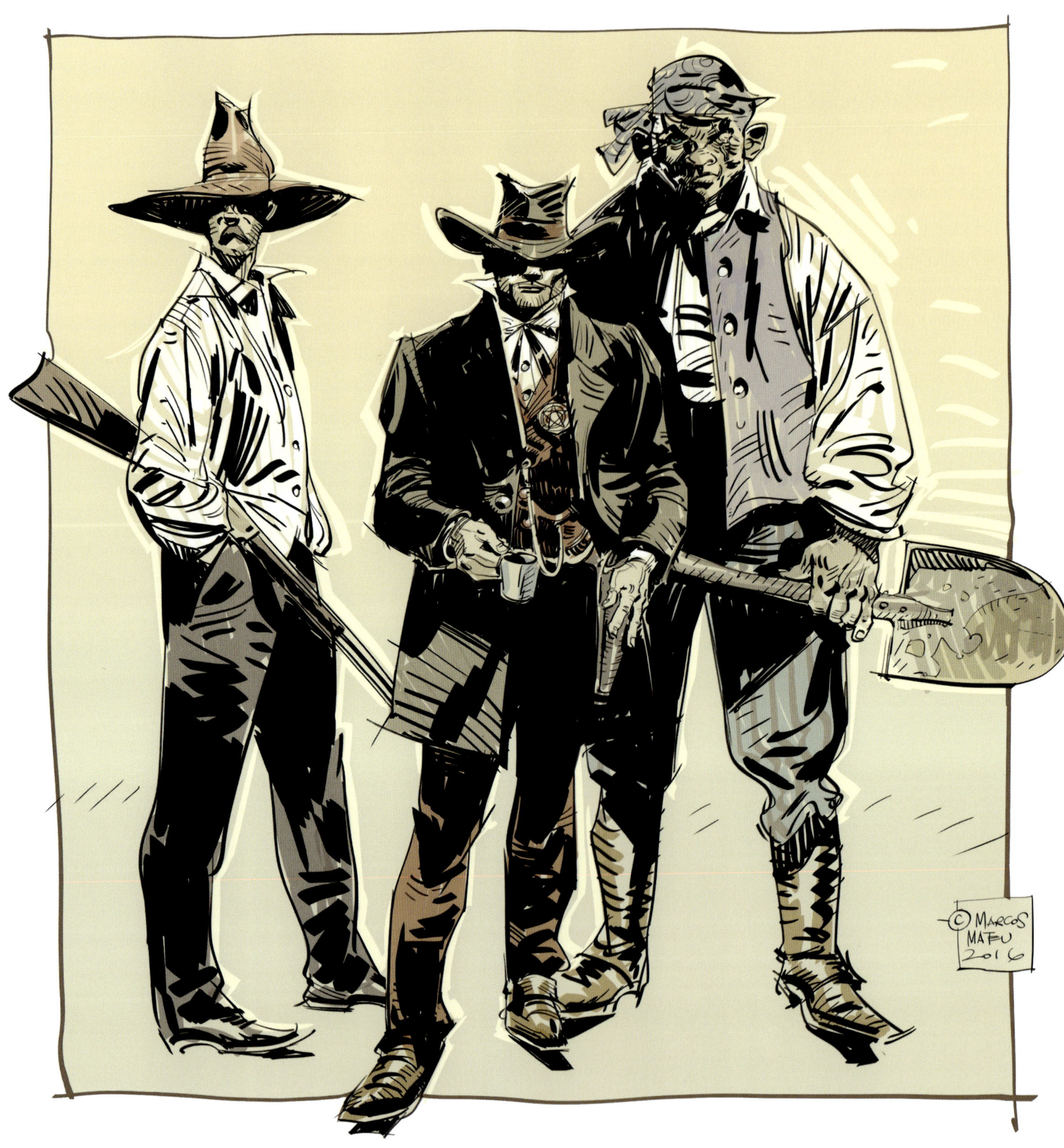
© MARCOS MATEU 2016

SOME GENERAL THOUGHTS ON DRAWING

On bees (and dogs).

We are definitely so lucky.

As creative-minded people, our lives are about playing for a living and **playing with a point of view and a passion.** As artists, we are offered a clear channel to express our own perception of reality—how we see things, the expression of who we are—through our work.

Whether in childhood or adulthood, at some point we start becoming aware that things are not necessarily as they appear to be at first glance. This can happen because of a special experience that triggers such awareness or as a result of a gradual process. For instance, we learn that a drawing goes well beyond the actual marks we put on paper (as important as these are). It's more about its **meaning and purpose**: about the world, the ideas, concepts, and emotions represented in the drawing and expressed through it.

When we draw a character, a landscape, or a general environment, we are not just drawing the thing itself, its physical state, we are, in fact, drawing a moment in the story: the action, happiness, anger, suspense, comedy, innocence, confusion, intimacy, and so many et ceteras. For this, we use a number of **visual devices**, such as lighting, composition, and facial and body expressions. We weigh the relative visual importance of one element versus another within a shot, make choices about brushstrokes (more or less smooth, broken, or dynamic), and consider how all images and panels play in continuity, one after the other. When we draw, it's about these **layers of emotions** and these **story moments** we represent in the imagery, which we create with a meaning and a purpose.

Being aware of these invisible layers gives us the opportunity to tell stories in a really compelling way. I sometimes think of it as the way bees see things—or the way dogs hear things, for that matter—compared to the way humans do. **Bees see the world differently.** They have the capacity to see ultraviolet light, allowing them to perceive more colors and patterns—layers of reality—than we can. This is the same case with dogs and their ability to hear sounds that we can't. These layers are invisible (and inaudible) to us yet are part of our reality.

Using **visual devices** such as the ones mentioned earlier, we manage to represent other types **of invisible layers of the reality** our characters are immersed in, going beyond the immediate visual appearance of things and going for **the essence of what these images actually represent and how they affect us.**

Taking the challenge

We are all imaginative, creative people: artists, scientists, bricklayers, astronauts, and newsstand vendors, anyone who enjoys and identifies with their line of work. The moment we take our work as an opportunity to express our vision of things, the output will be the product of creativity. It really isn't so much about what we do, but what type of experience we turn it into.

Working as a vendor at a street stall may at times be a monotonous activity, yet it can also be seen as an opportunity to interact with other people, make their daily trip to the stand a more fun and interesting experience, or to rearrange the items on the racks in a way that feels more appealing and exciting to the client. It also is a chance to learn how to deal with people in productive ways, ways that could be applied later on in a new job or business endeavor, if that's the desire.

If we intend to remain excited by life and the ability to communicate this excitement to others, we must not get comfortable or bored in our ways. If we get bored, we will bore people around us. In my first book, ***Framed Ink***, I wrote that we can only give what we have. Getting out of one's comfort zone and exploring the "out there" is a must.

One of the ways to do that is for us to routinely train in different art techniques and get to be as proficient in them as possible. That way we understand how to create and support our drawings, the actual physical representation of these stories and emotions on paper. The more we develop a technique, the more we can then forget about its more mechanical aspect and focus on the big game, the general strategies we follow in order to draw a story.

It really isn't so much about what we do, but what type of experience we turn it into.

Setting a destination

To get on the right track it is important to first **set up specific, practical goals.** They could include any of these: drawing anatomy, learning perspective, inking light and shadow, mastering facial expressions, or making things look dynamic. You could get even more specific with your goals depending on the project at hand: drawing airplanes, depicting sharks from different angles, or convincingly representing the smoke of an explosion. Then study and practice, study and practice until you possess the technical knowledge to reach those goals.

As you accomplish each, you will be able to resolve more artistic issues with relative ease at any given time. **Then move forward, take on new challenges, and try to leave no stone unturned.** Don't give up on anything until you have reached the furthest point you could reach with it for now, and then get ready to improve further.

To me the right attitude is to **always keep an avid eye on our goals**, the future ahead. As artists, we can always improve things if we keep practicing and trying to find answers to each and every question posed through our own work, as well as (good) outside influences and advice.

Turning walls into staircases

I remember when I decided to put a portfolio together and leave my hometown of Mallorca, Spain, to try my professional luck abroad. It all felt like a gigantic step for me, a gamble, all on one card.

I was preparing my portfolio for a long time, and then when I was done, I postponed the trip to work on it some more. And then I started all over again, and then again. I thought, *This is a one-shot deal, I better get this perfect.* But I could never find the right moment to get on a plane and go. A friend of mine observed all this and told me, "Why don't you just buy a ticket, go there, feel the place out a bit, and make some contacts. Then you can come back home with a better sense of what's going on, finish your portfolio, and then go again to try to get a job?"

The moment she said that, this enormous goal became much easier to confront, by facing incrementally, step by step. **All of a sudden, the wall became a staircase.** So I left home, took my portfolio, and I'm glad to say I found work on that first trip; that hypothetical second one was never necessary.

The point is, one way or another, this whole journey as an artist should be approached one step at a time. It's necessary to look toward the future eager to learn and to be better every day, **while still being excited to be at the place we currently are**, because it simply is a better place than the one we used to be at before.

It's necessary to look toward the future eager to learn and to be better every day, while still being excited to be at the place we currently are, because it simply is a better place than the one we used to be at before.

Developing an analytical mind

When constantly drawing it is not unusual to have occasions when we accidentally encounter success: like capturing a certain body pose in a convincing way as we had never done before, or that very special/meaningful expression in a character's eyes we previously never managed to achieve, or a way to represent appealing hair. It is important then to be determined to turn that "happy accident" into something we can control at will by systematically analyzing it, repeating it, thinking about it, and practicing it again until we manage to control that (originally) random occurrence, so that it becomes something that we can repeat any time we want.

This requires developing an analytical mind: getting to know why things are a certain way or cause a certain impression or emotional response by digging into them, dissecting them, and performing a full autopsy of them.

I have always had a hard time letting go of something, artistically speaking, before getting to the point that I believed I had a good understanding of it, a sense of that challenge having been finally resolved and now an integrated part of my system. It's like when we quickly browse through images (drawings, paintings, photographs) that our social media feeds are so packed with, or maybe a glance at an interesting, compelling detail as we walk past a location (a street corner, a storefront window, a certain arrangement within a patch of trees by a countryside road).

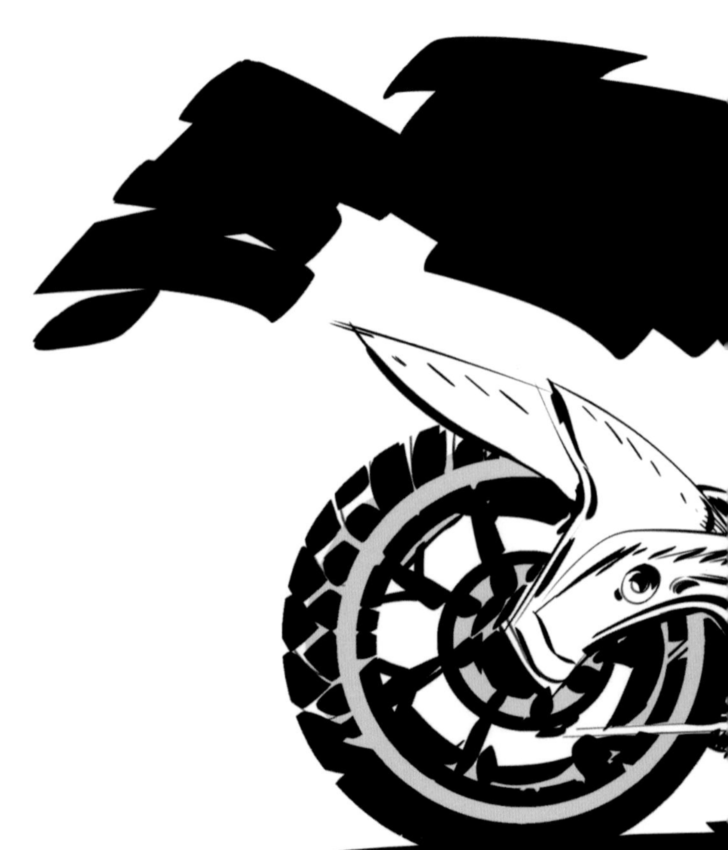

Dive into anything that motivates you enough to question, and don't let go. And when you find an answer to a question, add it to your always-growing "library of solutions."

There are moments here and there that I get an impression about an image I just briefly saw, whether pleasurable or dramatic, purposely dull, or something somehow special, **something that seems to tell a story** to me.

At that point I always have to go back and analyze why I got that impression. What is the secret to what makes that image special in a certain way, how did that moment manage to communicate that special emotion to me at a brief glance? Was it because of how light worked on it, creating harsh contrasts or rather a very flat feel to it? Is it because of the contrasting sizes of the elements in it? How things keep a visual balance or are arranged in dramatic diagonals? The quality and temperature of the colors? A fascinating play of reflections on a glass?

And then I spend as much time as I need diving into it and trying to understand. It's as if every one of these opportunities of acquiring new knowledge I would pass on would become a black hole in my rational library of awareness and understanding of how images work. If I were too lazy to go back for a few seconds to that particular image and analyze it, then I might also let the next time go and then the following and so on, and soon enough my growth as a visual artist would not be the same anymore.

I always think it is important to take on each and every challenge, to dive into anything that motivates you enough to question, and don't let go. And when you find an answer to a question, add it to your always-growing "library of solutions." In many ways, building this library can be fundamental in our trade, where we can pull from a number of previous experiences and potential solutions that we can use as a starting point in a new piece of work.

Whatever got any of us started in this field, once on this boat, we as artists will always find the time to think about drawing, practice drawing, read a book on art, and admire a painting. This interest might go from simple curiosity to serious enthusiasm and a constant need-to-do. It pushes us to explore, think, and get better at our craft every day. It's what leads us to observe things around us in a way that we can digest and then recycle or represent in a visual piece that tells us and others our point of view on things, how we see them, and what we think is important and what is not.

Albert Einstein said, **"Energy cannot be created or destroyed, it can only be changed from one form to another."** I believe the reality around us is here for us to do something with, take that energy and transform it into other (positive) things.

The experience of drawing

I started this introduction talking about how very lucky I believe we are. As kids, most people draw quite regularly. For some reason a high percentage seem to leave this behind as they come of age. I think that people who keep being creative past adolescence are the ones who keep believing dreaming is not only healthy, but that it puts us in touch with reality a lot more than we think sometimes. It's about the belief that there has got to be more than meets the eye.

Let's keep being the bees we were talking about, and let's keep enjoying the vast range of additional layers of reality that we know are there and turn/recycle them into something that will be on paper for a long time, new dots to be connected in this fascinating fabric in which we are immersed.

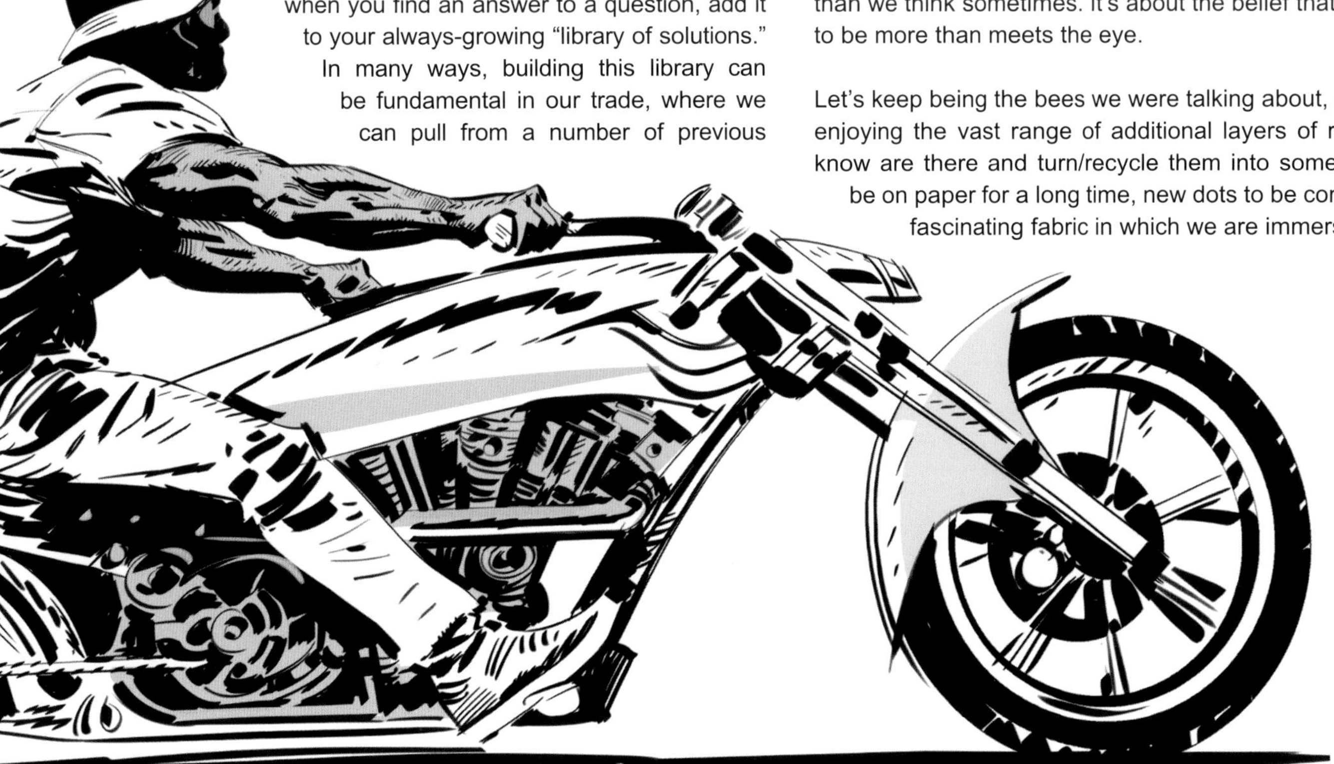

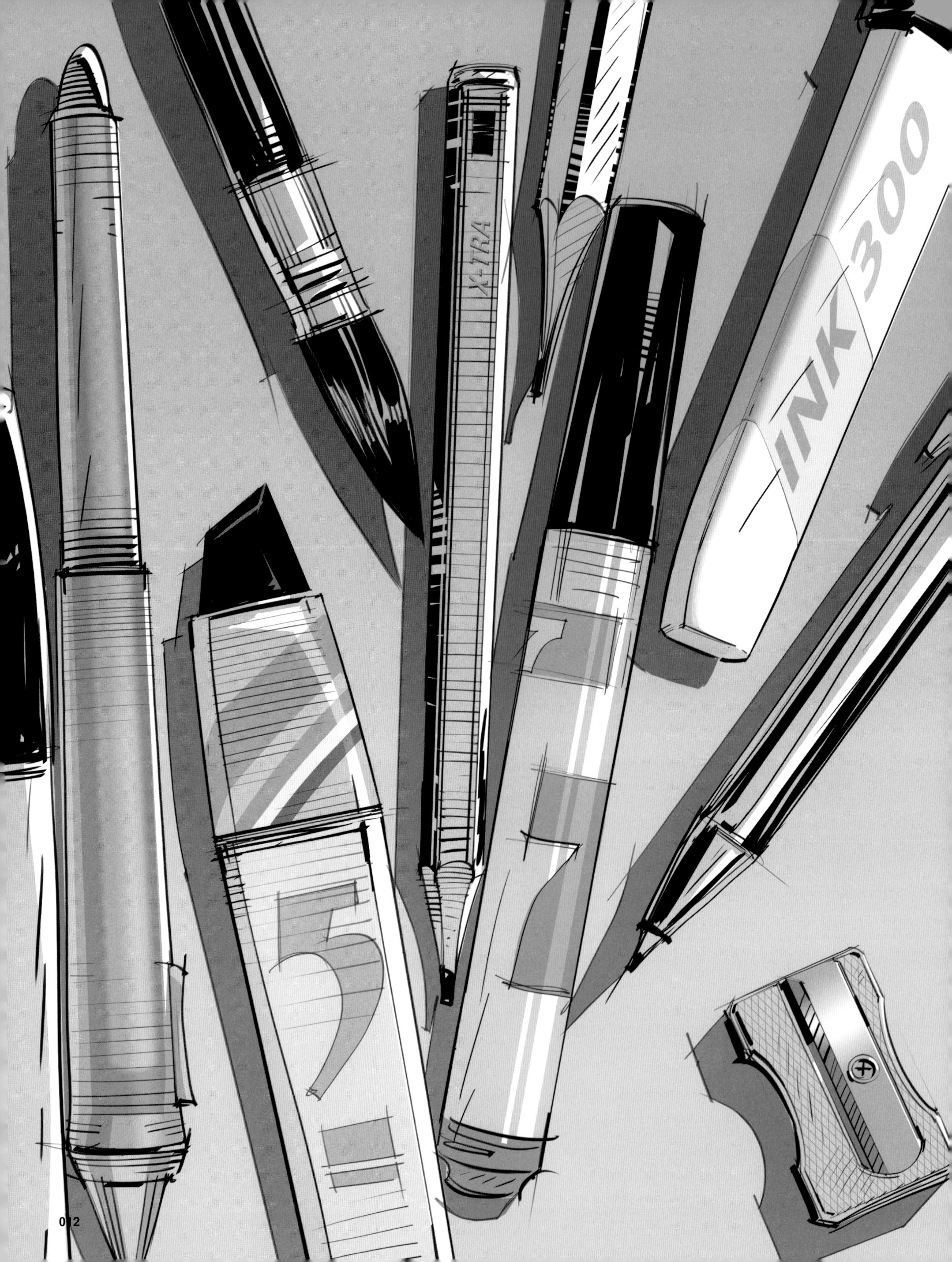
X-TRA
INK 300
5
7

TOOLS OF THE TRADE

Ball Pen

One of the things that makes our trade so personal and exciting is that the vehicle we use to communicate our emotions—the physical laying of lines, shapes, masses of ink, etc., themselves—has so much potential for beauty, and passion beyond its ultimate meaning as part of the story we are trying to tell.

The number of techniques we can use to put our artistic visions on paper has been greatly augmented in the last decades with the appearance of all things digital. Whether by imitating the good old traditional ways, or by offering completely new looks, they offer opportunities to experiment with, add to, or combine the means already available to us.

Given the fact that part of these new digital techniques focus on imitating traditional skills, the training, practice, and use of original, artisanal tools first are always recommended. The better we know and understand the real feel and subtleties of building an image from square one with a pen, pencil, brush, marker, and so forth, the richer our scope of options will become and the more proficient we will be at understanding the digital media and the things we can do with it. The more we know the more angles we see the same idea from, the more skills and abilities we develop as artists, the more dots we will be able to connect, and the more solid our work will be.

In the old days, when artwork was produced for commercial (printing) purposes, a lot of manual editing was or could be done: individual panels were replaced by cutting and pasting by hand and using Wite-Out on undesired ink areas. Nowadays editing can be done digitally after scanning the piece.

While I executed the traditional artwork in this book with ball pen and graphite (see specific tools below), different levels of editing were applied to my drawings. On the pages that follow, I explain in great detail how I used digital editing tools to finesse my work, and how to effectively apply them to your own.

Let's now take a look at the process and a number of solutions these various approaches have to offer.

Graphite pencils (different grades)*: Staedtler Mars Lumograph and Faber-Castell 9000*

Ball pens*: Daiso No. 76 0.7 mm ballpoint pen (blue) and Pilot Better ballpoint pen, fine point (black) Mars Plastic Eraser*

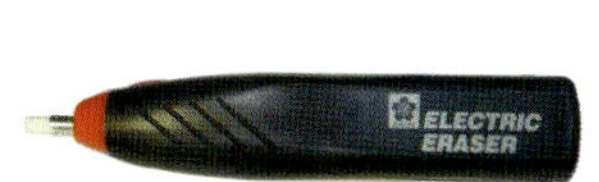

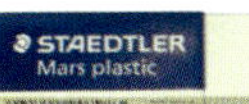

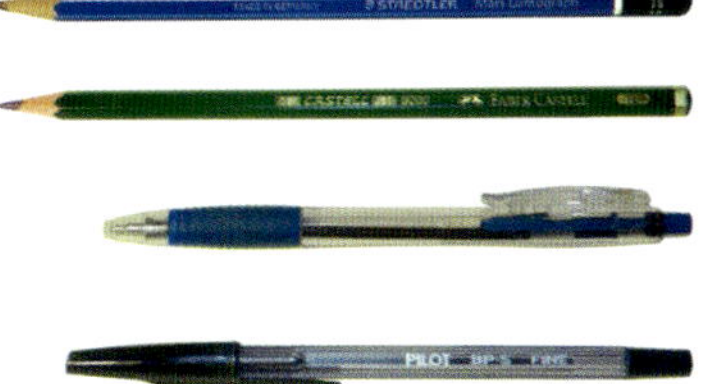

Tablet*: Cintiq pen tablet*

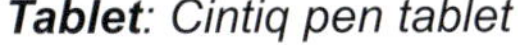

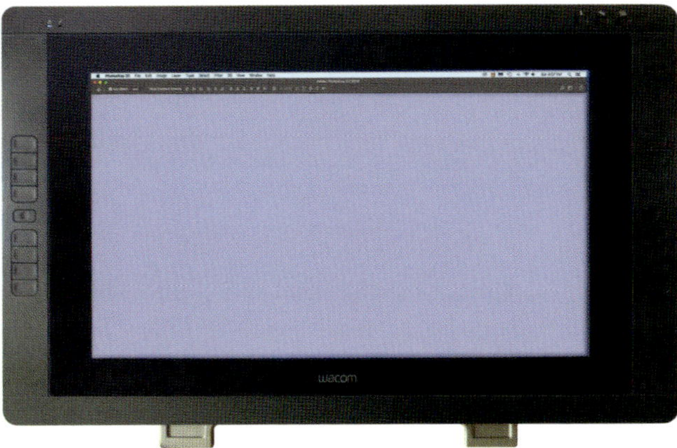

1

THE BALLPOINT PEN

It happened in Little Tokyo. Although it is easy to think of the ballpoint pen as only a tool of convenience, it is a device that can deliver unexpected levels of rich and interesting levels of line quality. From the most generic pen to the best brands in the market, it really is important to try a good number of them before starting a drawing, if time permits. The difference of line quality can vary a lot, and paying more money for a pen does not necessarily guarantee the line quality and/or results that you have in mind, especially depending on your artistic need of the moment and personal taste. To create the examples shown in this chapter I have used mainly two brands.

I remember once I had been looking for the "right quality pen" for a job, one that would offer me the softness, fluidity, and versatility that would somehow resemble a pencil, with the possibility of graphic and interesting differences in the flow of ink in one single stroke depending on the pressure and the angle of application. All that I had been trying at that point were actual brand names, but they were still too even and straightforward in the laying of the line, for my taste. With all that in mind, one day I was at a Japanese restaurant, happily eating my tempura. Little did I know, the answer would soon be on its way with the check.

The pen that came with it was really generic, but, boy, it felt nice. I could have drawn all day with that. So I talked to every waiter and manager available in the place until someone said where it cam from: Daiso, a Japanese chain store that sells a wide variety of goods at low prices.

I took a picture of the pen as reference, but the restaurant staff generously offered to give it to me so that I could get the exact same one at the shop. Indeed some of the pieces in this book are drawn with that type of pen, while for others I used a Pilot BP-S Fine Point, depending on the drawing.

So not only did I get introduced to a great pen—DAISO's No. 76 0.7 mm ballpoint pen—the food was also amazing.

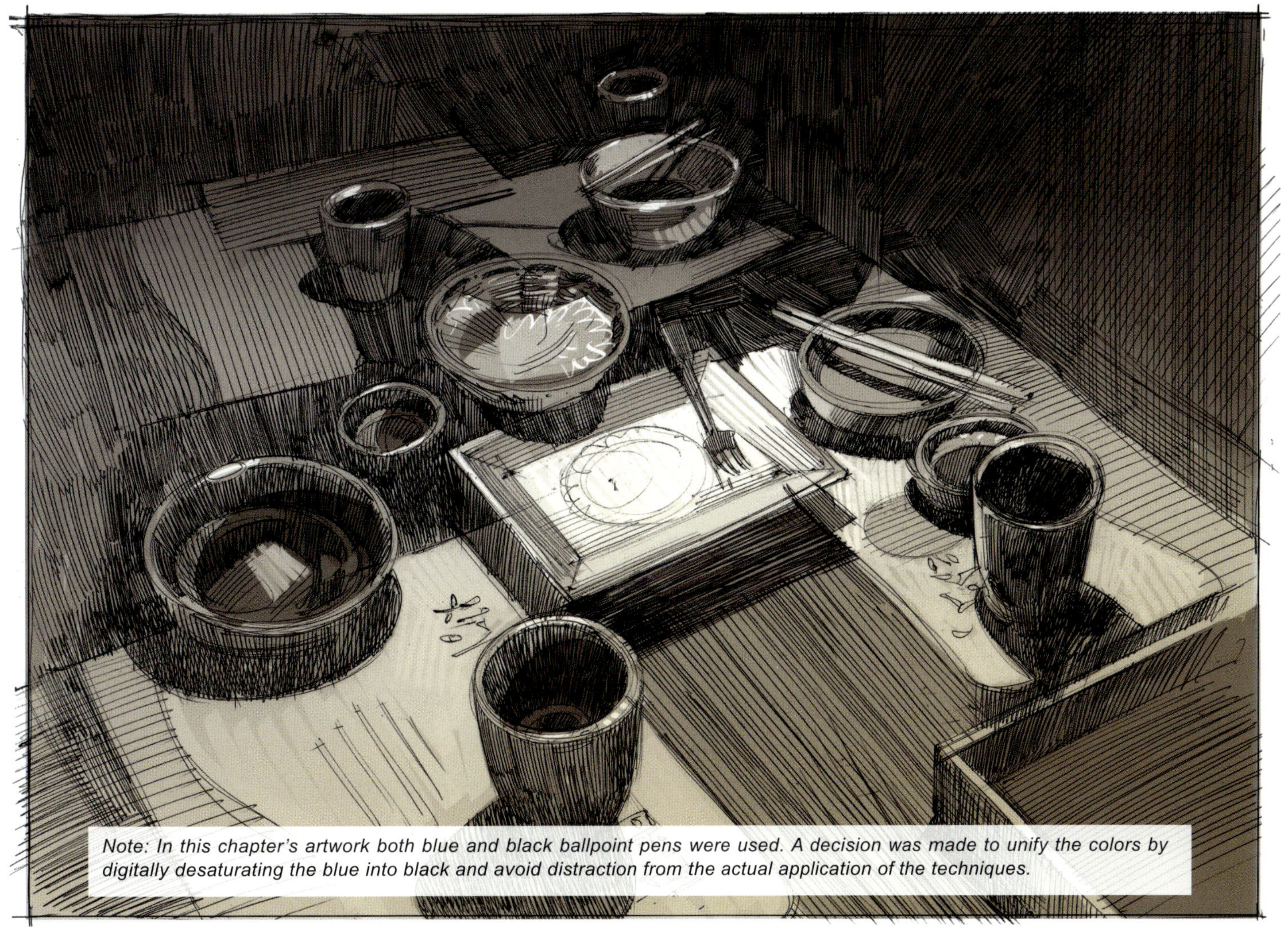

Note: In this chapter's artwork both blue and black ballpoint pens were used. A decision was made to unify the colors by digitally desaturating the blue into black and avoid distraction from the actual application of the techniques.

EXERCISING THE BRAIN-HAND CONNECTION

It is always good to warm up before starting on a piece. Like when you are playing a musical instrument, an essential part of the process is to get your mind and arm-hand connection flowing in the right direction, and this can take a while sometimes.

One of the things I usually do with this target in mind (and I'm talking not only about ballpoint pen drawing but also brush and ink, pencil, graphite, markers, and even digital) is an exercise in calligraphy. Just write with the tool of your choice, write a bunch of stuff, words, short sentences, long sentences, and loosen up your wrist, to warm up, creating a good (unconscious) connection, from brain to hand. Make all this second nature, automatic. It will reflect on your artwork. It's already a complex exercise to think ahead, while drawing, of a strategy: where to go heavier on shadows, what lines to make more prominent, how to create a good sense of dynamics, balance, etc. The hand should follow the thought as fluently and unconsciously as possible so that the artist can keep up with the complexity of creating artwork, but without the complications of trying to figure out too many important things while in motion. So let's get to writing and crazy spontaneous doodling, while making use of the type of line we want to use later on in our drawing. (See **fig. 1.1** below.) Write lowercase and capital letters, numbers, crazy good-looking/elegant lines, big curls, curves, straight lines, parallels, big, small, you name it, just let it flow big time.

Take into account that a good, graceful line will give-a lot-to the imagery we create. It is important to be willing to sacrifice some of the technical perfection we are usually aiming for in order to create a piece that is vibrant and alive, with a degree of spontaneity as opposed to something that looks unnecessarily slow and concerned.

We've all seen pieces that are technically perfect, until you realize that the overall work is just an exercise, and doesn't go beyond that. It does not involve us as it should, tell us that "something about somebody," and make us eager to see what's next. The curiosity of the moment can be satisfied only to fall in the next emotional moment.

DIRECTING THE LINE

Although I felt tempted to call this section "controlling the line" I finally opted for "directing." Essentially it comes down to the same principles, but "controlling" sounds too uptight, mechanical, and somehow void of a lively, intense, creative, and inspiring feeling.

"Directing" instead talks more about assertion, a literal sense of direction or knowledge and understanding of where to go depending on what you need for the job at any given time.

fig. 1.1

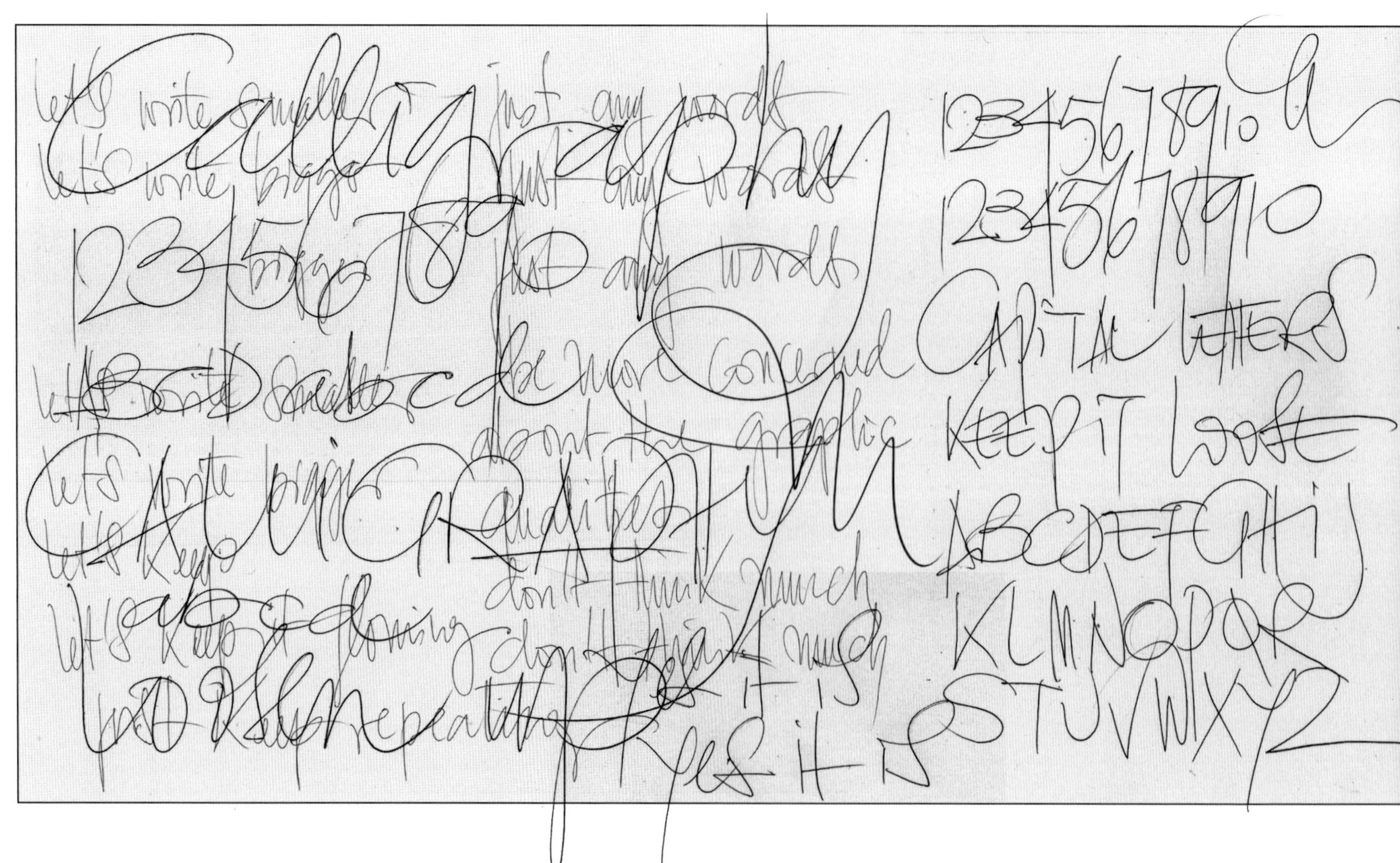

Fig. 1.2: Something you can do to integrate this into your system is to practice the following: create a number of cross points on both the left and right sides of your drawing surface. Put the tip of your ballpoint on one of the crosses to the left, point A. Without moving the pen at all, set your eyes on the cross point to the right of A (let's call it A"). Without moving your eyes at all, start moving the pencil towards A", while always looking at the final target! (If you are left-handed, reverse direction and go from point A" on right to point A on left.) Repeat this exercise between points B and B" and so on. You can also do it at different speeds—slower or faster—and see how that goes. You will see that, as with everything else in life, if you are set on a specific goal and focus on it all the time, your efforts will eventually lead you there.

fig. 1.2

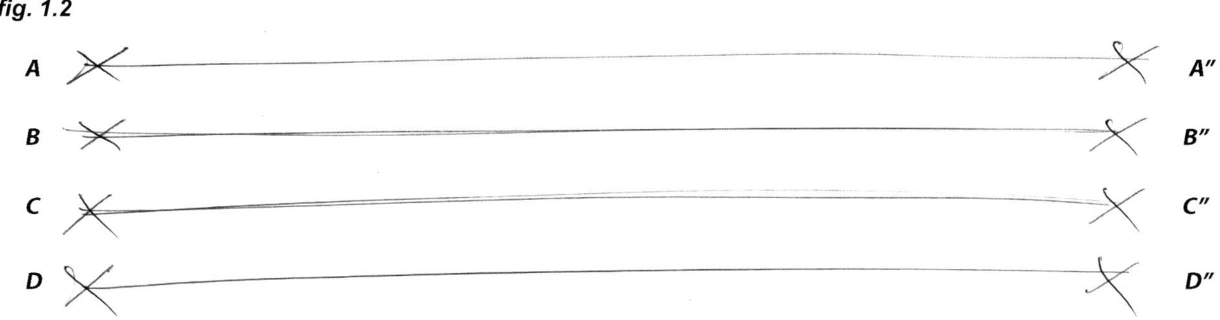

Another exercise I would always recommend in the execution of any technique is trying to combine different lines on paper within the same space, from drawing parallel lines (**fig. 1.3**) to a zigzag-type line that will allow us to quickly fill in spaces that need a darker tone (**fig. 1.4**).

fig. 1.3

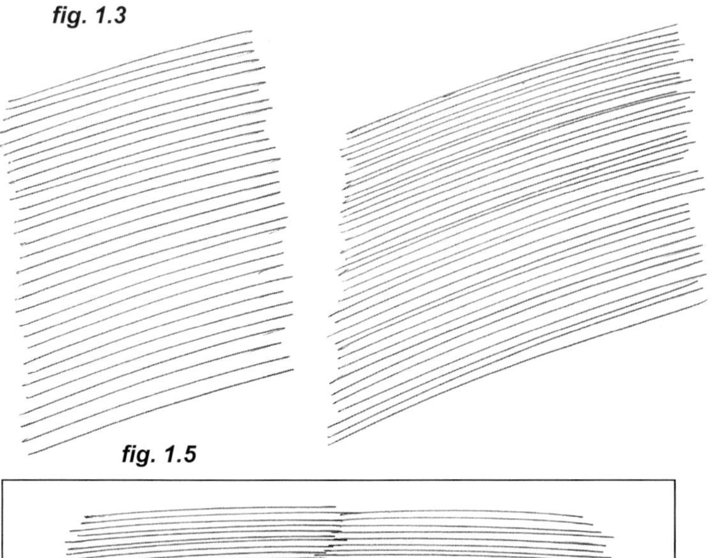

fig. 1.4

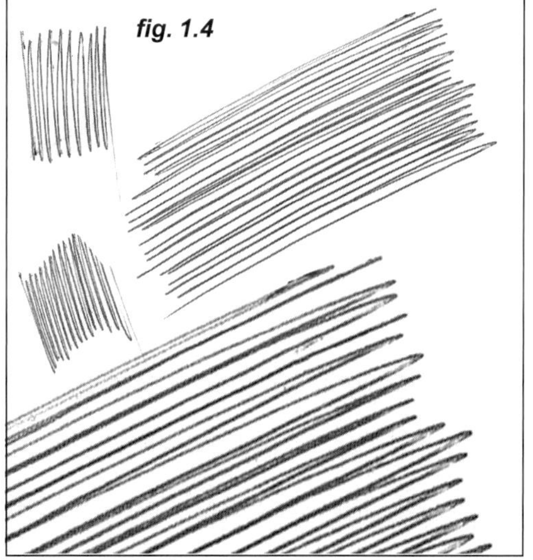

fig. 1.5

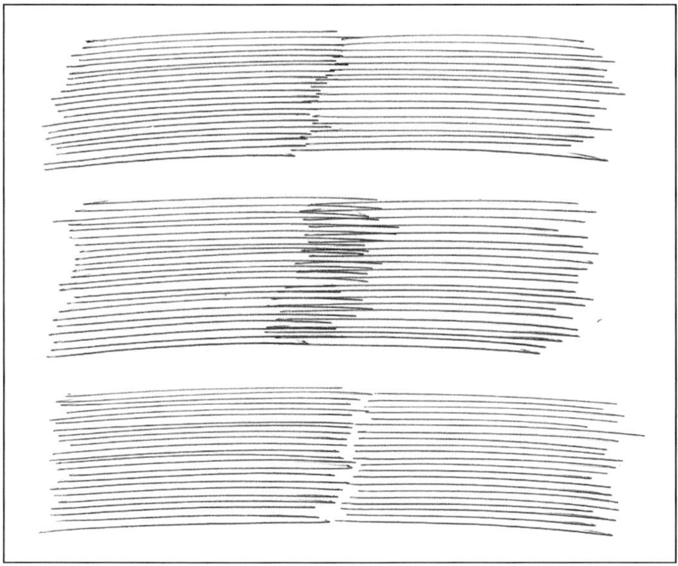

Fig. 1.5 Sometimes, depending on the length we need for a line, we will have to draw several lines in continuation in order to cover the required area (1). As much as possible try to minimize either the overlap between the segments (2), or the gap between them (3). Beyond the elegance and quality of the line, problems 2 and 3 are some of the potential issues that are more obvious whenever we look at our drawing as a whole from a certain distance. The way I usually draw these lines is by securing my elbow on the drawing board, as if it were the point/ needle of a compass, and take it from there.

fig. 1.6

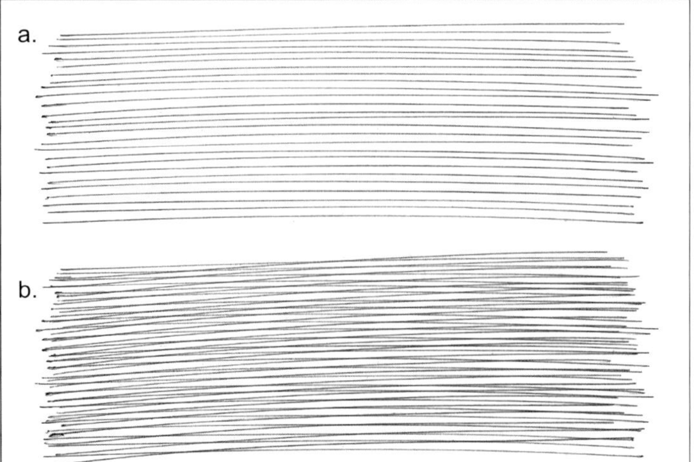

fig. 1.7

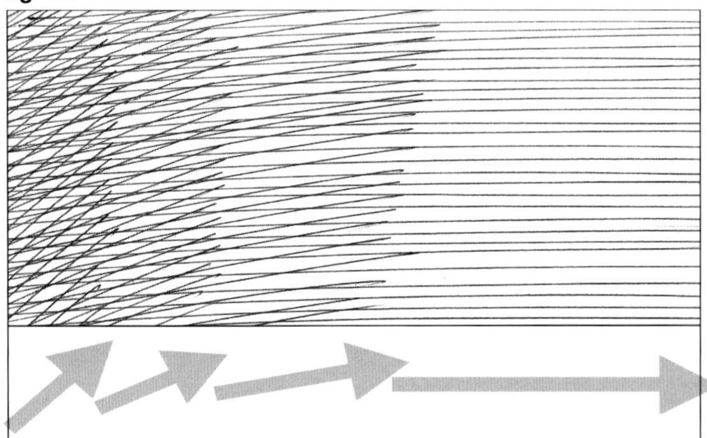

Fig. 1.6 a and b: Although I usually try to avoid crossing lines at different angles much (see **fig. 1.10** of restaurant table) to make an area darker, sometimes this device can become really effective. In these cases, I try to change the line's angle as little as possible so that it creates a smoother look, opposite to what a 90 degree crossing would feel like.

Fig. 1.7: Also useful when creating a gradation, I usually vary the angle of each new layer of lines just slightly from one to the next.

Fig. 1.8: Another exercise to practice is the consecutive darkening and lightning of areas within a single, continuous zigzag, so that again the transitions between lights and darks are progressive, smooth, and gradual.

Figs. 1.9, **1.10**, and **1.11**: A more organic and lively use of the line while using crosshatching is to progressively darken and brighten different areas; this can give a more credible look to subjects that are not purely geometrical or made of flat sides. Again, the pressure applied on the pen and the amount and density of pen strokes will become an important factor.

fig. 1.8

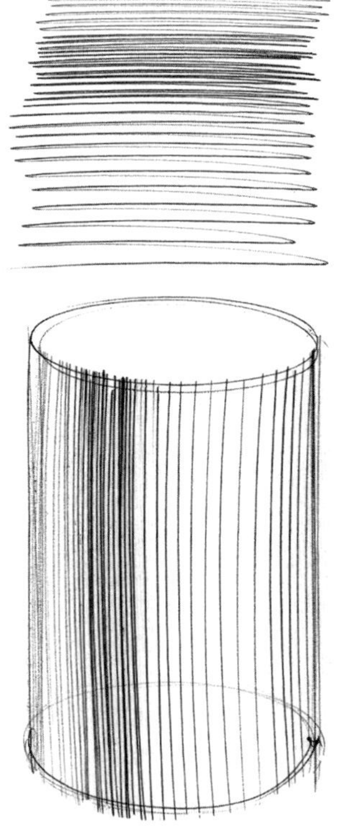

fig. 1.9

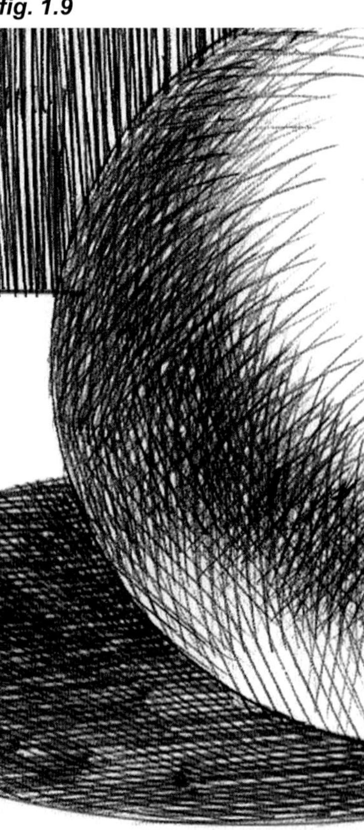

fig. 1.10

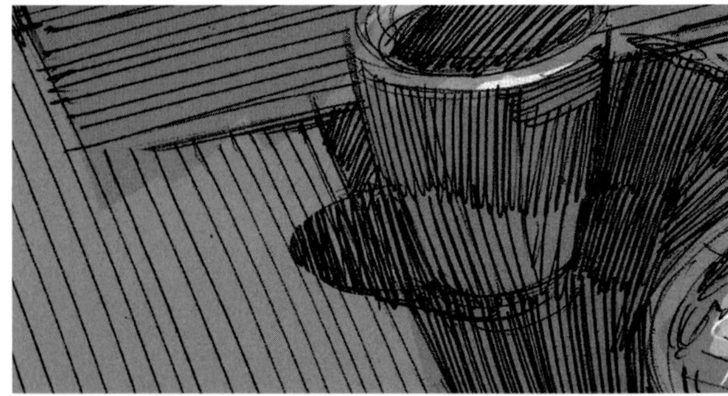

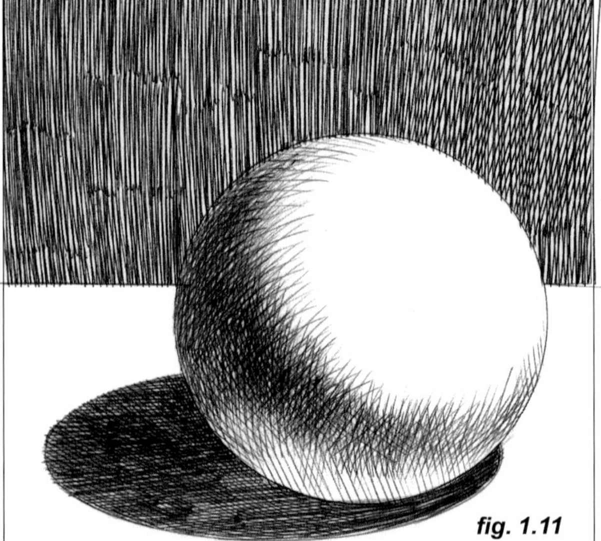

fig. 1.11

On this page you can see how I applied line direction to emphasize shape, volume, and construction.

Fig. 1.12: The straight lines defining the surface sides of these parallelograms help establish a solid sense of perspective. (For options on drawing longer straight lines, please refer to **figs. 3.18** and **3.19** on page 076.)

Figs. 1.13, **1.14** and **1.15**: The more organic lines in this still life show again how to sculpt these rounder shapes, more like in the previous page's example of the ball on a table.

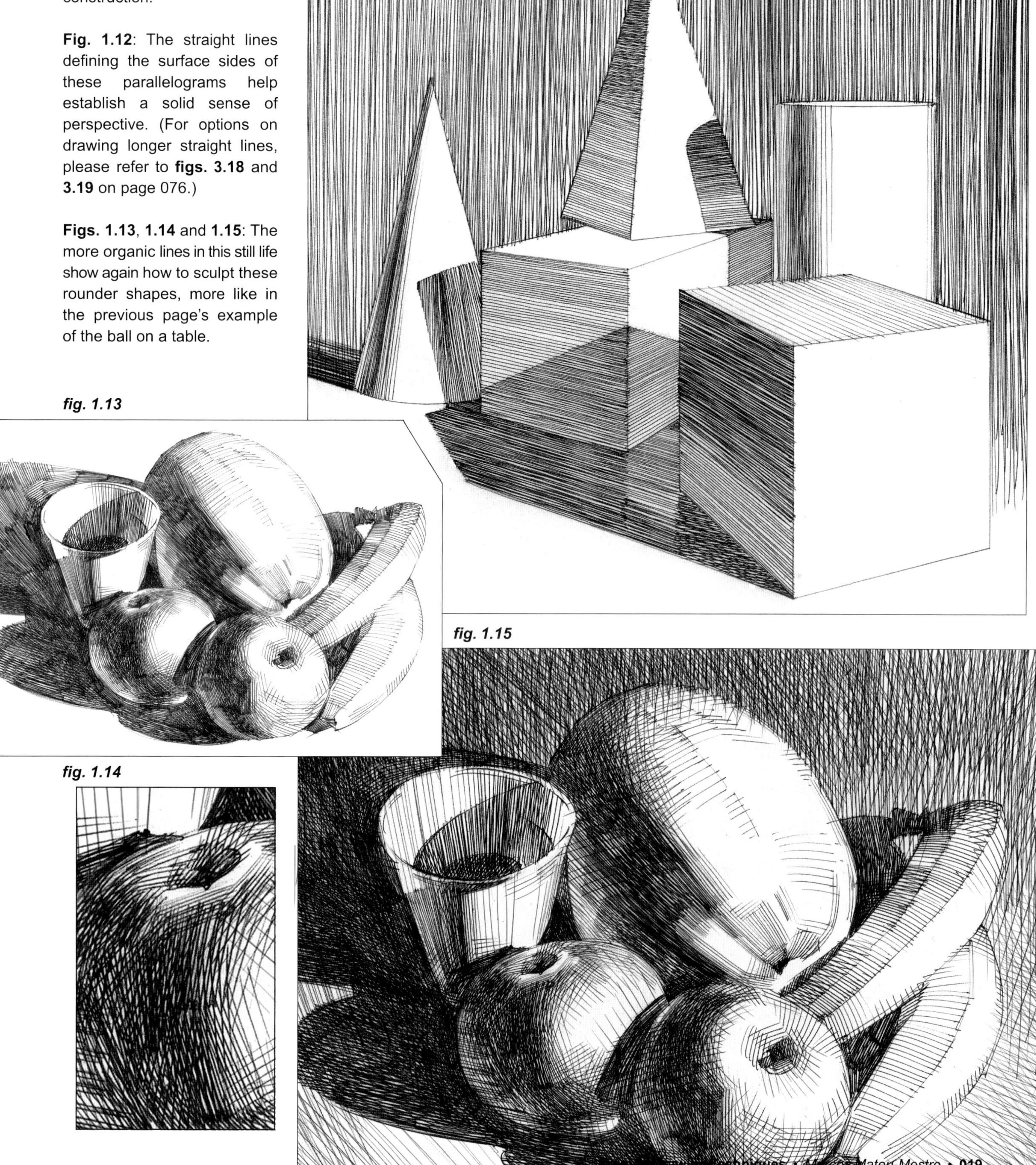

fig. 1.12

fig. 1.13

fig. 1.14

fig. 1.15

A BASIC BLOCKING EXERCISE

Figs. 1.16, **1.17** and **1.18**: In this quick exercise you will see the step-by-step buildup of a sense of volume and three dimensionality by establishing a clear separation between the main tonal areas–house in the background, bushes in the mid ground, and parked cars in the foreground; see also fig **1.21**.

Fig. 1.16, step 1: Although I already blocked the main tonal areas at this point, the level of contrast between values is not yet what I was ultimately aiming for. For instance, I haven't gotten to specific areas like windows.

Fig. 1.17, step 2: Once I established the main areas to work with, I started pushing for further contrast as well as defining more details.

Fig. 1.18, step 3: I finally pushed the values to the point that, even without details, I established a sense of lighting that felt believable, delivering a clear composition and sense of space at a quick glance.

Fig. 1.19: In this detail of the final drawing, you see how the value differences have been established by progressively adding layer after layer, wherever applicable, of ball-pen line work.

fig. 1.16

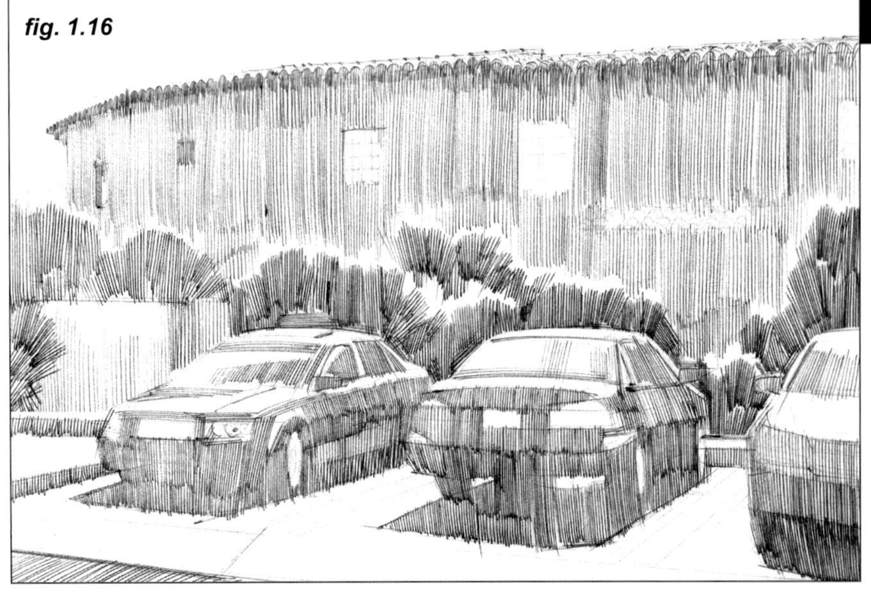

fig. 1.17

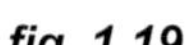

fig. 1.18

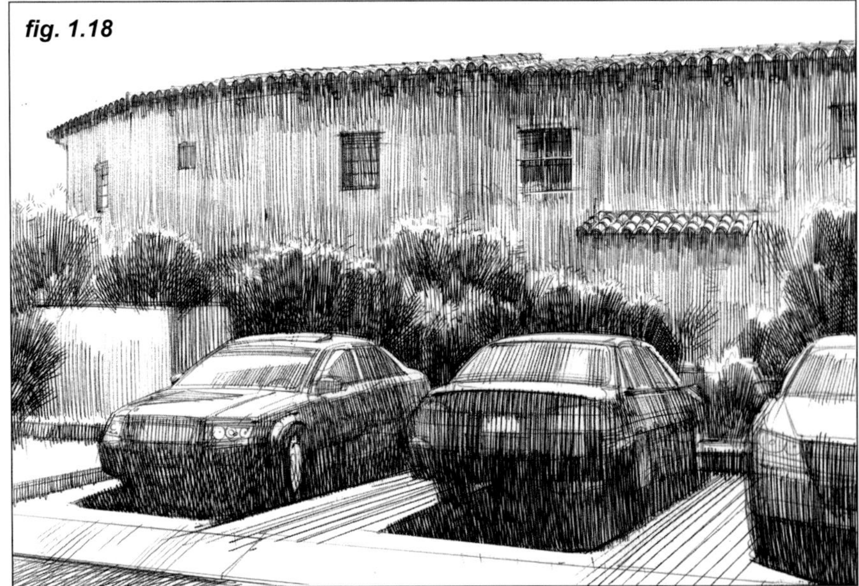

fig. 1.19

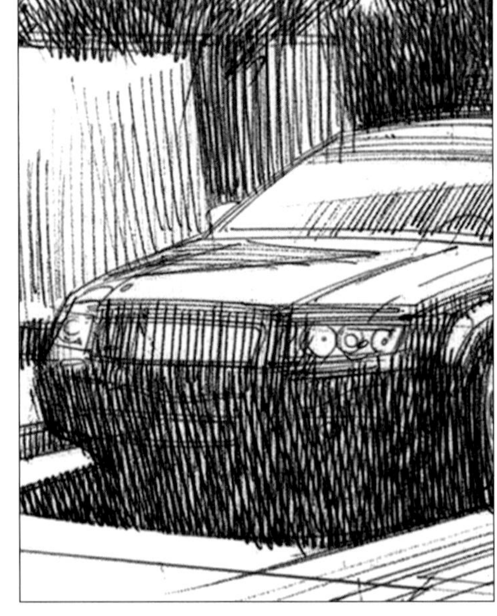

Fig. 1.20 (right): Instead of using consistent vertical lines, this new take on the same scene wraps the line around the three-dimensional bodies (cars, vegetation, buildings) to define their volumes.

Fig. 1.21 (tonal): Whether I actually draw the whole process step by step, as explained in the previous figures, or I visualize this process in my mind, it is important to see a scene in such a simplified way prior to execution.

fig. 1.20

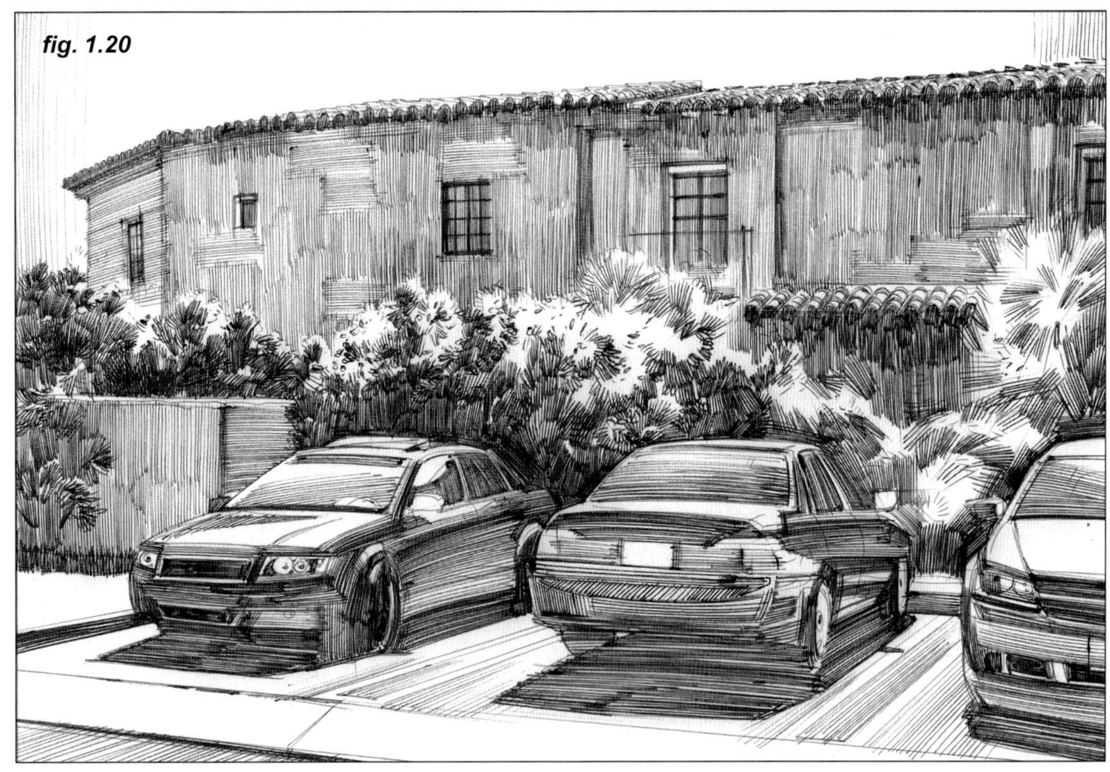

fig. 1.21

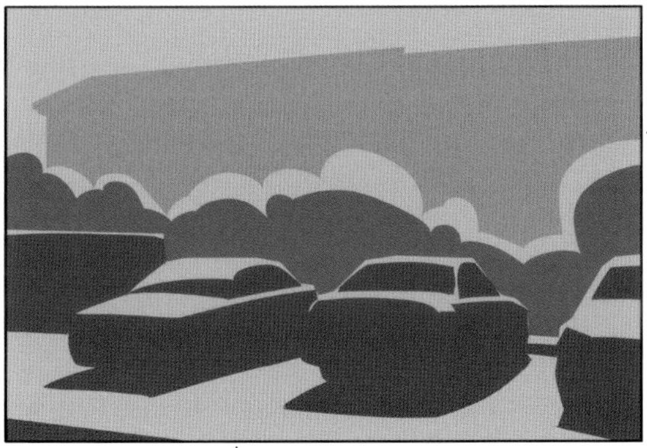

Figs. 1.22 to **1.25**: To practice how to establish solid structures through line work, you can draw geometrical figures and create line work that will literally wrap around such figures on their different planes, whether flat or curved. This is just a warm-up or way to create a good mind-to-hand coordination that you can then apply to your artwork.

Figs. 1.22, **1.23**, and **1.24** reflect a more methodical approach. After that, and with a solid understanding of the shape, you can move on to a more organic one (last **Fig. 1.25**).

fig. 1.22

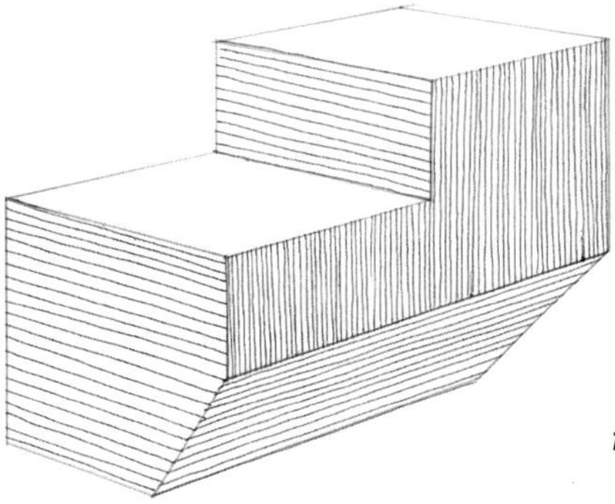

fig. 1.24

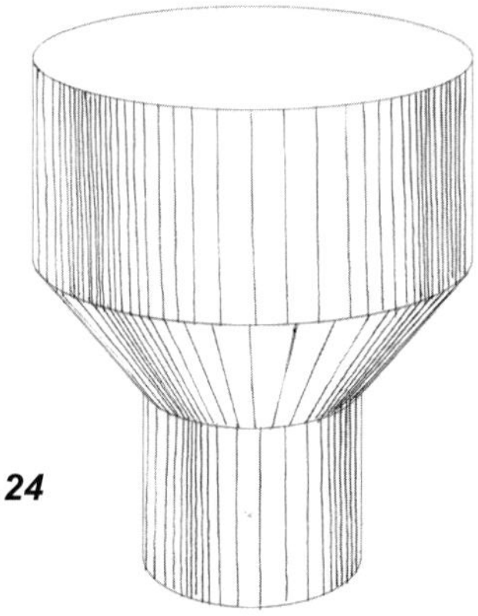

fig. 1.23

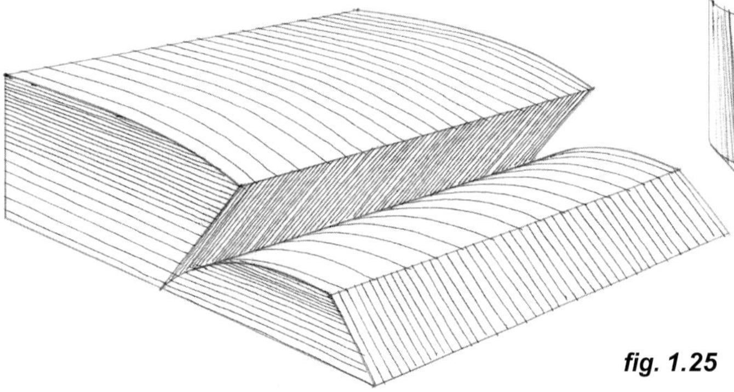

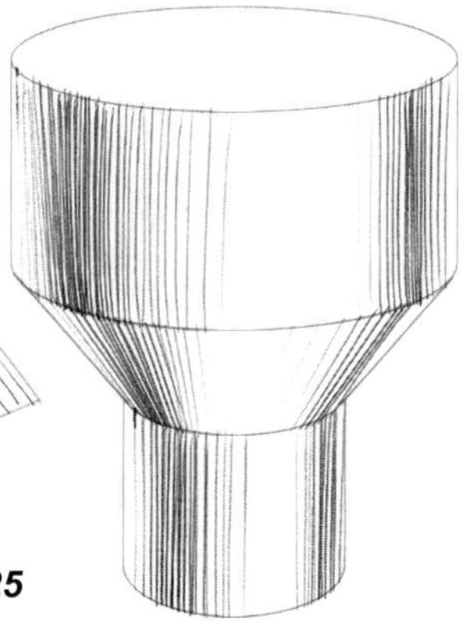

fig. 1.25

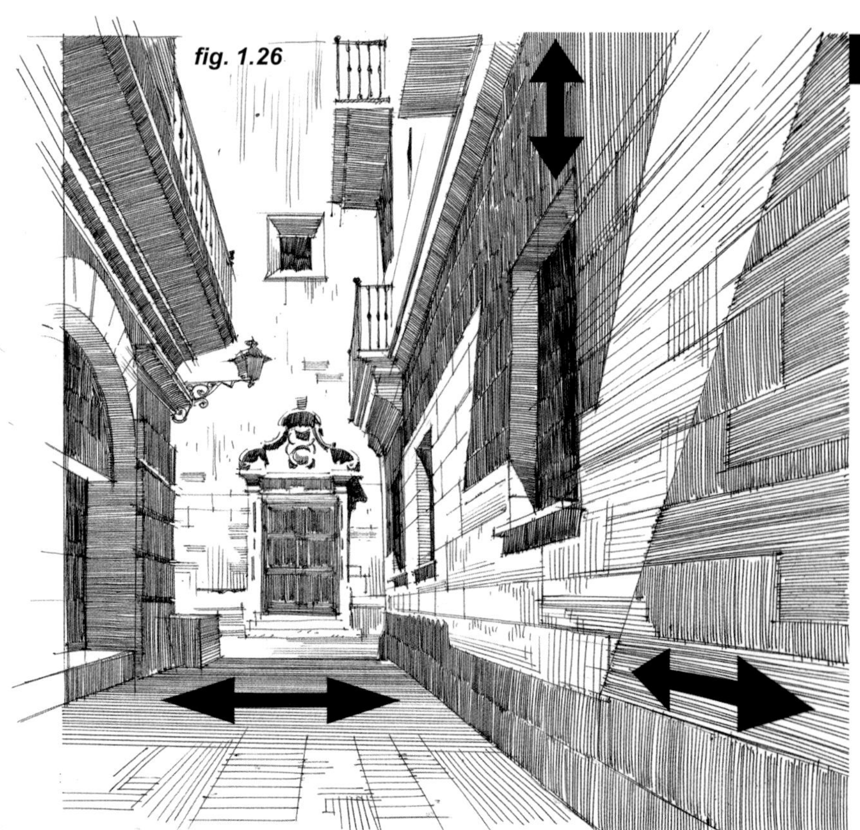
fig. 1.26

ARCHITECTURAL VS. ORGANIC

Figs. 1.26 and **1.27**, and **fig. 1.28**: The techniques seen in the previous spread, referring to the rendering of flat surfaces or polyhedrons, are seen here in action on more complex examples. See how the line direction adapts itself to the surface it is describing: the first one establishing the basic bone structure in terms of light, shadow, and plane direction. (for the longer vertical lines emphasizing the darker foreground, the use of a ruler can do the trick).

In this case, as opposed to the examples on the pages to come, the drawing is more of a technical style, and requires knowledge of perspective, as everything develops into a more geometrical fashion.

Figs. 1.29, **1.30**, and **1.31**: this more architectural approach can also be applied to organic subjects by previously breaking down the rounder surfaces into smaller, flat ones–see the flow of the arrows over the subject's surface, and also refer to **figs 1.22** to **1.25**, page 021.

fig. 1.27

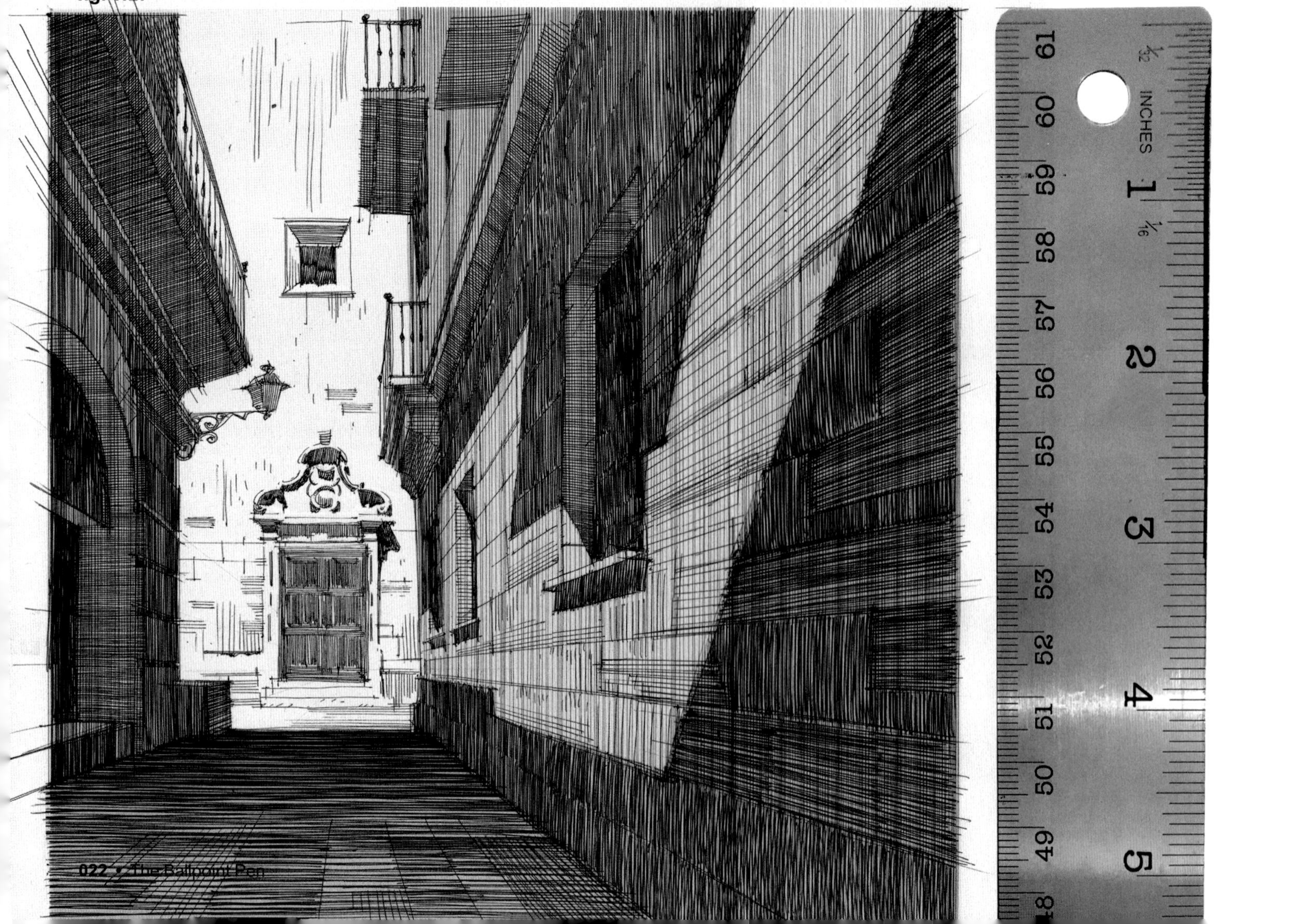

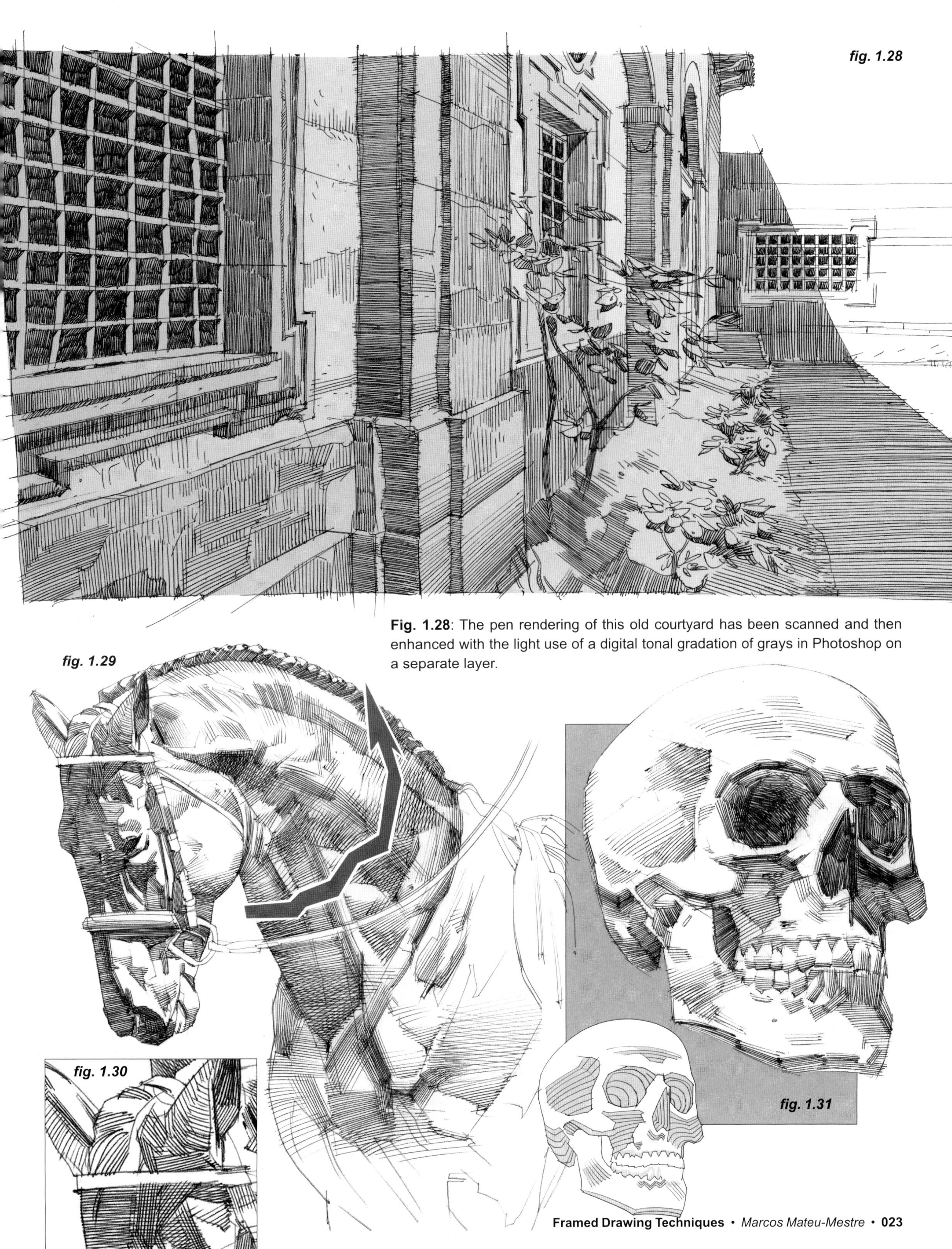

Fig. 1.28: The pen rendering of this old courtyard has been scanned and then enhanced with the light use of a digital tonal gradation of grays in Photoshop on a separate layer.

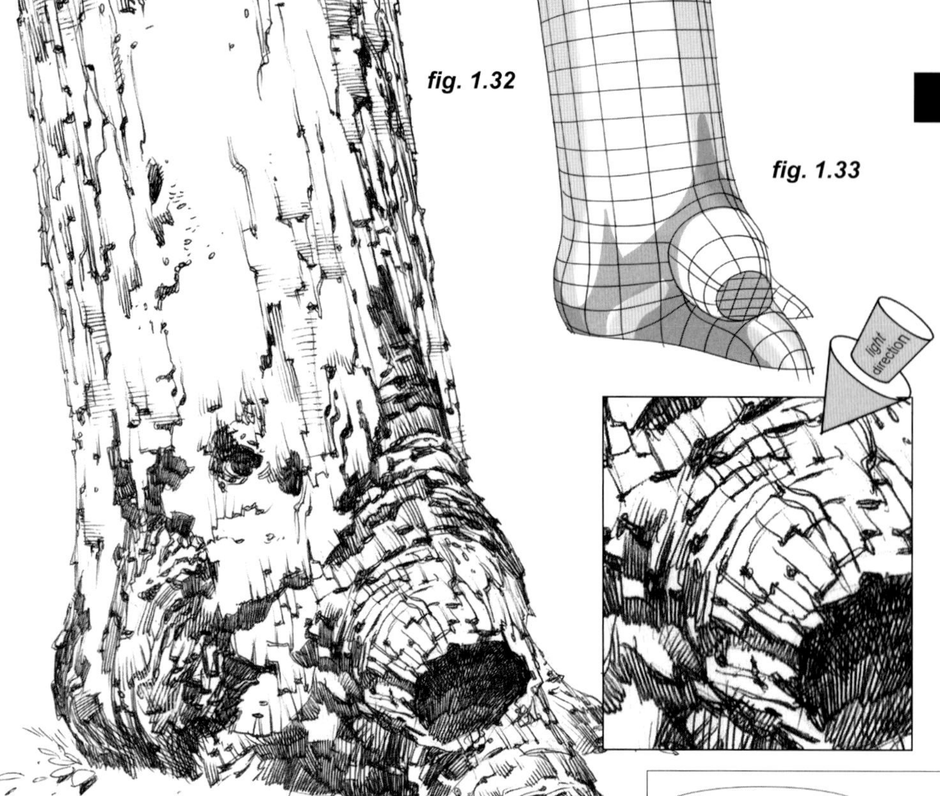

fig. 1.32

fig. 1.33

TEXTURES AND MATERIALS

When it comes to rendering textures, think in terms of light: how light affects texture and how texture dictates the way in which light affects the surface.

Figs. 1.32 and **1.33**: the texture of this tree trunk is rough, uneven, and matte. The contrast between its areas of light and shadow will tend to be sharp. Observe in the simplified wireframe version how the tones are grouped within certain areas to emphasize a sense of volume (especially the sides along the vertical trunk, as the chunks of bark appear more compact together to our sight as they go around) rather than being evenly distributed all over the drawing's surface, which would automatically flatten its look.

Fig. 1.34: This knight in literally shiny armor will offer a particularly clear view of the areas of highlight (1), half tone (2), core shadow (3), and reflected light (4), as seen simplified in the cylinder.

By contrast, the clay jars in **figs. 1.35** to **1.37** (next page top), gradate from light to a midtone and then shadow without offering much of a reflected light on the other side.

Technically, the first line pass (**fig. 1.35**) indicates the round volume of the amphora. The second pass (seen here separately in **fig. 1.36**) further emphasizes the shadowed areas.

Fig. 1.38 (wave): See how again the line-work direction follows the direction of the subject's surface.

Figs. 1.39, **1.40**, and **1.41** (inserts, bottom next page): These represent 1) the direction of the waves I mentioned before, 2) a simplified graphic, establishing a light (foam) to dark (water) gradation, and 3) the grouping of the main tonal areas, from the lightest at the waves' crest, which appear brighter the closer they are to the camera, to its darkest in the body of water itself.

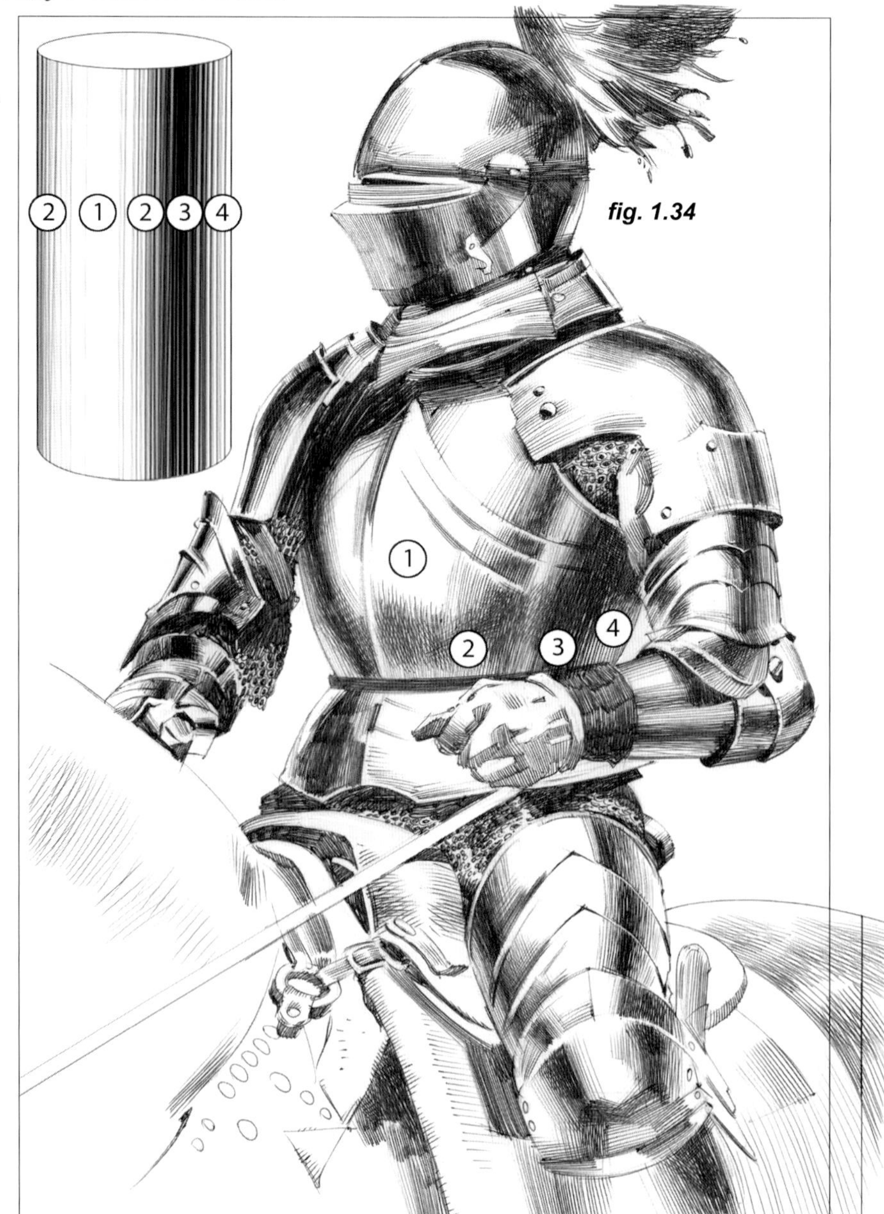

fig. 1.34

fig. 1.36

fig. 1.35

Fig. 1.35: The first line pass treats the amphora like a cylindrical body (see arrow's direction).

Fig. 1.36: The second is more sphere-like, with the line work usually pointing at the spotlight.

Fig. 1.37: Finally, here both layers are combined.

Fig. 1.37b: See in this detail how the line strokes follow the surface plane to enhance volume.

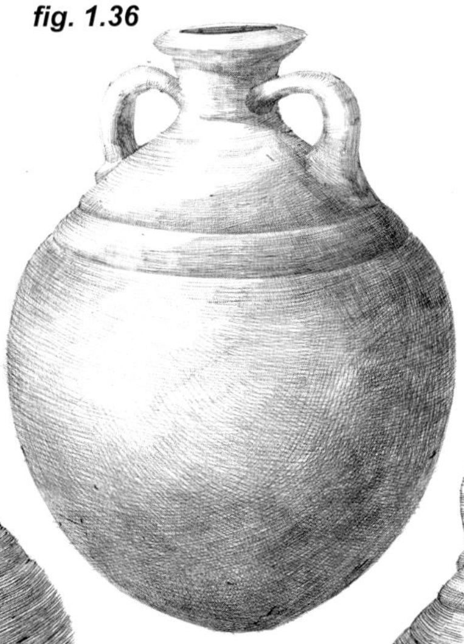

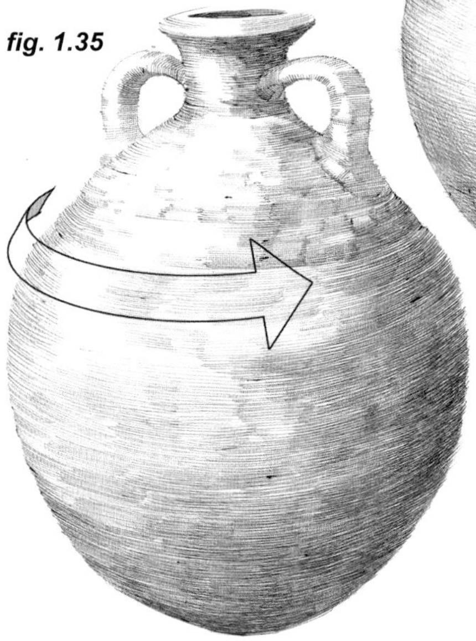

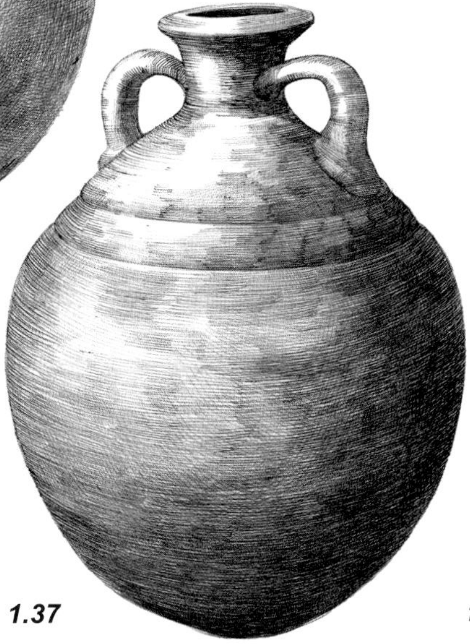

fig. 1.37

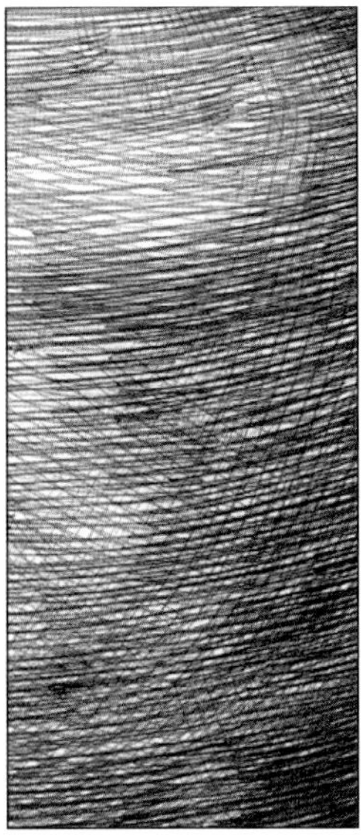

fig. 1.37b

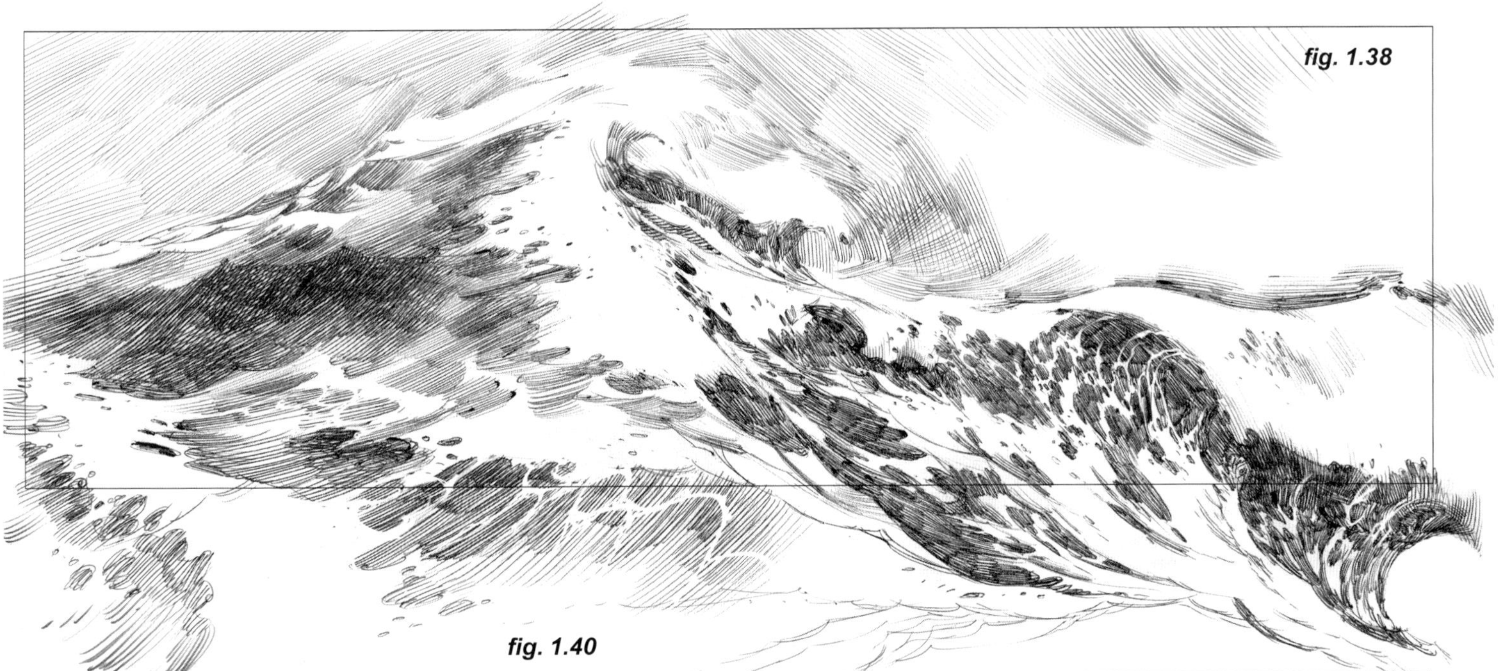

fig. 1.38

fig. 1.40

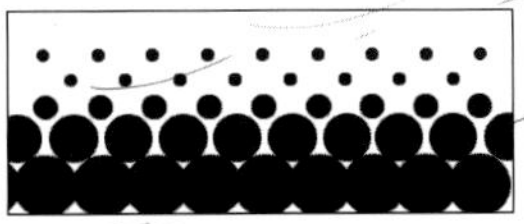

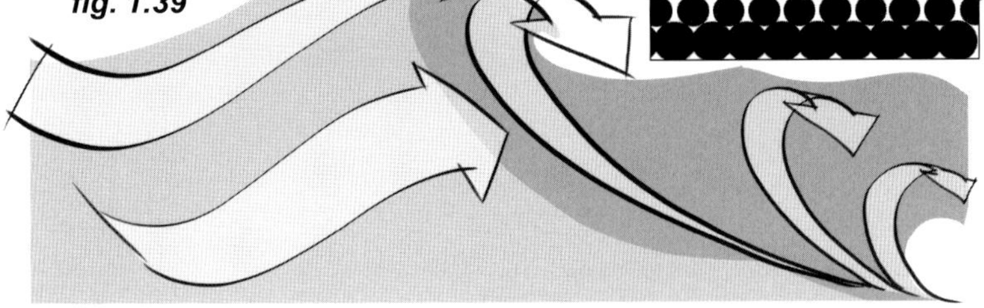

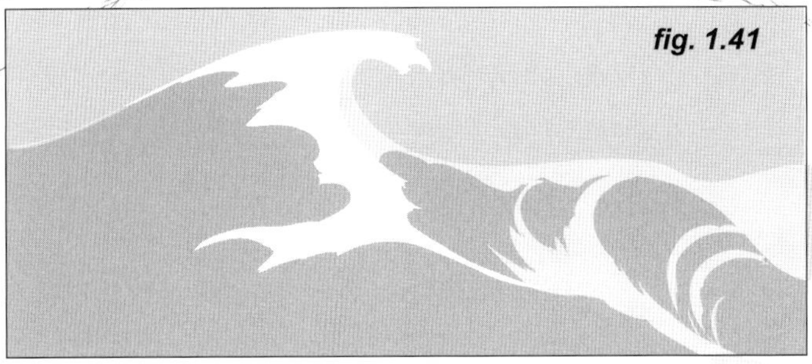

fig. 1.41

fig. 1.39

CREATING A FOREST

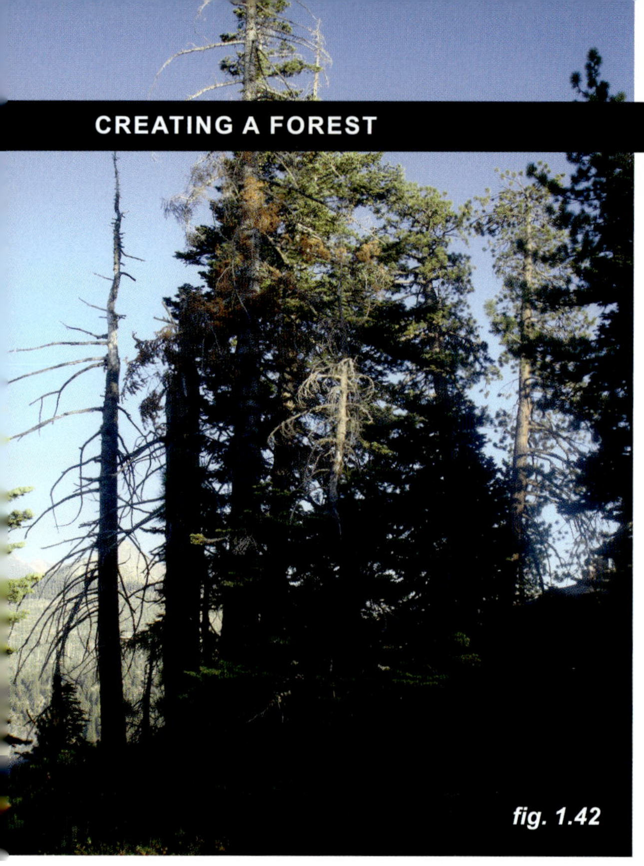

fig. 1.42

Fig. 1.42: This is the photo reference used for this illustration.

Figs. 1.43, **1.44**, and **1.45**: These three steps show the basic drawing and then, separately for clarity, the two consecutive layers that help punctuate the general darker areas and accents, mostly located at the bottom third of the final image.

All layers were drawn separately but on overlapped sheets of paper with the help of a light desk, and then scanned and digitally superimposed on "multiplied" (transparent) mode so the richness of all the line work shows together.

Figs. 1.46 and **1.47**: Observe that both the tree trunks and the foliage areas are not a mere flat render of their natural textures; they have been executed leaving clear, graphic areas of light (mainly center) and dark (mainly the left side) in order to bring up the life and volume of the scenery, rather than a flat, even, and boring render. (This drawing was done with a Pilot BP-S fine pen on copy paper).

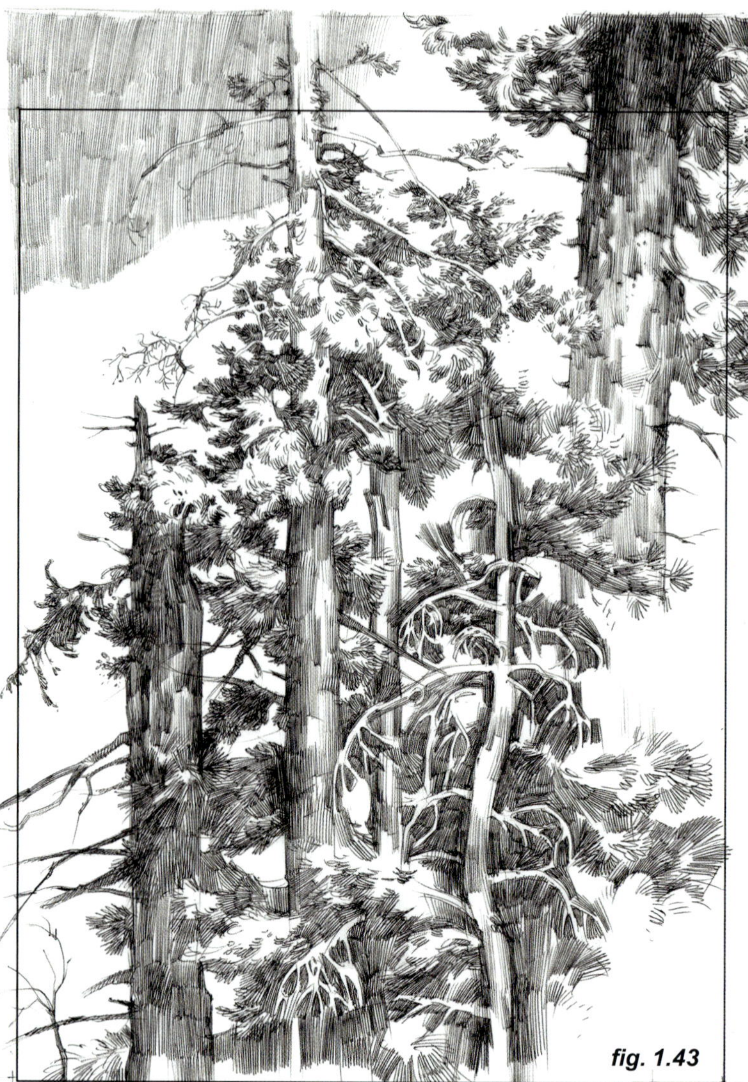

fig. 1.43

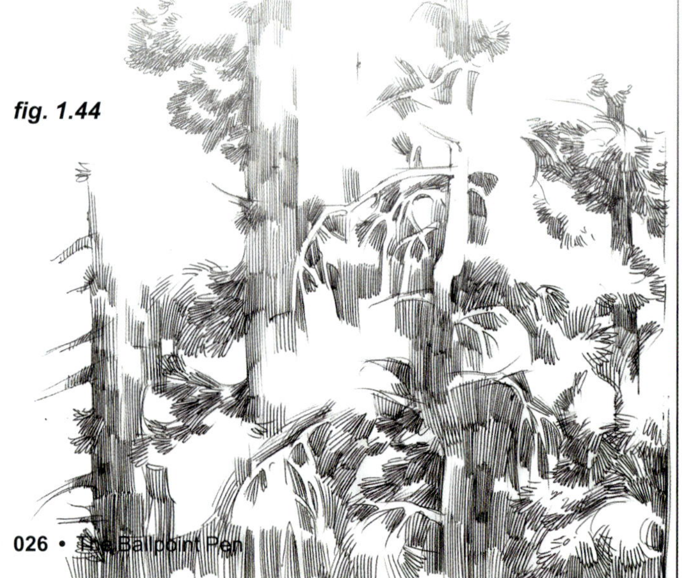

fig. 1.44

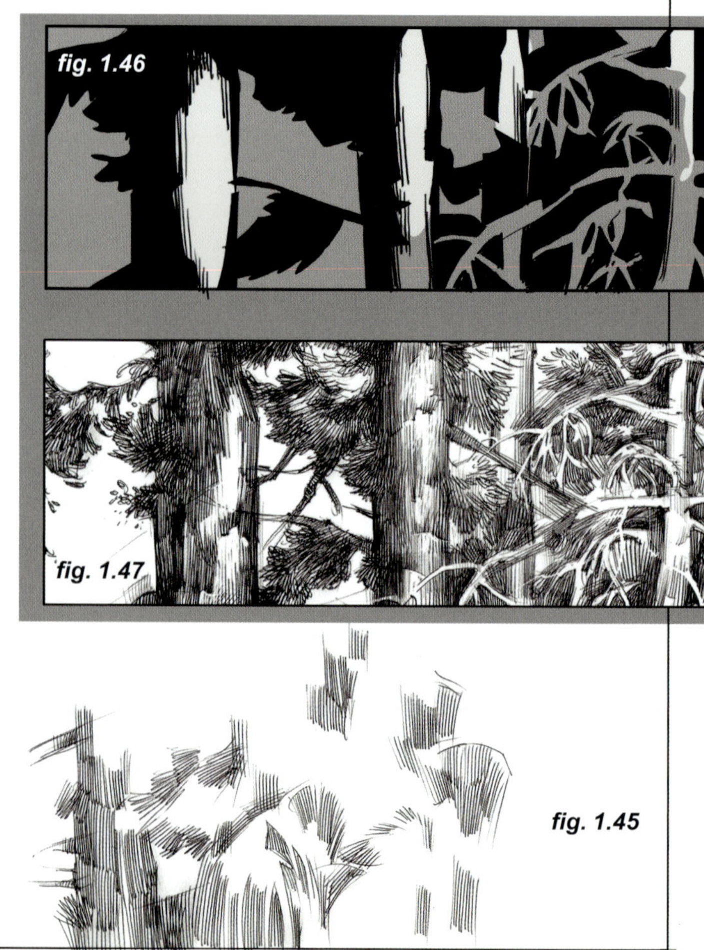

fig. 1.46

fig. 1.47

fig. 1.45

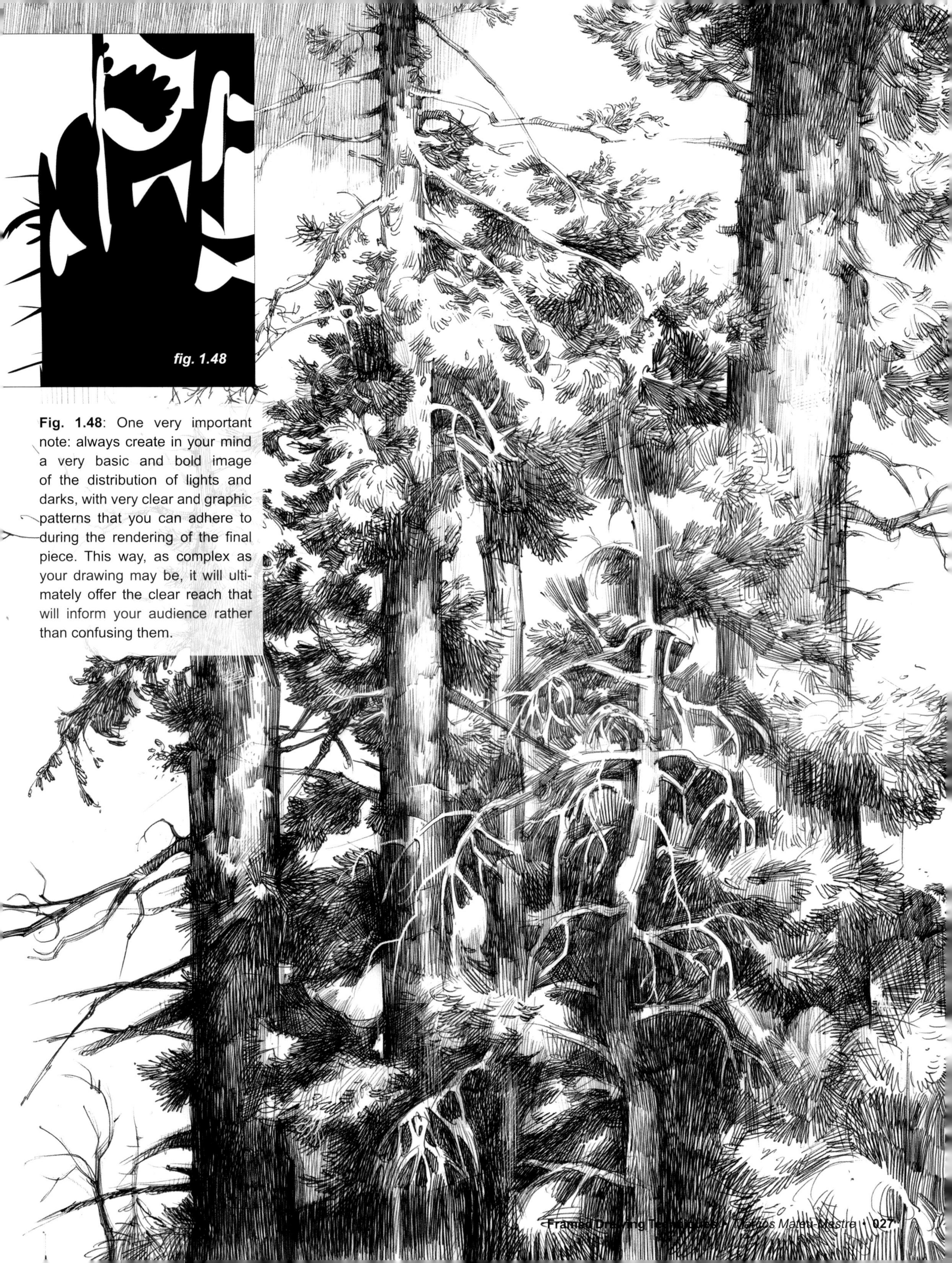

Fig. 1.48: One very important note: always create in your mind a very basic and bold image of the distribution of lights and darks, with very clear and graphic patterns that you can adhere to during the rendering of the final piece. This way, as complex as your drawing may be, it will ultimately offer the clear reach that will inform your audience rather than confusing them.

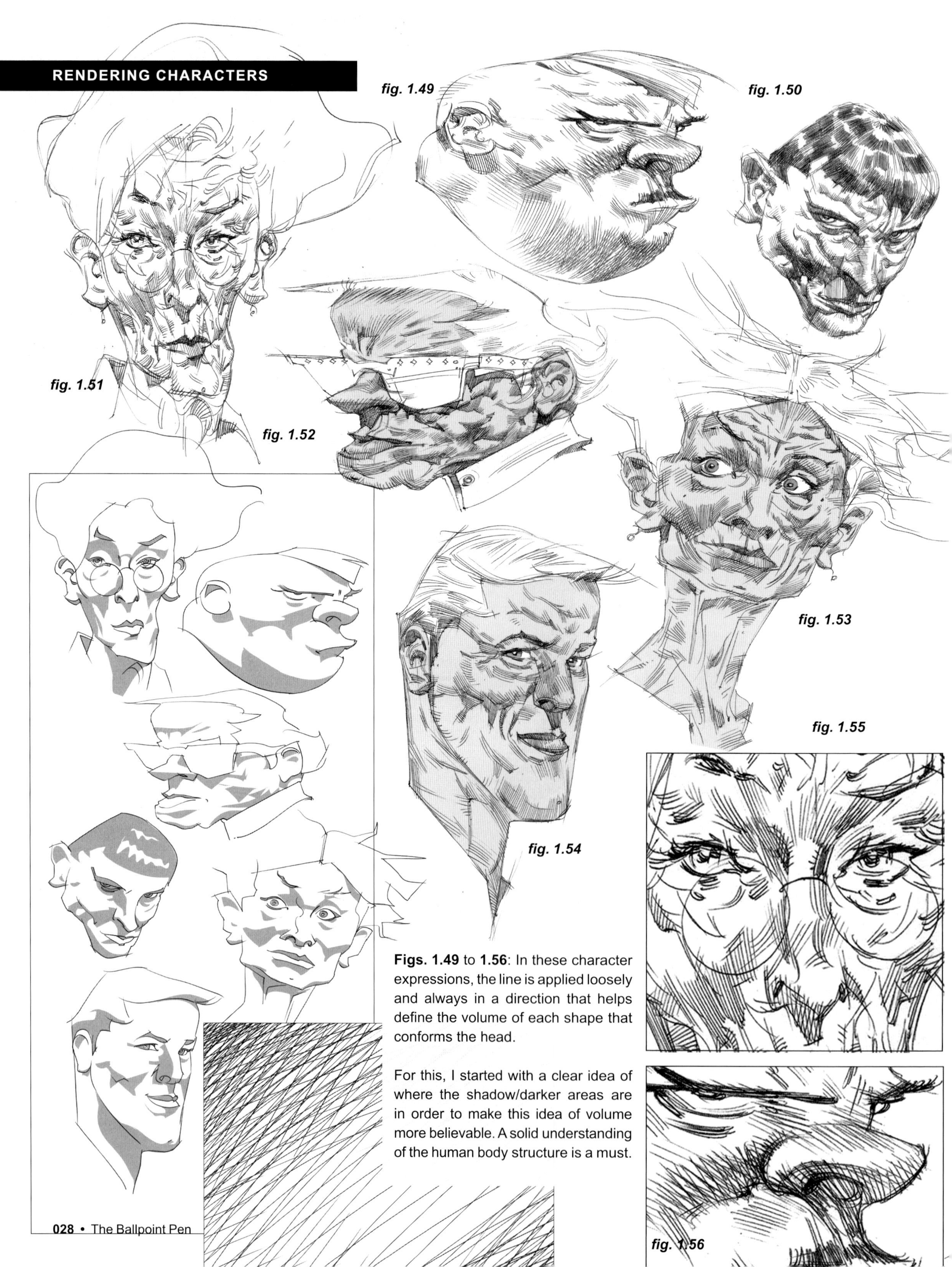

Figs. 1.49 to **1.56**: In these character expressions, the line is applied loosely and always in a direction that helps define the volume of each shape that conforms the head.

For this, I started with a clear idea of where the shadow/darker areas are in order to make this idea of volume more believable. A solid understanding of the human body structure is a must.

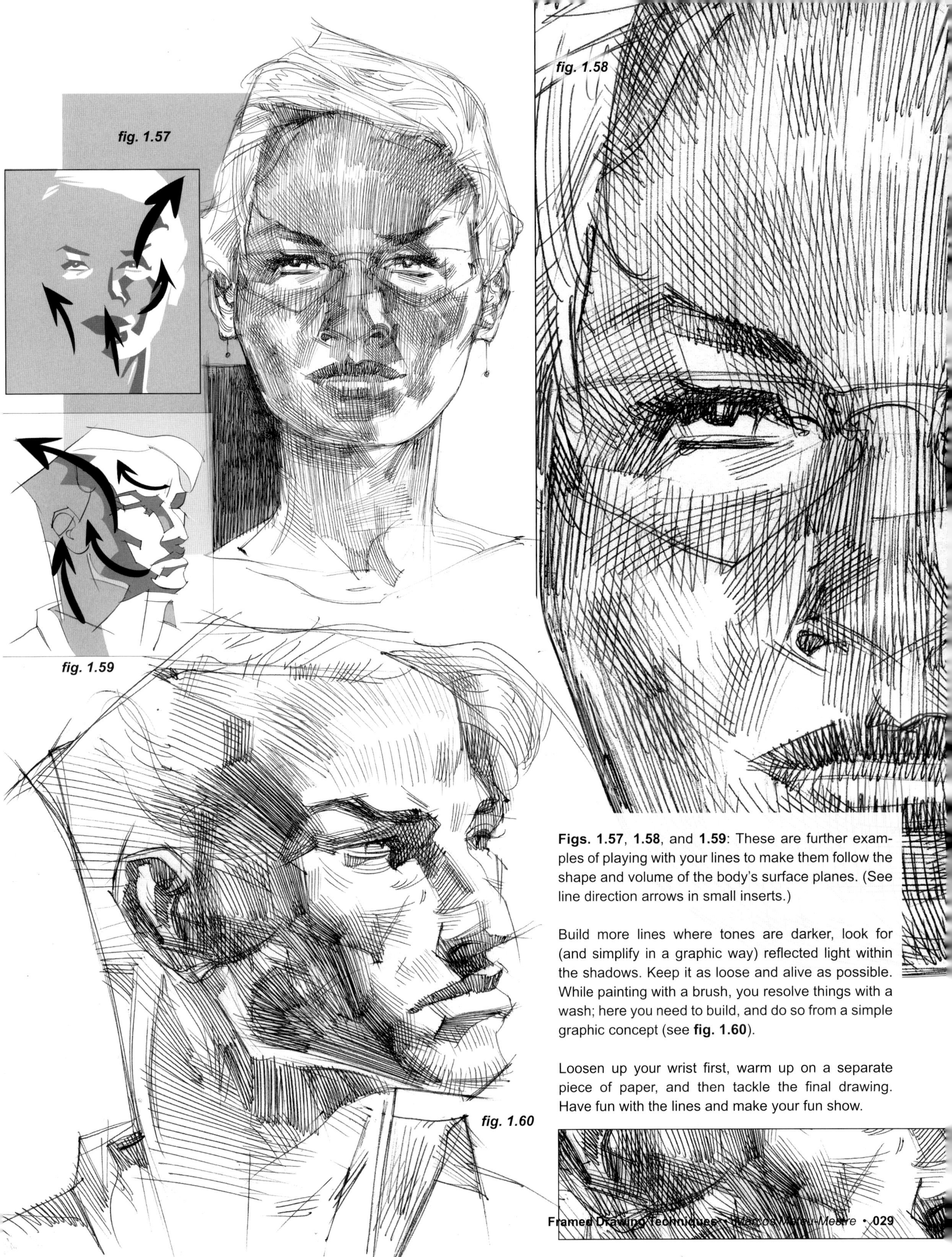

fig. 1.57

fig. 1.58

fig. 1.59

fig. 1.60

Figs. 1.57, **1.58**, and **1.59**: These are further examples of playing with your lines to make them follow the shape and volume of the body's surface planes. (See line direction arrows in small inserts.)

Build more lines where tones are darker, look for (and simplify in a graphic way) reflected light within the shadows. Keep it as loose and alive as possible. While painting with a brush, you resolve things with a wash; here you need to build, and do so from a simple graphic concept (see **fig. 1.60**).

Loosen up your wrist first, warm up on a separate piece of paper, and then tackle the final drawing. Have fun with the lines and make your fun show.

fig. 1.61

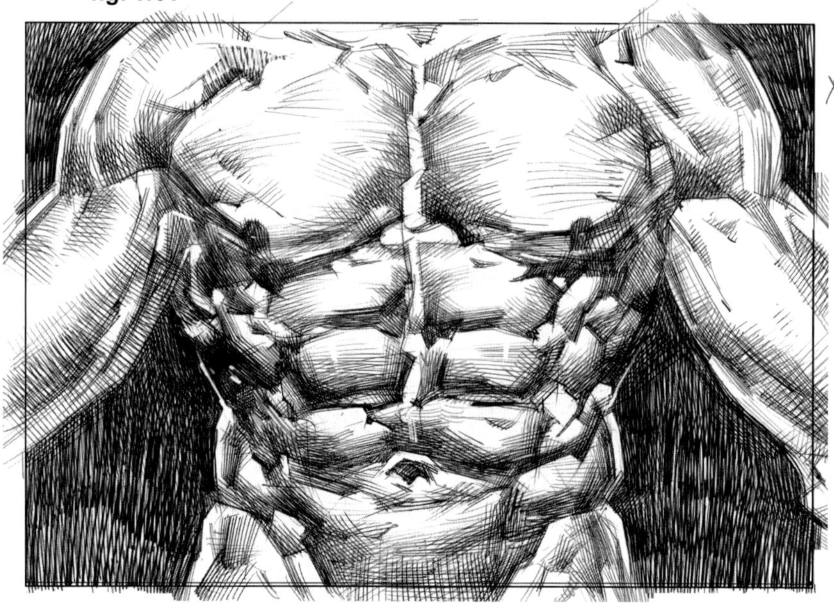

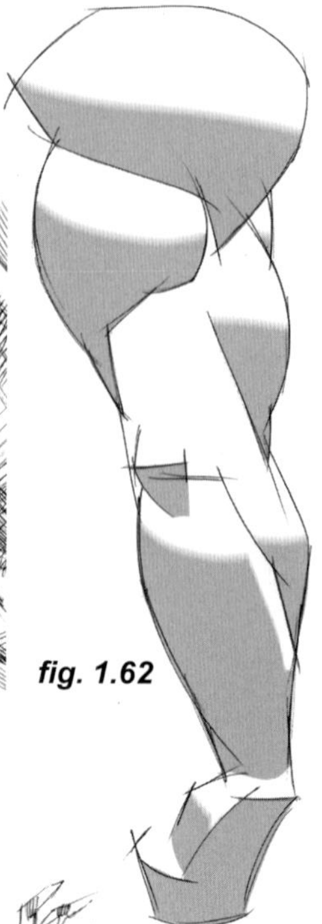

fig. 1.62

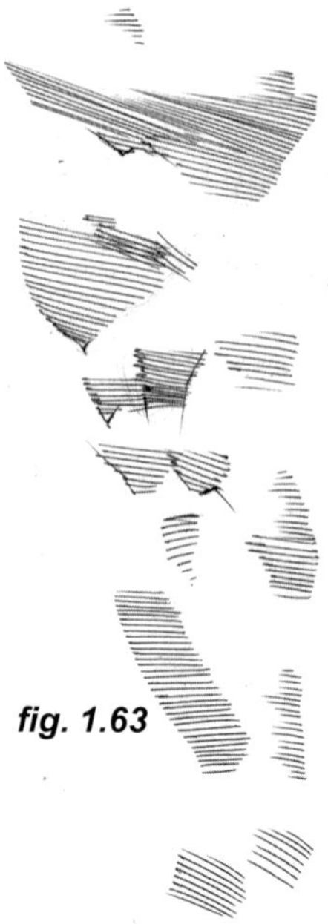

fig. 1.63

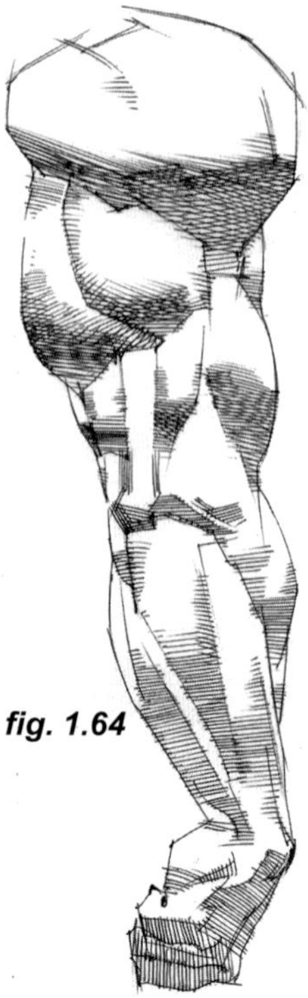

fig. 1.64

fig. 1.65

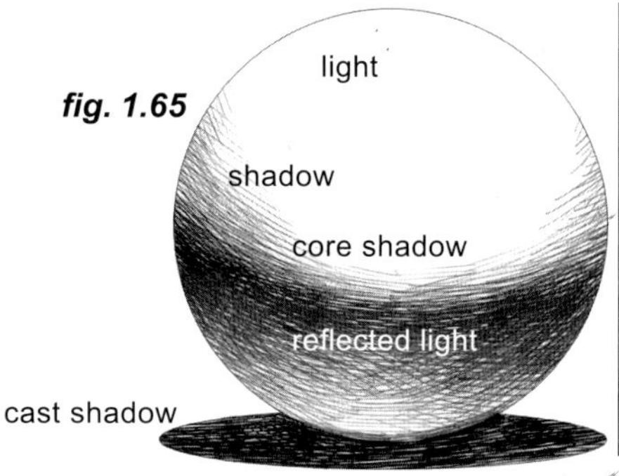

fig. 1.66

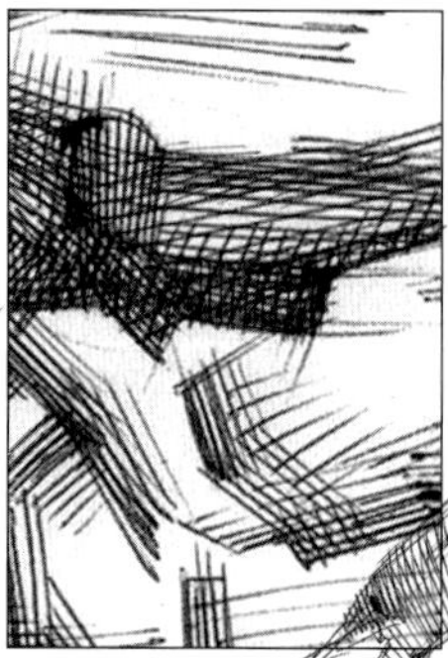

fig. 1.67

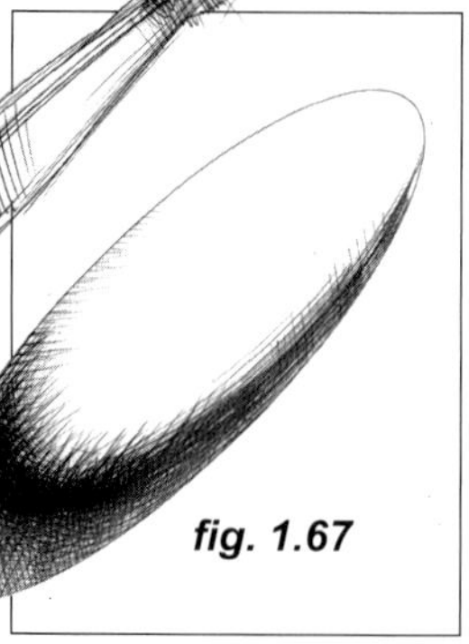

fig. 1.68

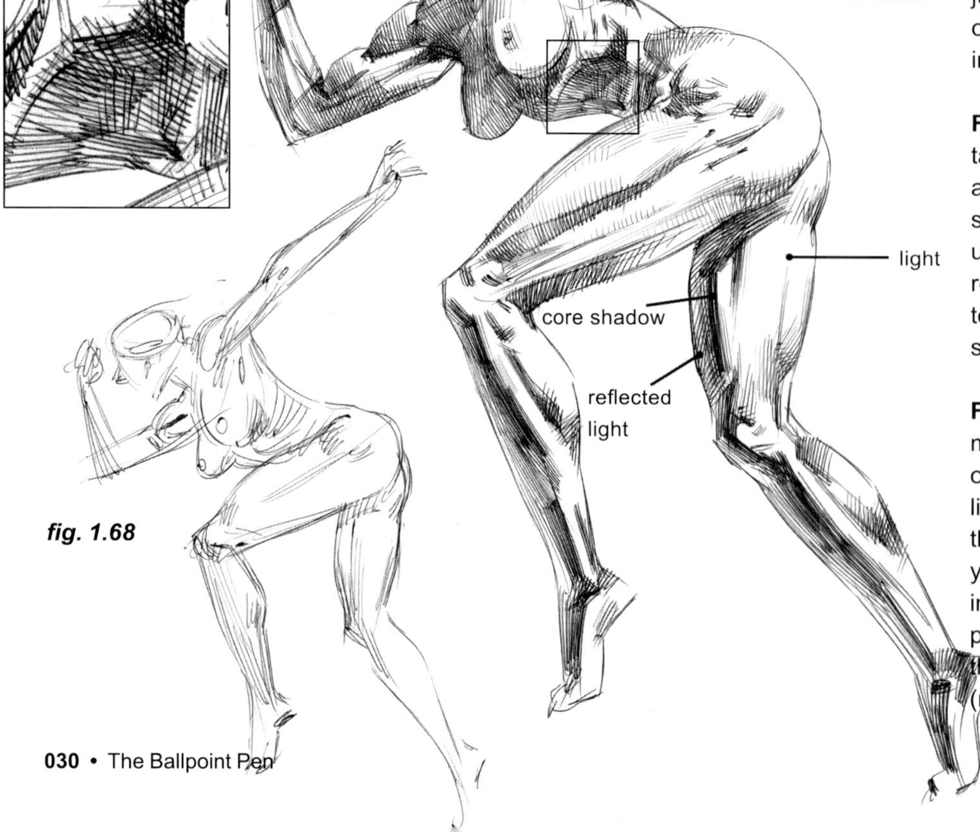

Fig. 1.61: While rendering this torso (top left) the idea of the volumetric rendering (**fig. 1.11**, page 018, and **figs. 1.65** and **1.67** this page) has been present throughout with all its elements, light, shadow, core shadow, reflected light, and cast shadow, as seen in more detail in the insert (**fig. 1.66**).

The three steps (**figs. 1.62**, **1.63** and **1.64**) show an understanding of the volumes and parts that compose the object being rendered prior to starting the job. Notice that just the shading by itself, without the outline of the arm (step 2), is enough to give a solid impression of the subject and its volume.

Fig. 1.68: First a quick sketch was drawn tackling a sense of dynamics, proportion, and anatomy. Then by imposing a new sheet of paper on the sketch and with the use of a light desk, the final drawing was rendered. See again the buildup of darker tones by the progressive overlapping of pen strokes.

Figs. 1.69 and **1.70**: When the drawing is meant to be printed rather than shown as an original, you can switch parts that you don't like out with new parts, and then compose them all together digitally. For this purpose, you can print the drawing and redo the improvements on a superimposed sheet of paper with the use of a light desk for it. Then the two layers are edited together digitally (refer to process example on page 064).

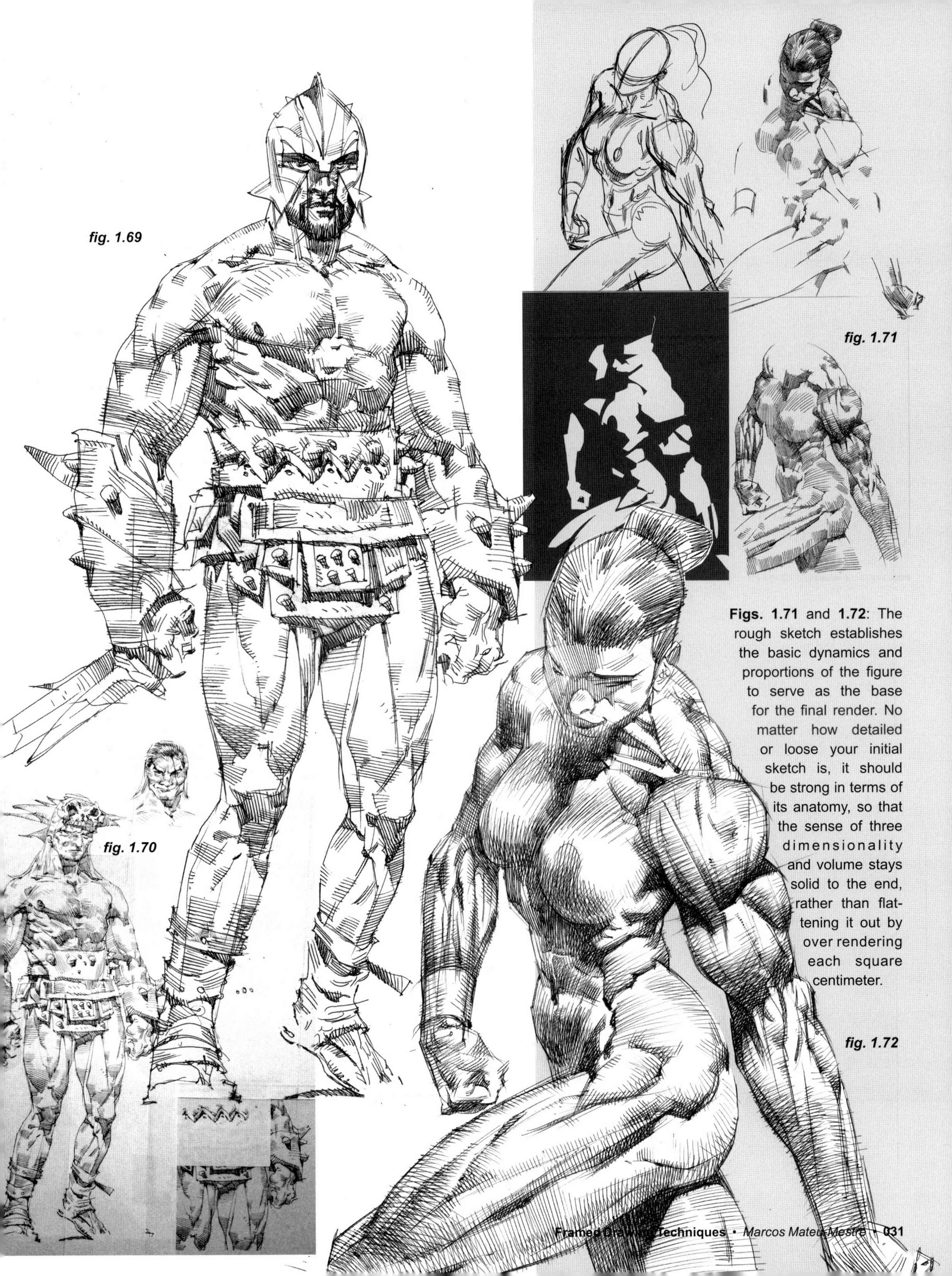

fig. 1.69

fig. 1.70

fig. 1.71

Figs. 1.71 and **1.72**: The rough sketch establishes the basic dynamics and proportions of the figure to serve as the base for the final render. No matter how detailed or loose your initial sketch is, it should be strong in terms of its anatomy, so that the sense of three dimensionality and volume stays solid to the end, rather than flattening it out by over rendering each square centimeter.

fig. 1.72

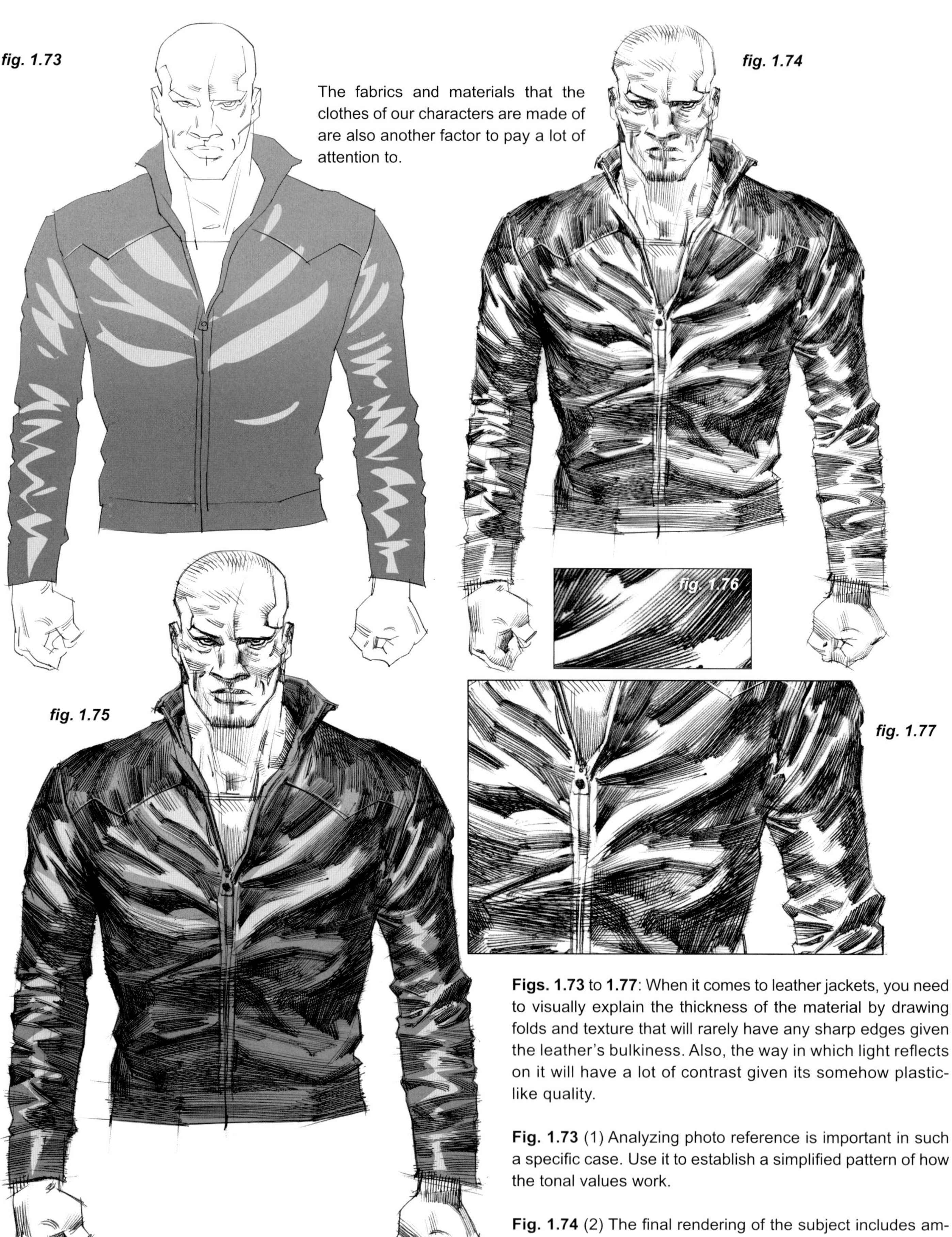

The fabrics and materials that the clothes of our characters are made of are also another factor to pay a lot of attention to.

Figs. 1.73 to **1.77**: When it comes to leather jackets, you need to visually explain the thickness of the material by drawing folds and texture that will rarely have any sharp edges given the leather's bulkiness. Also, the way in which light reflects on it will have a lot of contrast given its somehow plastic-like quality.

Fig. 1.73 (1) Analyzing photo reference is important in such a specific case. Use it to establish a simplified pattern of how the tonal values work.

Fig. 1.74 (2) The final rendering of the subject includes amplified details in **figs. 1.76** and **1.77**.

Fig. 1.75 (3) The previous layers are superimposed, line **1.74**) and tone (**1.73**), for a more realistic feel.

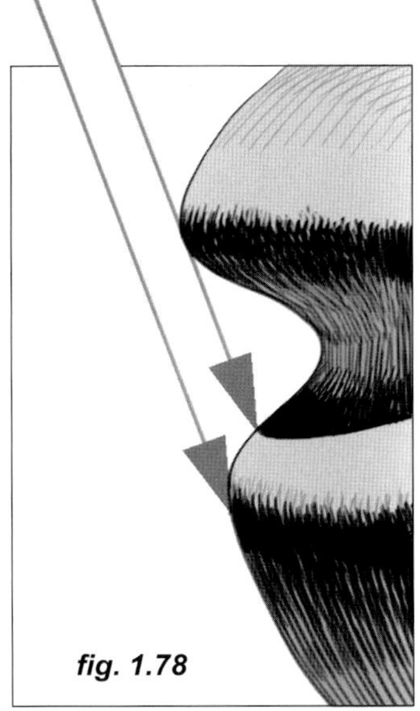

fig. 1.78

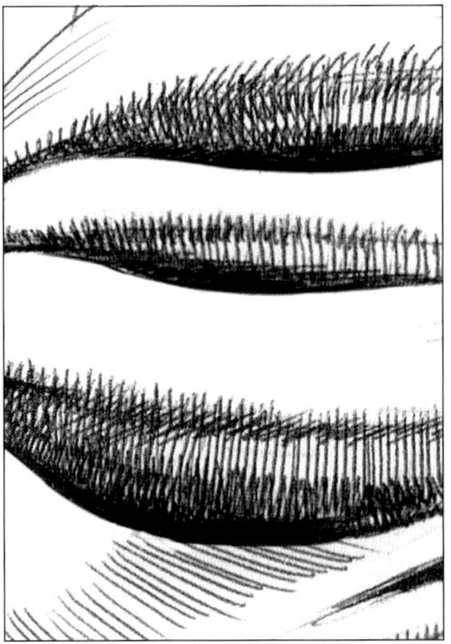

fig. 1.79

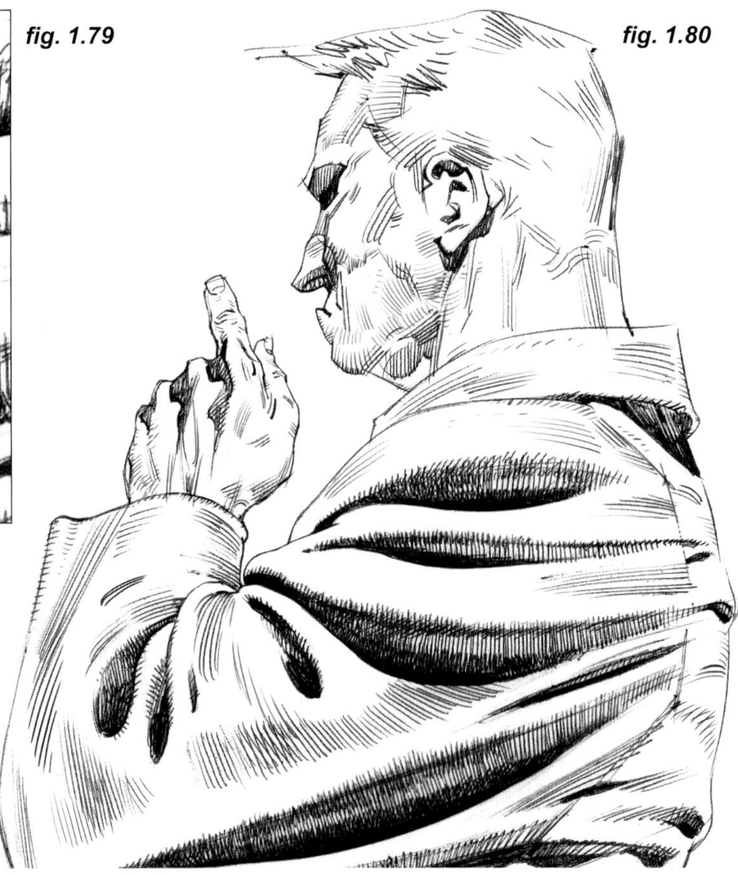

fig. 1.80

This other case represents a thick fabric coat, with a smoother, less reflective surface than a leather jacket. As the folds here also have a roundish, bulky aspect, light will have the time to play nicely on its surface, creating a full game of light, core shadow, and reflected light shadow.

You can see how this plays along in **figs. 1.78** and **1.79** in the side section and detail drawings.

Fig. 1.80 To the right shows the look of the final render. See how the light areas use up more real estate than the shadow ones, opposite to the previous "leather jacket" example in which the lesser amount of light areas make these appear more special, unique and shinier.

Fig. 1.81: Silk will come up with a different look and feel altogether. The fabric is thinner, the folds crispier and less bulky. The look somehow is a bit more metallic, which implies a strong, shiny quality wherever light hits its surface, creating visually graphic contrasts between the fabric's different areas, and directional planes (see arrows on **fig. 1.82** showing the more angular type of texture/surface compared to the previous cases).

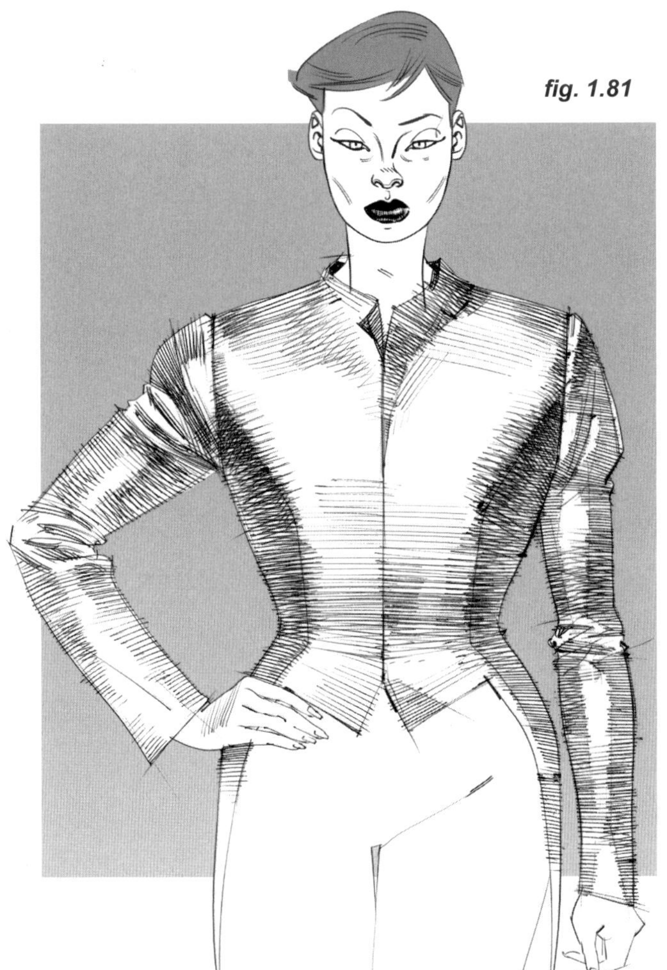

fig. 1.81

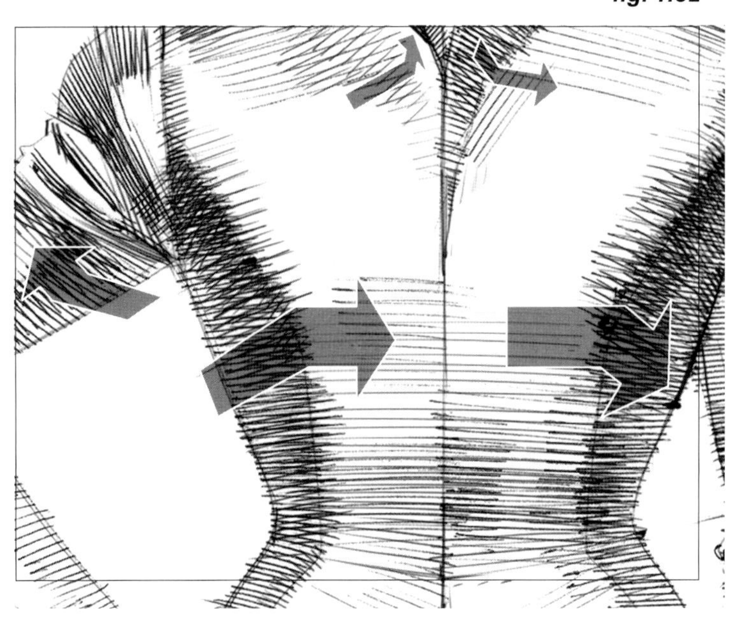

fig. 1.82

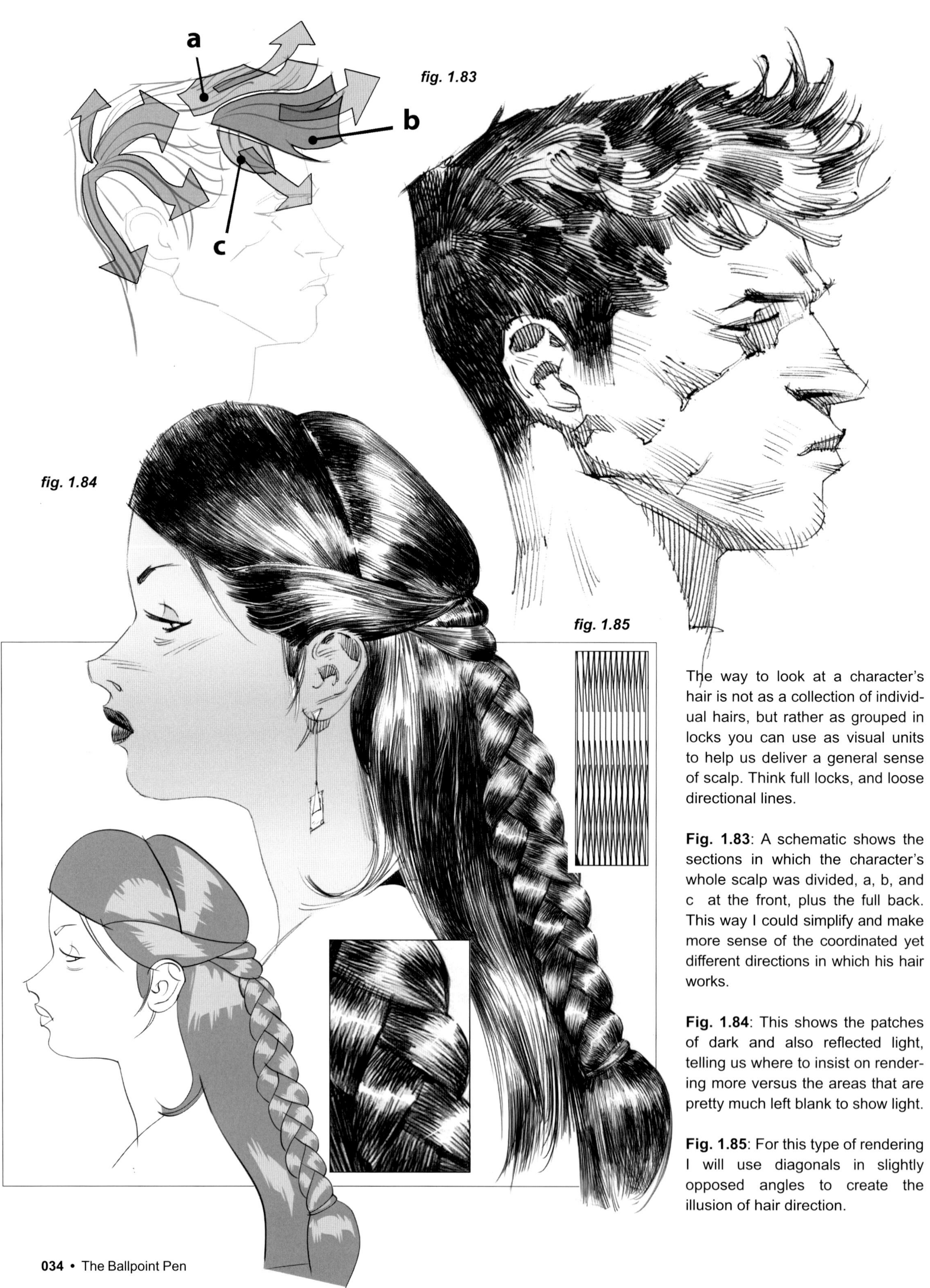

fig. 1.83

fig. 1.84

fig. 1.85

The way to look at a character's hair is not as a collection of individual hairs, but rather as grouped in locks you can use as visual units to help us deliver a general sense of scalp. Think full locks, and loose directional lines.

Fig. 1.83: A schematic shows the sections in which the character's whole scalp was divided, a, b, and c at the front, plus the full back. This way I could simplify and make more sense of the coordinated yet different directions in which his hair works.

Fig. 1.84: This shows the patches of dark and also reflected light, telling us where to insist on rendering more versus the areas that are pretty much left blank to show light.

Fig. 1.85: For this type of rendering I will use diagonals in slightly opposed angles to create the illusion of hair direction.

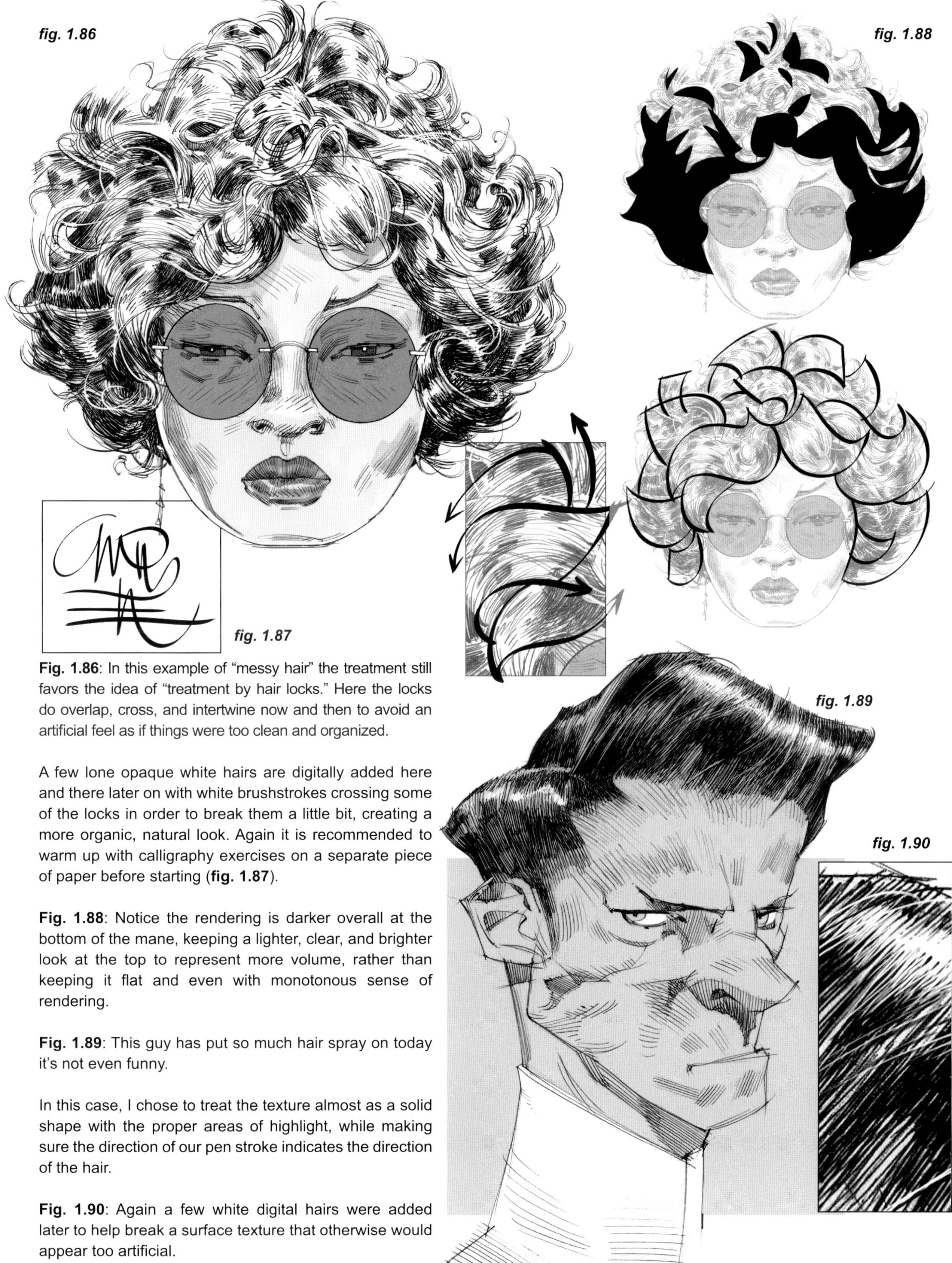

fig. 1.86

fig. 1.87

fig. 1.88

fig. 1.89

fig. 1.90

Fig. 1.86: In this example of “messy hair” the treatment still favors the idea of “treatment by hair locks.” Here the locks do overlap, cross, and intertwine now and then to avoid an artificial feel as if things were too clean and organized.

A few lone opaque white hairs are digitally added here and there later on with white brushstrokes crossing some of the locks in order to break them a little bit, creating a more organic, natural look. Again it is recommended to warm up with calligraphy exercises on a separate piece of paper before starting (**fig. 1.87**).

Fig. 1.88: Notice the rendering is darker overall at the bottom of the mane, keeping a lighter, clear, and brighter look at the top to represent more volume, rather than keeping it flat and even with monotonous sense of rendering.

Fig. 1.89: This guy has put so much hair spray on today it’s not even funny.

In this case, I chose to treat the texture almost as a solid shape with the proper areas of highlight, while making sure the direction of our pen stroke indicates the direction of the hair.

Fig. 1.90: Again a few white digital hairs were added later to help break a surface texture that otherwise would appear too artificial.

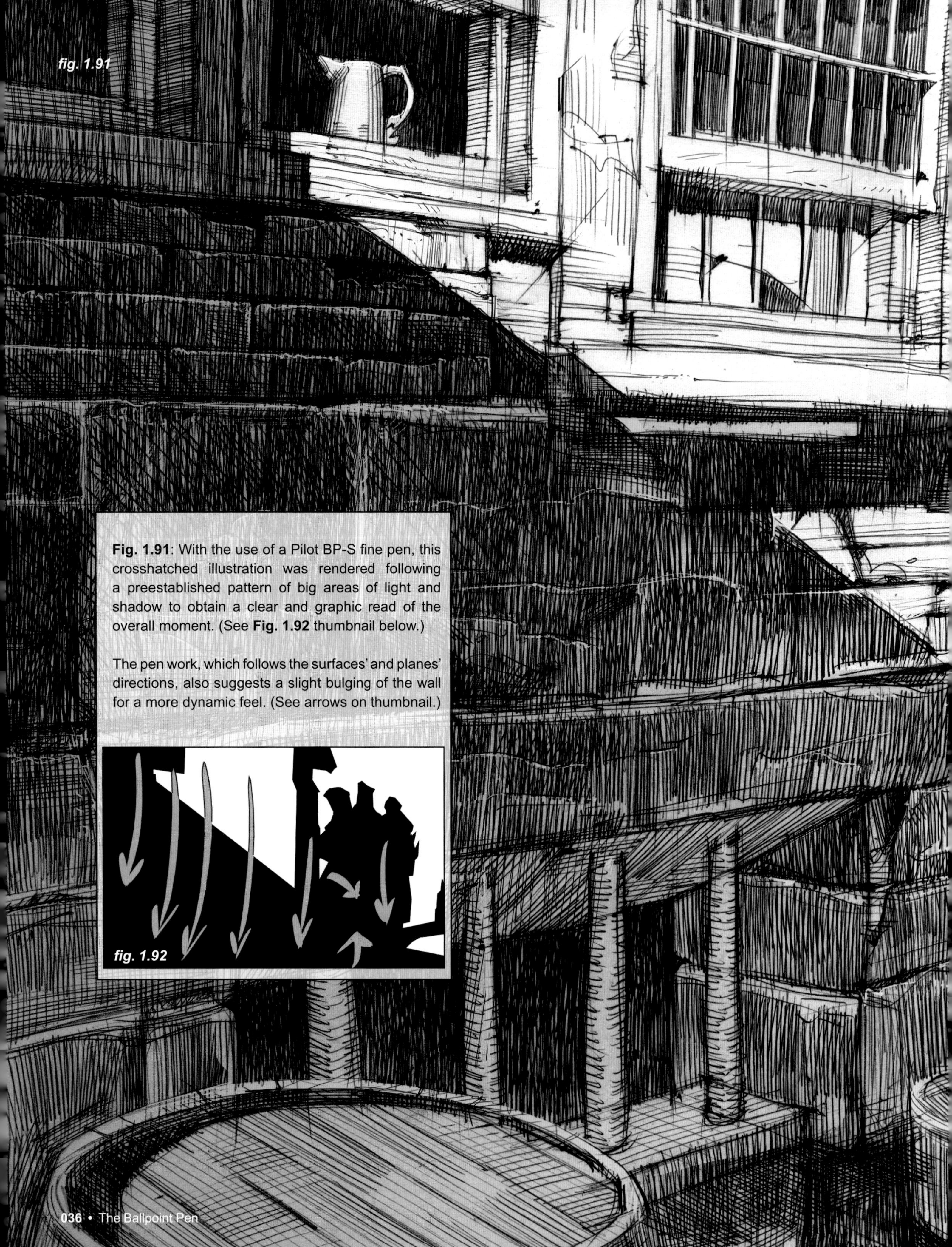

fig. 1.91

Fig. 1.91: With the use of a Pilot BP-S fine pen, this crosshatched illustration was rendered following a preestablished pattern of big areas of light and shadow to obtain a clear and graphic read of the overall moment. (See **Fig. 1.92** thumbnail below.)

The pen work, which follows the surfaces' and planes' directions, also suggests a slight bulging of the wall for a more dynamic feel. (See arrows on thumbnail.)

fig. 1.92

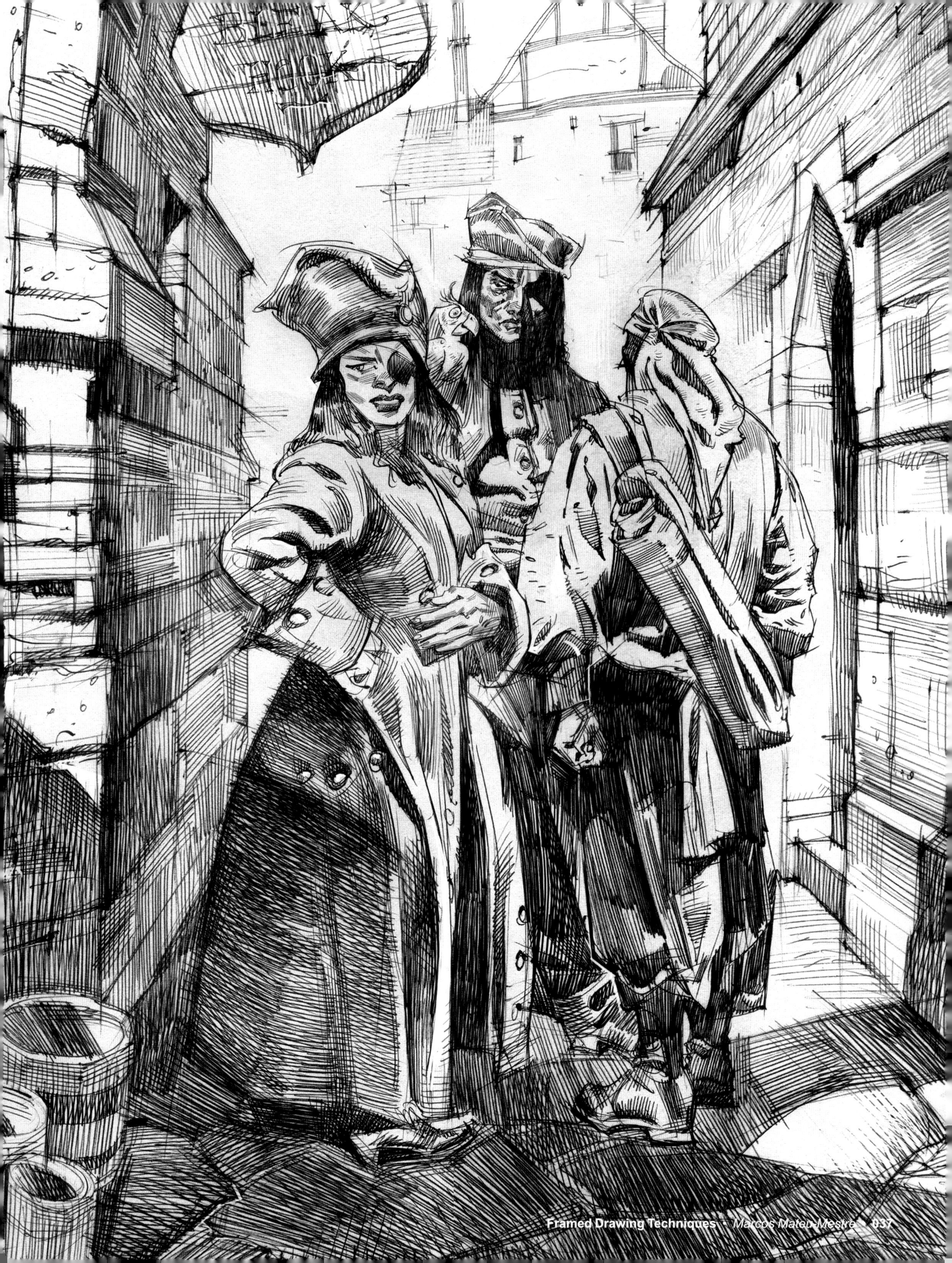
BLEAK
HOOK

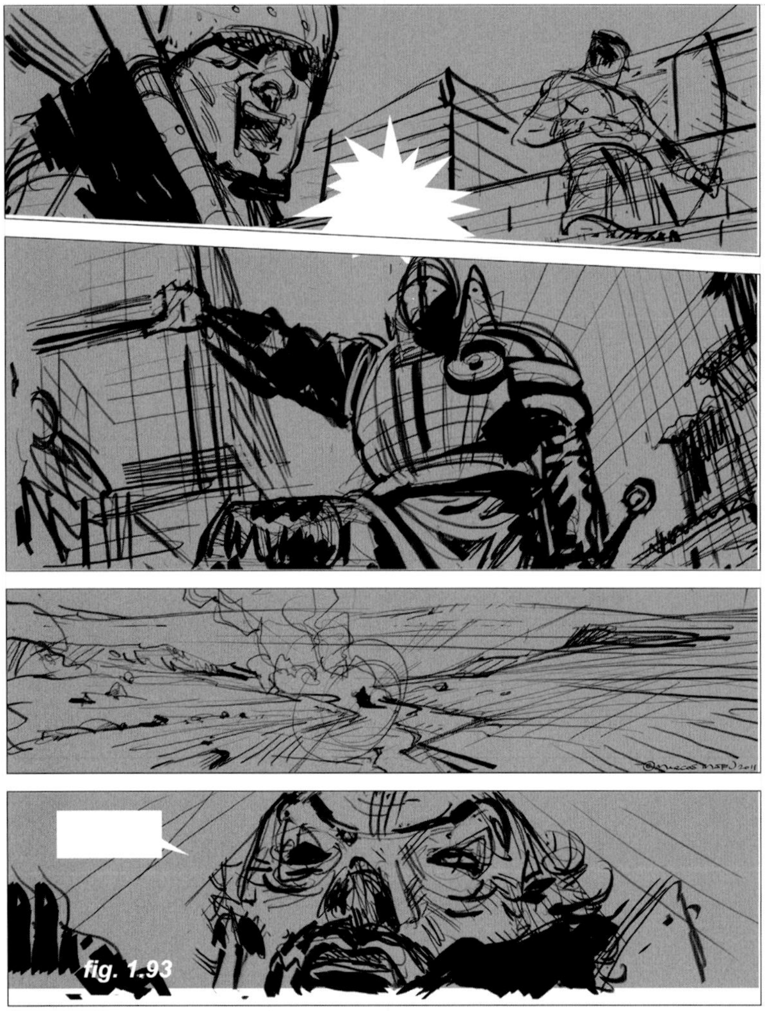

fig. 1.93

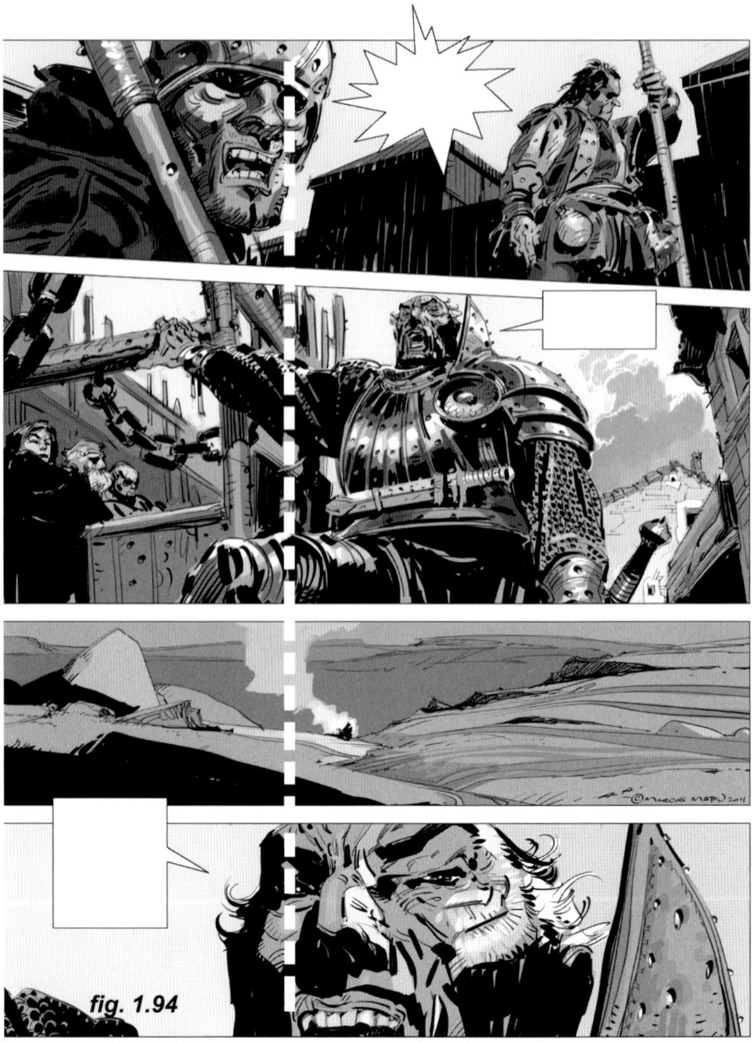

fig. 1.94

DIFFERENT TECHNIQUES, DIFFERENT RESULTS

These pages show the process of creating a graphic novel page from of my book *Trail of Steel: 1441 A.D.*: from the first layout sketch based on the script (**fig. 1.93**), to its final digital ink (**fig. 1.94**), and to a different rendering version in ball pen (**fig. 1.95** next page).

This ball-pen version shows how the choice of technique will affect the telling of the story itself.

The minutia and laborious look and feel of a pen can help emphasize the intricate, heavy nature of the medieval period shown here, a period when the sense of the passing of time was slower than now, allowing for a better chance to pay attention to detail. It can help us also to relate to that period by the use of one of the oldest and most traditional art techniques still available.

It can certainly be more appropriate for a story that happens say in medieval times rather than a science-fiction adventure. I'm not saying that the two do not belong together under any circumstances, as one can choose to focus on a futuristic time under a more baroque and complex eye, if it is our intention to aim for such a heavier feel of the visuals.

On this page, notice the rendering of elements previously seen in this book, like human faces (**figs. 1.51–1.60**, pages 028-029), metal (**fig. 1.34**, page 024), and clothing (**figs. 1.73–1.82**, pages 032–033), as well as chain mail, wood, natural terrains, and so forth.

Incidentally, and speaking of all visual narrative devices, see that the two characters involved in the dialogue (Condottiero Martin and one of his watchmen) "face each other" (not "crossing the line') even while appearing in different panels as well. See as well their placement in their respective panels, one favoring the left of his, the other his right.

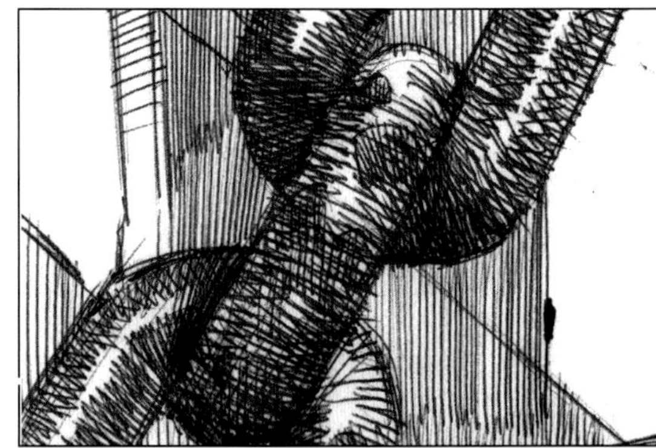

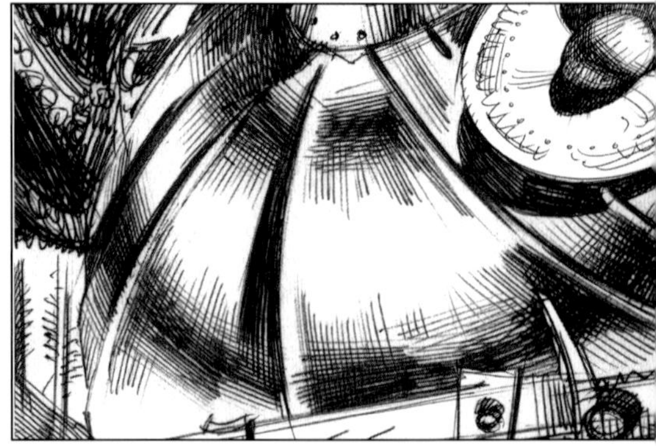

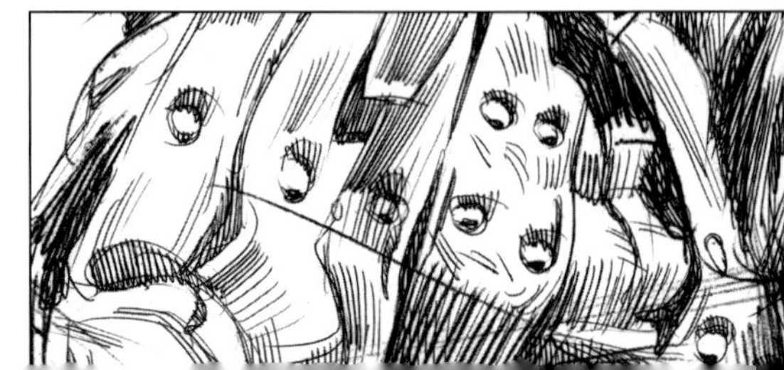

fig. 1.95

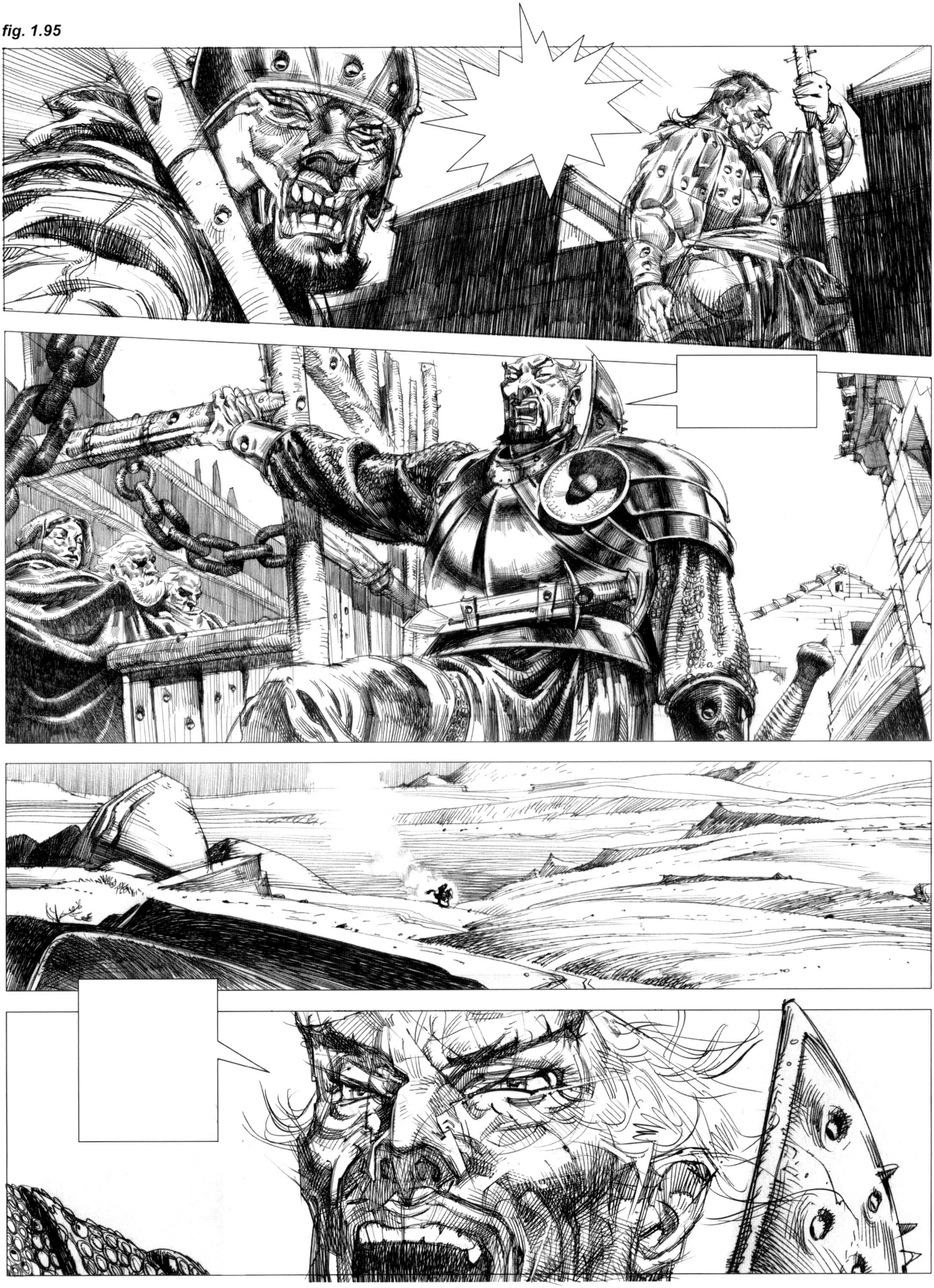

2

GRAPHITE PENCIL

While a graphite pencil cannot create the punching darks that an ink-based medium would, the range of tones and number of subtle nuances it achieves with seamless continuity can be spectacular. Its ability to move from one tone of the gray scale to another in flawless progression is a device an artist can use to achieve looks that are believable and realistic while keeping the energy of a hand-drawn piece of artwork.

Although these gradations can be achieved with the use of a single graphite pencil, there are a big range of pencil core qualities that is numerically ordered, from the hardest to the softest, between "9H" and "9B." The complete basic range is: 9H, 8H, 7H, 6H, 5H, 4H, 3H, 2H, H, HB, F, B, 2B, 3B, 4B, 5B, 6B, 7B, 8B, and 9B.

This hardness and softness depends on how much graphite is in the mix that conforms the core. The less graphite there is, the harder the core, the more graphite, the softer it is, and therefore the darker the mark that can be achieved.

Here are examples of how some of these pencils' grades translate on paper, with both flat and gradated renderings:

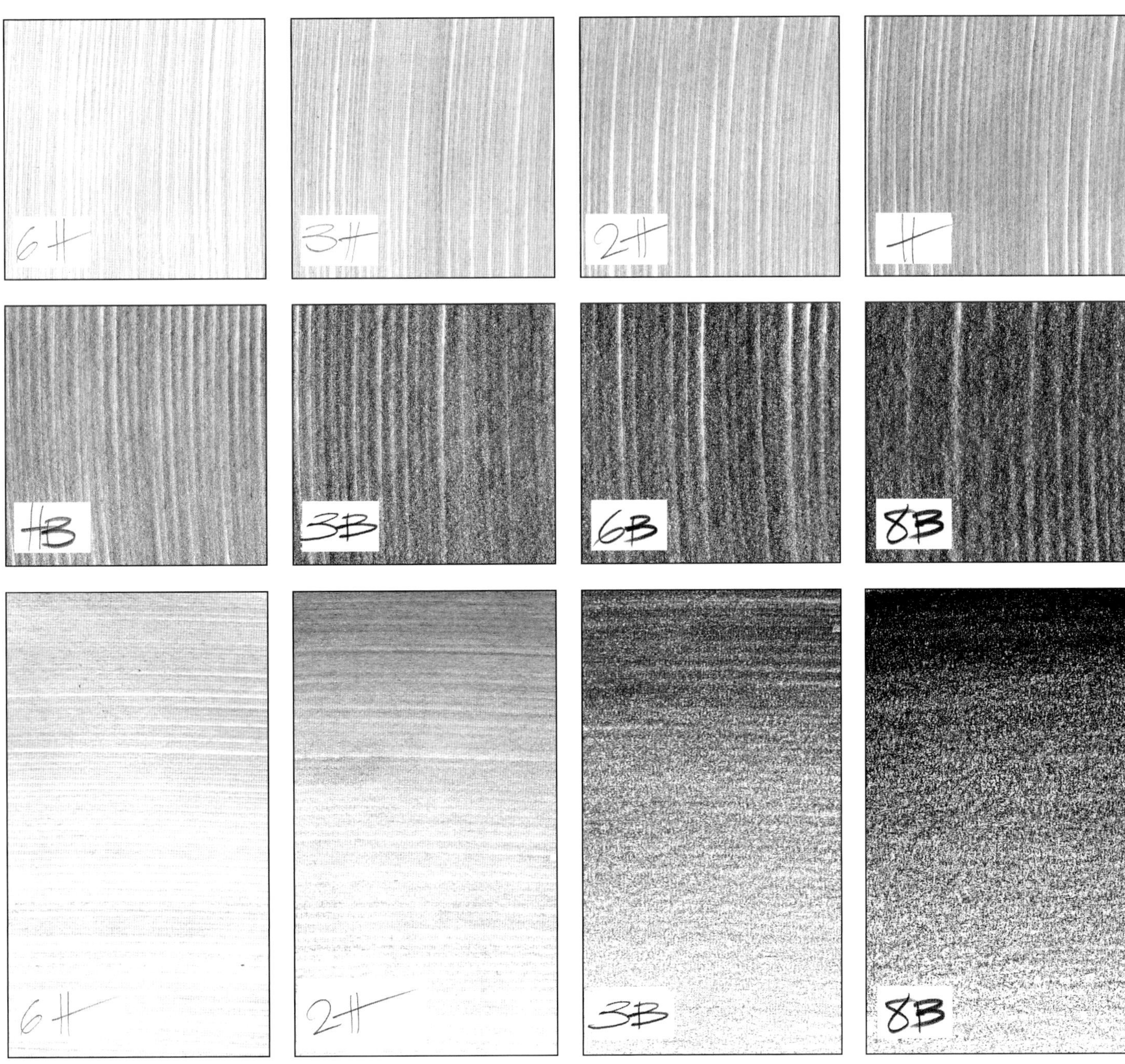

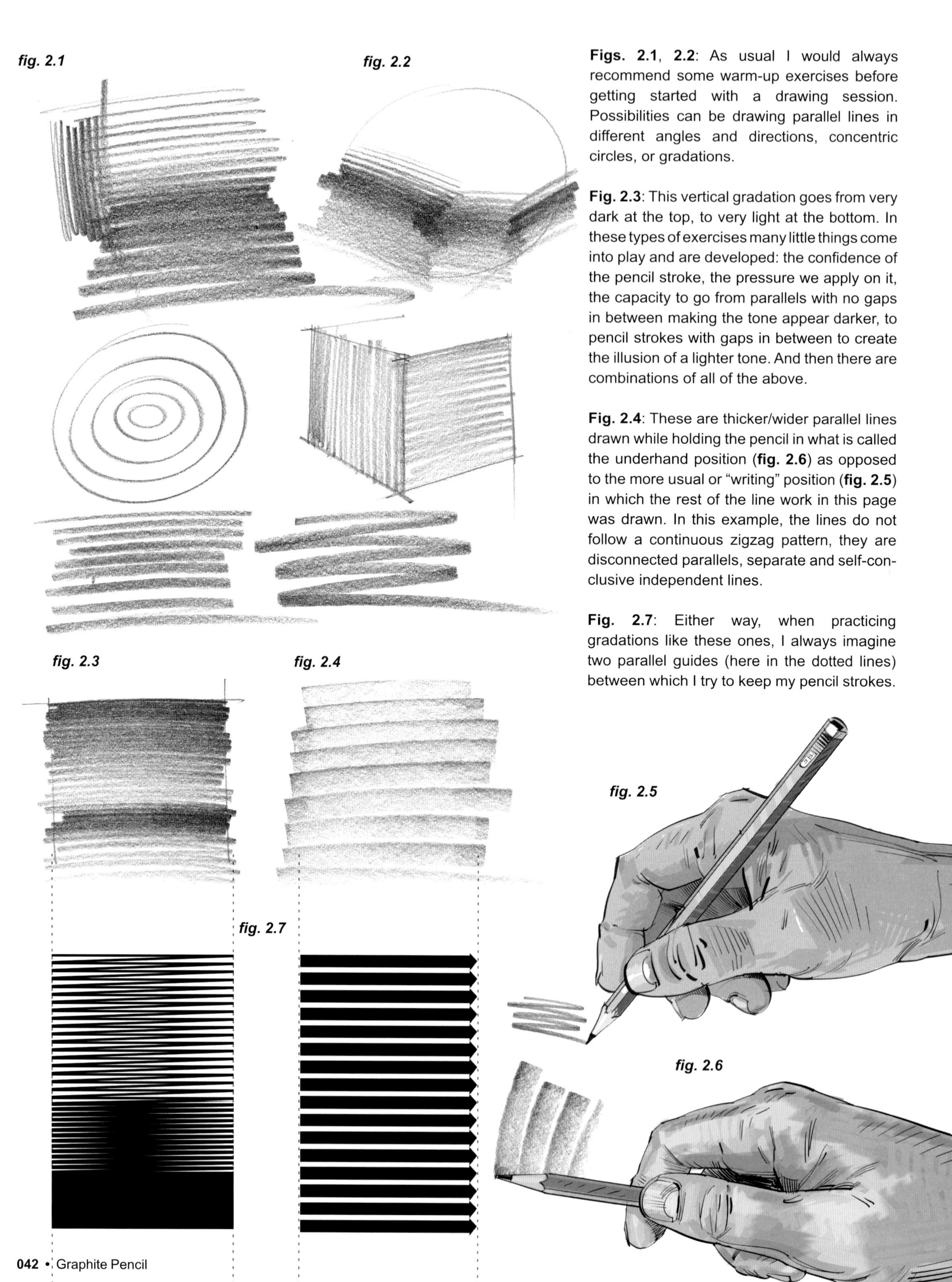

Figs. 2.1, **2.2**: As usual I would always recommend some warm-up exercises before getting started with a drawing session. Possibilities can be drawing parallel lines in different angles and directions, concentric circles, or gradations.

Fig. 2.3: This vertical gradation goes from very dark at the top, to very light at the bottom. In these types of exercises many little things come into play and are developed: the confidence of the pencil stroke, the pressure we apply on it, the capacity to go from parallels with no gaps in between making the tone appear darker, to pencil strokes with gaps in between to create the illusion of a lighter tone. And then there are combinations of all of the above.

Fig. 2.4: These are thicker/wider parallel lines drawn while holding the pencil in what is called the underhand position (**fig. 2.6**) as opposed to the more usual or "writing" position (**fig. 2.5**) in which the rest of the line work in this page was drawn. In this example, the lines do not follow a continuous zigzag pattern, they are disconnected parallels, separate and self-conclusive independent lines.

Fig. 2.7: Either way, when practicing gradations like these ones, I always imagine two parallel guides (here in the dotted lines) between which I try to keep my pencil strokes.

fig. 2.8

fig. 2.9

Generally I aim for two main types of rendering: a more uniform one and one where the direction of the pencil strokes is evident and becomes part of the dynamics, energy, and dramatic tension of the image I am working on.

Fig. 2.8: This is an example of a flat, more "uneventful" shading rendered with the help of a 3B grade pencil. A way to achieve this look is explained in the following images.

Fig. 2.9: Start by creating a uniform block of graphite with as big a surface as you can. After that, create another "twin" one right next to it. Then, in step two, bring them together by masking the apparent line between the two previous blocks, with the creation of a subtle overlay of yet another block of graphite at the center, which covers the said "line of encounter" between the first two blocks. And then repeat steps as needed.

Take into account that by overimposing all of these layers you will progressively achieve a darker tone in your rendering. Because of this, you would need to start your first layers at a lighter tone than intended as a final look or result, so that by applying the next layers you will finally achieve the tonal intensity you originally had in mind as a final goal.

fig. 2.10

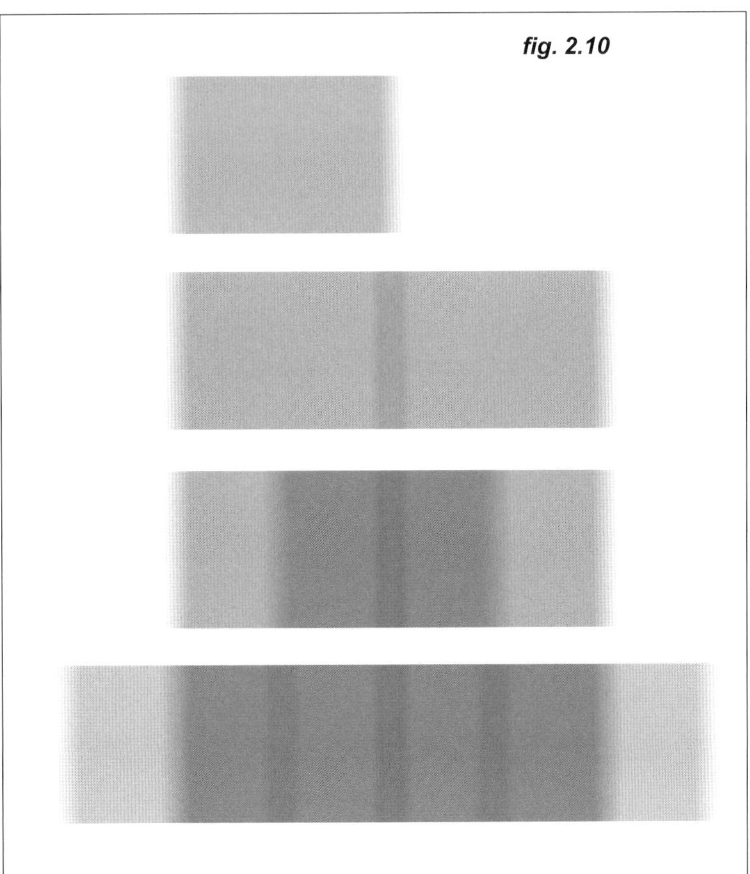

fig. 2.11

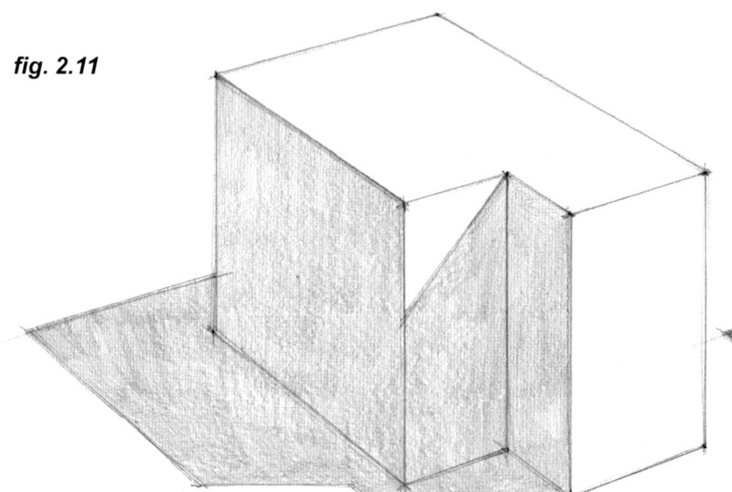

fig. 2.12

fig. 2.13

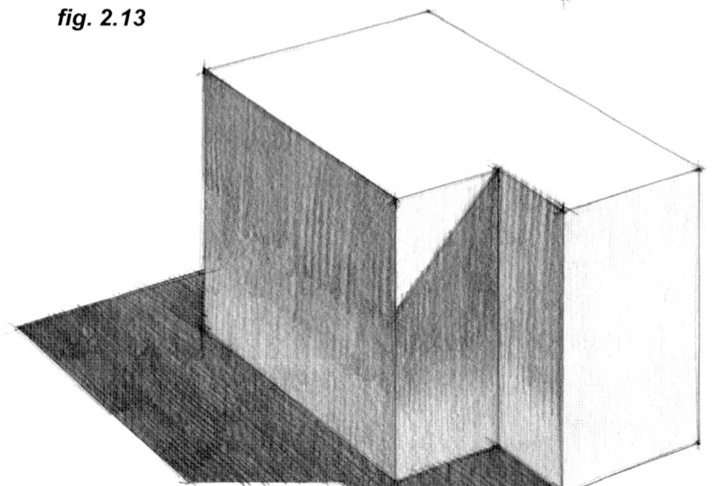

These three steps show the process of rendering by adding successive layers of graphite.

Fig. 2.11: The shading here clearly separates the model in two basic areas: light and a flat, mid-gray shade.

Fig. 2.12: The second step separates the shadow areas in two, the medium and the darkest, by adding layers of graphite.

Fig. 2.13: The third pass gets into the final accents and gradations within shadows to show some reflected light where needed, as well as further separation between the model's different planes, where needed.

Figs. 2.14 and **2.15**: The same system of building up the tonal intensity of each area requires the addition of consecutive layers as seen in these two examples. It is always recommended to start with exercises where the limits between different tonal areas (numbered) are sharp and well defined for a simplified approach.

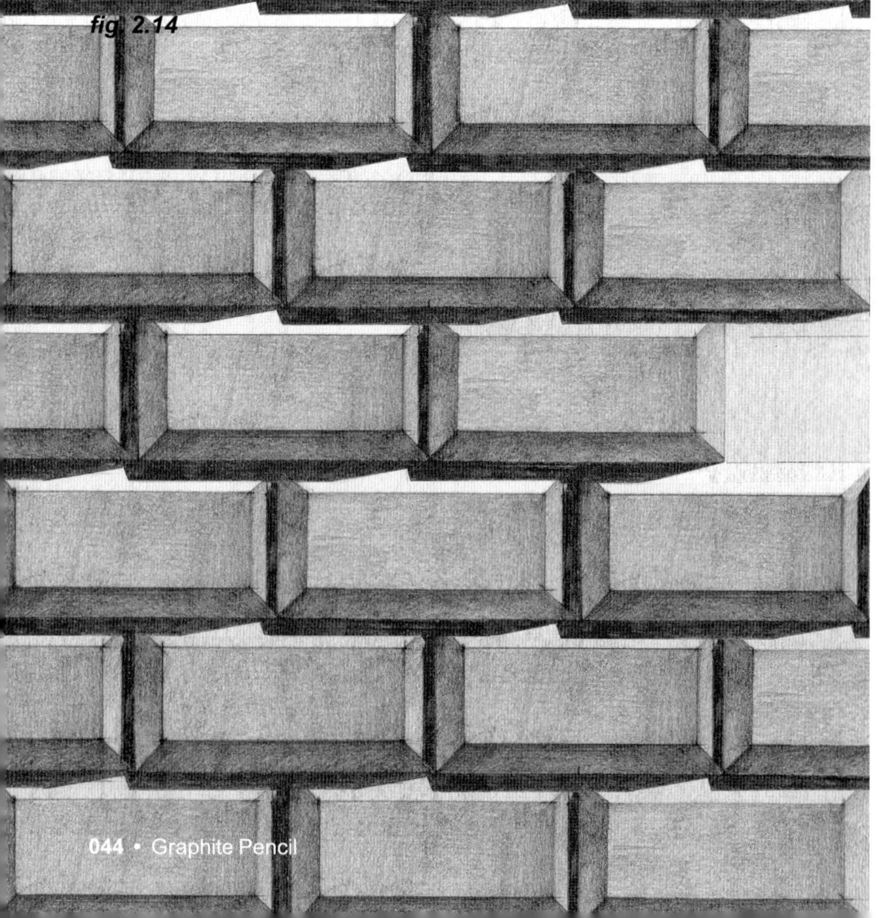

fig. 2.14

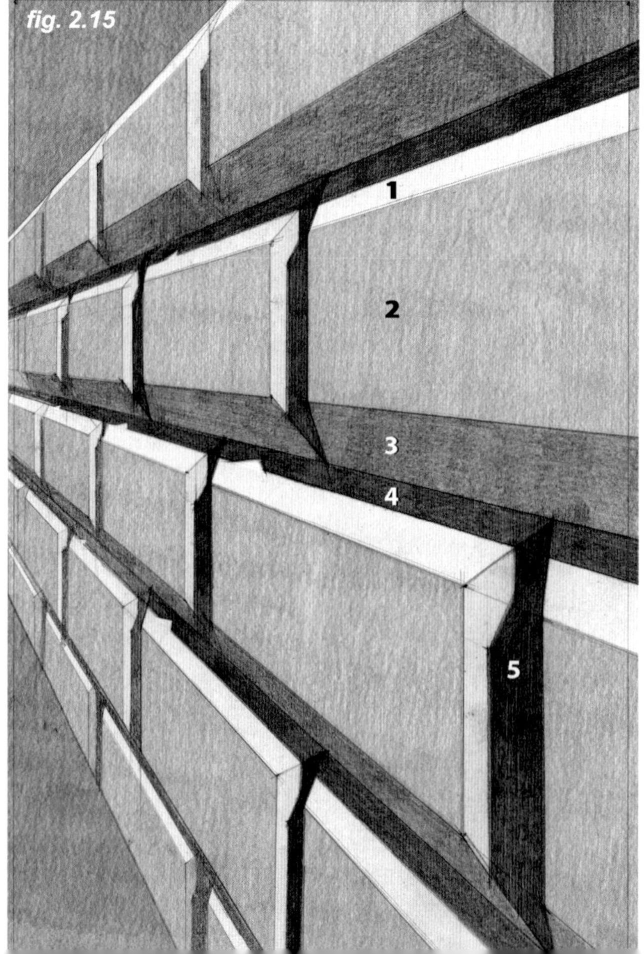

fig. 2.15

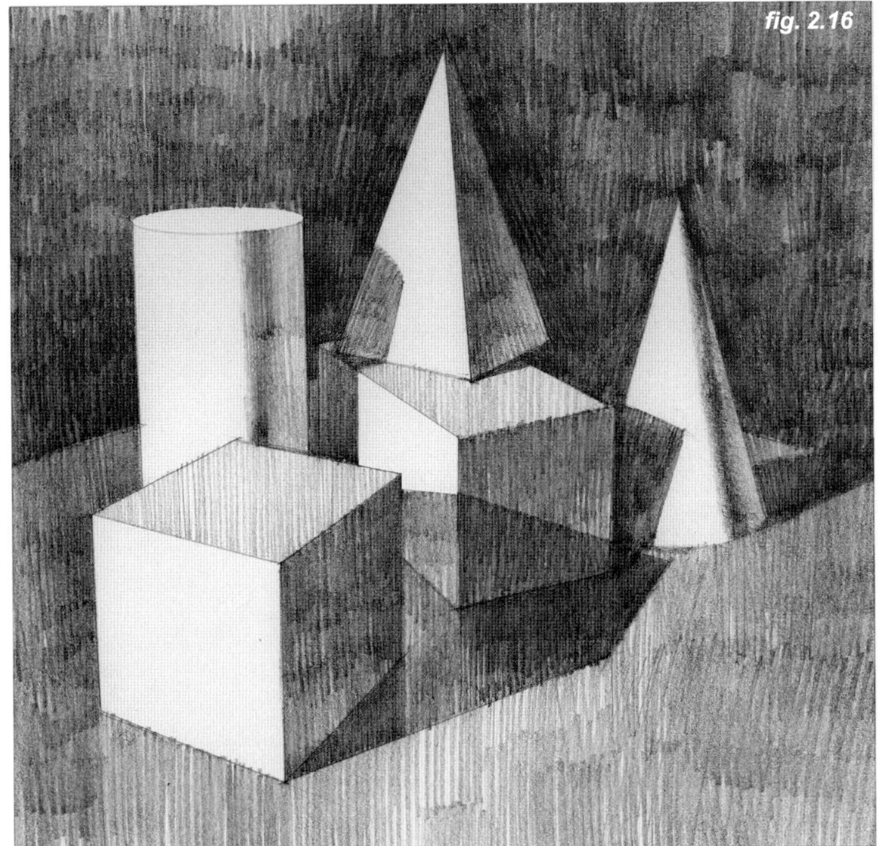
fig. 2.16

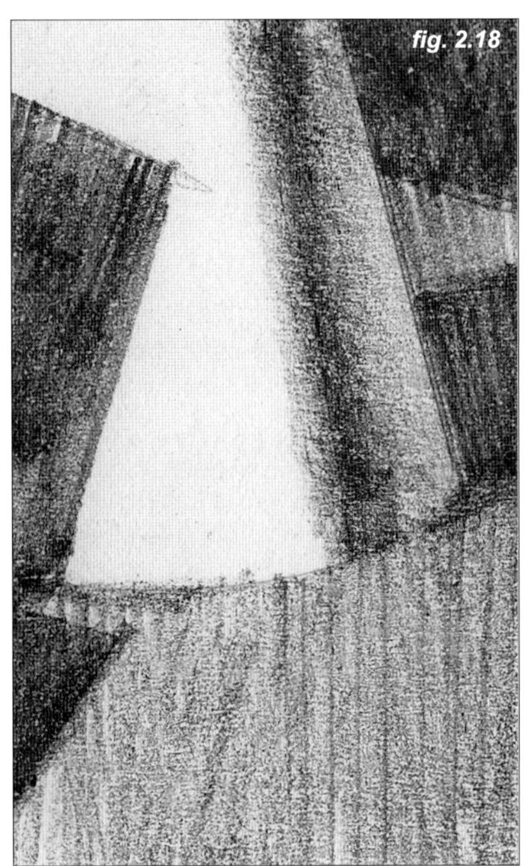
fig. 2.18

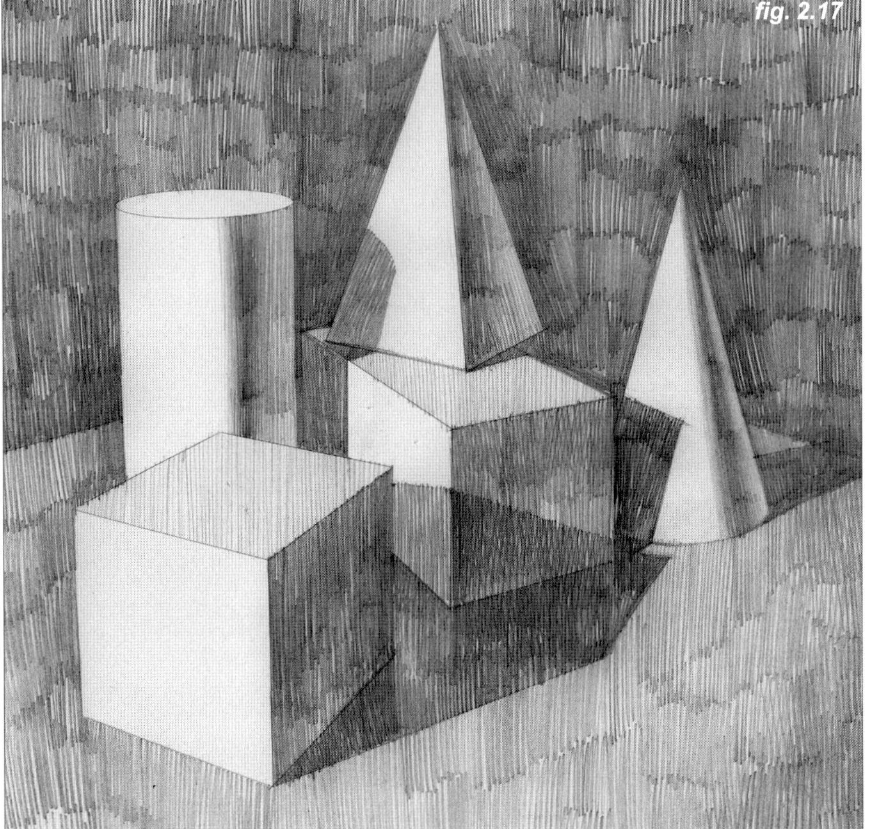
fig. 2.17

Putting these basic techniques into practice, **figs. 2.16** and **2.17** are graphite-pencil versions of a still life similar to the one seen in **fig. 1.13** (page 019). While the essential approach is the same as when using a ball pen, graphite allows us to play with tone in a more controlled manner, not only by the application of extra layers of pencil strokes whenever needed, but also by being more effective when it comes to applying pressure in order to obtain lighter, darker, softer, or sharper tones.

The detail seen in **fig. 2.18** shows the use of the aforementioned techniques, as well as the stroke direction to adapt to the depicted shapes and volumes.

The first version (**fig. 2.16** top left) was executed with a 2B pencil, the second version (**fig. 2.17**) with an H pencil. These show the resulting difference, from softer-edged and more intense in tone (2B), to an overall sharper and lighter feel (H).

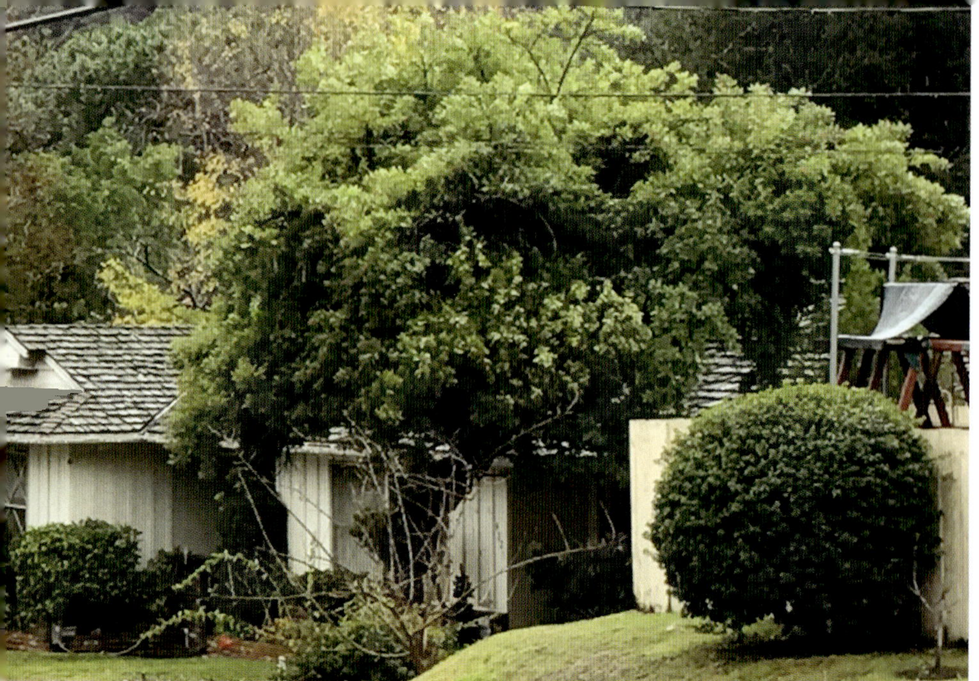

Figs. 2.19 to **2.20**: The images on this page illustrate the thinking process by which to see a subject: by simplifying the most basic shapes and separation of volumes, shown through lights and shadows, and then evolving from there, to a more complex understanding of our subject.

Fig. 2.21: The final drawing reflects (as does **fig. 2.20**) an uneven distribution of masses of light and shade that helps the drawing look more volumetric, as opposed to how an even and flat leaf-pattern-oriented rendering would.

Fig. 2.22: This insert shows how a certain "calligraphy" of the pencil helps create an overall illusion of foliage.

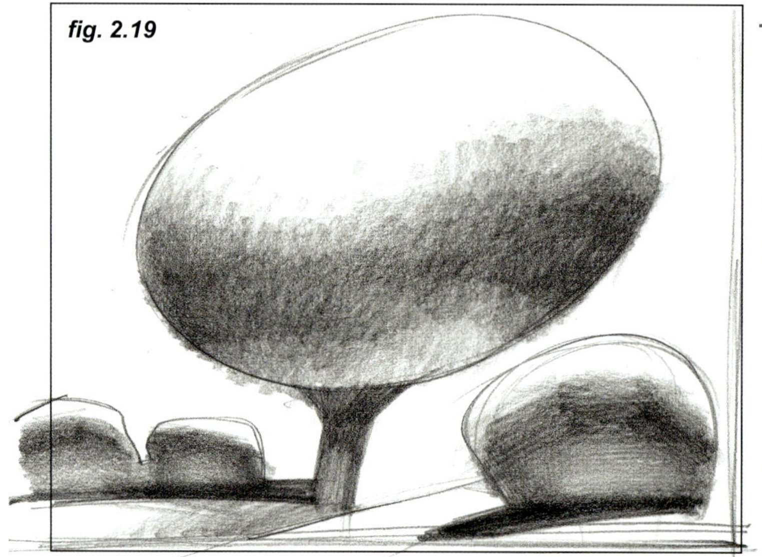

fig. 2.19

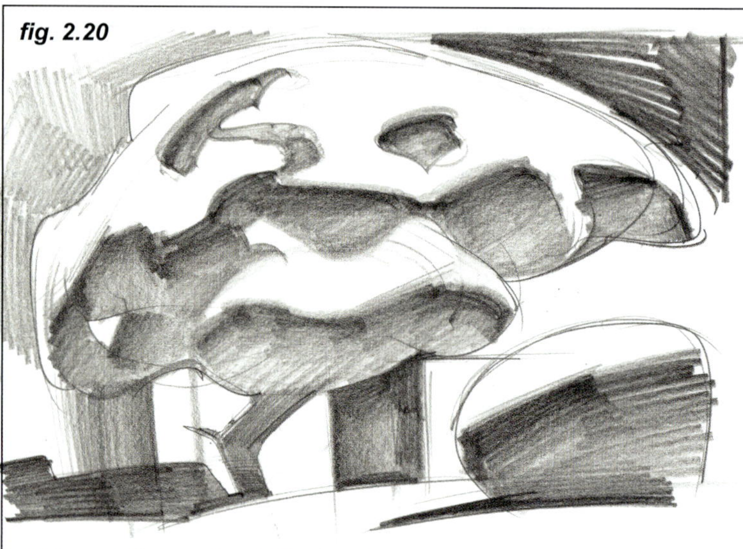

fig. 2.20

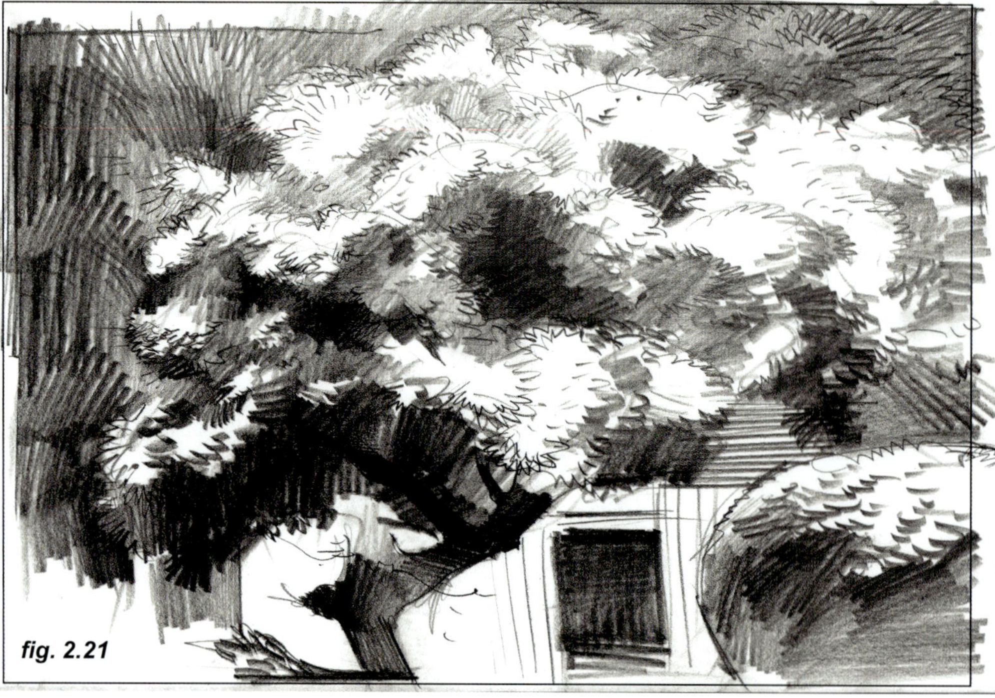

fig. 2.21

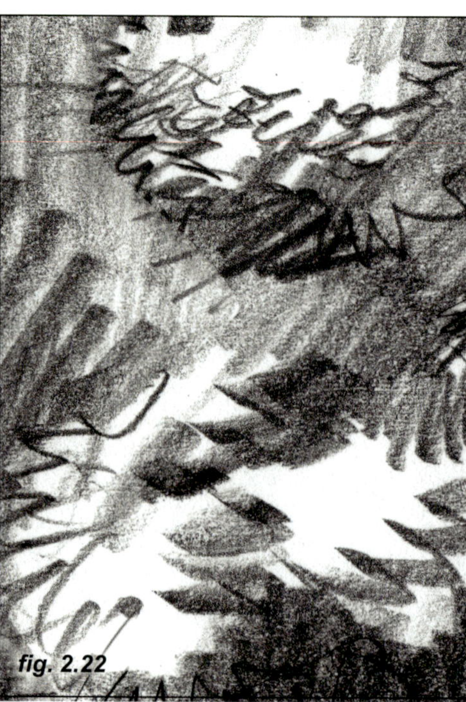

fig. 2.22

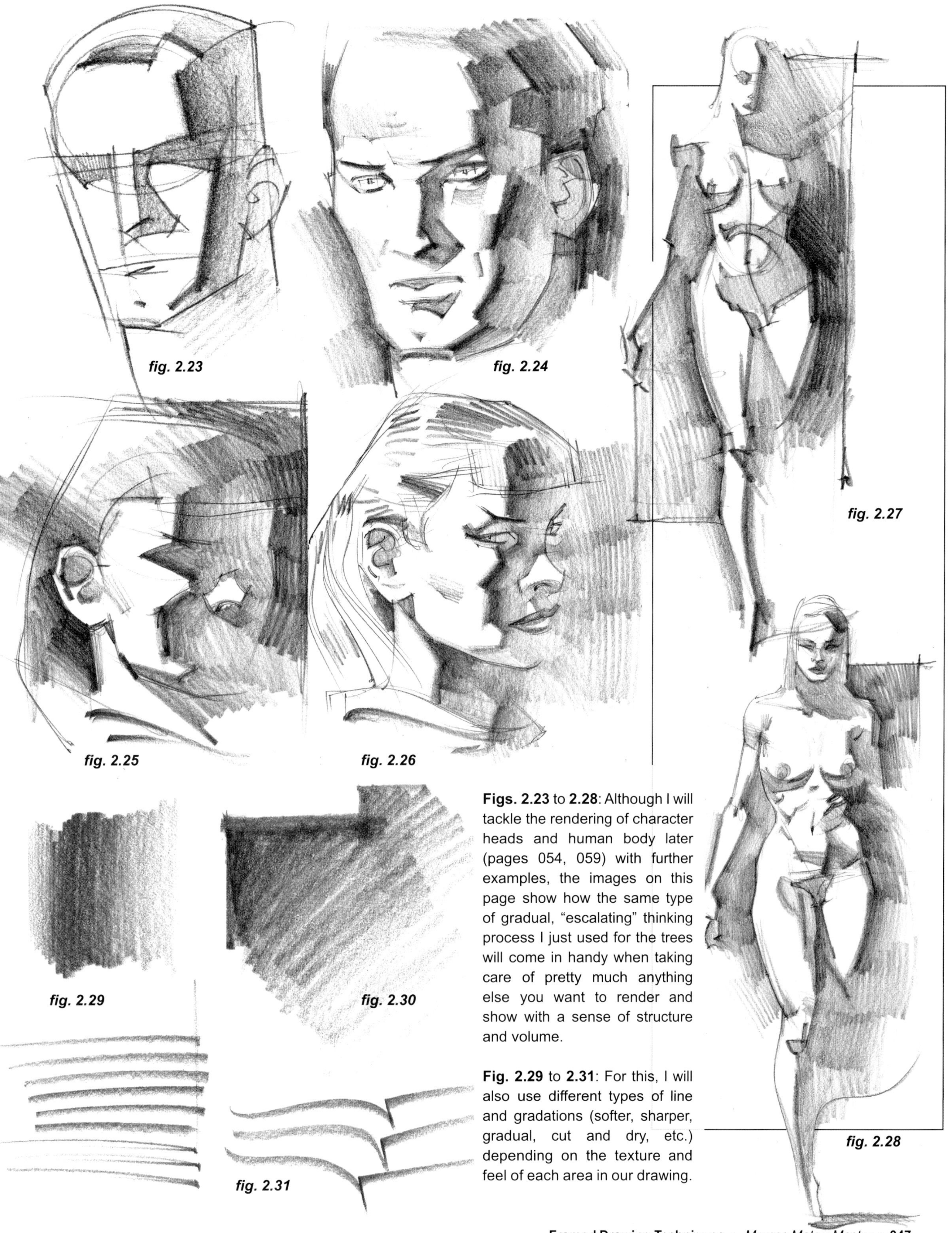

fig. 2.23

fig. 2.24

fig. 2.25

fig. 2.26

fig. 2.27

fig. 2.28

fig. 2.29

fig. 2.30

fig. 2.31

Figs. 2.23 to **2.28**: Although I will tackle the rendering of character heads and human body later (pages 054, 059) with further examples, the images on this page show how the same type of gradual, "escalating" thinking process I just used for the trees will come in handy when taking care of pretty much anything else you want to render and show with a sense of structure and volume.

Fig. 2.29 to **2.31**: For this, I will also use different types of line and gradations (softer, sharper, gradual, cut and dry, etc.) depending on the texture and feel of each area in our drawing.

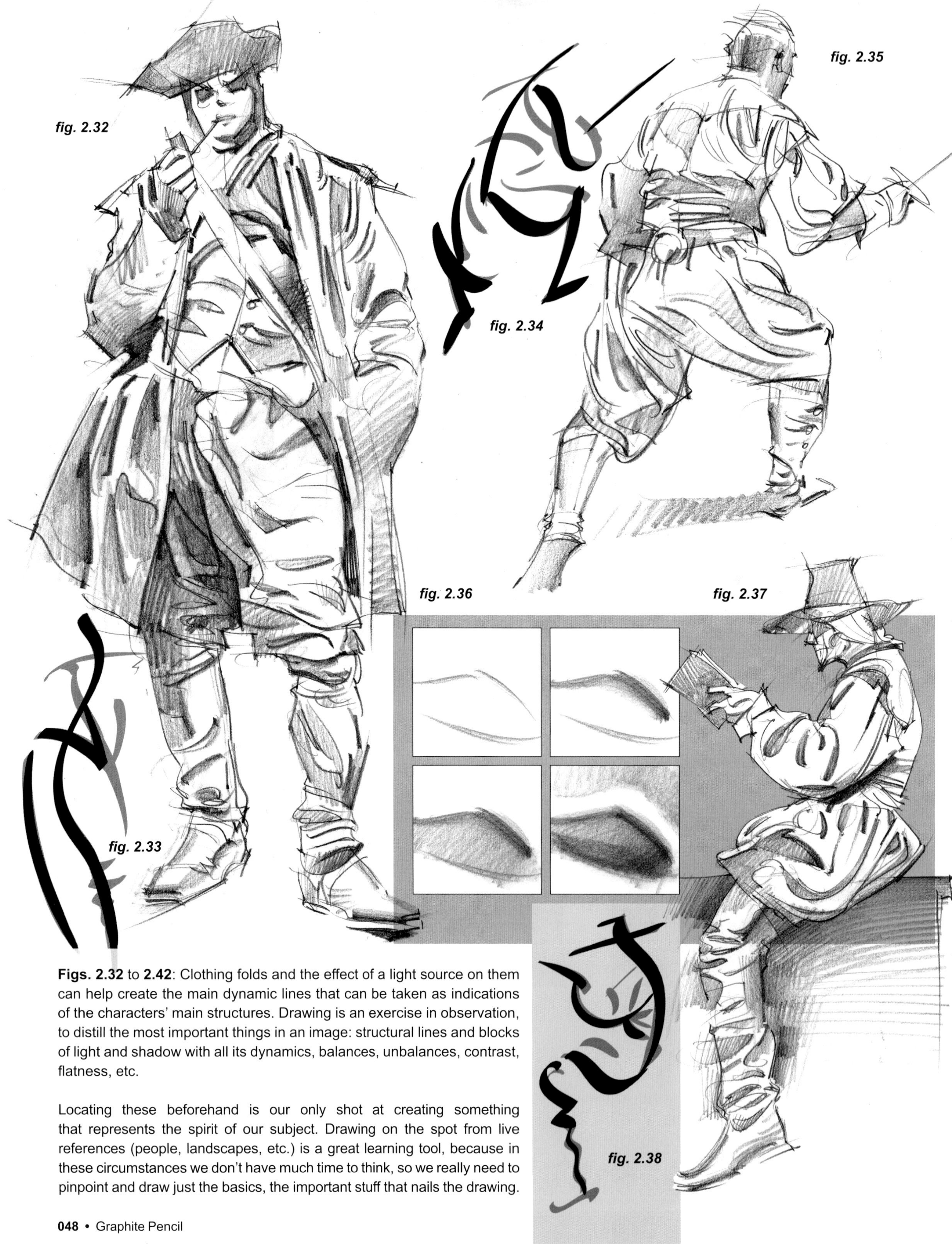

Figs. 2.32 to **2.42**: Clothing folds and the effect of a light source on them can help create the main dynamic lines that can be taken as indications of the characters' main structures. Drawing is an exercise in observation, to distill the most important things in an image: structural lines and blocks of light and shadow with all its dynamics, balances, unbalances, contrast, flatness, etc.

Locating these beforehand is our only shot at creating something that represents the spirit of our subject. Drawing on the spot from live references (people, landscapes, etc.) is a great learning tool, because in these circumstances we don't have much time to think, so we really need to pinpoint and draw just the basics, the important stuff that nails the drawing.

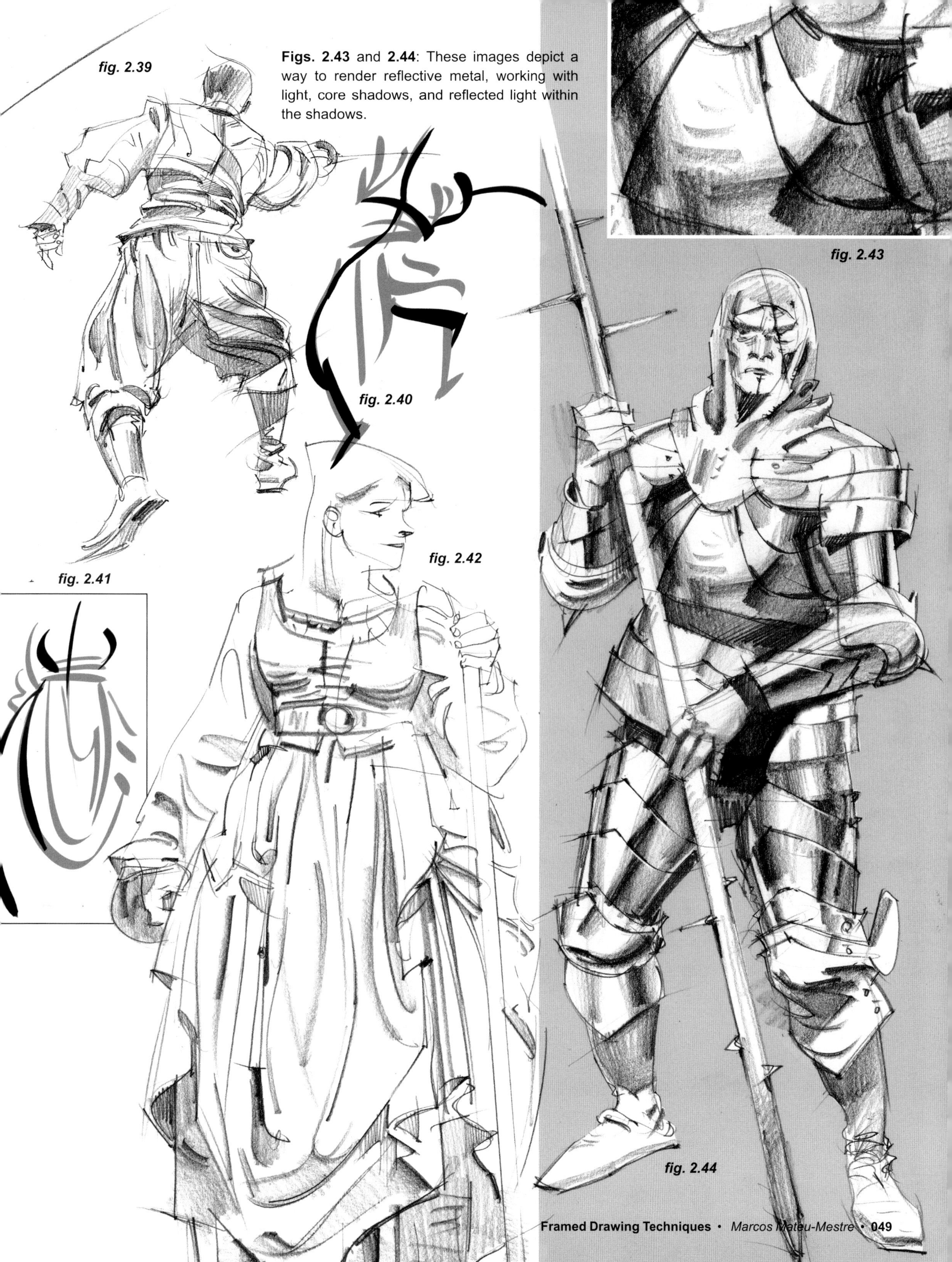

Figs. 2.43 and **2.44**: These images depict a way to render reflective metal, working with light, core shadows, and reflected light within the shadows.

fig. 2.39

fig. 2.40

fig. 2.41

fig. 2.42

fig. 2.43

fig. 2.44

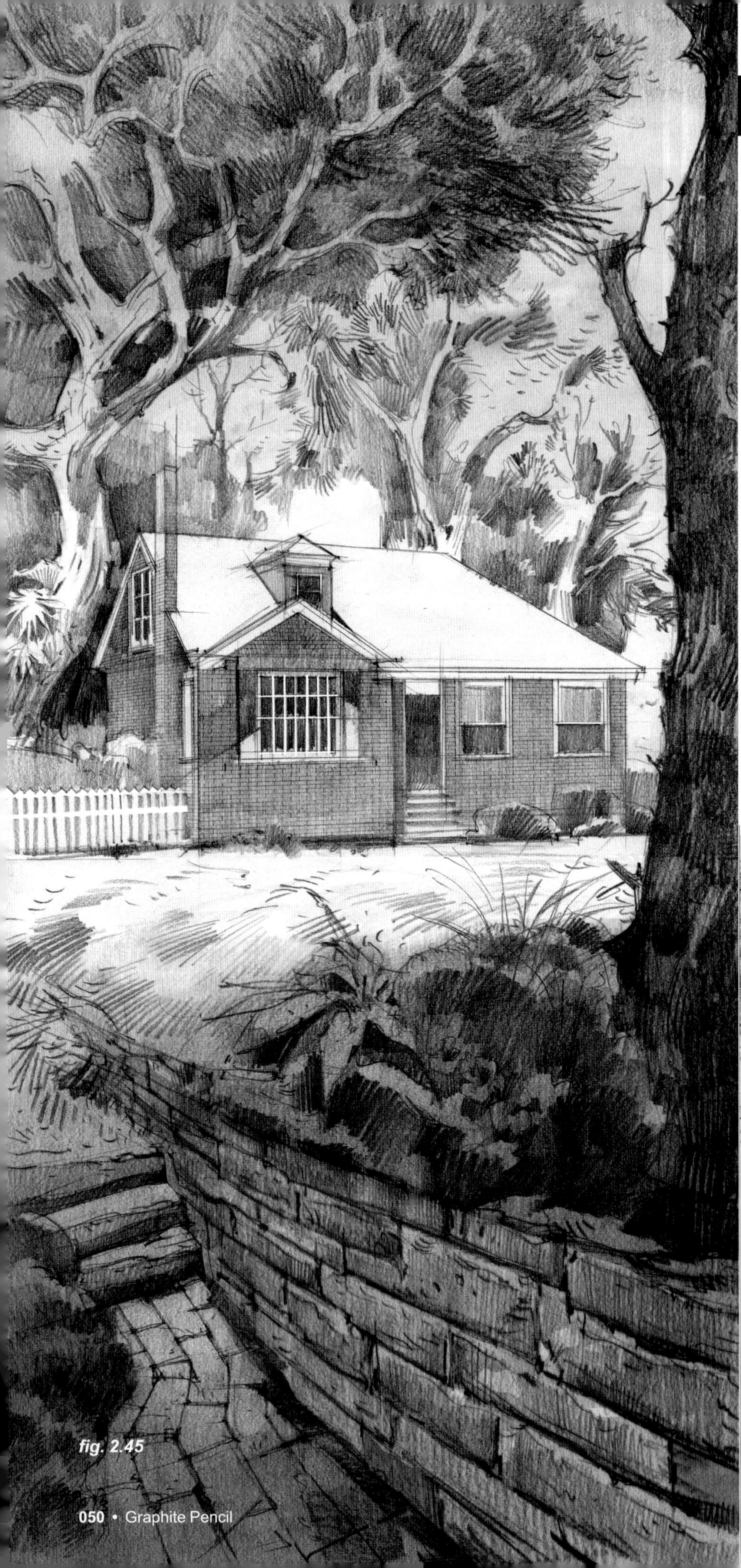

A SENSE OF DIRECTION AND STRUCTURE

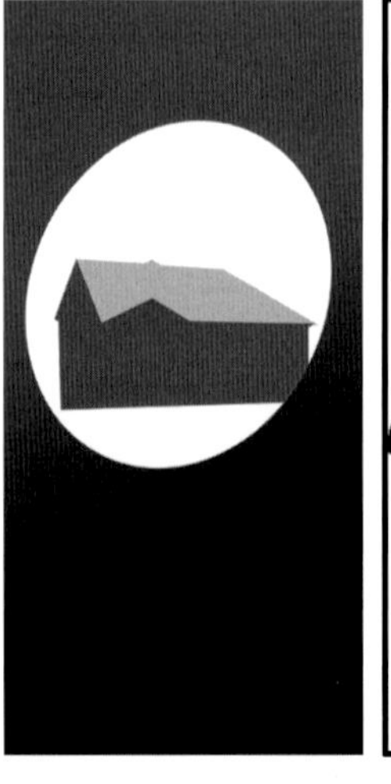

fig. 2.46

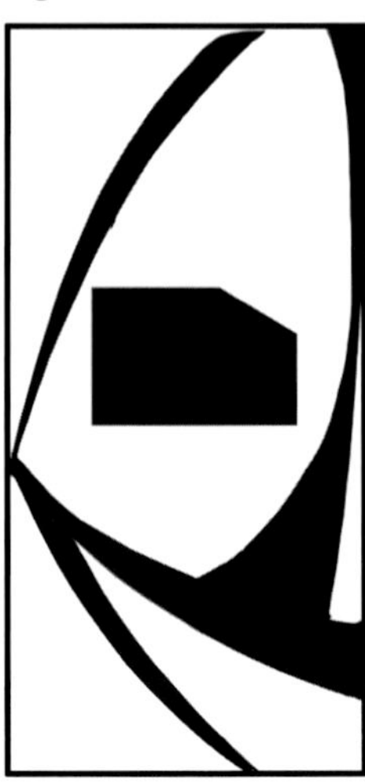

fig. 2.47

Figs. 2.46 and **2.47**: Applying these basic concepts to more complex scenes, let me start off by grouping the elements from a compositional and line-dynamics point of view in a way that will read clearly. Lights and darks will be achieved by the amount of pressure: applying more on a specific (darker) area, less for a lighter area, or simply by leaving blank pools of light as breathers.

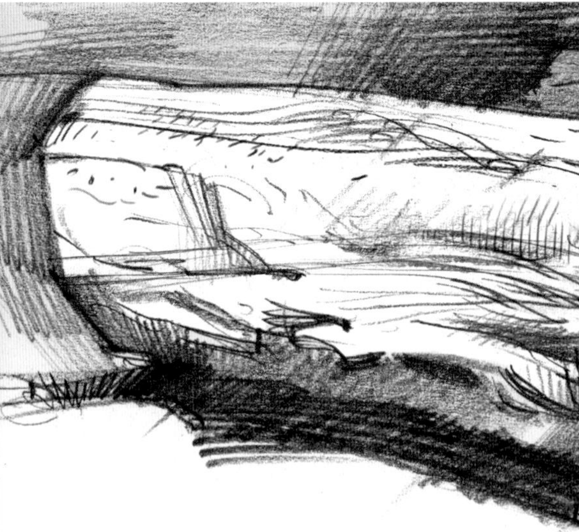

Figs. 2.48, **2.49** and **2.50**: The graphite pencil stroke's direction will help us describe shape and volume, whether more organic (treetops) or more structural and architectural (brick wall).

Fig. 2.51: The rough groves and fibers of this dry fallen trunk are visually explained by the use of dry and sharp-edged lines.

fig. 2.45

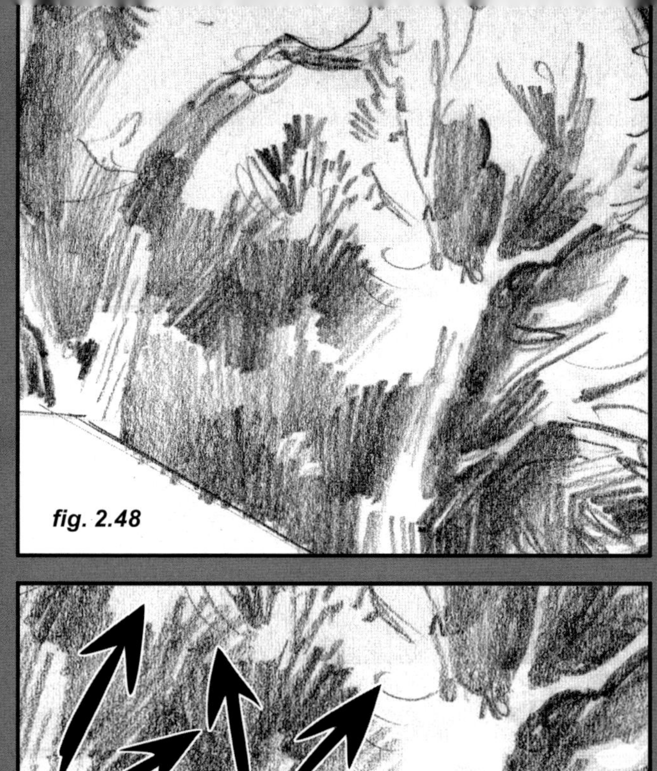
fig. 2.48

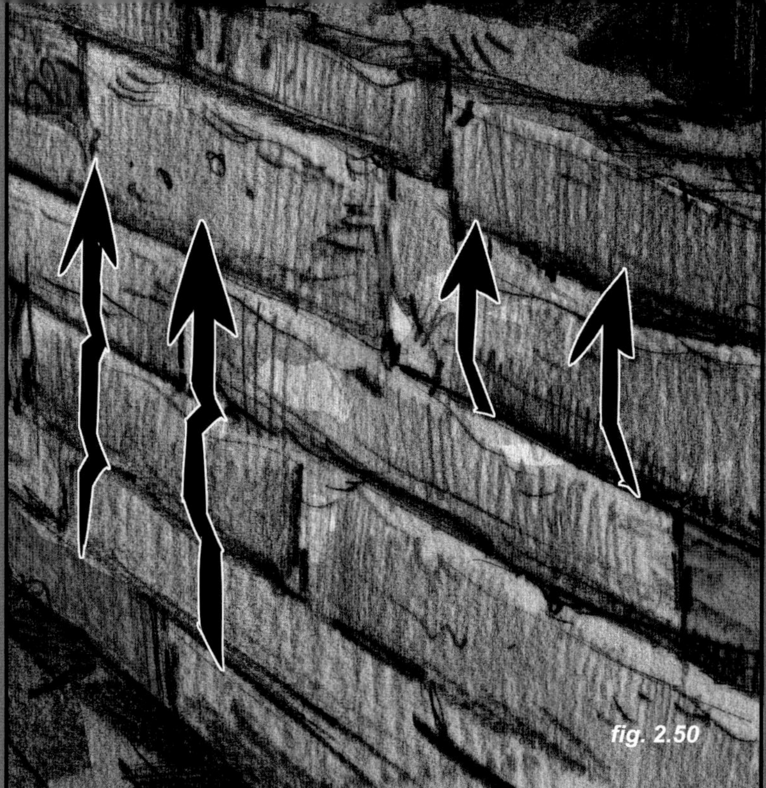
fig. 2.50

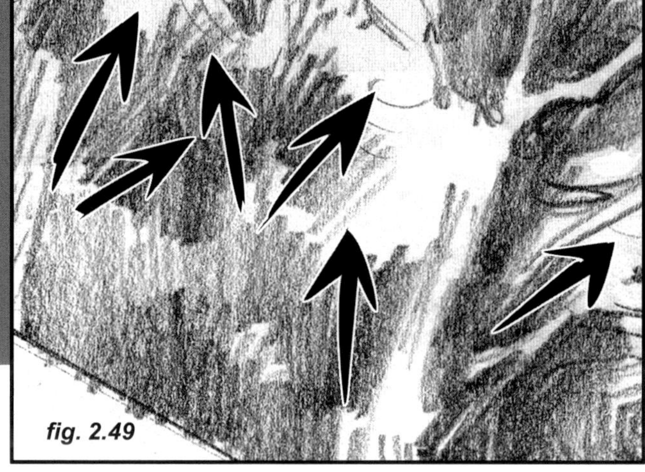
fig. 2.49

fig. 2.51

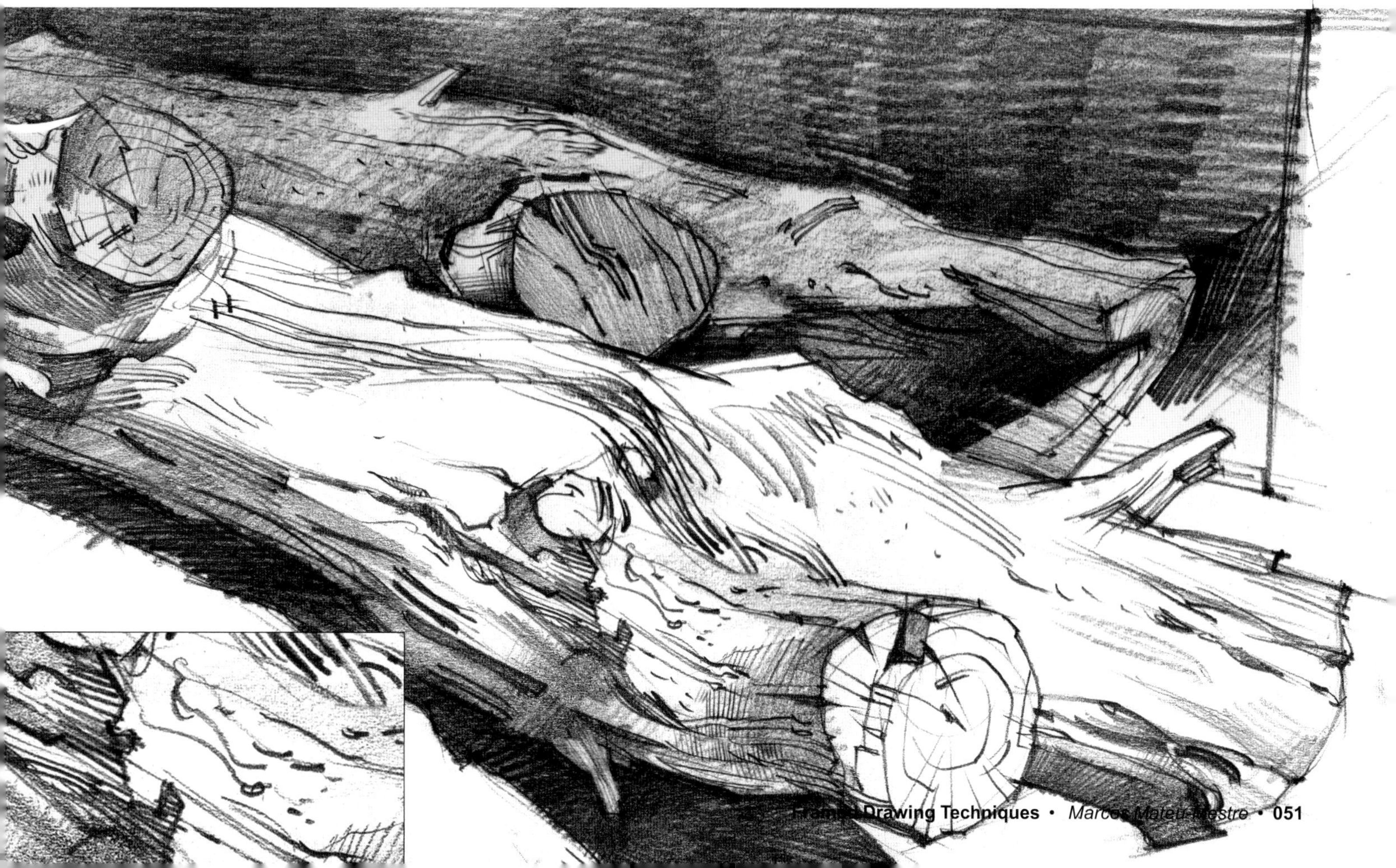

FROM REFERENCE TO FINAL ART

By observing the volumes of the different parts of this car, the angles in which the lines containing these areas go, and the areas of negative space (**fig. 2.53** and also *Framed Perspective Vol. 1*, Chapter 11), you are able to establish the proper basic guidelines around which to render this car's tonal values.

Fig. 2.54: The darkest (right) side of the car was the first area to be established. Given its forced perspective, the tonal nuances were more concentrated in a smaller area, essentially darker at the top and bottom and reflected light in the middle.

Once that was secured, the left half was developed more freely, more energetically, taking advantage of the broader, more dynamic perspective of that side.

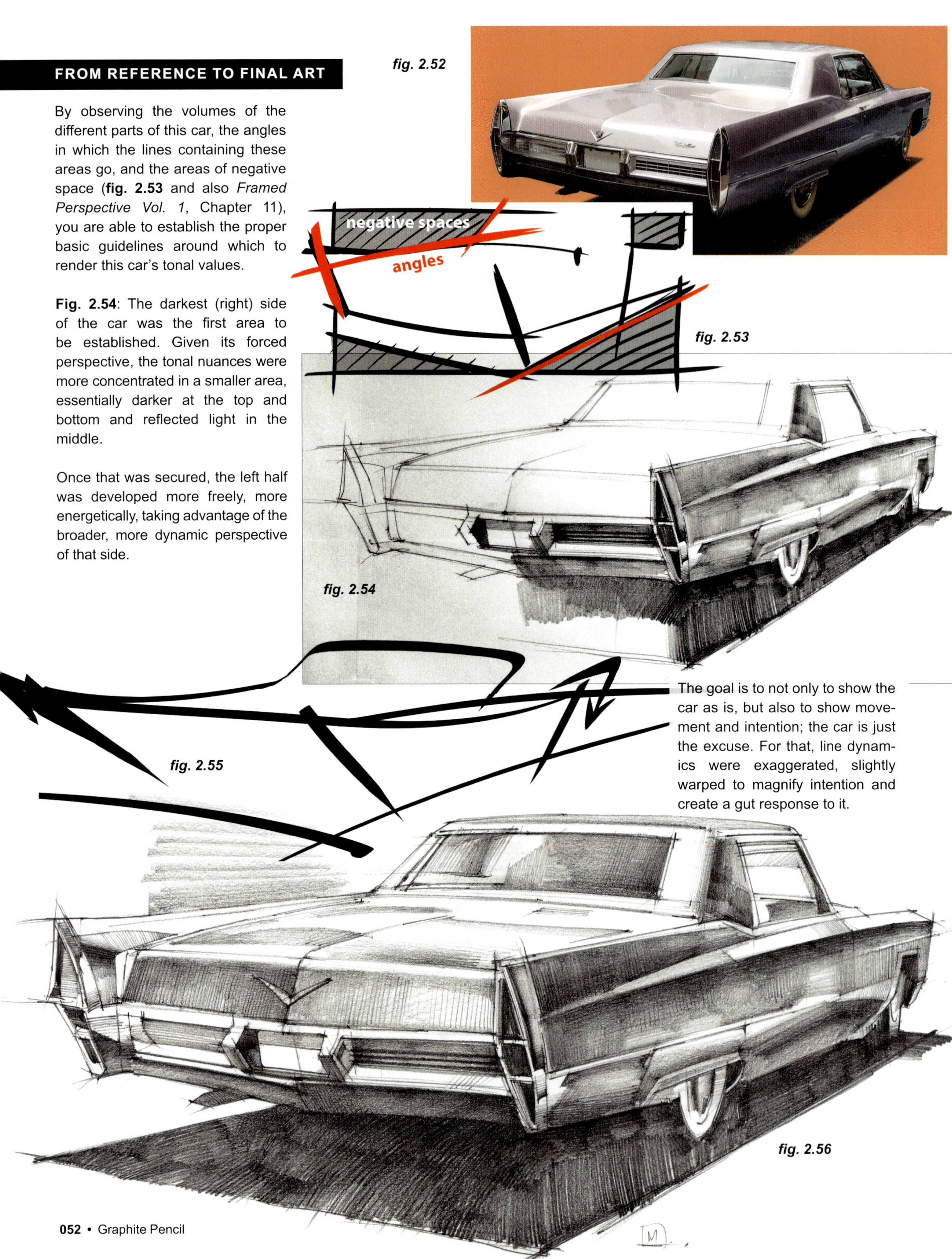

fig. 2.52

fig. 2.53

fig. 2.54

fig. 2.55

The goal is to not only to show the car as is, but also to show movement and intention; the car is just the excuse. For that, line dynamics were exaggerated, slightly warped to magnify intention and create a gut response to it.

fig. 2.56

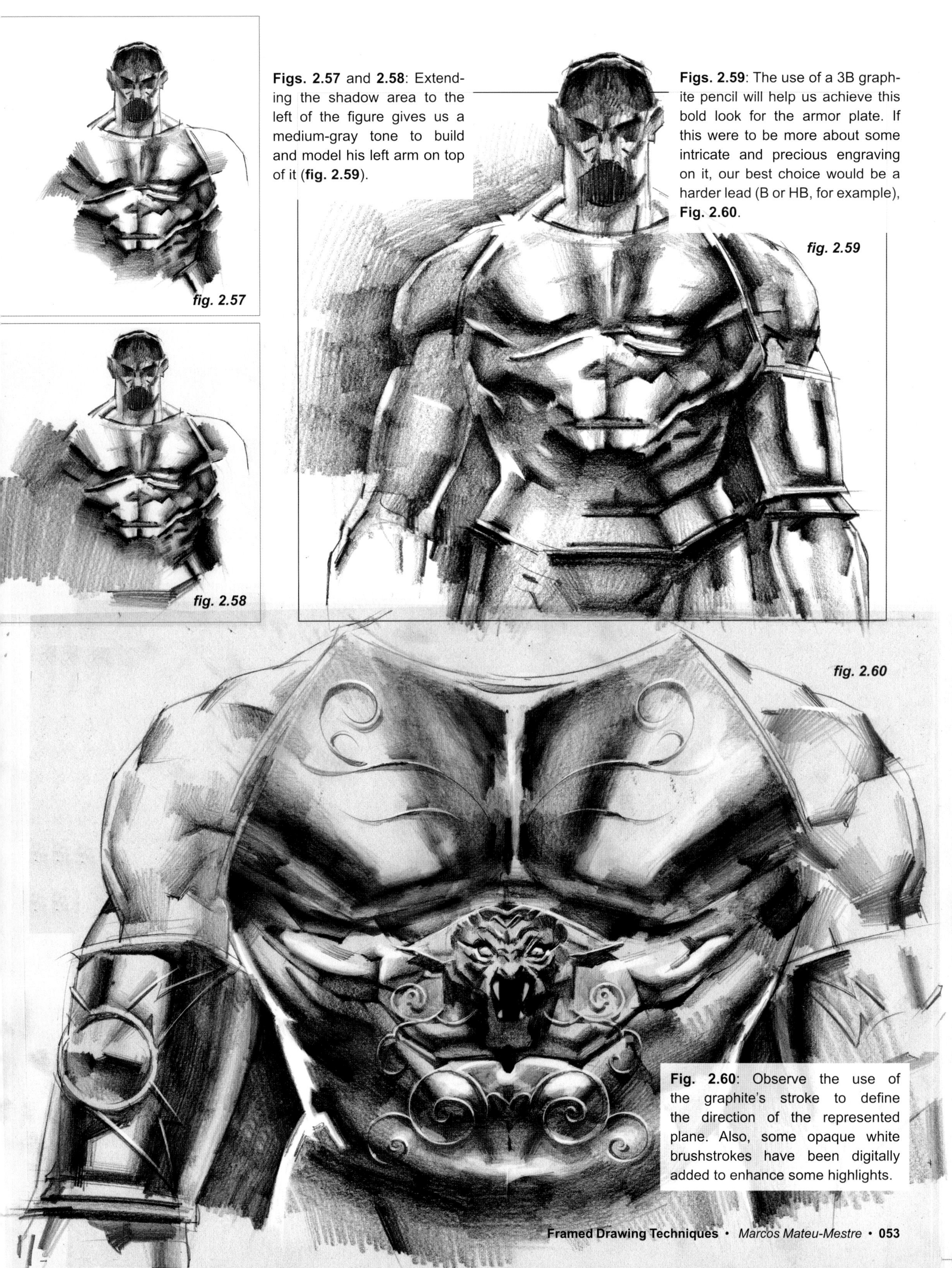

Figs. 2.57 and **2.58**: Extending the shadow area to the left of the figure gives us a medium-gray tone to build and model his left arm on top of it (**fig. 2.59**).

Figs. 2.59: The use of a 3B graphite pencil will help us achieve this bold look for the armor plate. If this were to be more about some intricate and precious engraving on it, our best choice would be a harder lead (B or HB, for example), **Fig. 2.60**.

fig. 2.57

fig. 2.58

fig. 2.59

fig. 2.60

Fig. 2.60: Observe the use of the graphite's stroke to define the direction of the represented plane. Also, some opaque white brushstrokes have been digitally added to enhance some highlights.

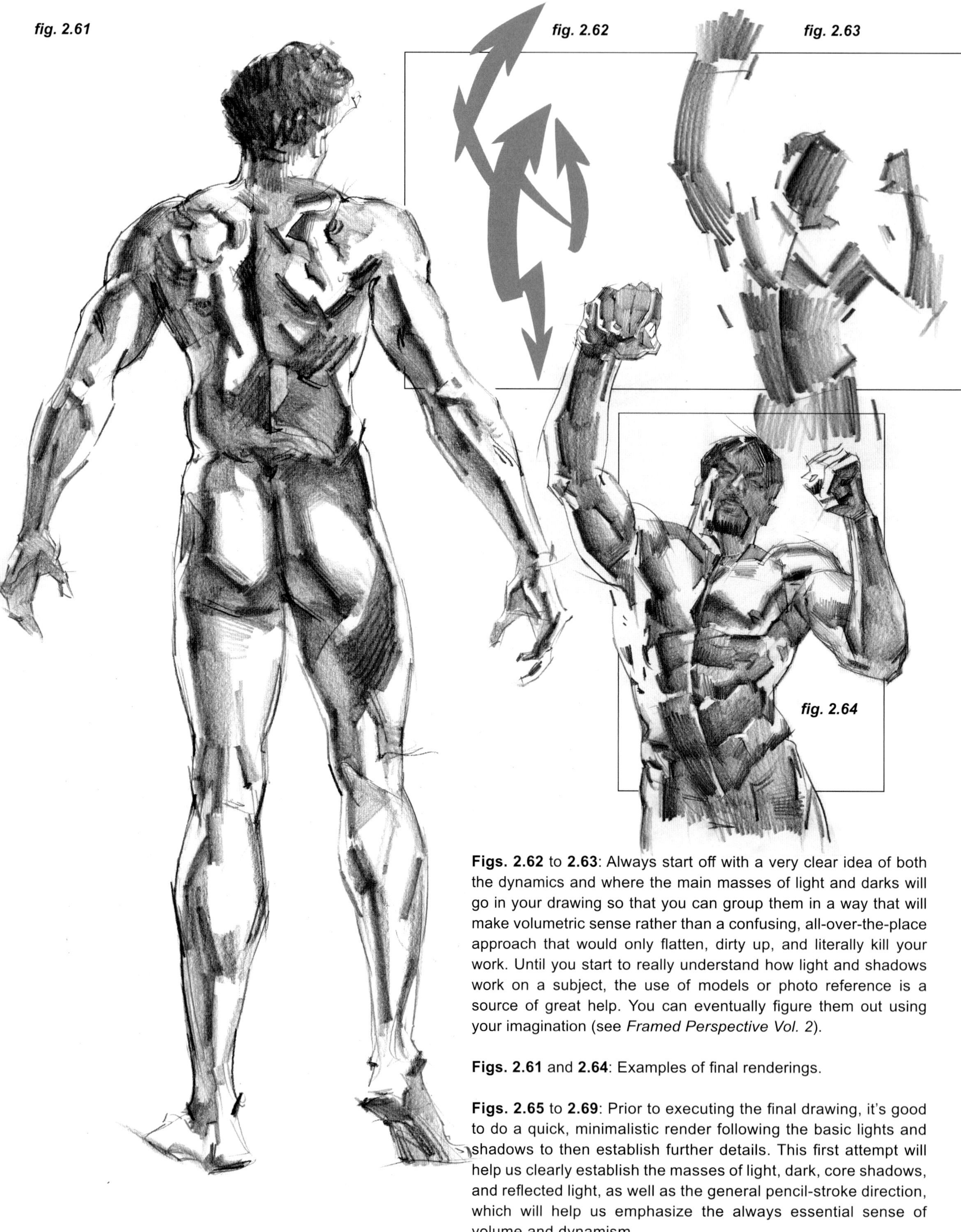

Figs. 2.62 to **2.63**: Always start off with a very clear idea of both the dynamics and where the main masses of light and darks will go in your drawing so that you can group them in a way that will make volumetric sense rather than a confusing, all-over-the-place approach that would only flatten, dirty up, and literally kill your work. Until you start to really understand how light and shadows work on a subject, the use of models or photo reference is a source of great help. You can eventually figure them out using your imagination (see *Framed Perspective Vol. 2*).

Figs. 2.61 and **2.64**: Examples of final renderings.

Figs. 2.65 to **2.69**: Prior to executing the final drawing, it's good to do a quick, minimalistic render following the basic lights and shadows to then establish further details. This first attempt will help us clearly establish the masses of light, dark, core shadows, and reflected light, as well as the general pencil-stroke direction, which will help us emphasize the always essential sense of volume and dynamism.

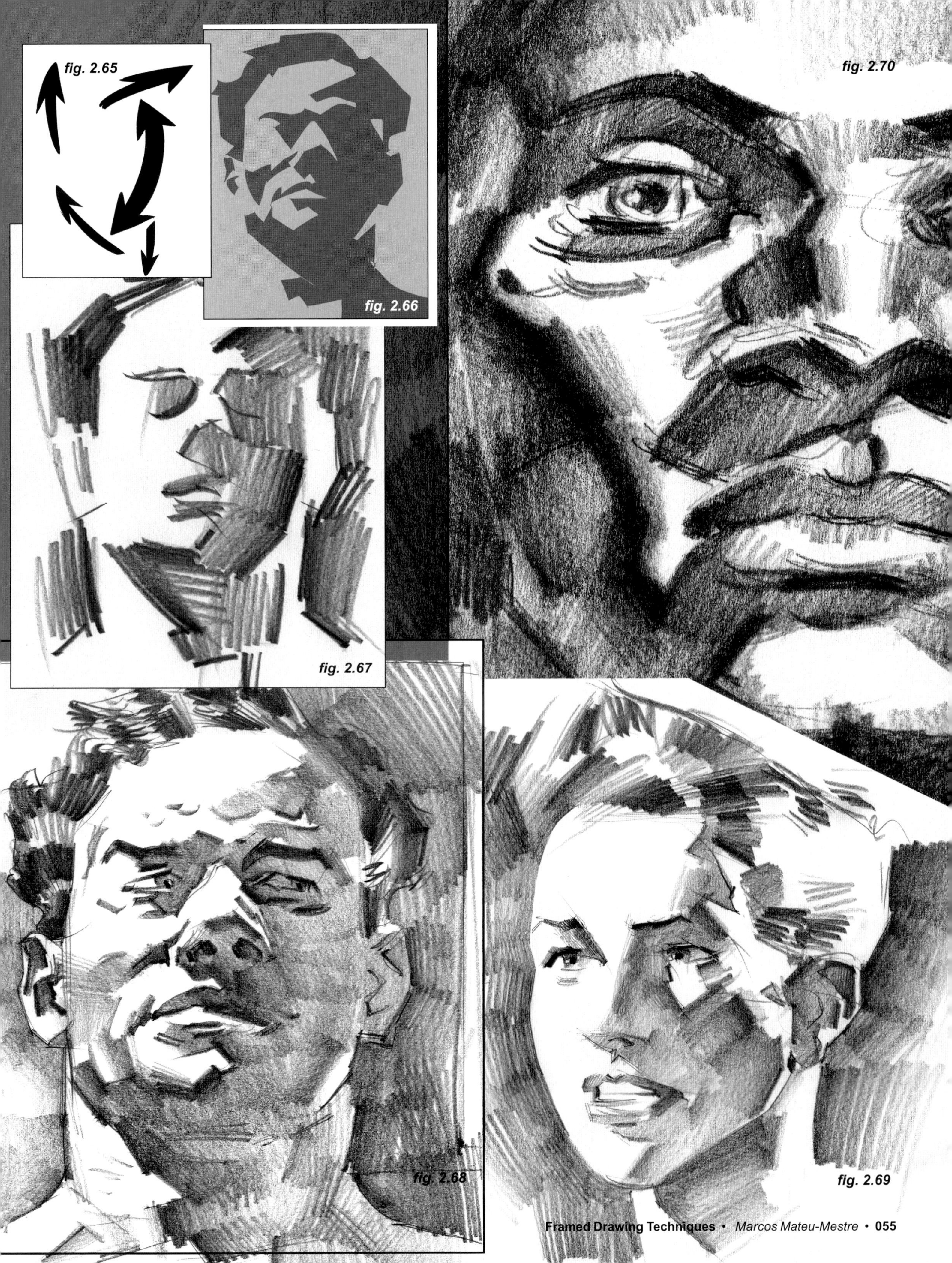
fig. 2.65
fig. 2.66
fig. 2.67
fig. 2.68
fig. 2.69
fig. 2.70

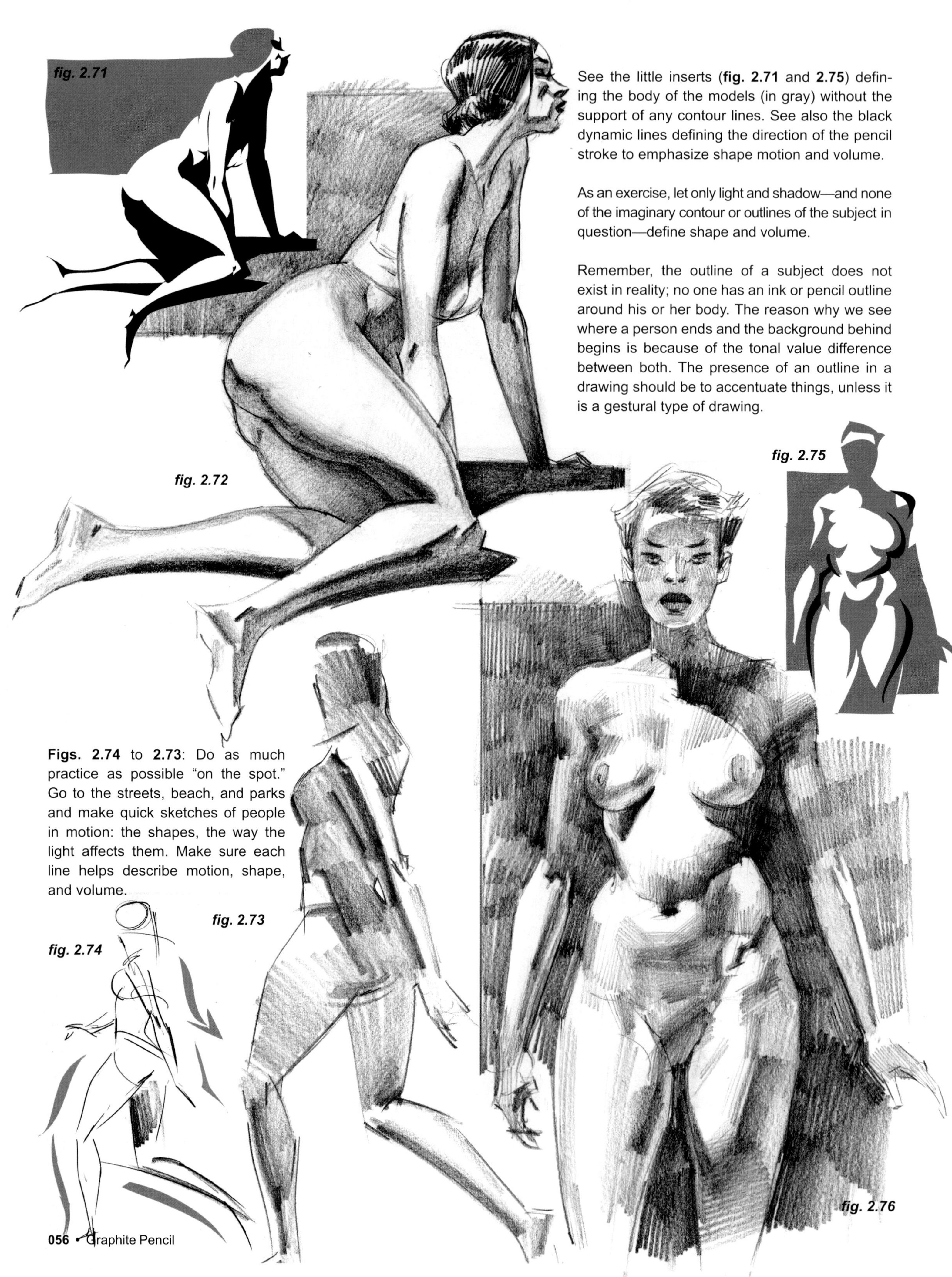

See the little inserts (**fig. 2.71** and **2.75**) defining the body of the models (in gray) without the support of any contour lines. See also the black dynamic lines defining the direction of the pencil stroke to emphasize shape motion and volume.

As an exercise, let only light and shadow—and none of the imaginary contour or outlines of the subject in question—define shape and volume.

Remember, the outline of a subject does not exist in reality; no one has an ink or pencil outline around his or her body. The reason why we see where a person ends and the background behind begins is because of the tonal value difference between both. The presence of an outline in a drawing should be to accentuate things, unless it is a gestural type of drawing.

Figs. 2.74 to **2.73**: Do as much practice as possible "on the spot." Go to the streets, beach, and parks and make quick sketches of people in motion: the shapes, the way the light affects them. Make sure each line helps describe motion, shape, and volume.

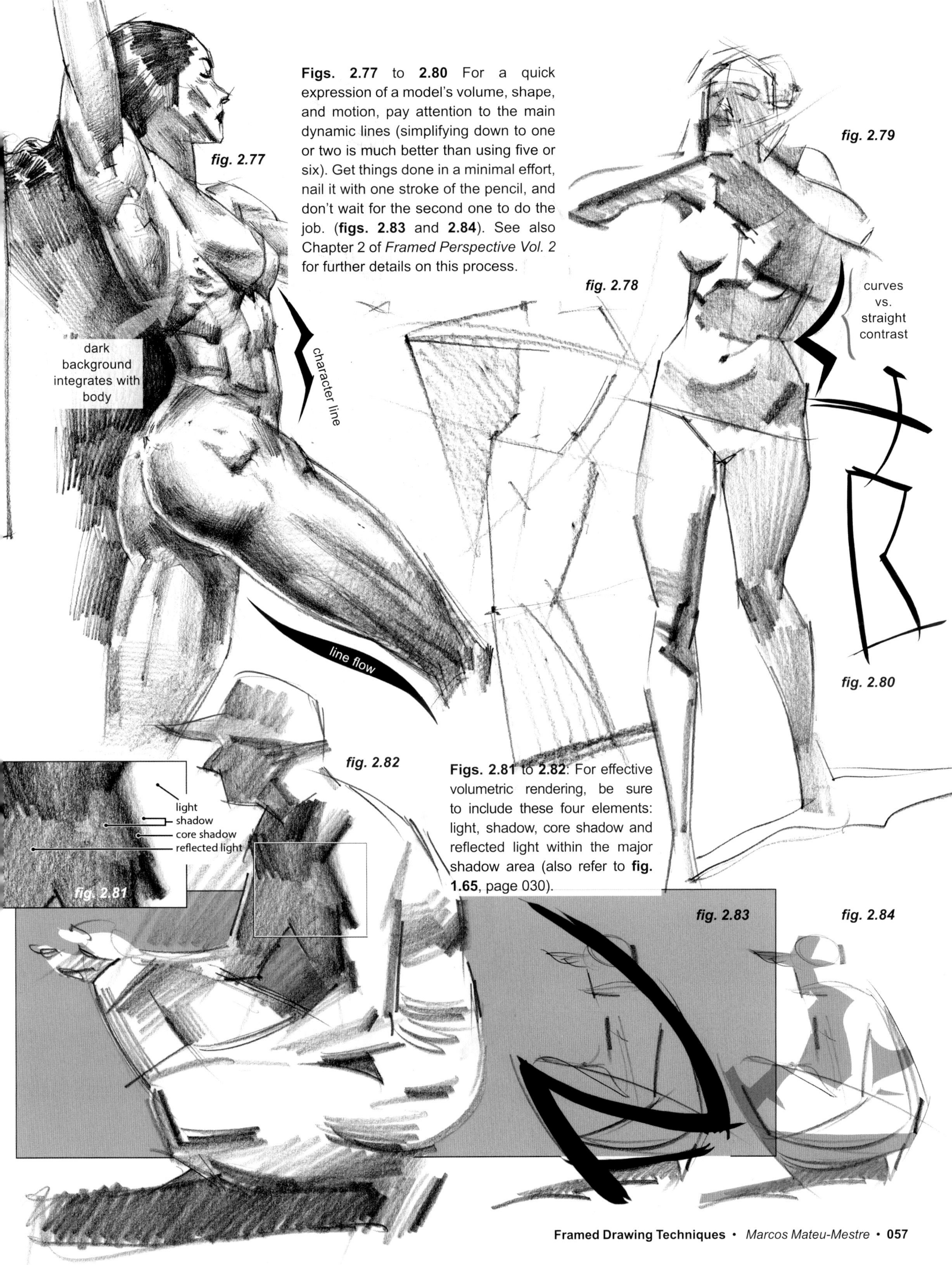

Figs. 2.77 to **2.80** For a quick expression of a model's volume, shape, and motion, pay attention to the main dynamic lines (simplifying down to one or two is much better than using five or six). Get things done in a minimal effort, nail it with one stroke of the pencil, and don't wait for the second one to do the job. (**figs. 2.83** and **2.84**). See also Chapter 2 of *Framed Perspective Vol. 2* for further details on this process.

Figs. 2.81 to **2.82**: For effective volumetric rendering, be sure to include these four elements: light, shadow, core shadow and reflected light within the major shadow area (also refer to **fig. 1.65**, page 030).

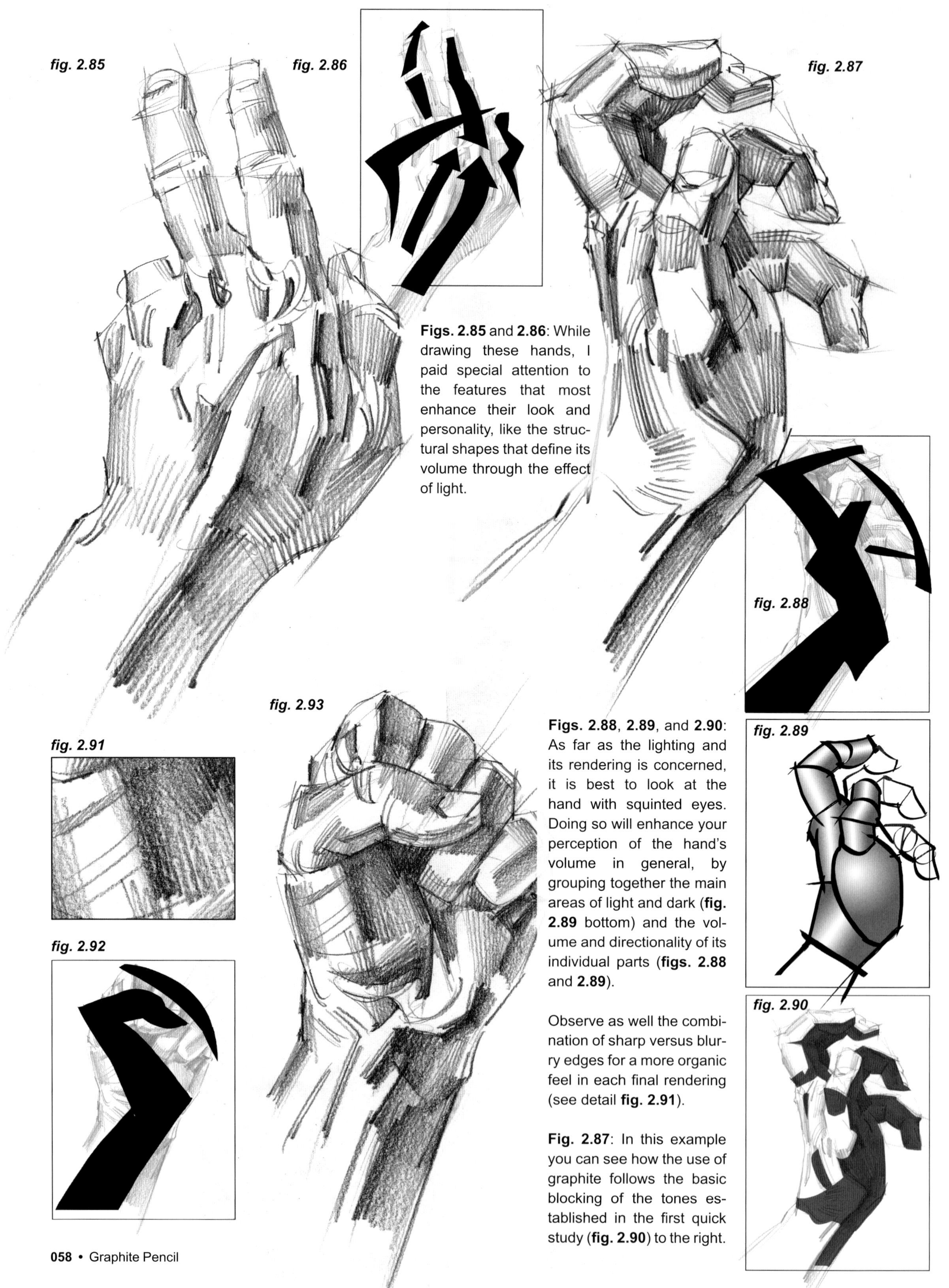

Figs. 2.85 and **2.86**: While drawing these hands, I paid special attention to the features that most enhance their look and personality, like the structural shapes that define its volume through the effect of light.

Figs. 2.88, **2.89**, and **2.90**: As far as the lighting and its rendering is concerned, it is best to look at the hand with squinted eyes. Doing so will enhance your perception of the hand's volume in general, by grouping together the main areas of light and dark (**fig. 2.89** bottom) and the volume and directionality of its individual parts (**figs. 2.88** and **2.89**).

Observe as well the combination of sharp versus blurry edges for a more organic feel in each final rendering (see detail **fig. 2.91**).

Fig. 2.87: In this example you can see how the use of graphite follows the basic blocking of the tones established in the first quick study (**fig. 2.90**) to the right.

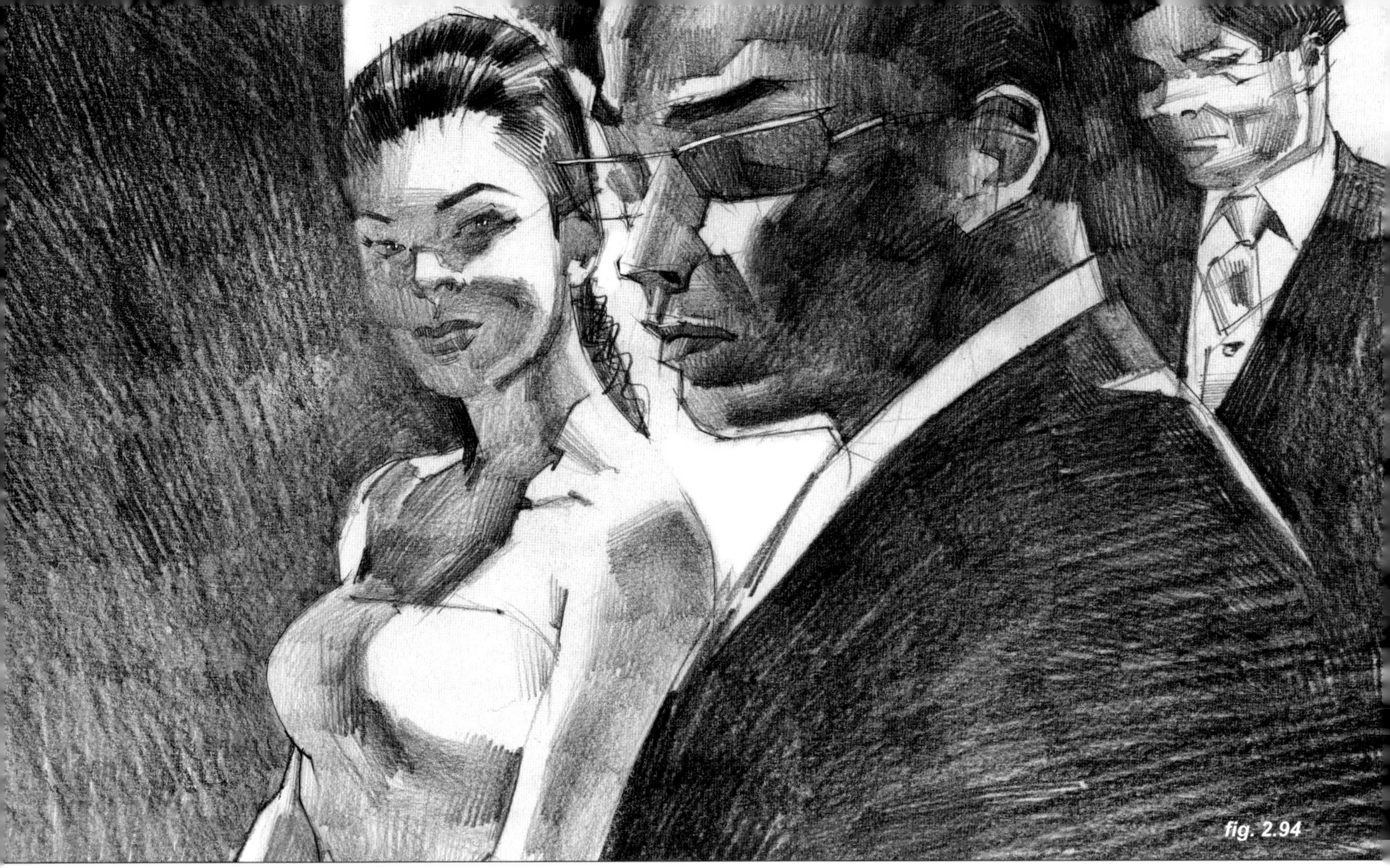

fig. 2.94

fig. 2.95

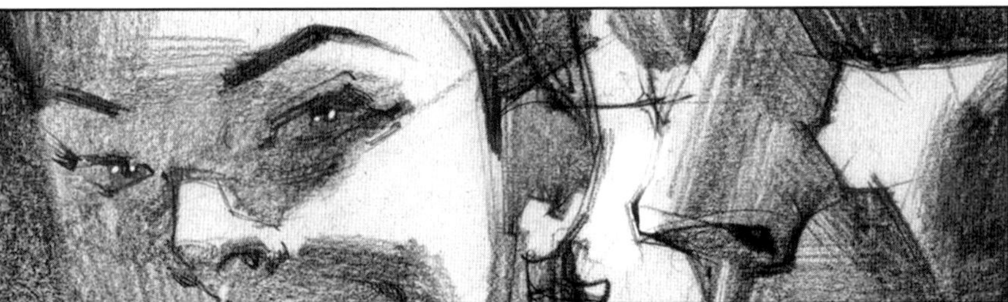

fig. 2.96

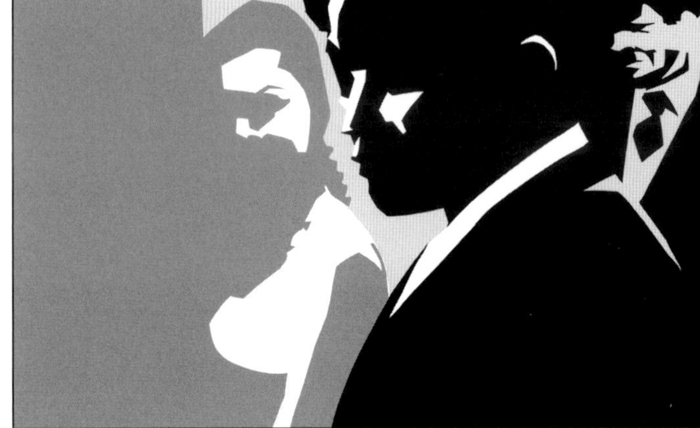

Fig. 2.94: Notice again in this example how the use of graphite follows the basic blocking of the tones established in the first quick study (**fig. 2.96**) to the right.

Obviously as I render the panel I will include many subtleties and nuances in each shading block, while always having in mind the decisions previously made so that I keep a strong and graphic sense that keeps each and every area in the order of importance and visual clarity it requires. (Here, darker in the foreground, lighter in the background).

Fig. 2.97: The general direction of the actual pencil strokes follows a purposeful pattern that helps give the overall image a sense of order and balance.

While I will usually apply several layers of graphite for each area of the drawing, that doesn't mean all pencil strokes will exactly follow this dynamics pattern (shown by the arrows). In fact, many will cross and intertwine (**fig. 2.98**, little insert), but the main line intention will obviously do so.

This rendering was executed with a 3B and a 4B pencil.

fig. 2.97

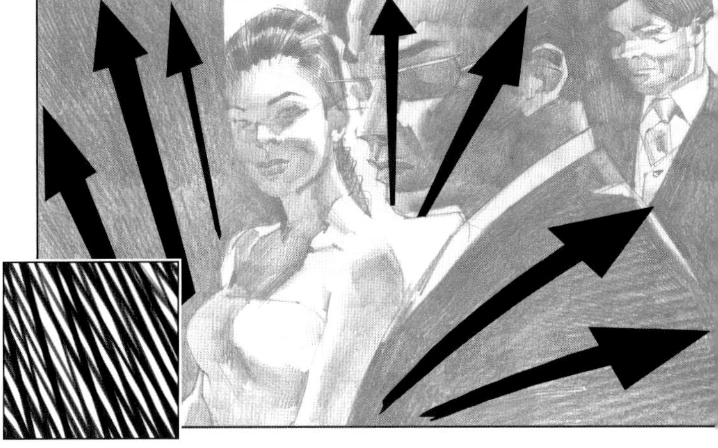

fig. 2.98

THE THOUGHT AND DRAWING PROCESS

Even though the chosen tool for the final rendering of this illustration was graphite pencil, other techniques were used on the way to reach the final goal.

Here are a few previous sketches and tryouts done with the help of a ball pen, based on a simple idea: an action shot where foreground characters are defending themselves against a number of assailants.

fig. 2.99

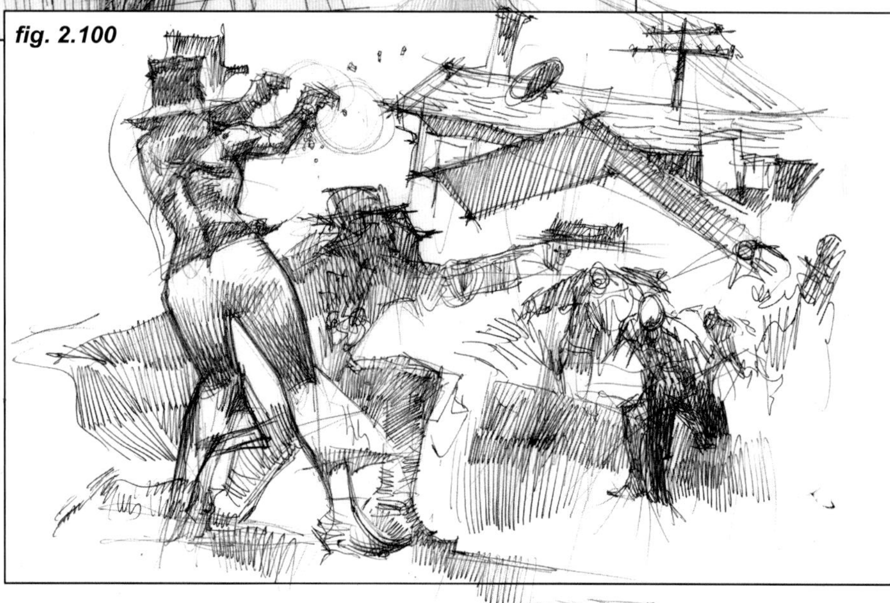
fig. 2.100

Fig. 2.99: In the first attempt, a female undercover police officer in the foreground is taking action with the support of a number of agents. (Please disregard the unrelated sketches on the same piece of paper!)

Fig. 2.100: The foreground character now has a closer ally; they are both defending themselves against a zombie attack coming from a derelict old house in the background. The whole shot is seen from a three-quarter angle. Both characters are shooting in different directions—she shoots away from the camera, he does so parallel to the lens—suggesting they are attacked from different angles.

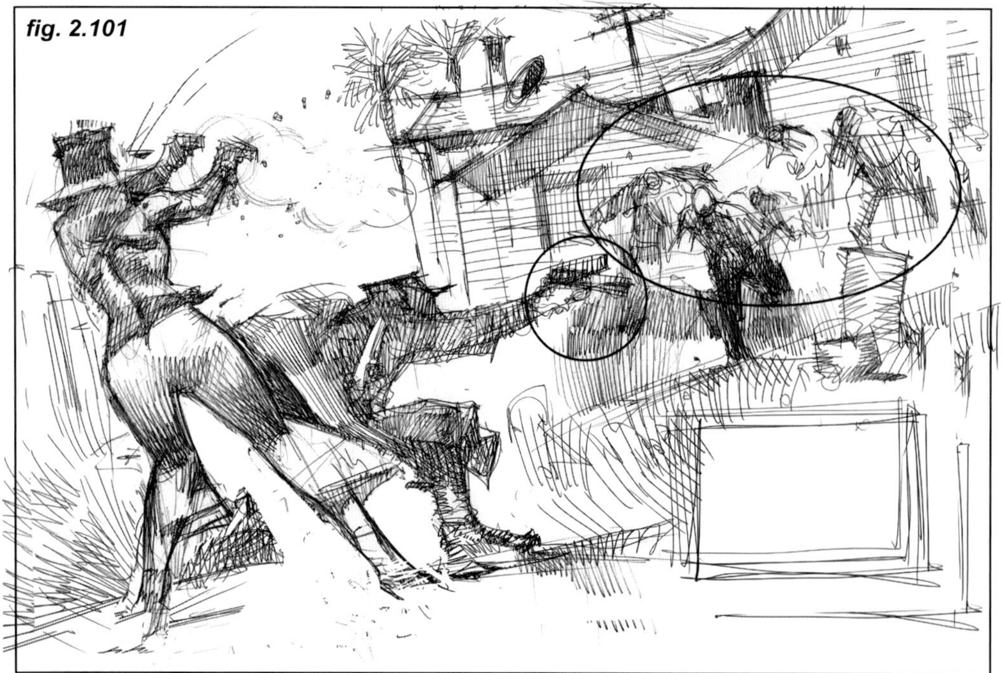
fig. 2.101

Fig. 2.101: Same shot but this time the Dutch angle that was previously leaning to the right has been inverted and instead leans toward the left, so the house is now higher in the frame, and so are the attacking zombies. This makes the latter appear more lethal as they have the visual upper hand. Also, they used to be located "under the man's gun," but now they are above it, again emphasizing their control and superiority within the action. (See the circled areas.)

The whole image has been stretched a bit horizontally as well, so it is wider now, punching more into the dynamism of the scene.

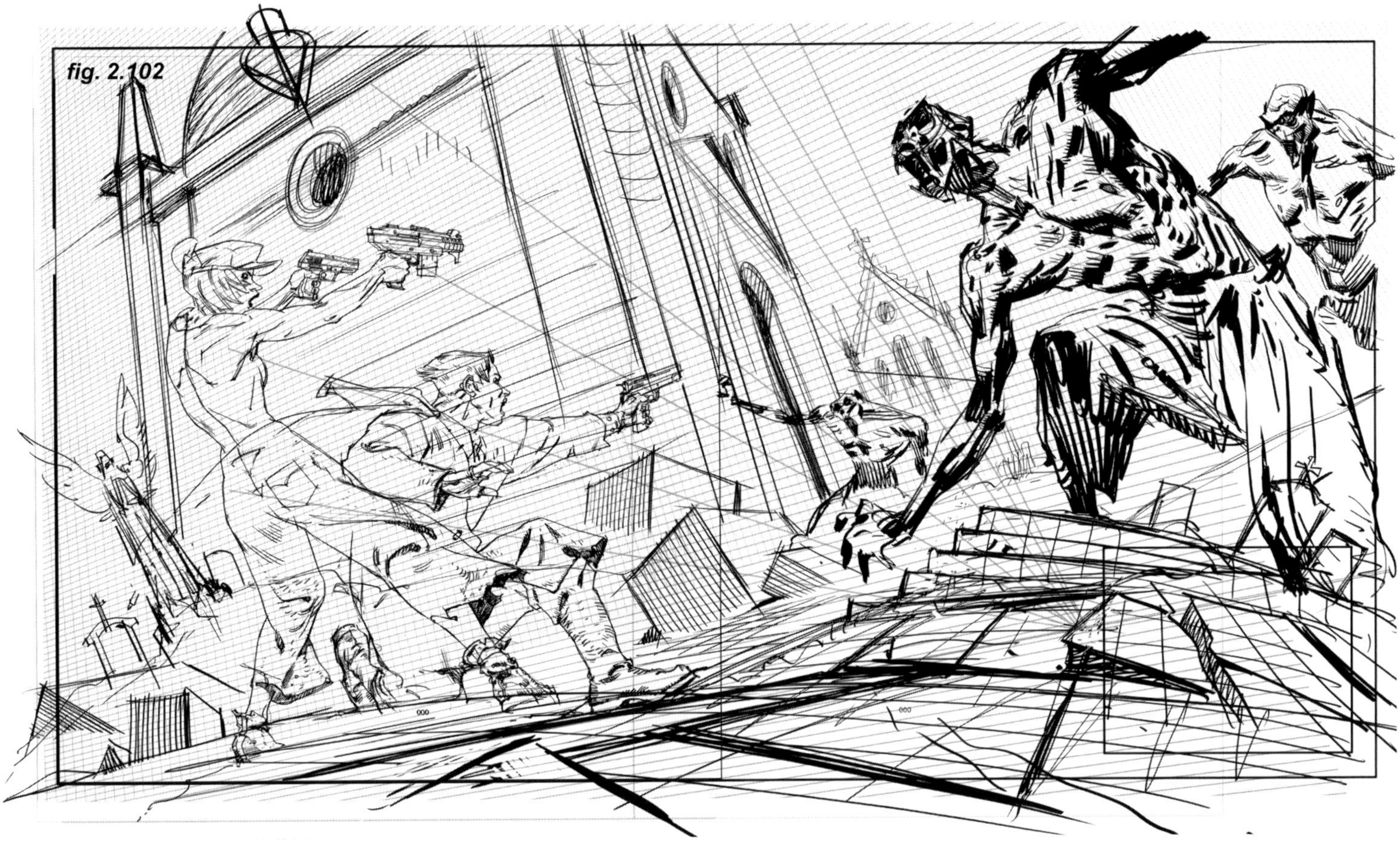

fig. 2.102

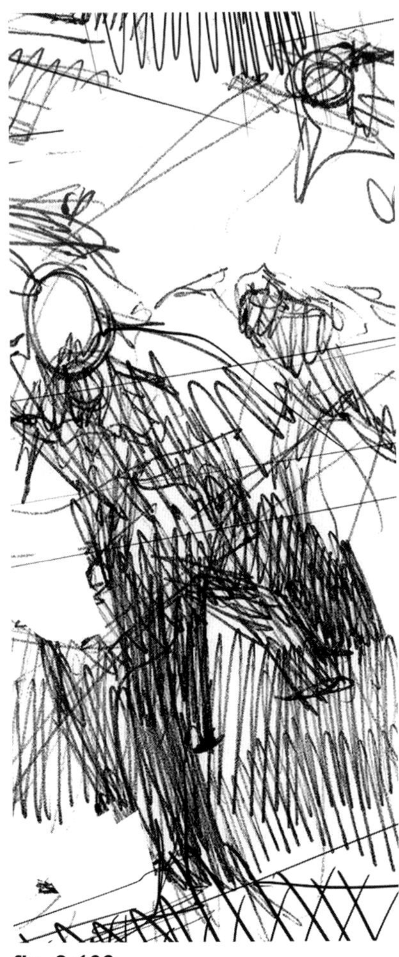

fig. 2.103

Fig. 2.102: During the "warm-up" process toward a final idea, the next step was to scan the previous image (**fig. 2.101**) and play and build on it digitally. Now the derelict house became an old, gothic cemetery.

For this new sketch I created a perspective grid that would help me support the design of the pantheon and all other structures and characters in the background.

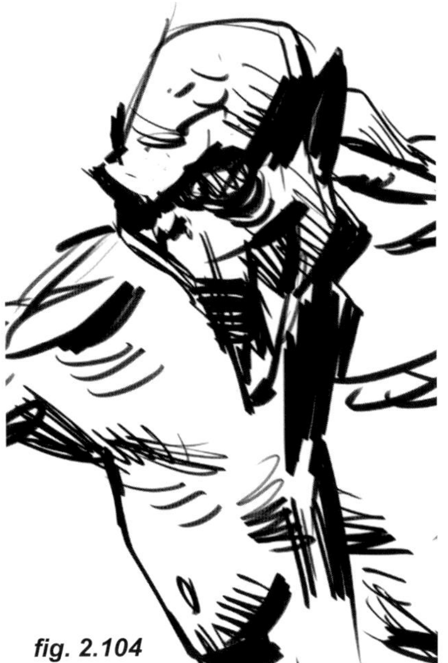

fig. 2.104

The use of any technique is good at this stage as long as it helps us play with the idea **Figs. 2.103** and **2.104**.

The idea to bring the zombies closer to the camera and make them look gigantic was in order to give me more capacity for detail when it came time to render the final illustration with graphite. Graphite is a beautiful medium that can give us an amazing range of tonal gradations and options. At the same time, and because of the quality of its line, it is a bit more imprecise than, for example, an ink pen. For this reason (and in this case), the bigger and the more graphic the shapes are, the more you will be able to bring up all the juice a good graphite pencil rendering can give us.

In general, the composition for the two human characters remained the same, their poses, their attitude, and also the Dutch angle I settled for in the previous version.

At this point the visual research process (including online websites, books, etc.) has already started for things like weaponry, the cemetery's gothic style architecture, etc.

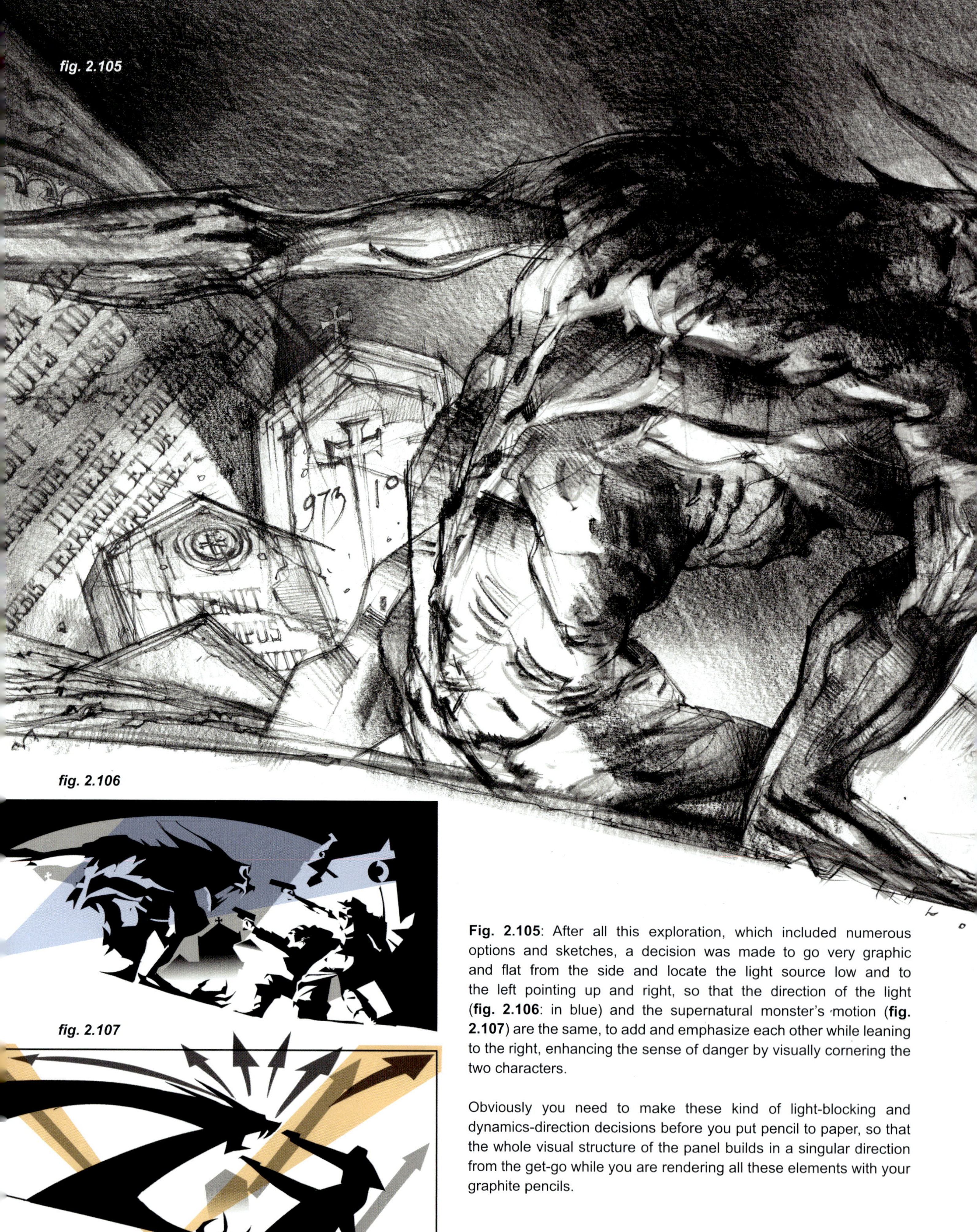

fig. 2.105

fig. 2.106

fig. 2.107

Fig. 2.105: After all this exploration, which included numerous options and sketches, a decision was made to go very graphic and flat from the side and locate the light source low and to the left pointing up and right, so that the direction of the light (**fig. 2.106**: in blue) and the supernatural monster's motion (**fig. 2.107**) are the same, to add and emphasize each other while leaning to the right, enhancing the sense of danger by visually cornering the two characters.

Obviously you need to make these kind of light-blocking and dynamics-direction decisions before you put pencil to paper, so that the whole visual structure of the panel builds in a singular direction from the get-go while you are rendering all these elements with your graphite pencils.

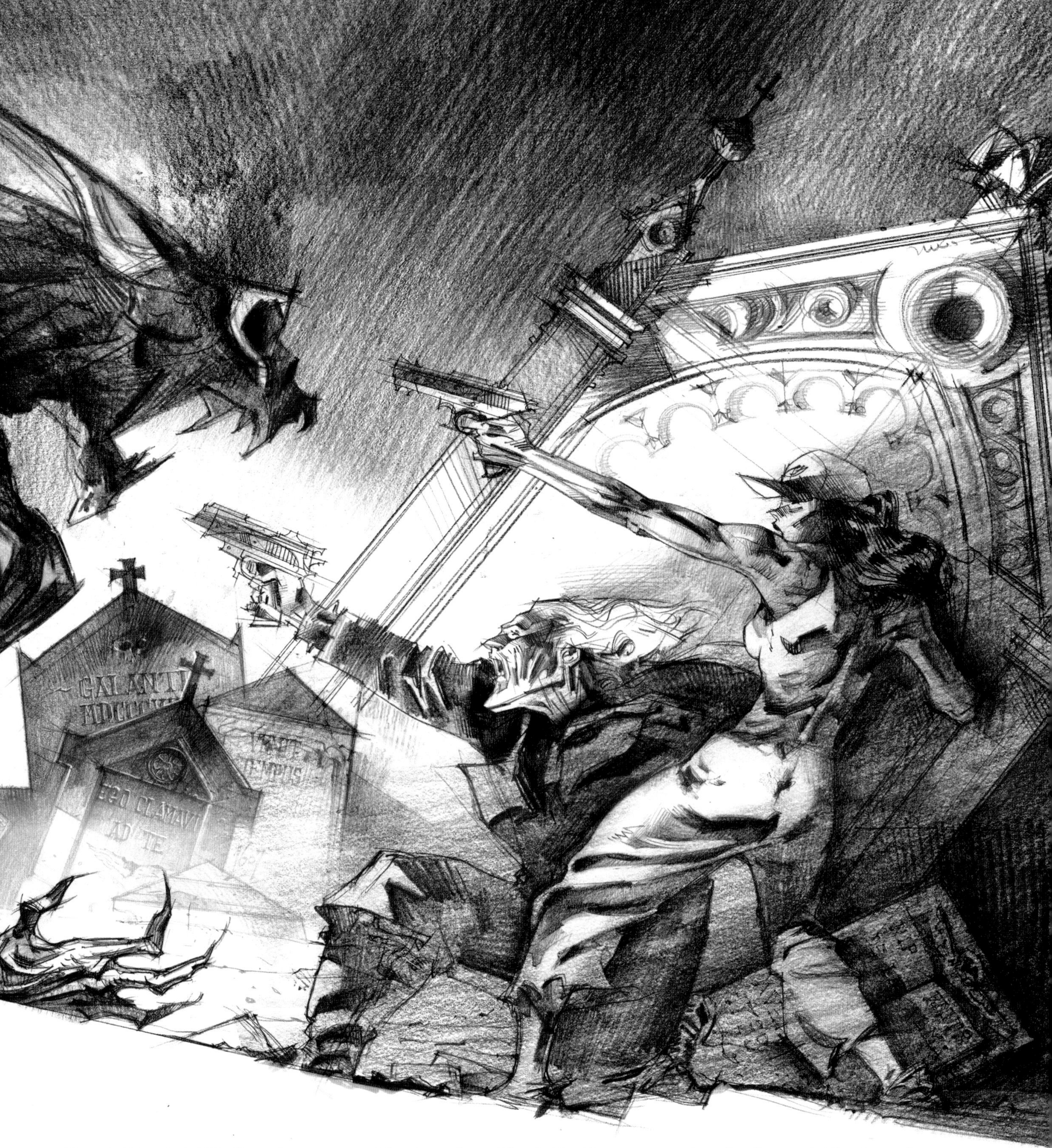

Figs. 2.106 and **2.107**: Show the essence of the dynamics of the shot, how the main shapes (darkest) attack/react, creating tension. The medium-tone arrows indicate the direction of the graphite render emanating out from the center of the action just like sunrays.

The lightest-tone arrows describe the angle/direction of both the big tombstone/wall to the very left and the pantheon to the very right. These two angles describe a "V" shape that emphasizes the explosive dynamics of the moment.

The rendering details of this image are analyzed in the next page.

When rendering, try to keep a healthy balance between a loose, playful, interesting line and a level of tightness that will describe the shape, volume, and tone of all subjects in your drawing.

Here, once the drawing was scanned, I used that as the base to then retouch the parts I wasn't completely happy with (see also page 31). In the old days, this would be achieved by erasing or cutting off the undesired parts then replacing them with a new rendering. Now, once scanned, a much cleaner digital version of this process does the trick.

Here is an example, **Fig. 2.108** (below, frame 1): This new "head, shoulder, arm, and chest" rendering for the male character was created to replace the original one in frame 3. For that I printed out the problematic area*, taped (with removable tape) a blank sheet of copy paper on the printout, and then laid both now superimposed sheets onto a light desk, reworked the area that needed to be on the blank paper, and then scanned this new version (frame 1).

**Sometimes, if the area to be reworked requires an extra level of detail, you can print it out at a bigger size, say for example 125 percent or 150 percent of the original. At these sizes you can better refine and elaborate the new rendering.*

This scan was then digitally placed on the original drawing as a transparent overlay, underneath which I created a new layer with a solid white area–frame 2–(to digitally "erase" the undesired part of the original drawing). This white area became the blank space on which I laid down the new/final drawing.

After this new piece is scanned, I reduced it back to the original file size so that it fit perfectly back on the original drawing. (Note: Past a 150-percent enlargement, you will need to be careful that the new work is not much more detailed than the one you want to replace, because that would create an obvious discrepancy between both renderings.)

NEXT PAGE

Fig. 2.109: The bottom of the carved letters was specially darkened to show "underlighting," otherwise the letters would look like they are simply printed on the stone.

Fig. 2.110: Digitally adding graphite layers on top of each other that have been rendered on a separate piece of paper can sometimes help give the right level of richness to a specific area of a drawing.

Fig. 2.111: The irregularity of a graphite rendering can be enhanced by selecting that desired area and applying a Sharpening filter from the Photoshop Filter menu to it, so that the surface appears rougher, like in the case of this tombstone.

Fig. 2.112: To create a sense of depth and distance between the monster's hand and the tombstones in the background, a semi-opaque layer of white was digitally superimposed and its edges diffused with either a 'Gaussian' or a 'motion blur' filter.

Fig. 2.113: An example of how line direction helps achieve a better, more convincing sense of volume.

Figs. 2.114 and **2.115**: A more refined, detailed work was performed on the characters' heads as they are the focus of attention. Whereas the knee, for example, has been rendered a bit more roughly and dynamic, just enough to describe volume, light, and motion so it doesn't take away from the narratively more important areas.

Fig. 2.115: As seen in **Fig. 2.20** (page 46) the use of darker core shadows and reflected light within the shadow next to it can create a very interesting sense of three-dimensionality.

Fig. 2.116: For architectural elements, you can go ahead and ruler in the main lines to then apply the more organic freehand render on top of it, producing an interesting contrast.

Pencils used in this piece were well-sharpened 8B and 6B.

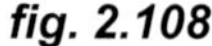

fig. 2.108

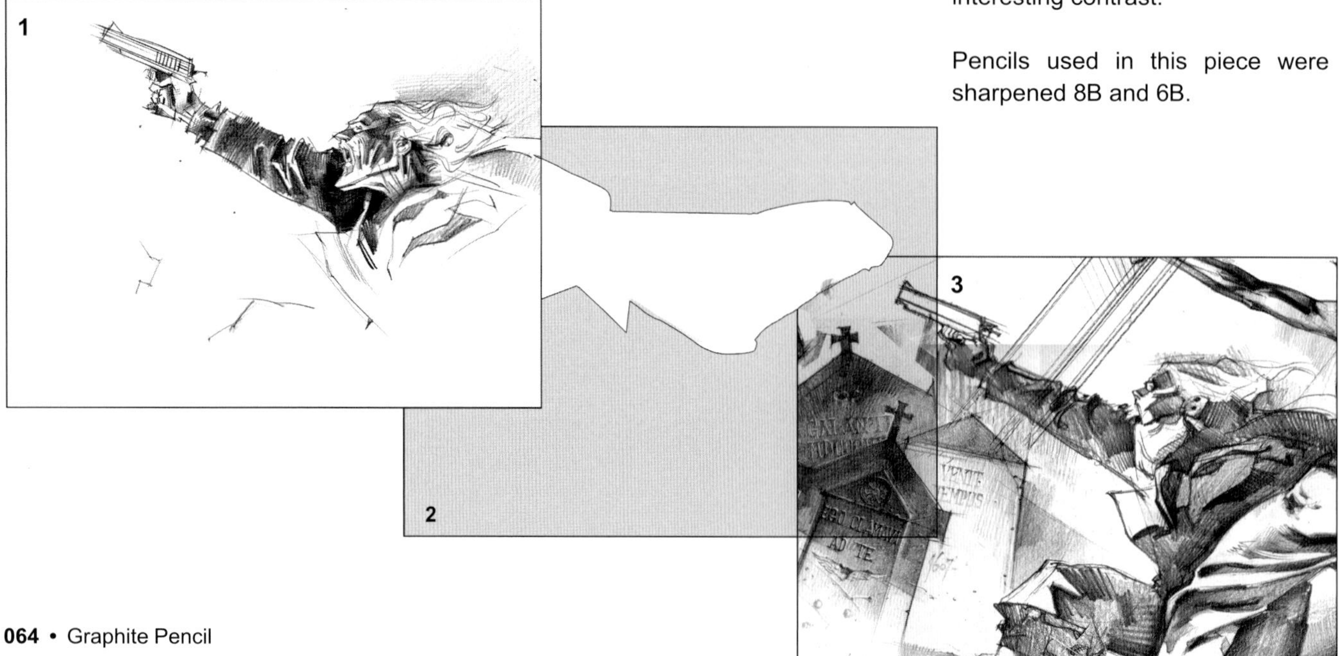

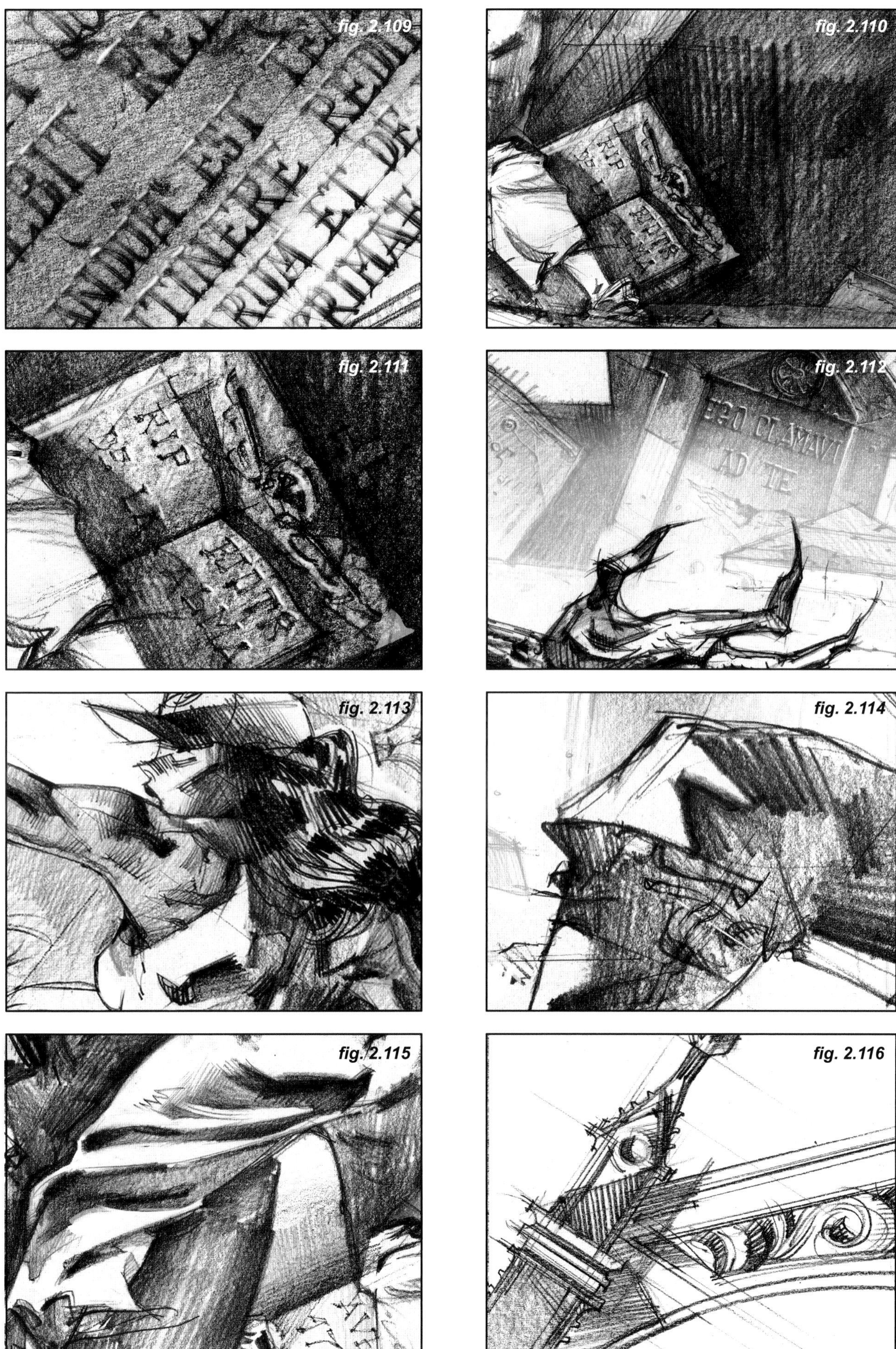
fig. 2.109
fig. 2.110
fig. 2.111
fig. 2.112
fig. 2.113
fig. 2.114
fig. 2.115
fig. 2.116

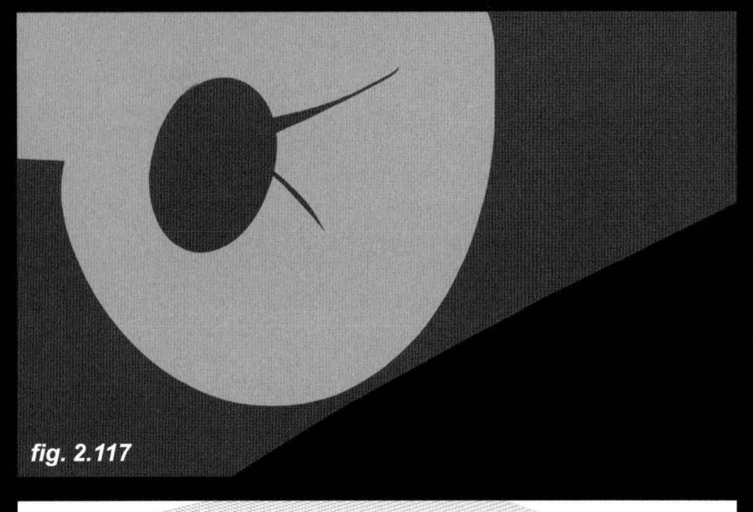
fig. 2.117

fig. 2.118

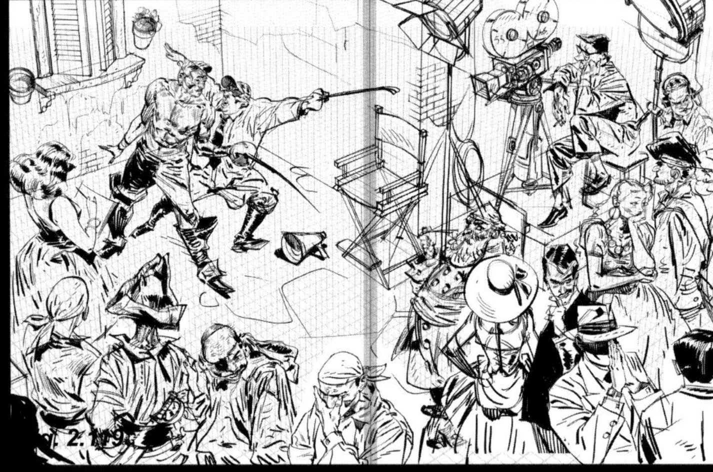
fig. 2.119

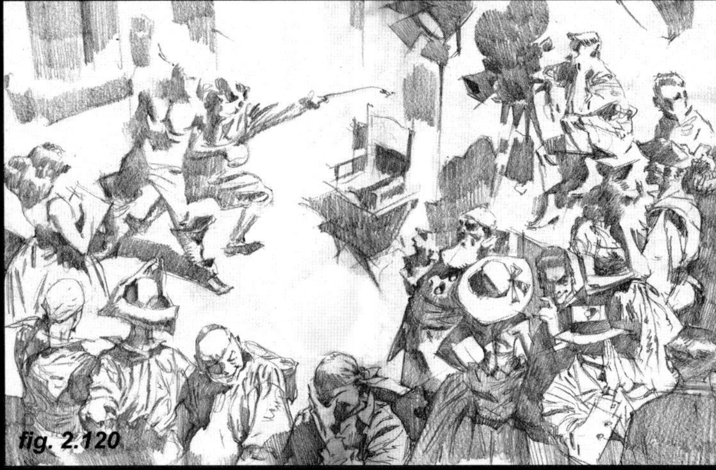
fig. 2.120

It is time for an illustration depicting an early Hollywood film shoot.

As always, start drawing the moment you have a rough idea of what you want and need in your shot. In this case, I have a director getting mad at the actor who just doesn't get it right after 375 takes, and a surrounding cast of supporting actors and extras fed up with the situation.

As the usual "first thing," let's imagine a schematic composition that will serve to clarify the situation. In **Fig. 2.117** see the basic positioning of all elements: the actor and director being isolated as the center of attention (top left) and the dynamic lines depicting the sword and the riding crop shooting out in opposite directions (up vs. down). Everyone else is in a crowd on which a convenient shadow will drop (bottom right of the illustration) to help better frame the whole thing.

Fig. 2.118: One of the items that will literally provide solid ground for this drawing is a well-constructed, three-vanishing-points perspective grid. (See *Framed Perspective Vol. 1 and 2*).

Fig. 2.119: In this case I started with a digital-ink sketch that clearly stated most of the details that helped define the characters and tell the story. (**figs. 2.121** to **2.126**: See details on top half of next page, where the expressions have been clearly determined at this stage already). Since the shot has been thought out as a double-page spread, I made sure that the central vertical area (band in gray) does not contain any vital information.

Fig. 2.120: This shows how, after using the previous ink sketch as an underlay on a light desk, I have foreseen, without major detail yet and without much use of character outlines, where the shadows and lights will go to make volumetric sense of all the elements in the shot (mostly characters), within the basic light and dark visual structure previously designed in the basic composition (**fig. 2.117**).

Figs. 2.127, **2.128**, **2.129** and **2.131**: For the game of light and shadows, the choice was to go quite obvious on the light, core shadow, and reflected shadow rendering. See how within the shadows themselves there is a lot of tonal variations that define the shape and volumes of whatever they contain, in most cases without even the use of line to separate the different areas. (See the shadows on the main actor's torso in **Fig. 2.127**). See also, for example, how the shadow of the white beard's bottom and the pirate's jacket (**fig. 2.131**) blend with each other so that the issue here is not beard vs. jacket but light vs. shadow (See *Framed Ink*, for light-shadow rendering).

Observe as well in **Fig. 2.130** that the graphite pencil stroke in the render of the wall behind the chair follows the vertical perspective of said wall, so that render emphasizes its shape and direction.

See final, full render, **fig. 2.133** on pages 068-069.

fig. 2.121

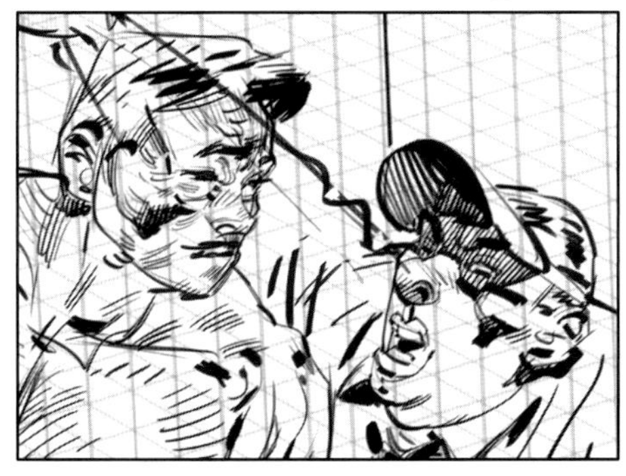

fig. 2.122

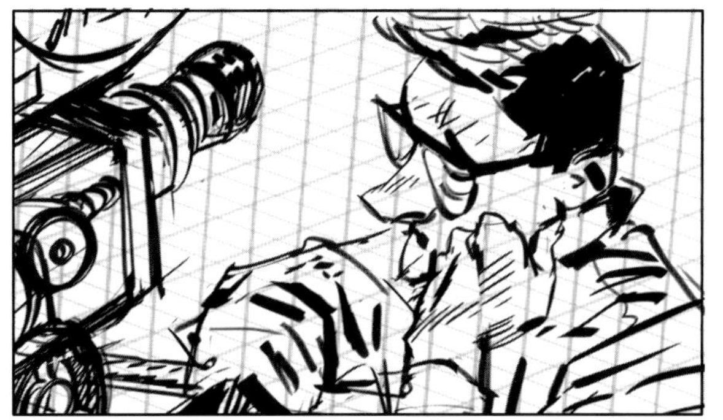

fig. 2.123

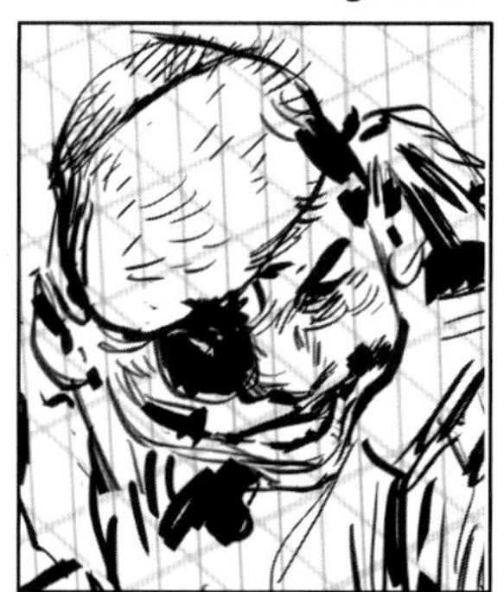

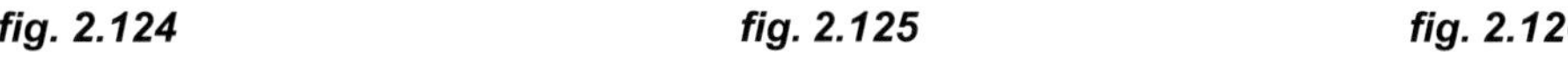

fig. 2.124

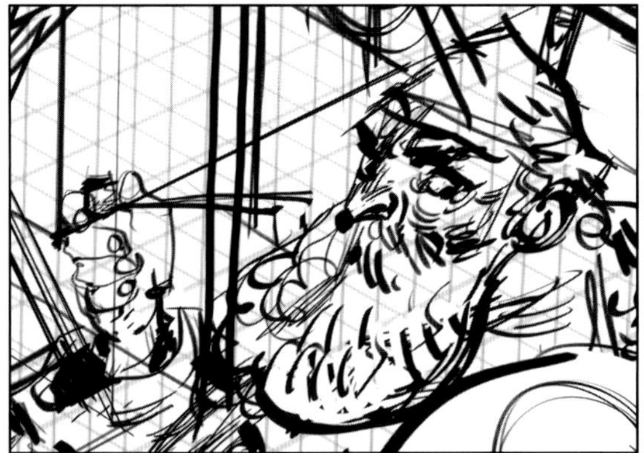

fig. 2.125

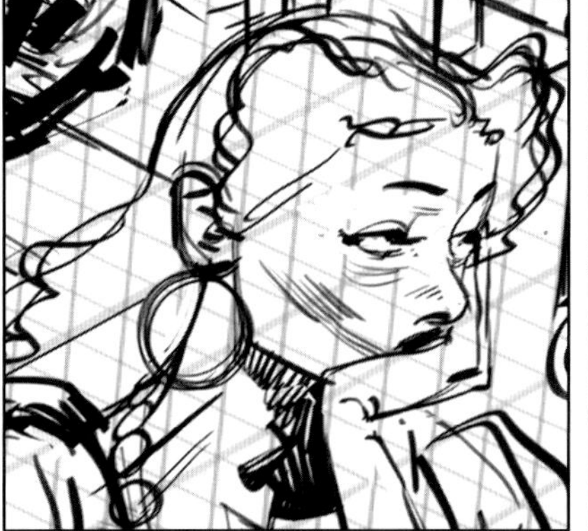

fig. 2.126

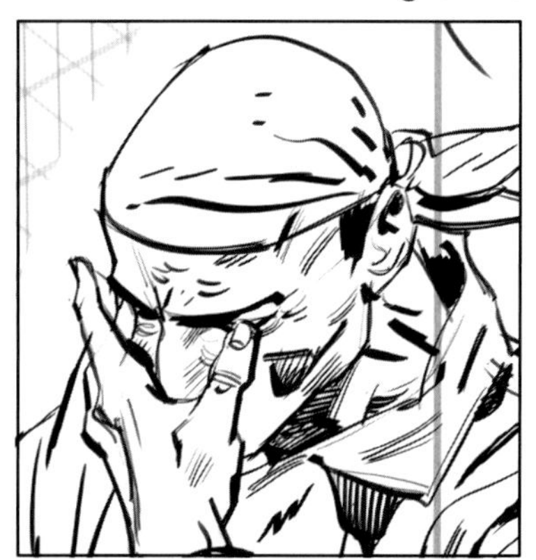

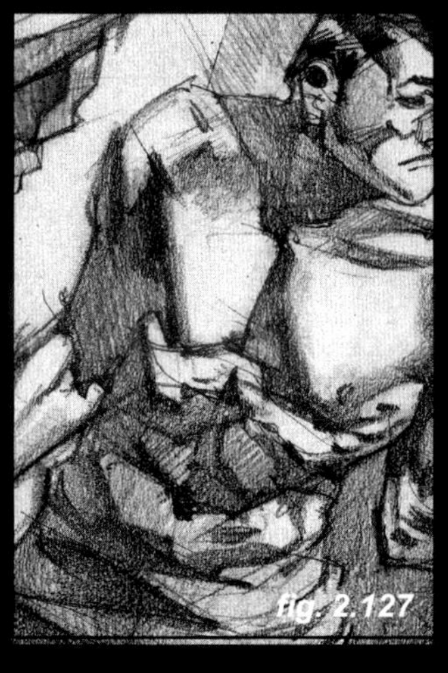

fig. 2.127

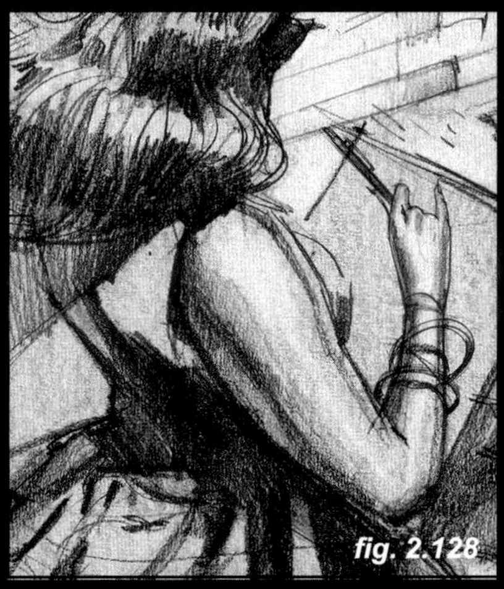

fig. 2.128

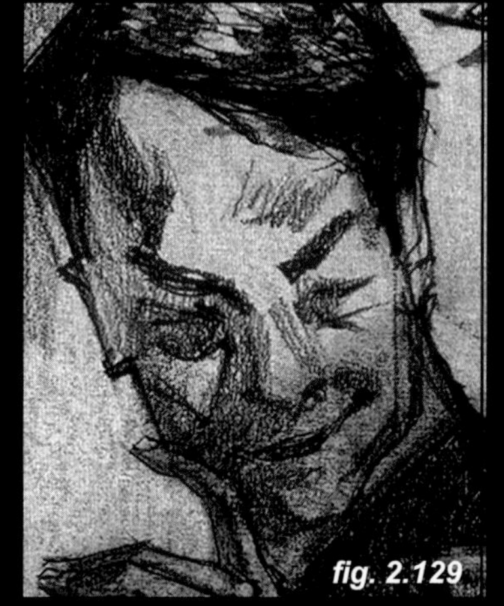

fig. 2.129

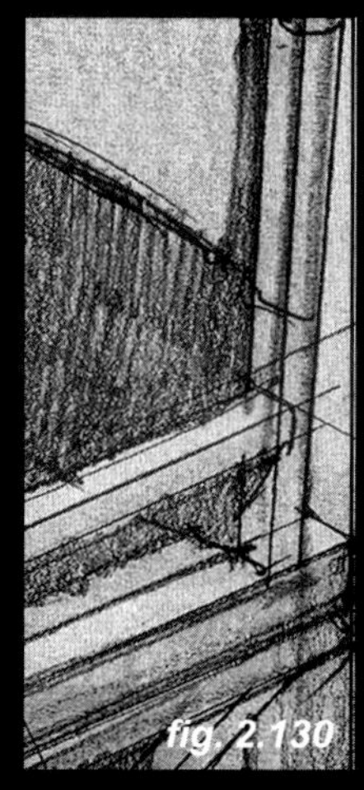

fig. 2.130

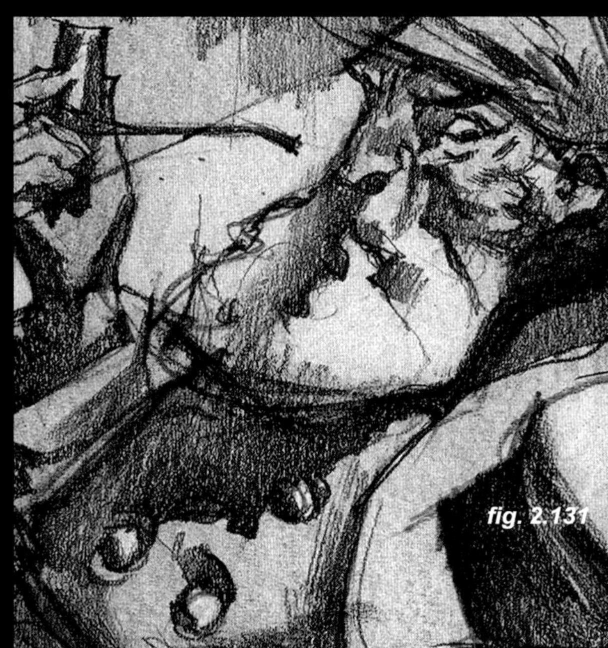

fig. 2.131

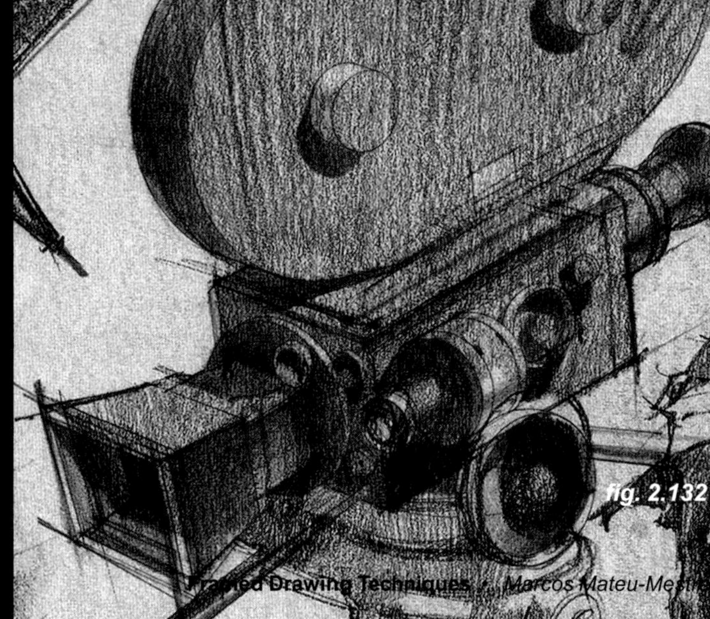

fig. 2.132

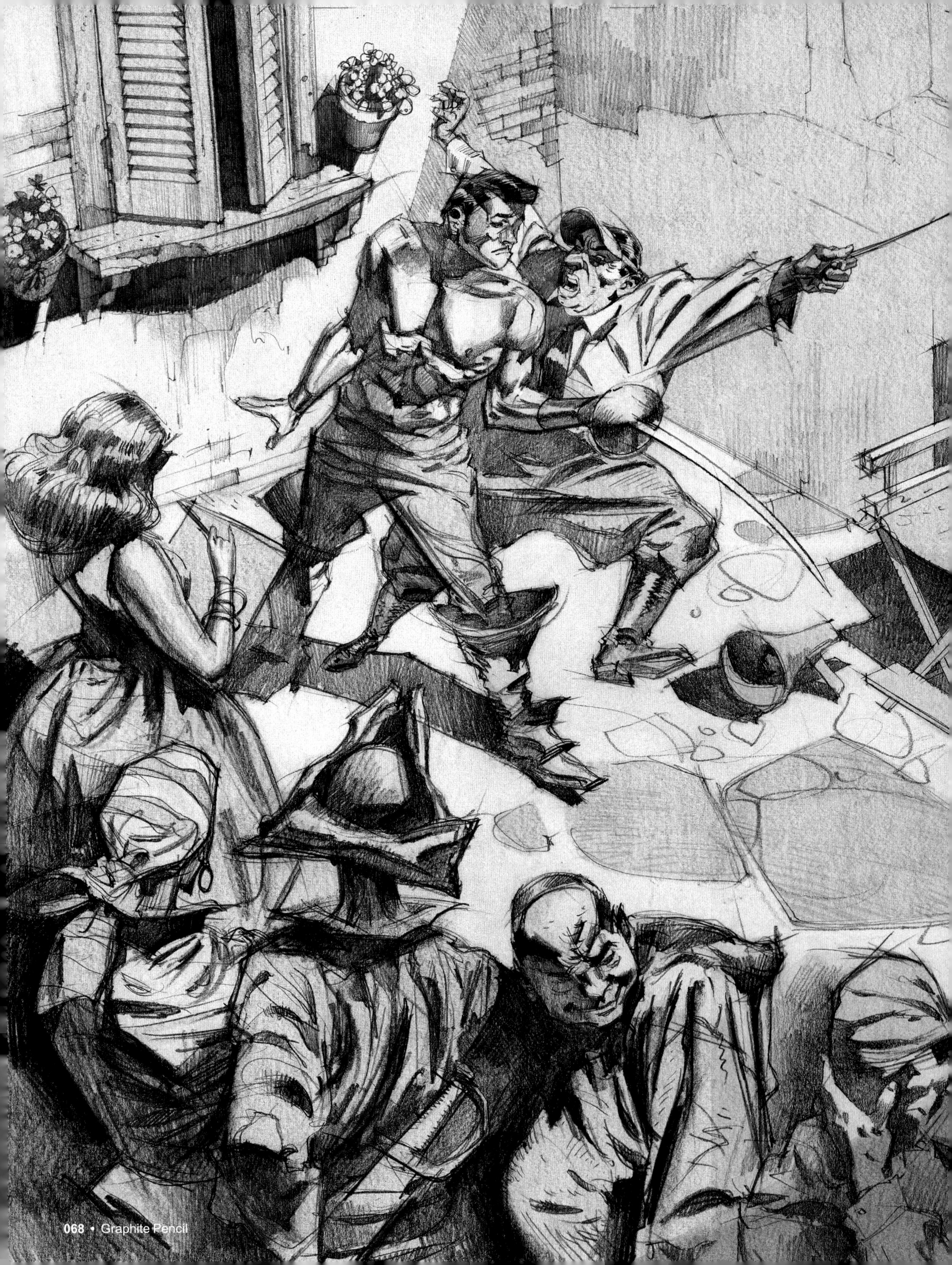

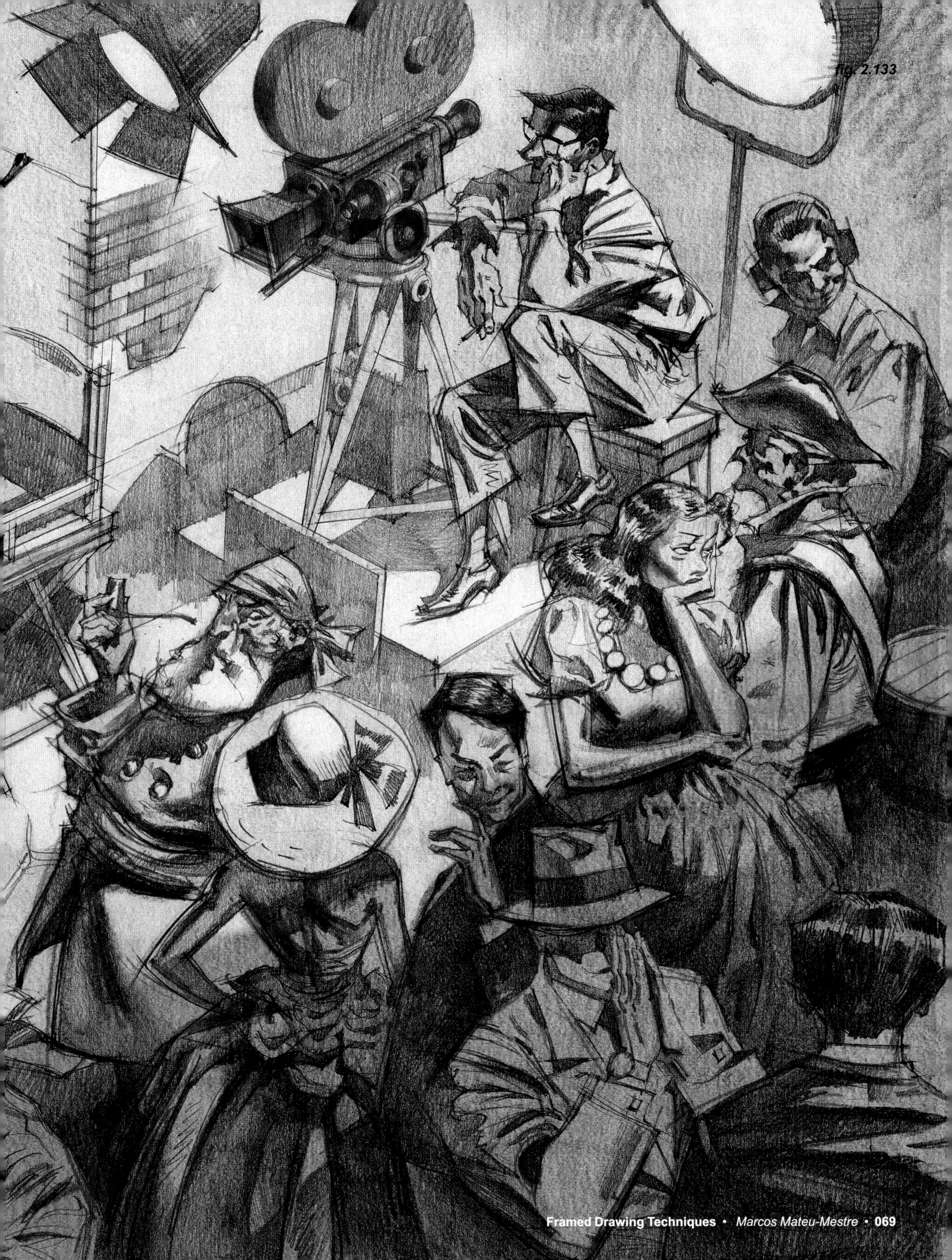

Fig. 2.133

fig. 2.134 *fig. 2.135*

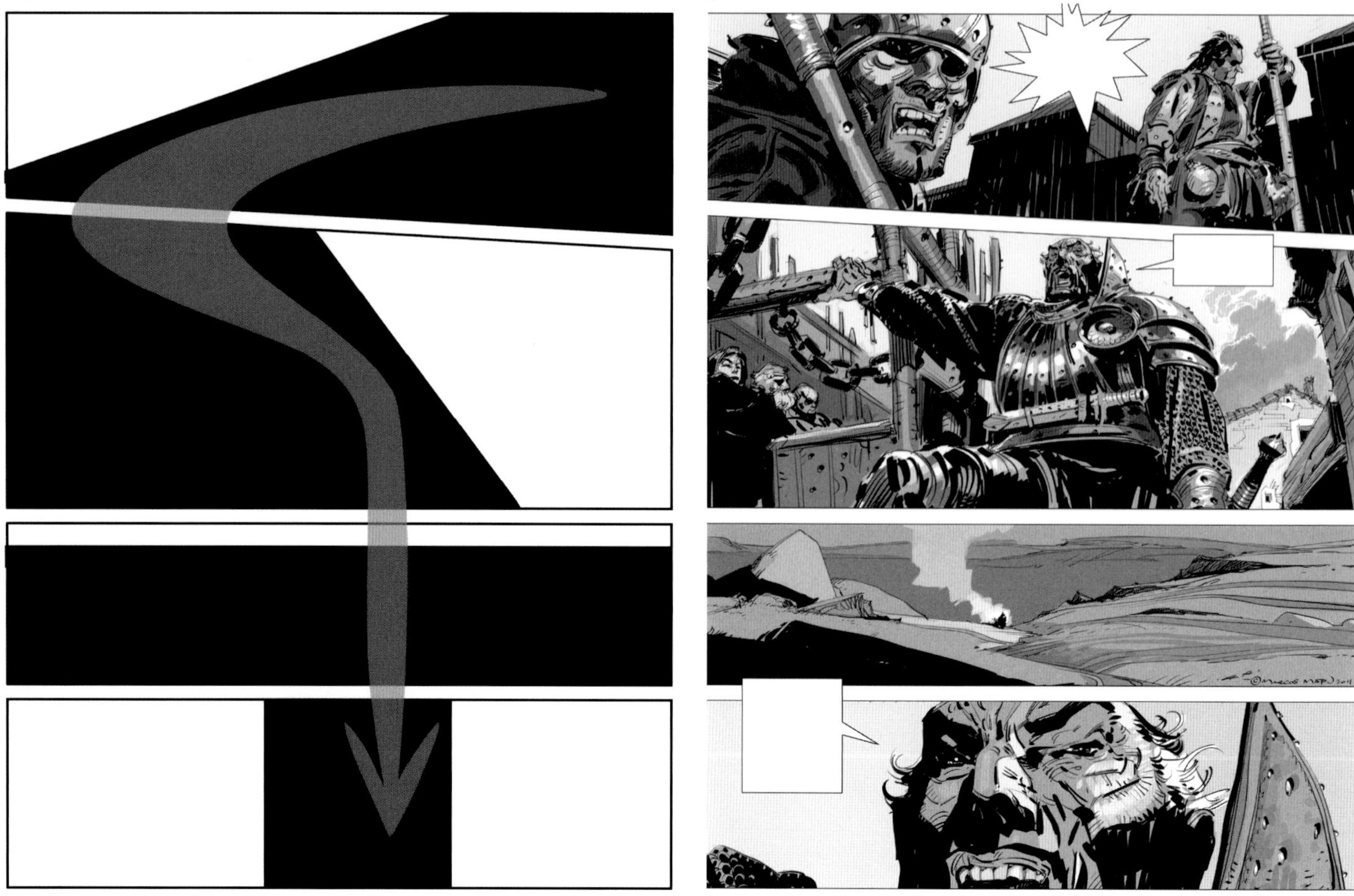

Figs. 2.134 and **2.135**: The graphic-novel page previously seen on pages 038-039 is now together with its layout schematic that shows how the essential dynamics of the page works. A rhythm is established that goes right, left, then flat, and finally drops vertical to bring the beat to a stop, almost like the motion of a leaf falling from a tree.

The character galloping in the distance in panel 3, although in quite a neutral angle, is still traveling in a direction that slightly indicates a left-to-right path toward Condottiero Martin (the leader of the pack in the story), again establishing a visual sense of dialogue with him as they 'face' each other.

Also, observe how in both the defensive wall in panel 1 and the wooden side of the cart background (panel 2 left), the rendering stroke follows the overall direction of the plane on both subjects, reinforcing a sense of three-dimensional construction.

Fig. 2.136: Here is the page rendered in graphite pencil, demonstrating how it can be used to depict various textures and materials as seen in previous sections of this book (reflective metal, wood, rocky terrain, skin, fabrics, etc.), and that by adapting the stroke of the pencil (in terms of softness, dryness, sharp contrast, gradations, etc.), you can obtain the desired effects.

Notice how other visual narrative devices are being used in the rendering of this page, like the drawing where Condottiero Martin in panel 4 isn't contained in a frame anymore, visually expanding in a way that "claims territory" while other characters are inside panels that do have boundaries, in the shape of line frames. This way a visual contrast between hierarchies and levels of power within the story is established.

Overall, the rendering of these images has been, despite the sense of formal detail in them, executed with a subtle dynamic stroke in order to keep up the sense of pace and action of the story.

Do not forget when it comes to rendering comic panels, ideally you should do it in a way that matches the sense of the story (historical, comedy, science fiction, etc., through the choice of fast vs. more detailed line, emphasizing dynamic gesture vs. general chiaroscuro, etc.) and still communicates to the audience a sense of energy big enough that it will grab them and drive them from one panel to the next, so that they don't get stuck in each individual frame, which would break the flow of the story.

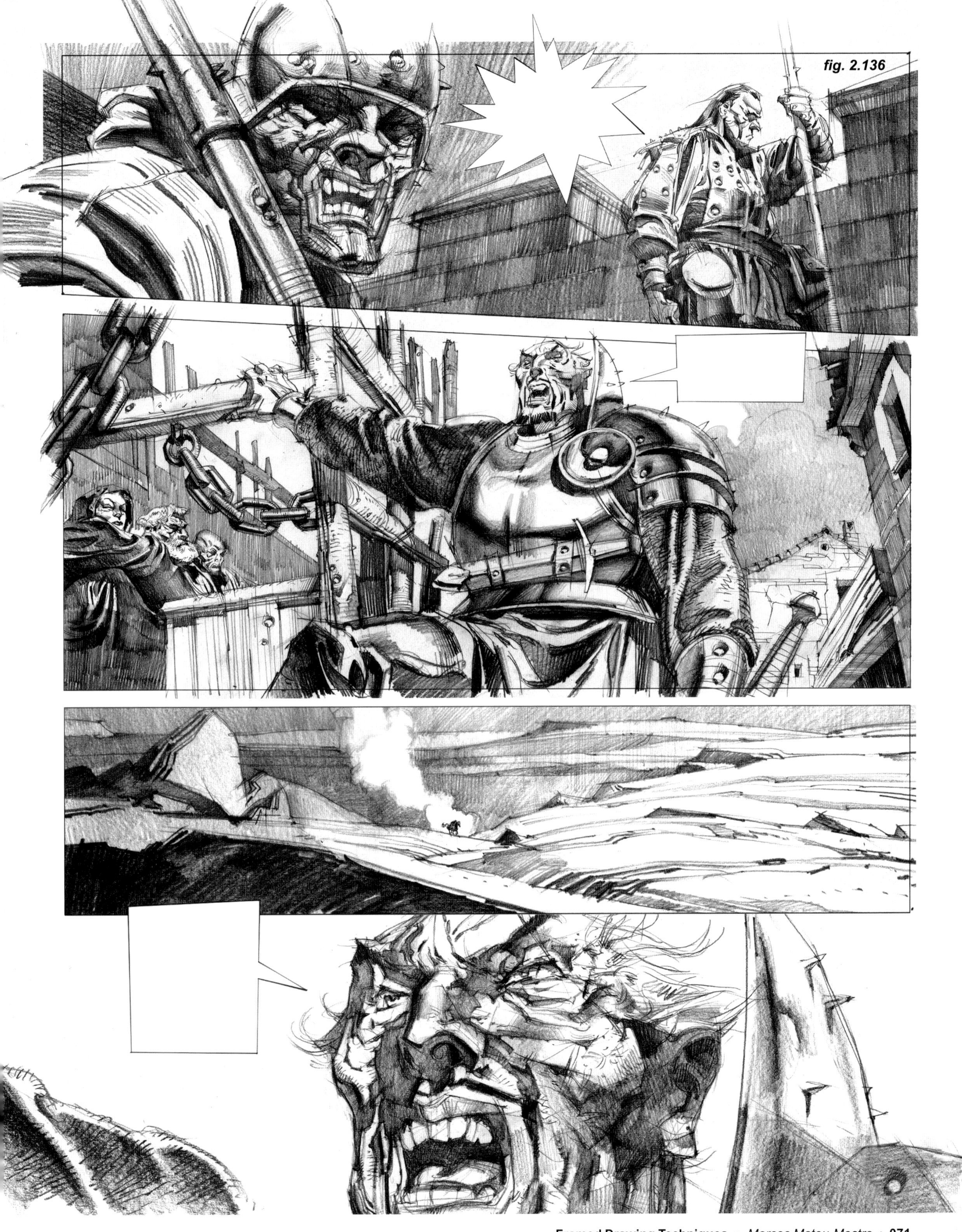
fig. 2.136

Fig. 2.137: Recall the zoom tip on page 064. Given the long-shot nature of panel 3, a separate, more detailed drawing of the horseman was drawn, so that once scanned and reduced to fit in the drawing, it would be more than just a blob in the center.

fig. 2.137

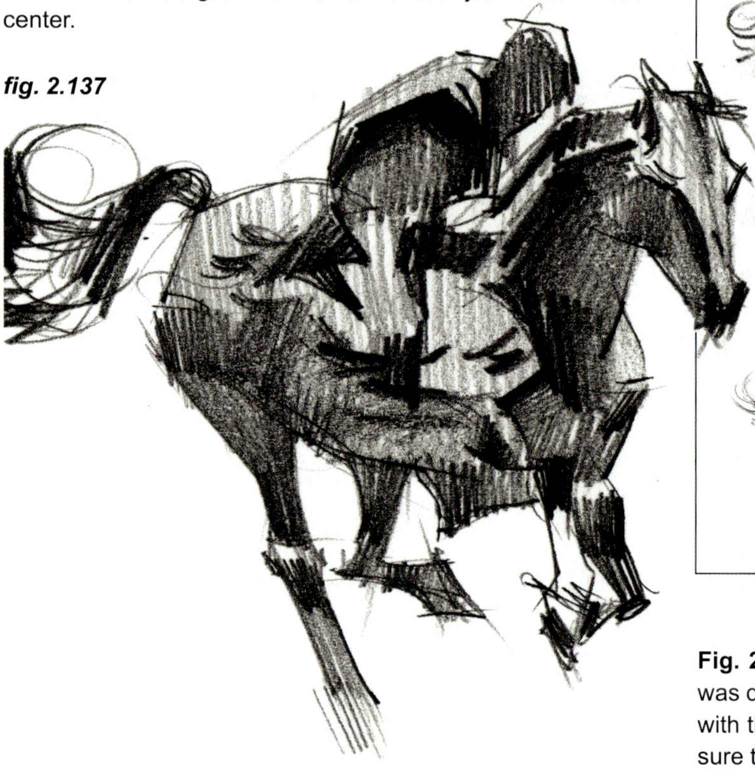

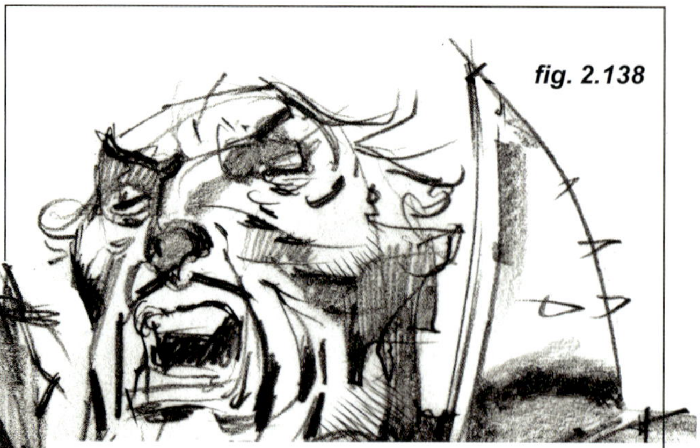

fig. 2.138

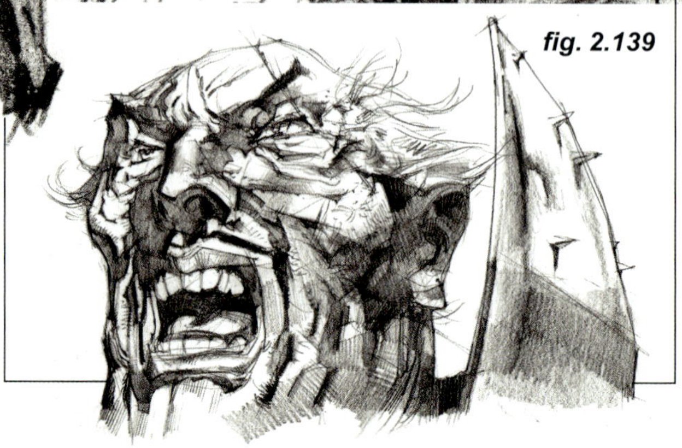

fig. 2.139

Fig. 2.138: The drawing of Condottiero Martin's head in panel 4 was directly based on an enlarged printout of the same in panel 2, with the help of a light desk to keep visual consistency and make sure that the final shot in the page feels like I just directly cut in on him with the camera.

Fig. 2.140: It is usually the case that an original graphite drawing does have a punch and vibration that a scanned or printed copy somehow doesn't quite have, and to make up for this, sometimes you can slightly push the contrast out of the scans digitally.

Figs. 2.141 and **2.142**: Another way to achieve bigger visual contrast of a scanned image is by copying the drawing's layer (in red: drag the layer down to the Layer icon, and it will automatically be copied right on top of the original).

After that, I change the top layer from Normal to Multiply, making it transparent. You can also adjust the copied layer's opacity to bring the overall contrast down a bit if needed. Here I brought it down to 40 percent for the sake of instruction.

fig. 2.141

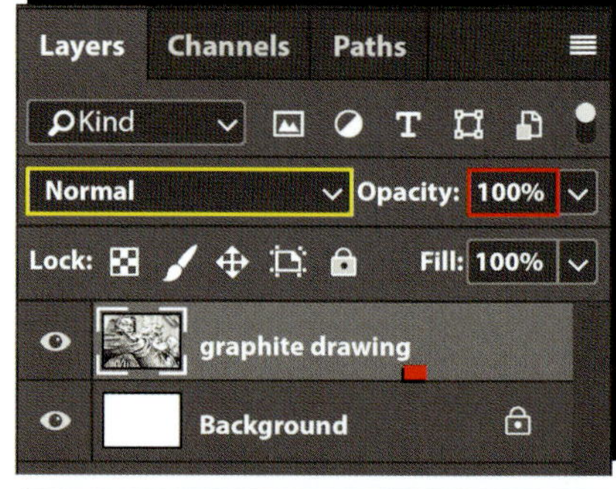

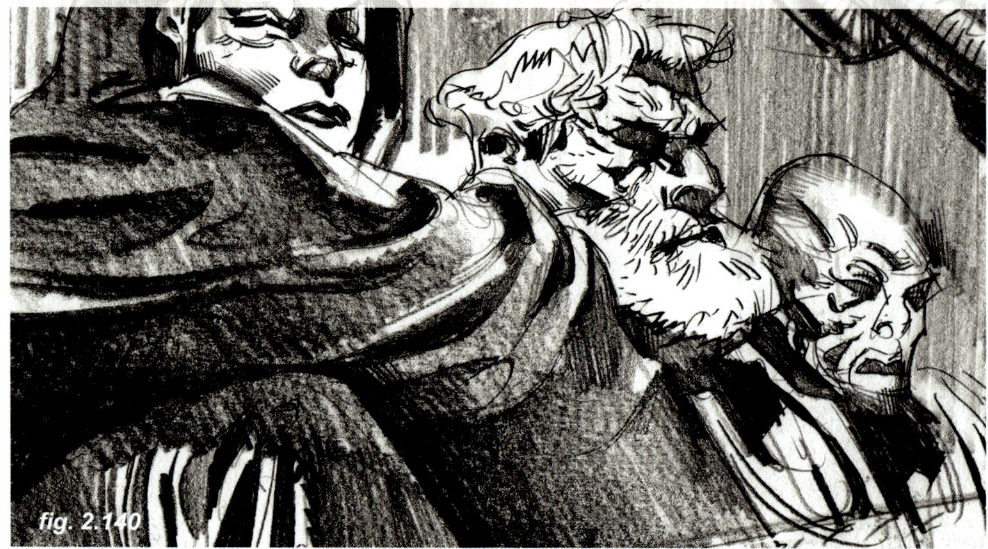

fig. 2.140

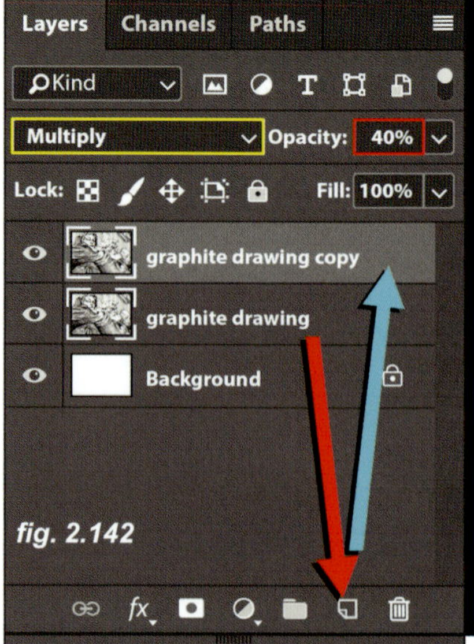

fig. 2.142

3

THE DIGITAL WAY

THE BASICS, AGAIN

So here we are, in the digital age, the one that changed everything years ago, and yet digital tools do not (nor will they ever) completely substitute the array of traditional tools we have available to us.

In fact, what they provide are simply more devices that, just as the others, we will need to use based on our straight knowledge of drawing, lighting, composition, anatomy, perspective, architecture, expression, storytelling, flow, dynamics, and so many etceteras. All of these will always constitute the strong skeleton on which we will build our visuals, regardless of the tools or techniques we decide to use for them.

The particularity of the digital way—besides its capacity for quick editing and ability to try many different options by adding disposable layers in a record amount of time—is the potential boldness of it. It can be used as an inking tool that can look very close to a traditional brush and ink, or a marker for graphic novels or storyboards, for example, or more painterly when used as multitonal (see Chapter 4, page 108 of this book), with all the grays available to us between black and white, as it would be more attuned with a visual development piece for a film, whether animated or live action.

The two digital approaches I will be focusing on in this book are the "inking way" and grayscale tonals.

BLACK AND WHITE / THE INKING WAY

The look of an image created this way is particularly bold and graphic, and in order to achieve these looks there won't be much need for elaborate or complex brushes. I tend to use (exclusively) the basic "round-dot" brush, which I usually slightly distort depending on the needs of the moment.

Next, see a few variations together with a screenshot of the Photoshop brush setups (for reference) as well as some written and drawn practical tryouts of each brush to show their look and results.

Obviously these are just suggestions, and it's always a great idea to explore further based on one's needs and sense of style.

fig. 3.1

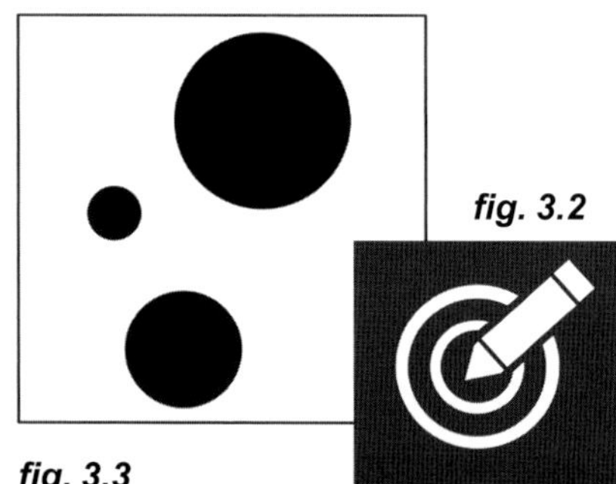

fig. 3.2

#1 | The basic round brush

It's just a circle brush—here used with "shape dynamics" and "smoothing" checked, "hardness" to the maximum and "spacing" to the minimum—that we can increase or decrease using the left and right bracket keys to adjust the line we need to draw at that point. The pressure put on the pen at each moment will also make a difference in the thickness of the line and within the same brushstroke. See the Wacom tablet settings used to produce the artwork in this book, **Fig. 3.10**.

Fig. 3.2: Make sure you activate the pen pressure icon as well so that the beginning and end of each stroke have a nice smooth feel to them.

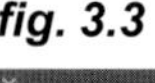

fig. 3.3

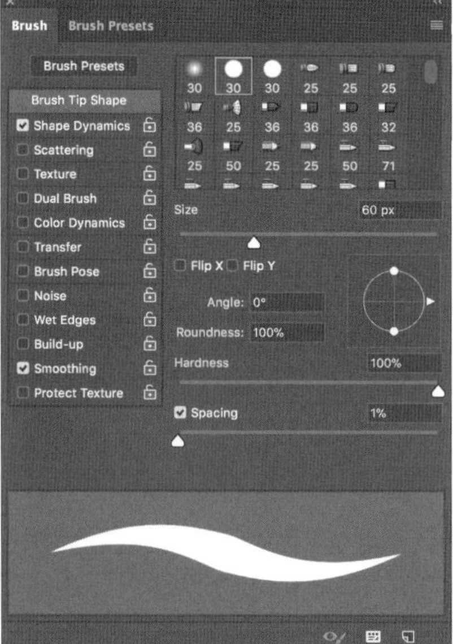

fig. 3.4

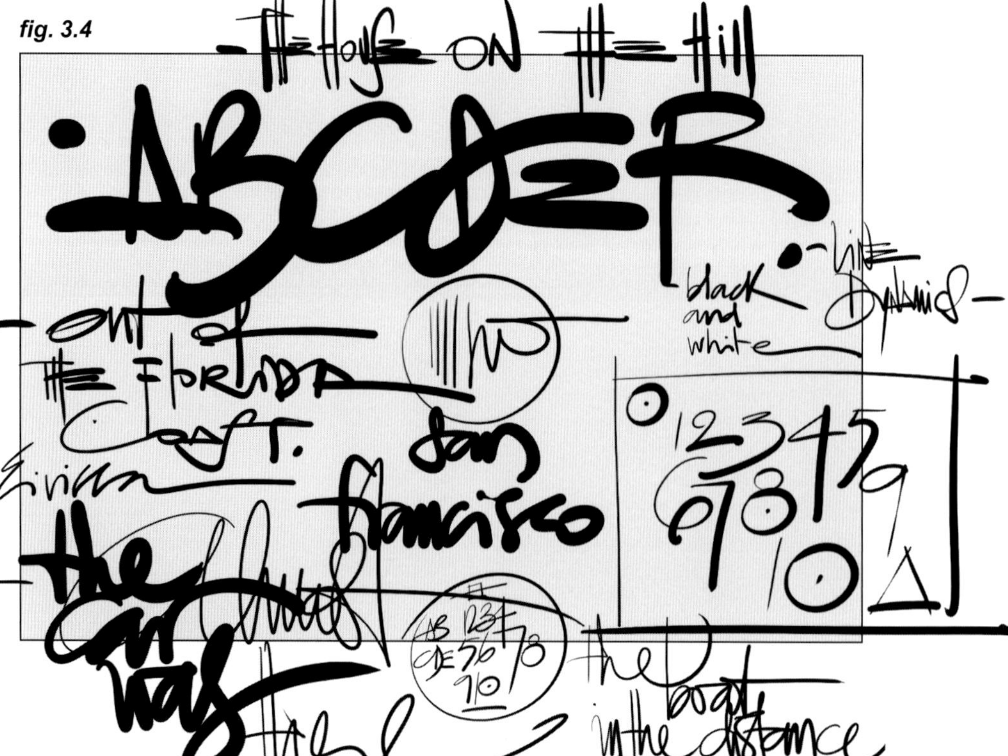

#2 | Stretching horizontally

Squeezing the #1 round brush we can form horizontally stretched, "grain-of-rice" looking brushes (**figs. 3.5** and **3.6**) to obtain graphic results such as the ones in **Fig. 3.7**. Again, these settings are for reference only and can vary accordingly to the needs or stylistic taste for the narrative moment. You can observe how this sort of squeeze offers the ability to have thick and thin stretches on the same brushstroke.

fig. 3.5

fig. 3.7

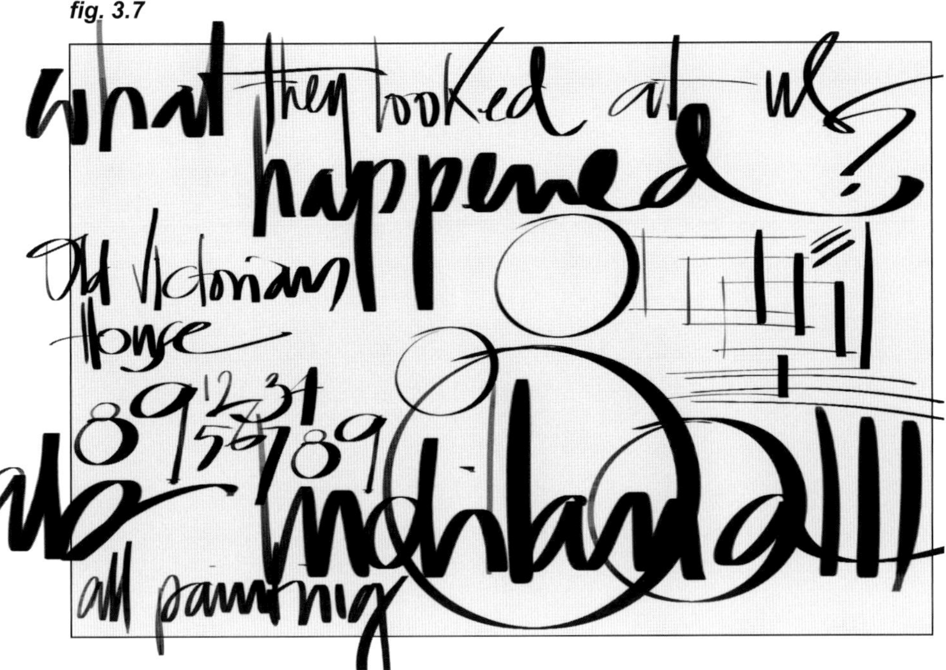

fig. 3.6

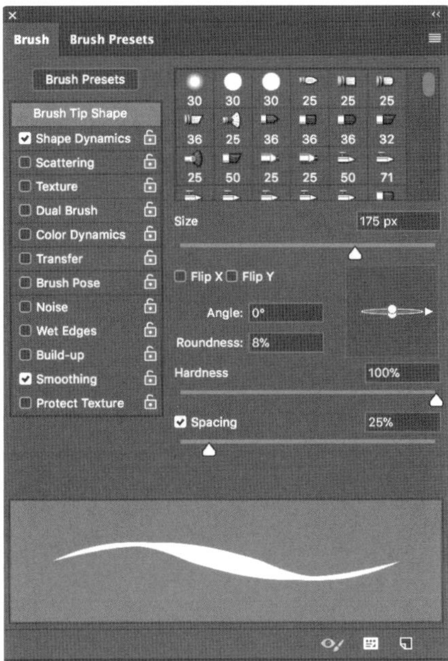

#3 & #4 | The diagonal tilt

Time for a squeeze and a tilt (either to the left, **fig. 3.8**, or to the right, **fig. 3.9**). All these are options that give an extra punch and interest to the resulting line of an otherwise pretty common brush (**figs. 3.11** and **3.12**).

fig. 3.8

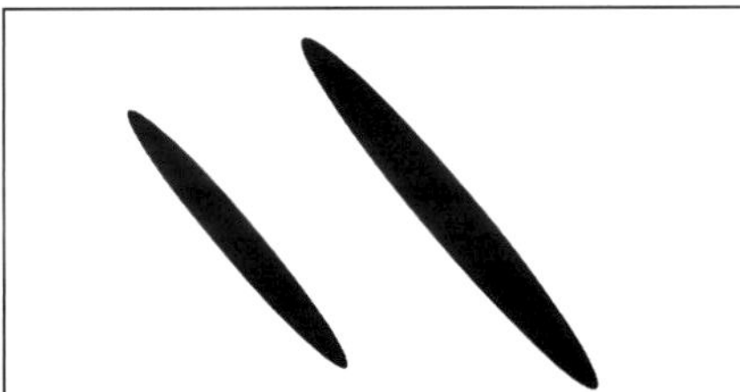

fig. 3.9

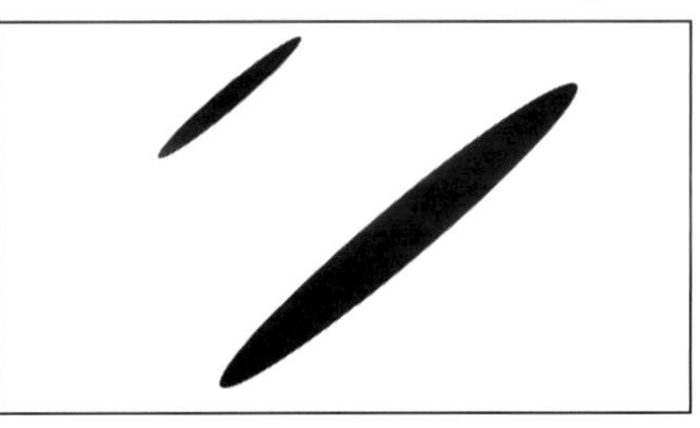

fig. 3.10

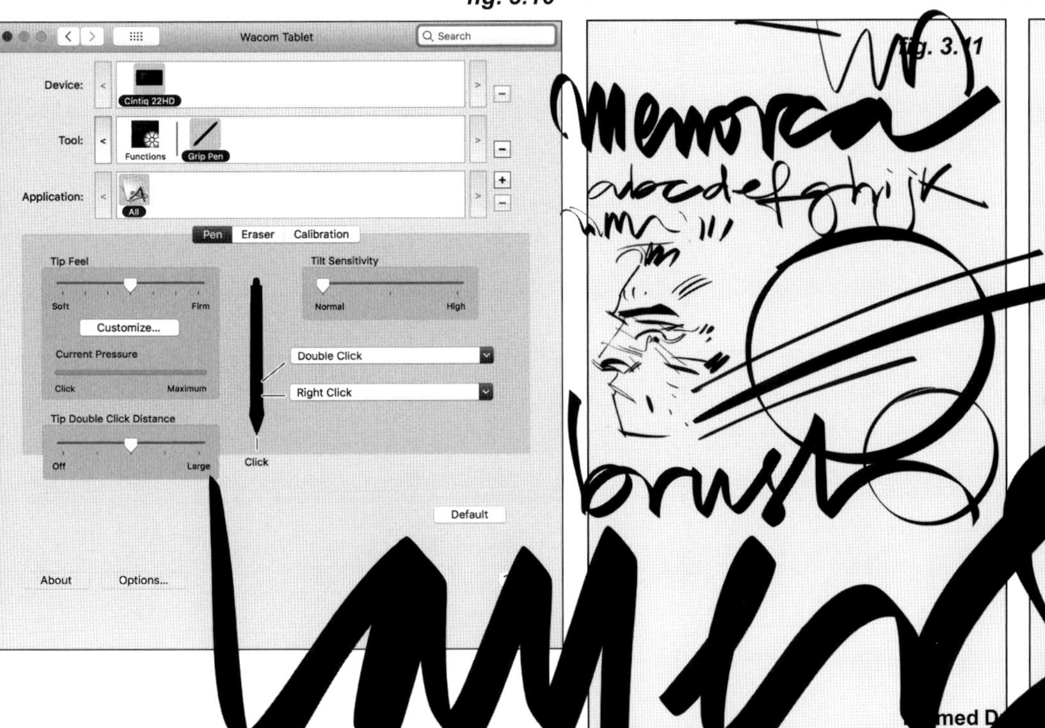

fig. 3.11

fig. 3.12

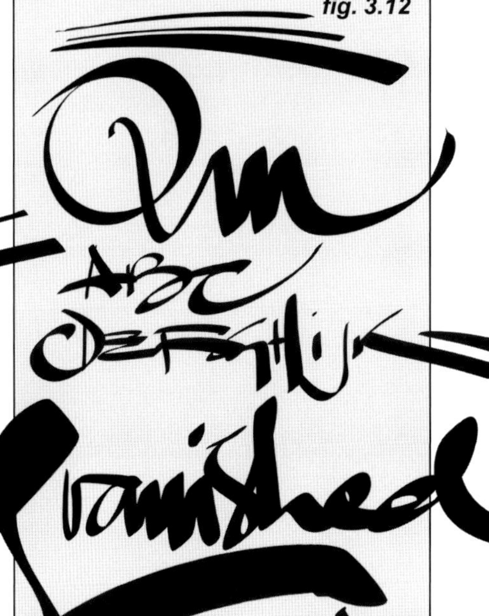

After seeing the basic use of the "Ink-like" brush, let's now get into how to use these for practical purposes. There are many ways and variations to utilize to get things done, but as long as they are visually clear, gracefully executed, and deliver the narrative message you are trying to convey, they are all valid. Everything else is a matter of taste and opinion. Here are a few examples of how to create organized line work:

Fig. 3.13: A hard black-and-white line gradation obtained by the use of consecutively smaller/thinner brushes (achieved by changing the width of the brush by the number of its pixels on the go, with the short keys { or }).

Fig. 3.14: If your intention is to design a shadow tone by drawing parallel lines that, although drawn by freehand, try to look as straight and vertical as possible, you might find that either your wrist or your elbow—depending on where you draw from—can act as a compass needle (**fig. 3.17**), making you draw the pretended straight lines in a slightly curved fashion, no matter how much you try to avoid it.

Fig. 3.15: A possible solution to this is to draw a second group of parallels with the same curvature, and then use the tool "Edit/Transform/Flip Horizontal" on it, so that now the curvature of this second batch of lines curves in the opposite way (**fig. 3.15**).

Fig. 3.16: Next, you can superimpose both sets of lines so that the slight curvature of one compensates for the slight curvature of the other, balancing out an overall sense of verticality.

Another way to create a nice looking set of long parallels is by drawing a set of parallels with a length you feel comfortable and confident with (**fig. 3.18**). Then select it and stretch the selection vertically (**fig. 3.19**) so that you end up with the same set of lines, only longer and with a more "straight" look, yet still keeping part of this "hand drawn"/not perfectly straight" look to it that will fit in better within the context of a more organic piece of artwork.

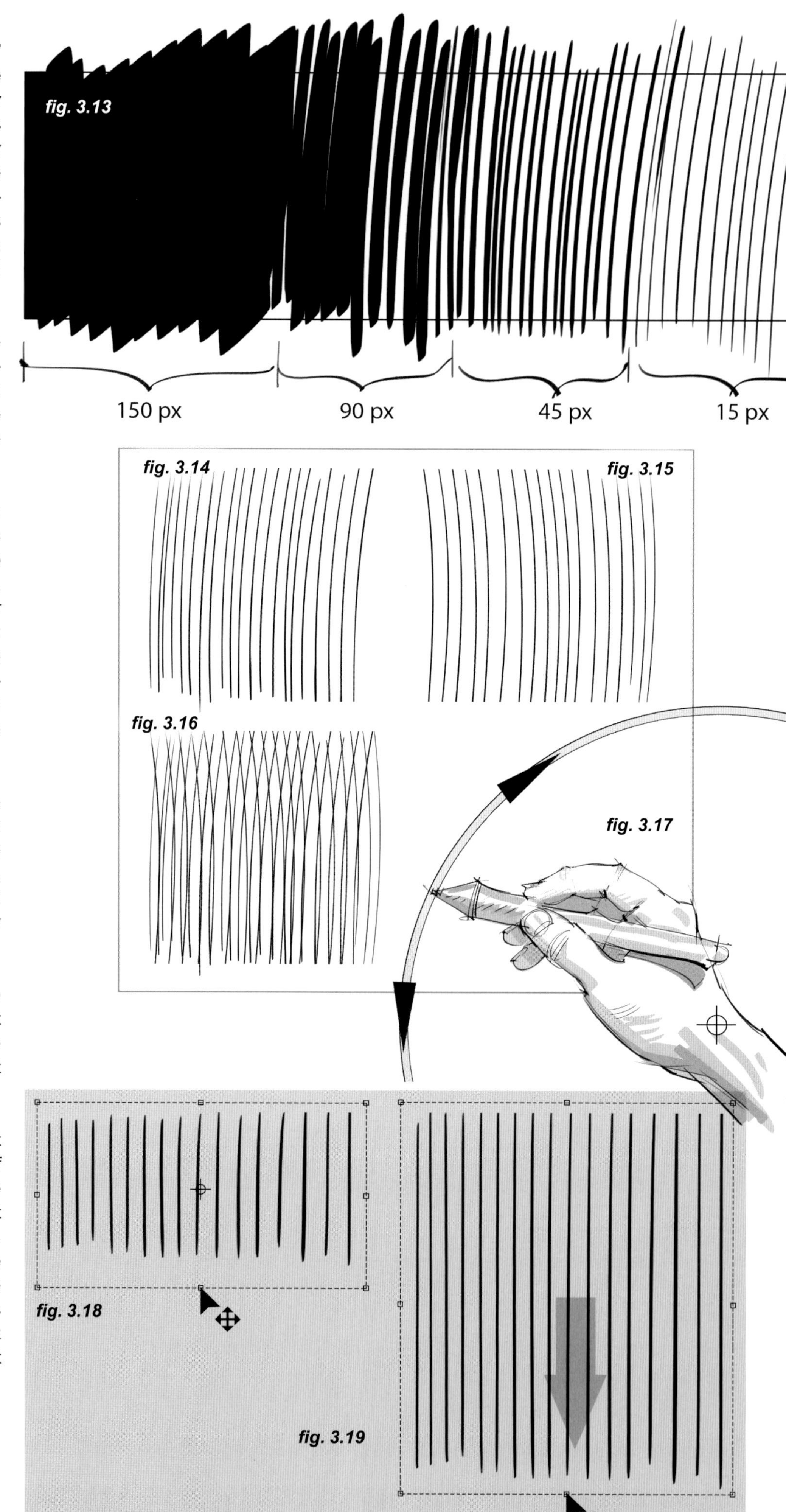

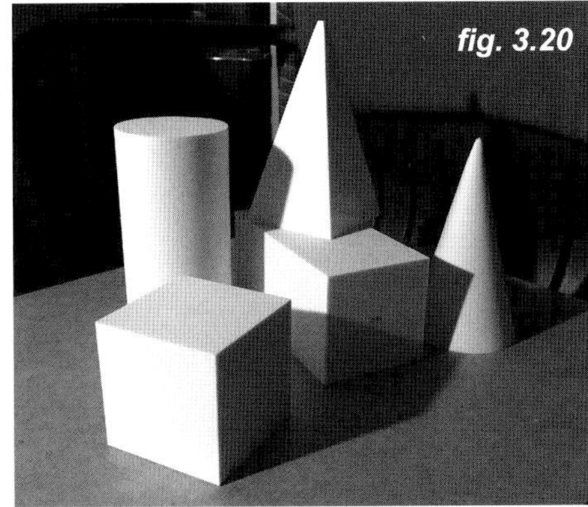

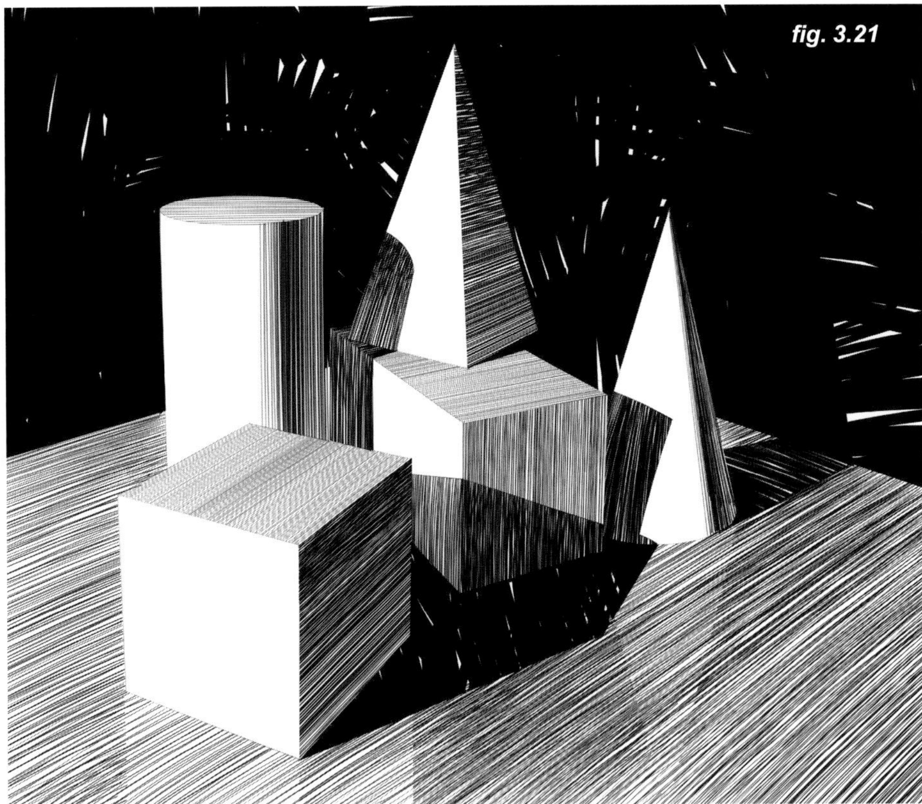

Fig. 3.20: Going back to the same basic example I used for previous techniques, it's always interesting to compare how the same subject looks when rendered in different media.

Fig. 3.21: This is the subject when digitally rendered to look inked. Take into account that usually there is never one valid answer to a challenge.

The dark background was rendered with a thick (50 px) brush. Some gaps were left between the lose brushstrokes here and there to let such dark mass breathe a bit, and give it a more freehand, organic feel.

Although all line work in this drawing was digitally rendered freehand, given its architectural nature, I opted for a more formal, regular, geometrical look.

It is important for all brushstrokes, independent from thickness and other properties, to look and feel like they belong to the same "visual family," rather than appearing to belong to different images or contexts.

Then again, all sets of parallels were drawn on a different layer according to the technique explained in **Figs. 3.18** and **3.19** and then digitally placed within the corresponding surface through the help of the 'skew' and 'distort' tools within the 'edit/transform' menu in Photoshop.

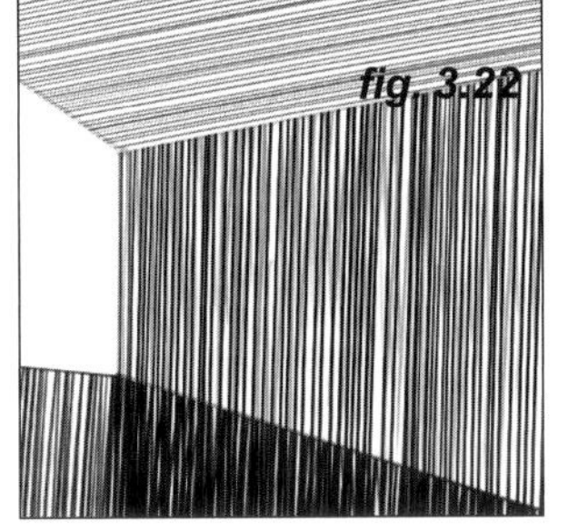

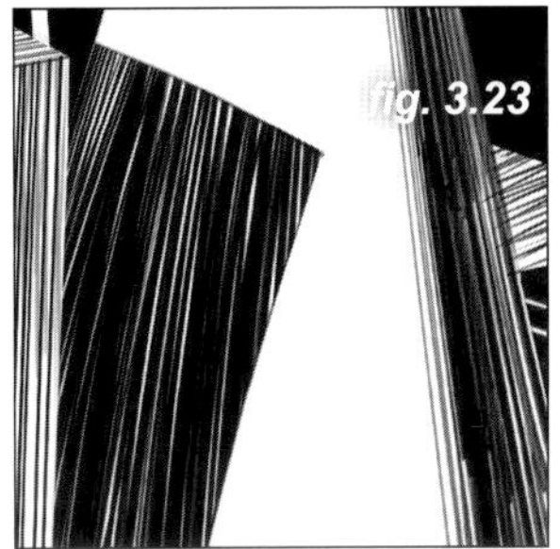

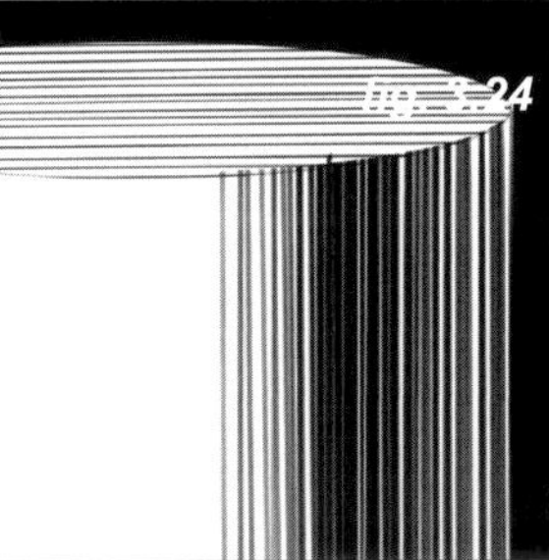

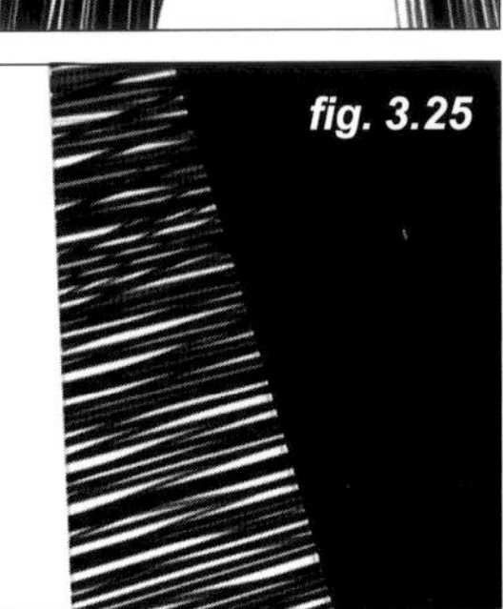

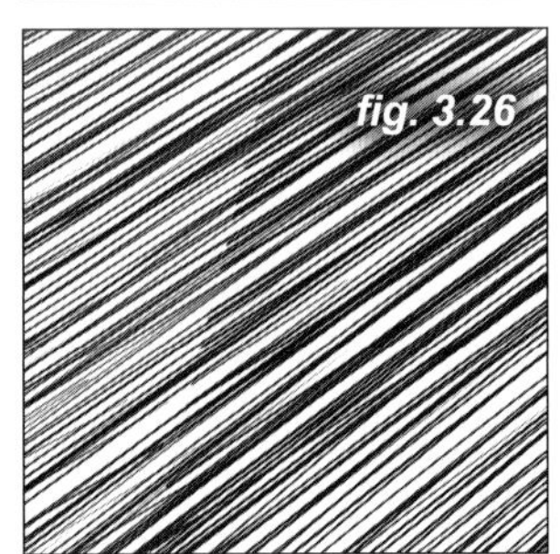

DETAILS

Fig. 3.22: See how different brush thicknesses have been used for different shadow intensities, sometimes superimposing more or less layers of lines to achieve a darker or lighter shade.

Fig. 3.23: When rendering the shadows on the cone, all lines were following its surface's shape, therefore pointing all of them toward the top tip of the figure.

Fig. 3.24: Here's another example of different tones achieved with different brush thicknesses. After the stretching of the lines (explained earlier) has been done, you can then rotate such set of parallels in the needed direction.

Fig. 3.25: The lines on the pyramid's side also follow the direction of its perspective. They may be drawn beyond the edge during the sketch phase, but the parts of the lines that extend outside the edges should be deleted before finalizing.

Fig. 3.26: The subtle reflections of the lit sides of these polyhedrons and the cylinder and cone on the table are achieved by drawing more layers of lines on the darker areas, leaving the lighter ones less rendered.

Before I get into more details and nuances, let me make one thing clear: details are, the vast majority of the time, a second read, something that will hit us a few seconds later. The first read is more important. We only have one chance to make a good first impression, so let's work on this.

This first impression reveals what's going on in the scene and where to look. It provides key information to the audience in order to follow the story and indicates the mood of the scene. Are things dynamic, poetic, funny, dark, or dramatic? And by comparison, are they brighter/darker than the previous or following moment? Are things getting better or worse in the story?

To practice creating a strong first impression, one of the best exercises you can do is to get a model to work from (photographic or live), and try to extract the bare-bones information based on shadows and light, simplify the existing contrast to the maximum, do it all with a thick brush and use only masses of light and dark. Don't use an outline to define the limits of an object simply because one doesn't exist; an outline only presents itself when light hits in a way that an edge or limit of an object is defined by the contrast of light and shadow.

Here are a few examples of "first-impression" exercises I did with the photo reference used and the artwork produced. You can see where the information reflected in the drawing actually comes from and how it has been "extracted" from the source.

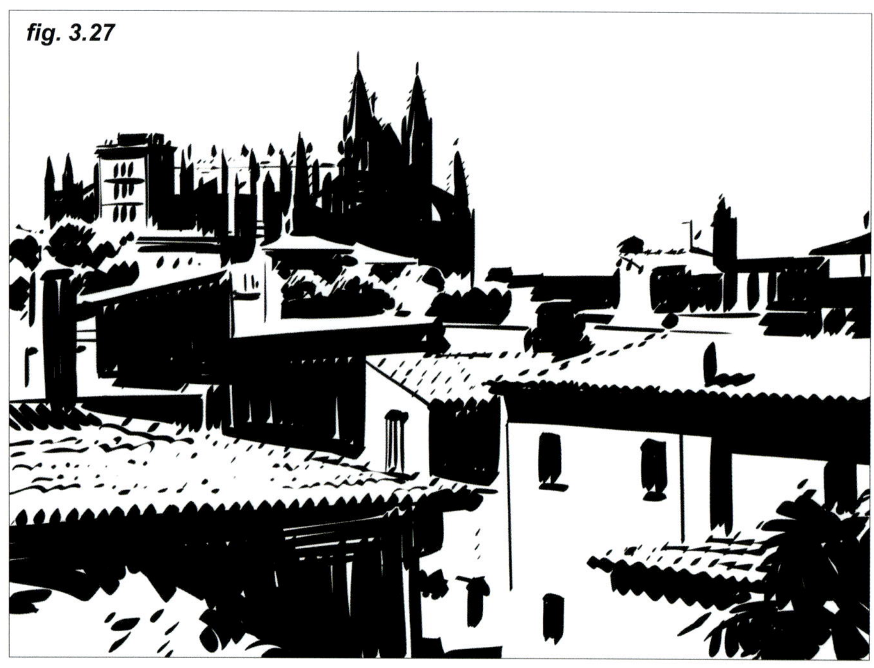

fig. 3.27

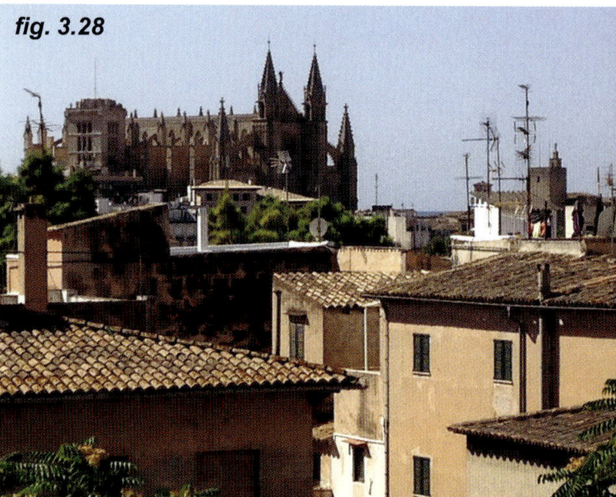

fig. 3.28

Drawing exercise

Figs. 3.27 to **3.30**: Now you try it using a thick brush at the same width throughout the exercise. Look at the image, squinting your eyes to observe where the darker shades are (either shadows or dark local color), and then put this on your canvas. Shadows that are together blend into each other without separation regardless of whether they belong to completely different objects. The lines you'll see are not outlines but the shadows of drainage pipes, roof tile shadows, etc.

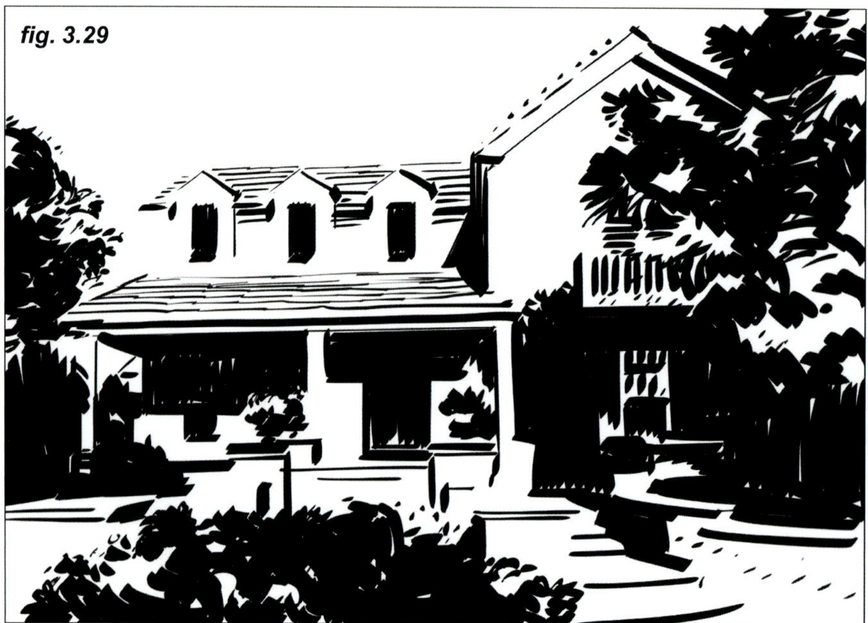

fig. 3.29

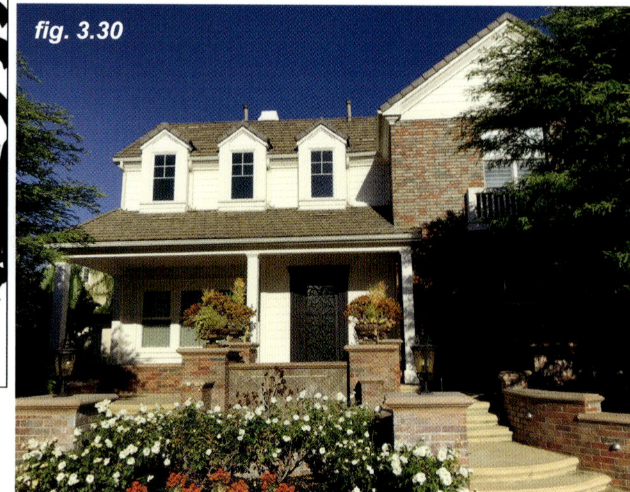

fig. 3.30

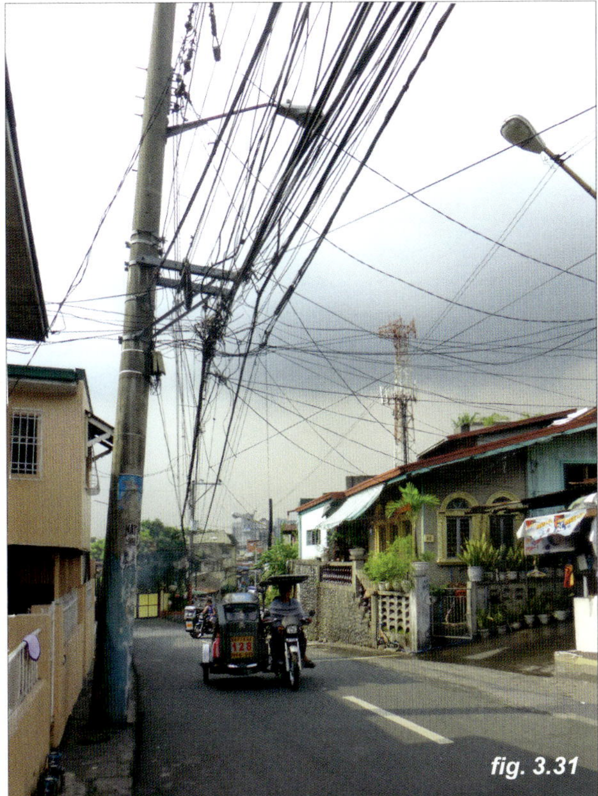

fig. 3.31

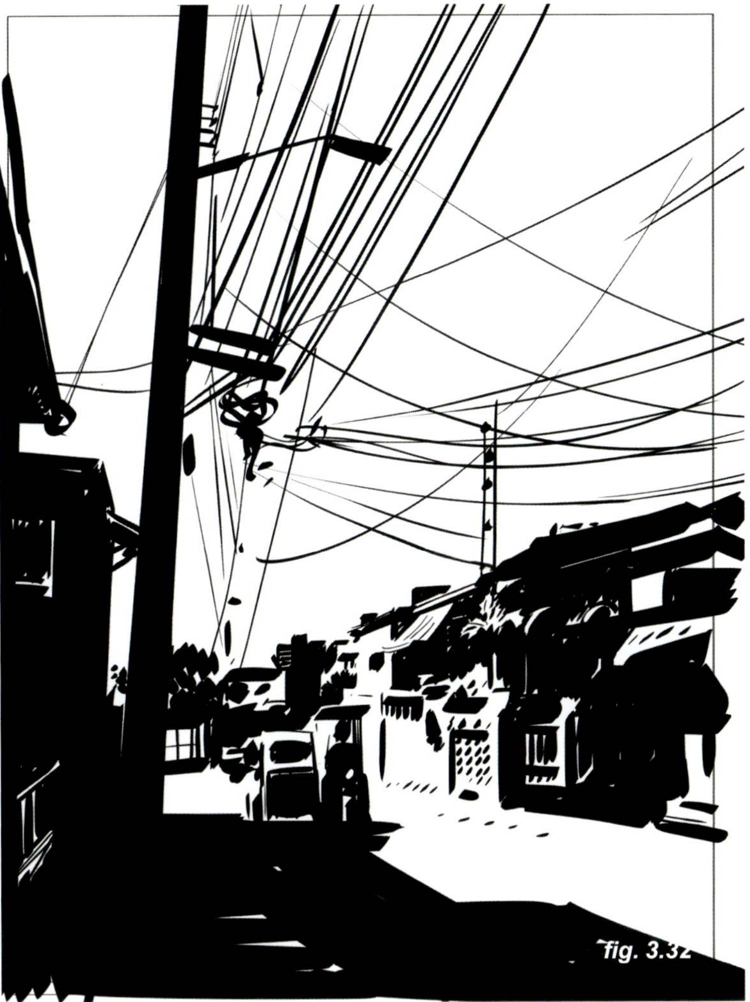

fig. 3.32

Figs. 3.31 and **3.32**: With my options being only black or white, here I greatly exaggerated the existing tones. The buildings on the left and the shadow they cast on the pavement become one dark mass. It is the same with the other side of the street where darks have been greatly contrasted and accentuated.

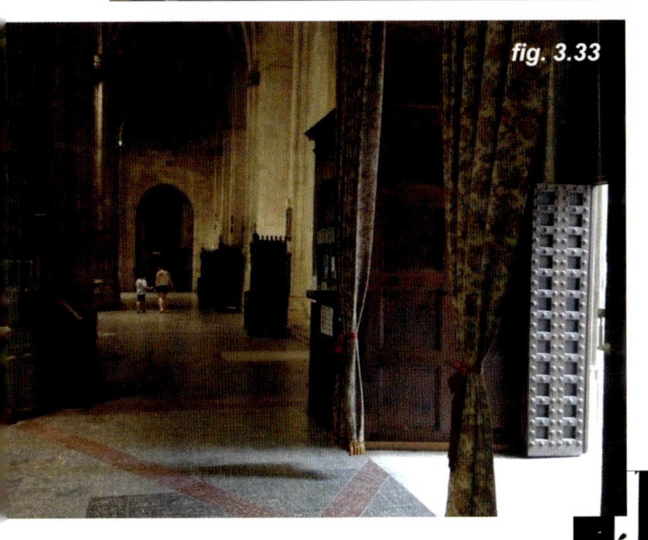

fig. 3.33

fig. 3.34

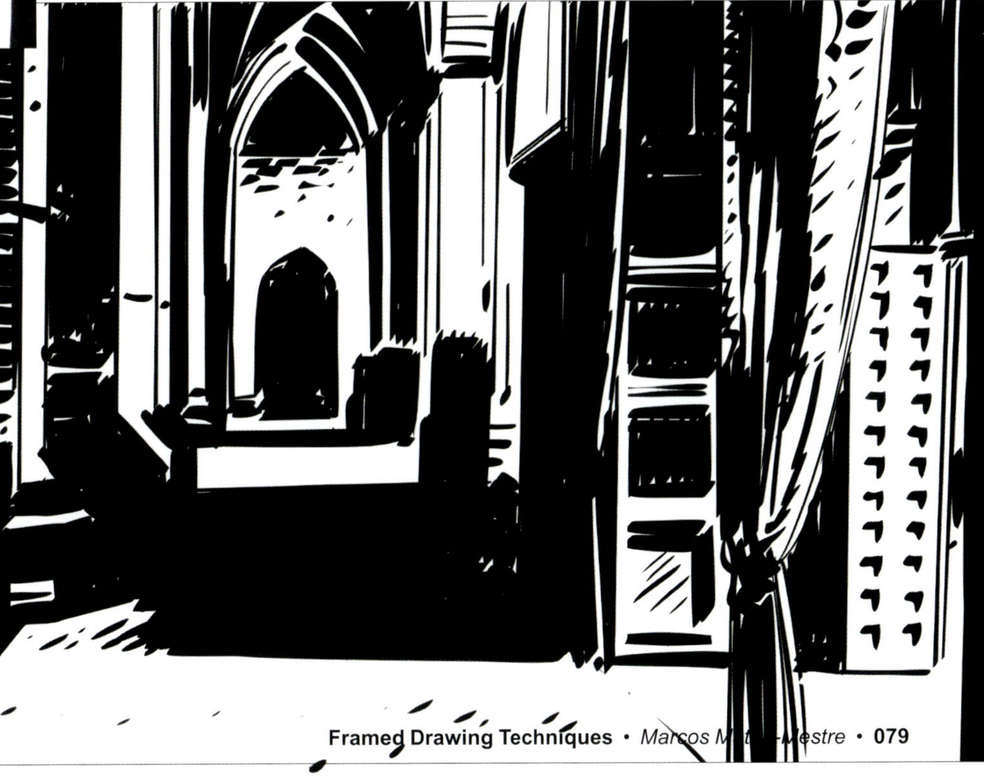

Figs. 3.33 and **3.34**: The most delicate moment in this type of exercise is to decide on the treatment of middle tones. Will they become part of the blacks or whites? This will depend on whether the midtone is closer to black or white in the first place. Another thing to take into consideration is how much a black or white tone will help in the general readability of the image and the overall sense of balance. When performing these types of exercises, the recommendation is always to start with models/reference that have a clear separation between lights and darks and then move on to others with more subtle tones.

The first thing an artist needs to pay attention to when inking a panel (whether digitally or traditionally), is the general sense of lighting in the scene and the subsequent distribution and balance or imbalance of blacks and whites on our working surface.

The next focus of interest will be the sense of texture, the rhythm in the execution of lines and patterns. These will vary depending on the material depicted (metal, stone, plastic, etc.), and will give a strong layer of believability to your work if properly executed. Let's put these into practice.

Figs. 3.35 and **3.36**: A fairly common visual subject in many stories, vegetation is always an interesting item to use, with a strong sense of rhythm and the potential to serve as a great framing device. You can use a stretched brush (see page 075) to draw this subject. Its very different length and width (very narrow yet very long) will give us the option to create a vibrant line with different degrees of thickness at every step in the same stroke. These palm leaves are a good example of this.

Fig. 3.37: Use the same brush to create more regular-looking leaves. Notice how I always use the thicker part of the line where the shadow would be, which is usually the bottom of the subject (same device I used in the palm's drawing). See how a thick brushstroke on the leaves underneath helps create a sense of depth and three-dimensionality, as the shadows projected on them by the leaves right above indicate. (See additional example on page 084).

Other elements like the leaves' veins will usually fall as secondary to the image and are therefore indicated by thinner lines, either by the straight use of a thinner brush or by using less pressure on the current, or a combination of both.

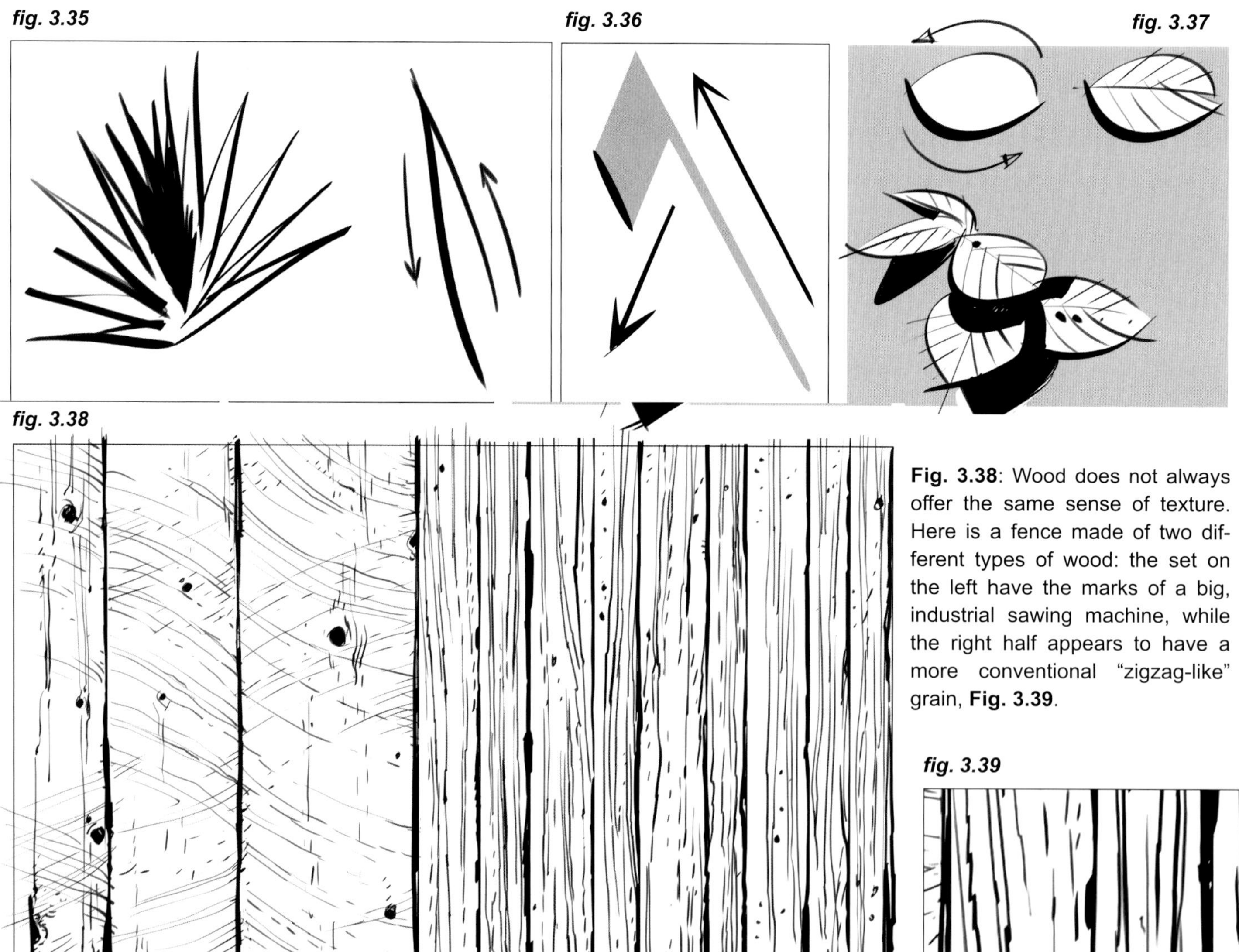

fig. 3.35

fig. 3.36

fig. 3.37

fig. 3.38

Fig. 3.38: Wood does not always offer the same sense of texture. Here is a fence made of two different types of wood: the set on the left have the marks of a big, industrial sawing machine, while the right half appears to have a more conventional "zigzag-like" grain, **Fig. 3.39**.

fig. 3.39

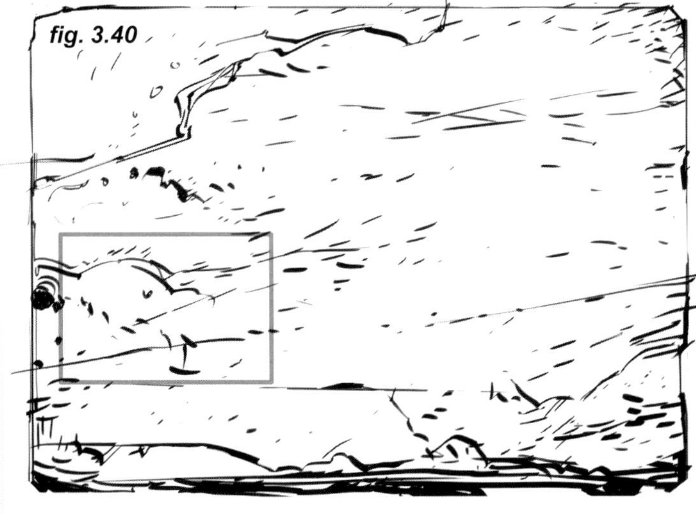

fig. 3.40

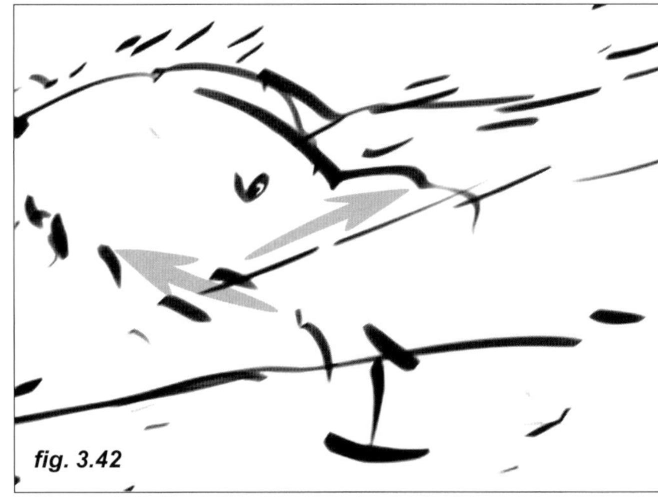

fig. 3.42

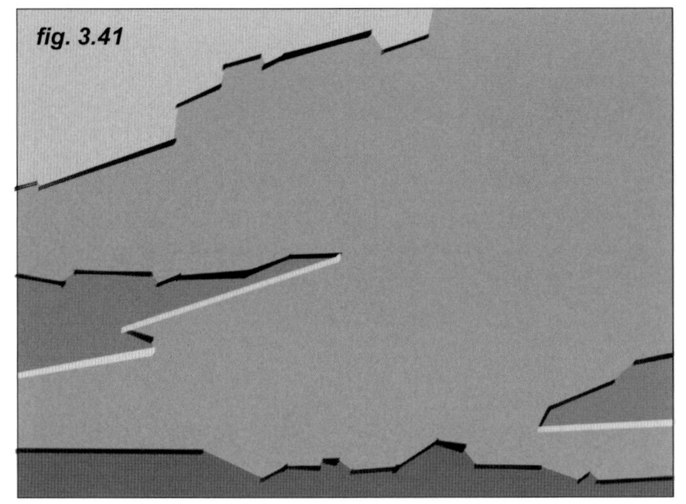

fig. 3.41

Texture on wood normally feels relatively soft to the eye while smoothly streaming along surfaces. Harder surfaces like ones of rock and stone will usually appear less graceful to the eye (**fig. 3.40**). Overall, I still need a sense of visual organization within this roughness. **Fig. 3.41** shows how the textural feel of a brick (top left) is enhanced, by subdividing its total surface into highs and valleys. Again, the use of a thicker line right underneath the depression's edge helps create the visual illusion of a step and subsequent lower plain below that area.

Fig. 3.42: Shows an enlarged detail of **Fig. 3.40**. Although the majority of textural lines will have the tendency to go in a similar direction, the use of minor lines running in opposite directions will help create a feeling of roughness. (See gray arrows.)

Figs. 3.43 and **3.44**: As per the look and feel of clothing folds (of which there can be many different varieties), this drawing shows how a more graceful, somehow calligraphic line can be our best bet when it comes to depicting the shape of fabrics on a body, whether human or inorganic. As folds will create lights and shadows, the use of thicker and thinner lines is again a good element to consider. Additional examples are on pages 106–107.

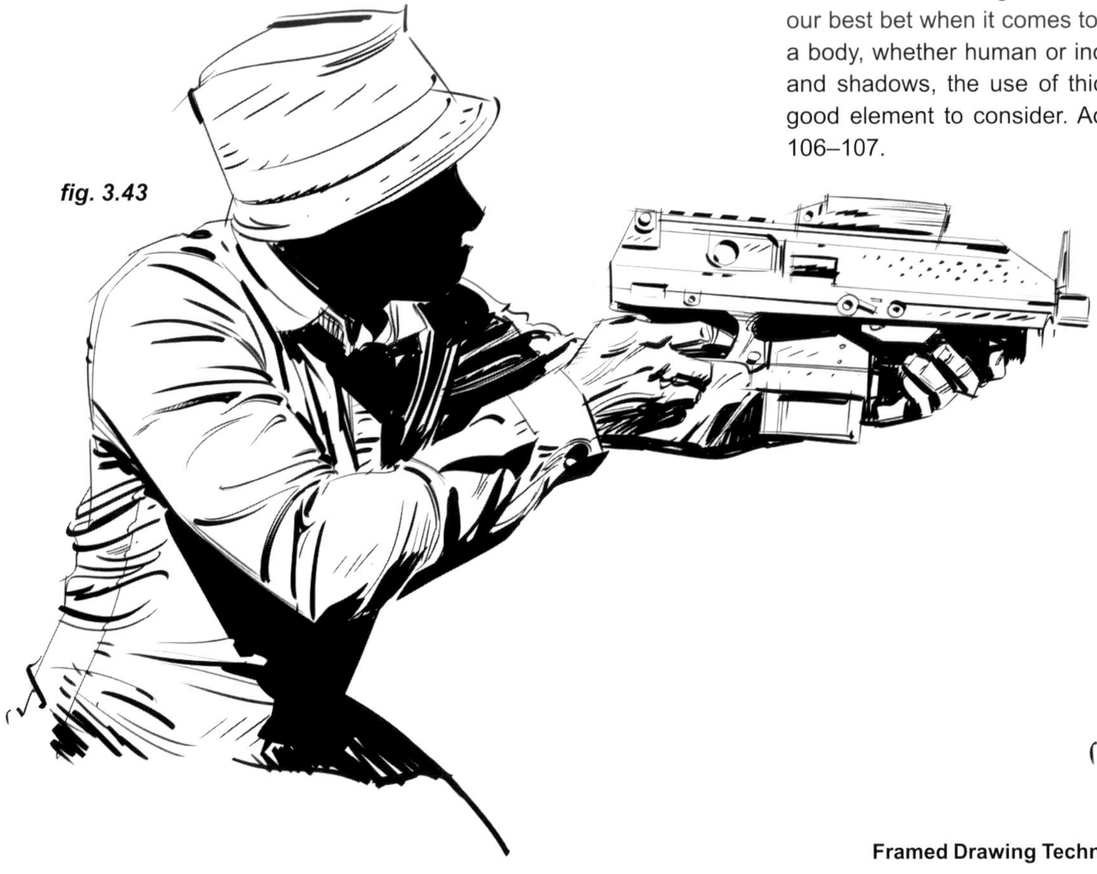

fig. 3.43

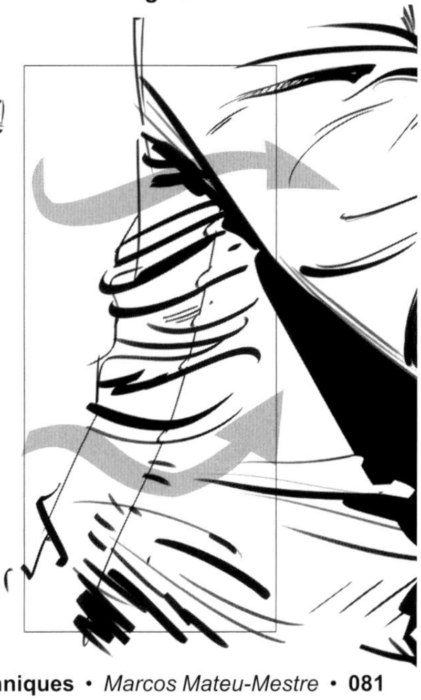

fig. 3.44

INKING SPECIFIC EXAMPLES OF VEGETATION

Let's start with some trees, essentially a trunk, branches, and leaves, with all the variety of possibilities these imply.

Fig. 3.45 and **Fig. 3.47**: The first example is a bare, leafless tree.

Obvious things to pay attention to here are:

- The main trunk is thicker than the rest.
- The branches are at least a little thinner than the main trunk.
- Both the main trunk and branches start off thicker and end thinner.

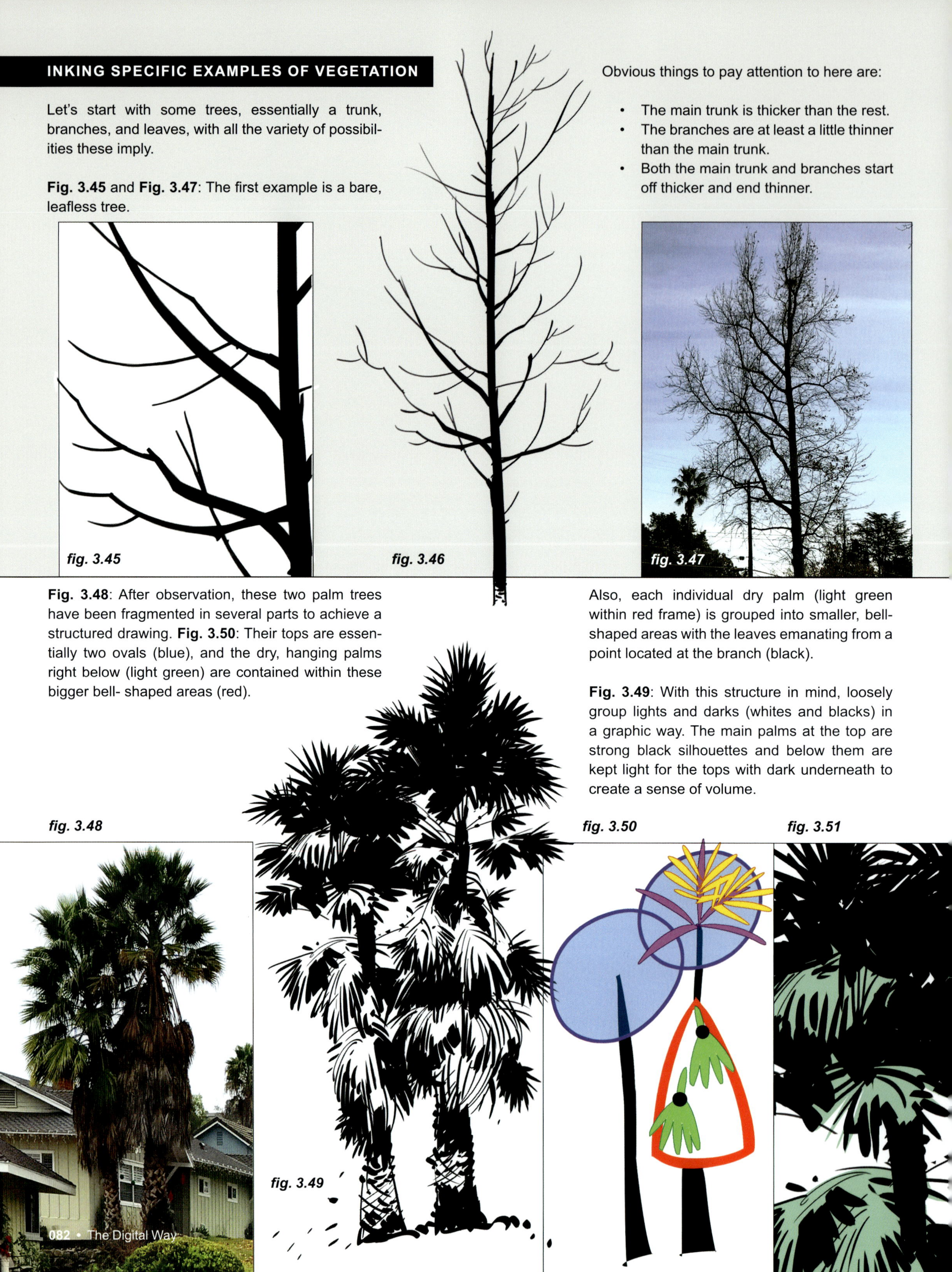

fig. 3.45

fig. 3.46

fig. 3.47

Fig. 3.48: After observation, these two palm trees have been fragmented in several parts to achieve a structured drawing. **Fig. 3.50**: Their tops are essentially two ovals (blue), and the dry, hanging palms right below (light green) are contained within these bigger bell- shaped areas (red).

Also, each individual dry palm (light green within red frame) is grouped into smaller, bell-shaped areas with the leaves emanating from a point located at the branch (black).

Fig. 3.49: With this structure in mind, loosely group lights and darks (whites and blacks) in a graphic way. The main palms at the top are strong black silhouettes and below them are kept light for the tops with dark underneath to create a sense of volume.

fig. 3.48

fig. 3.49

fig. 3.50

fig. 3.51

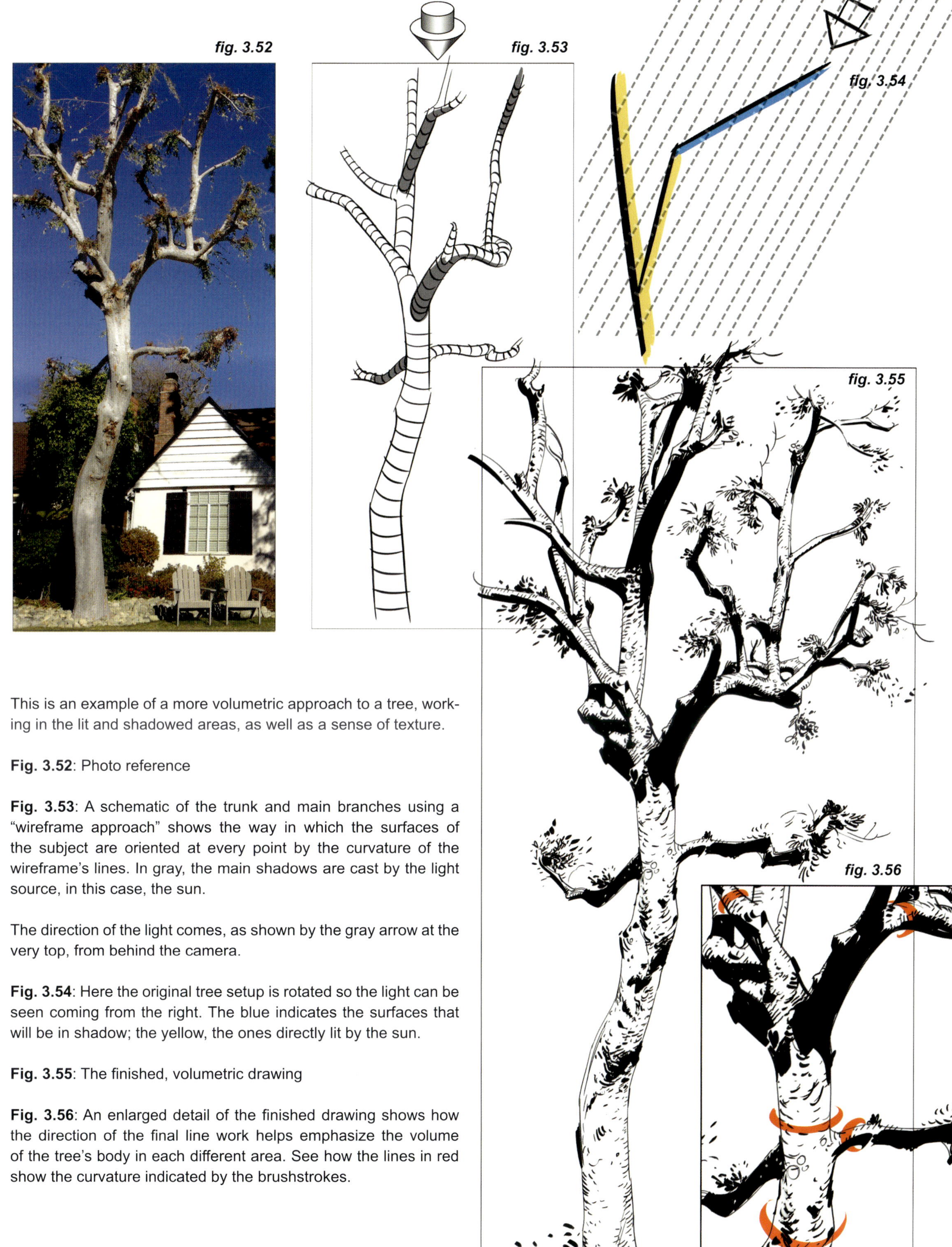

This is an example of a more volumetric approach to a tree, working in the lit and shadowed areas, as well as a sense of texture.

Fig. 3.52: Photo reference

Fig. 3.53: A schematic of the trunk and main branches using a "wireframe approach" shows the way in which the surfaces of the subject are oriented at every point by the curvature of the wireframe's lines. In gray, the main shadows are cast by the light source, in this case, the sun.

The direction of the light comes, as shown by the gray arrow at the very top, from behind the camera.

Fig. 3.54: Here the original tree setup is rotated so the light can be seen coming from the right. The blue indicates the surfaces that will be in shadow; the yellow, the ones directly lit by the sun.

Fig. 3.55: The finished, volumetric drawing

Fig. 3.56: An enlarged detail of the finished drawing shows how the direction of the final line work helps emphasize the volume of the tree's body in each different area. See how the lines in red show the curvature indicated by the brushstrokes.

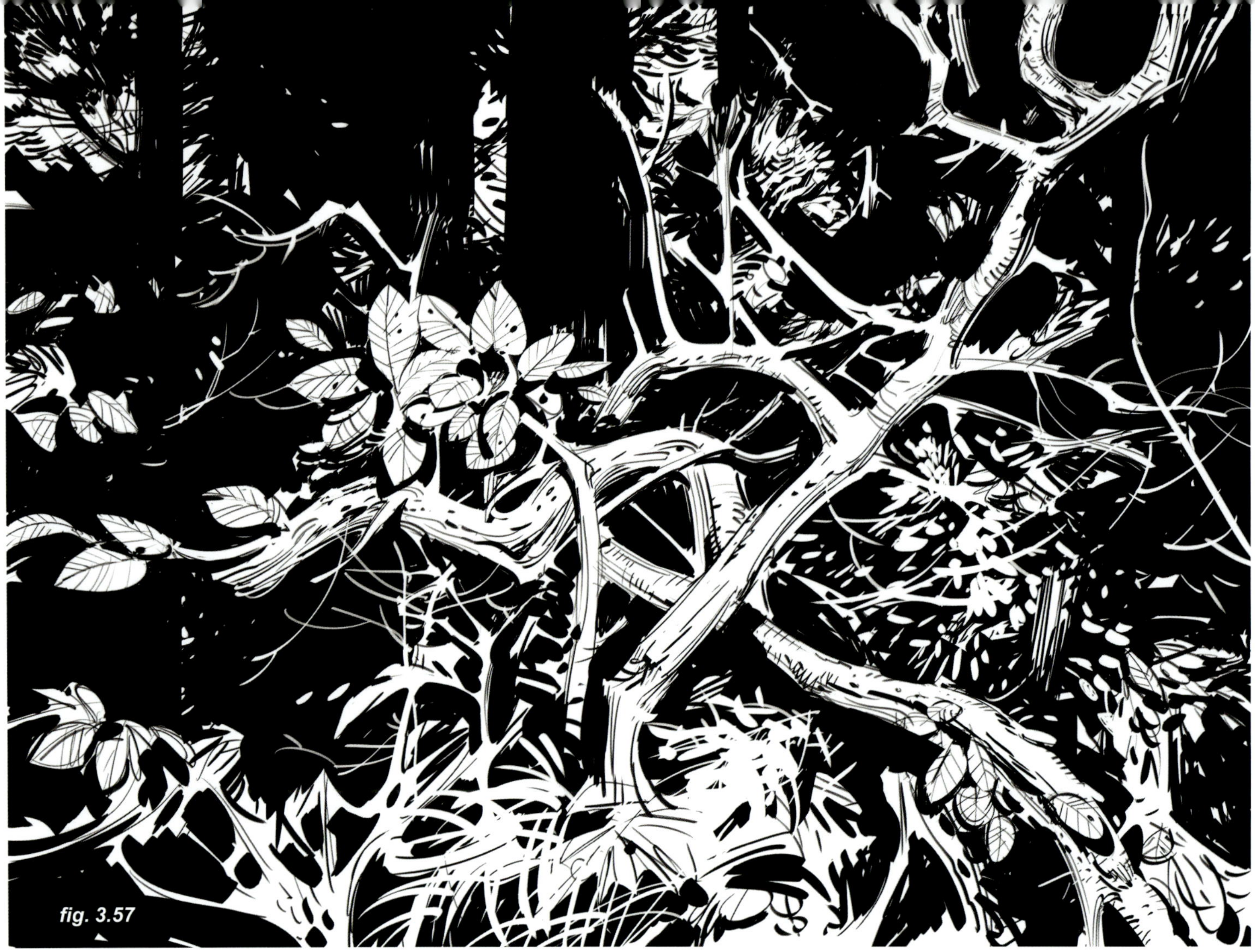

fig. 3.57

fig. 3.58

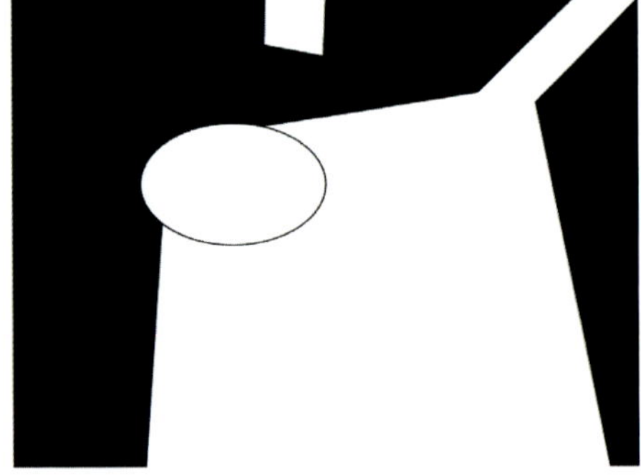

Fig. 3.57: When putting a scene together, a structured sense of order within all the elements contained is a must to have your image rendered in a way that is clear. Our storytelling artwork is there to deliver and move on to the next frame. A panel can appear complex in its rendition, but the structure underneath it will need to be clear and concise. I always recommend taking a few physical steps back from the page you're working at, and look at it from a distance. If from there you can see what's going on, what the main masses of light and dark are, where you are supposed to look at (the center of attention), and the flow from one panel to the next works well (so that nothing gets in the way when moving your eyes on the page), then you have done a good job.

Fig. 3.58: Shows the main light and dark pattern as based on the reference seen in **Fig. 3.60**.

fig. 3.59

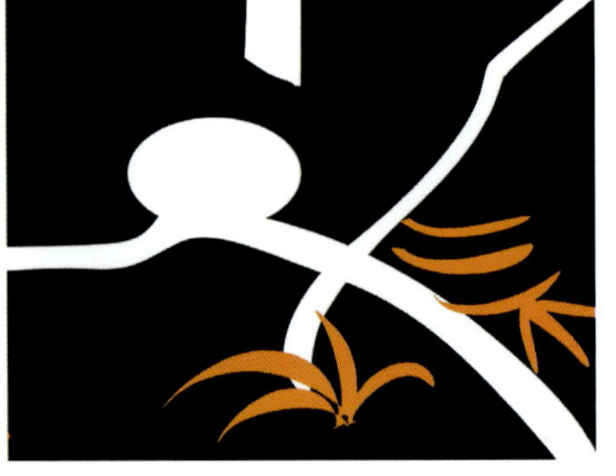

Fig. 3.59 indicates the three basic elements: the two crossing foreground trunks and the bunch of leaves contained within the light oval. As long as these main focal elements are clearly rendered with the right amount of detail, the rest can be a bit more abstract, within reason, as "the facts" are already clearly stated: leaves, branches, etc.—meaning, a forest.

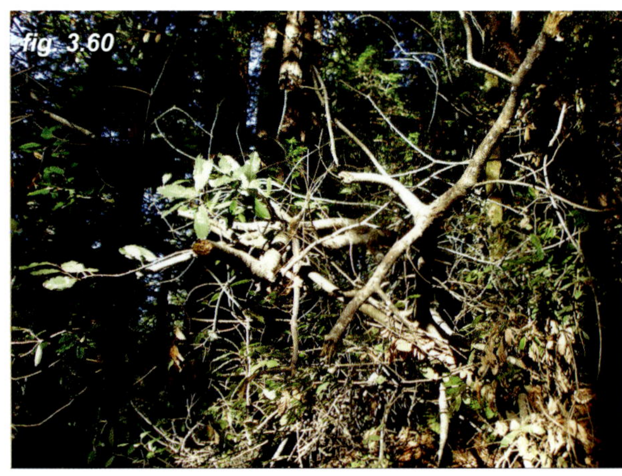

fig. 3.60

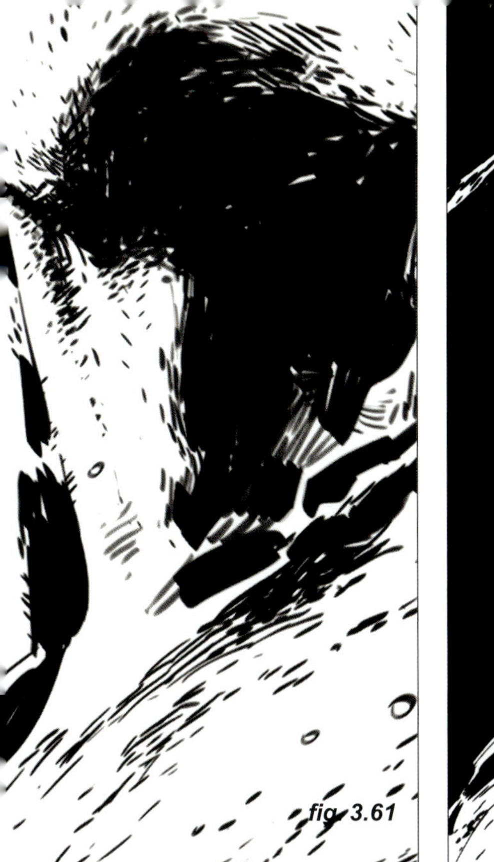

fig. 3.61

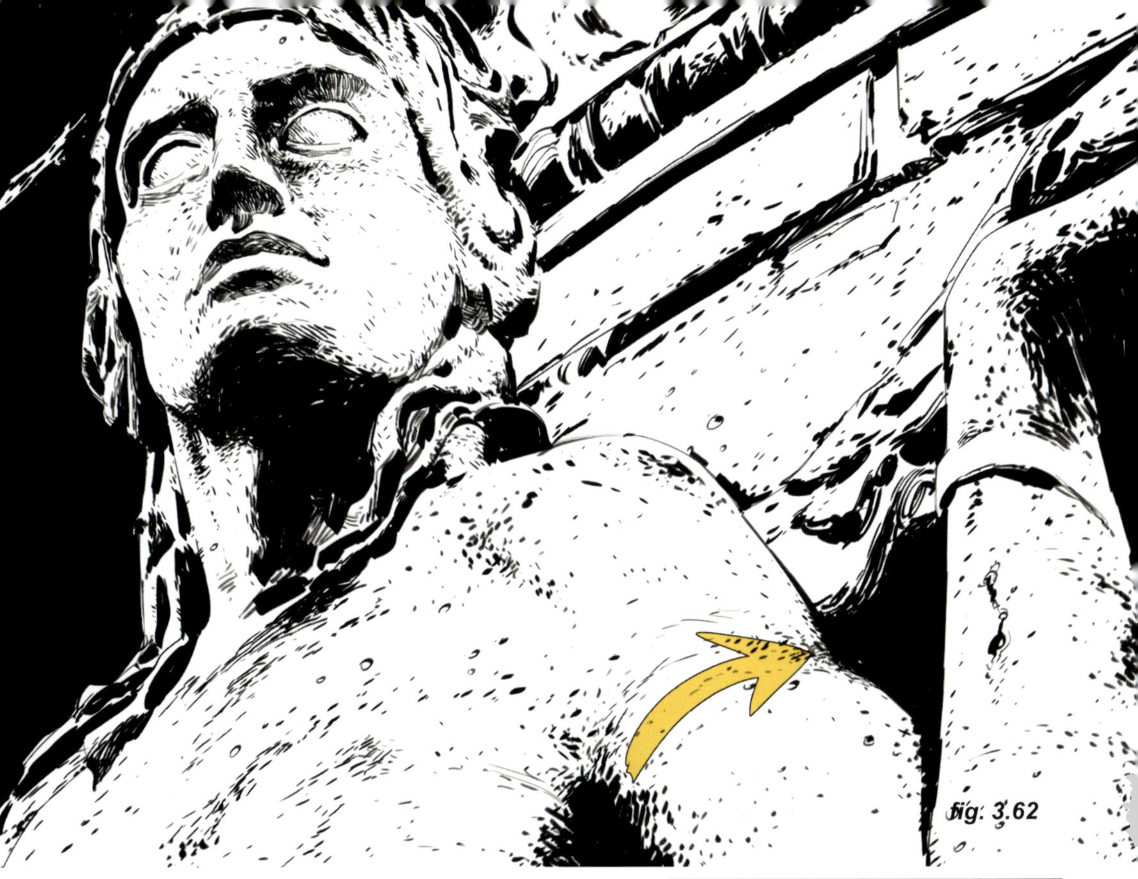

fig. 3.62

fig. 3.63

ROCK AND STONE

Figs. 3.61 and **3.62**: A close-up of a bust and its detail. Besides grouping into areas of light and shade and the following of the volumetric lines, the orange arrow guides the dots or brushstrokes applied following the roundness of the arm. The way the texture has been applied here, offers a rather monotonous, lifeless look, with most of the dots representing the surface's porosity being similar in shape and size (see **Fig. 3.63**).

Figs. 3.66 and **3.64**: If this sculpture were in fact a human character, the organic feel of the texture would be represented by a more sophisticated looking render based on longer, more curved, elegant, dynamic and organic lines, strategically leaving blank spaces wherever the person's fresh skin offers a shining quality look to it.

fig. 3.64

Fig. 3.65: See how a very graphic result can be achieved with these backlit desert rocks if the dry "rock" texture is applied only at the top edge, where the sunlight is reflected, leaving the rest as bold dark shapes.

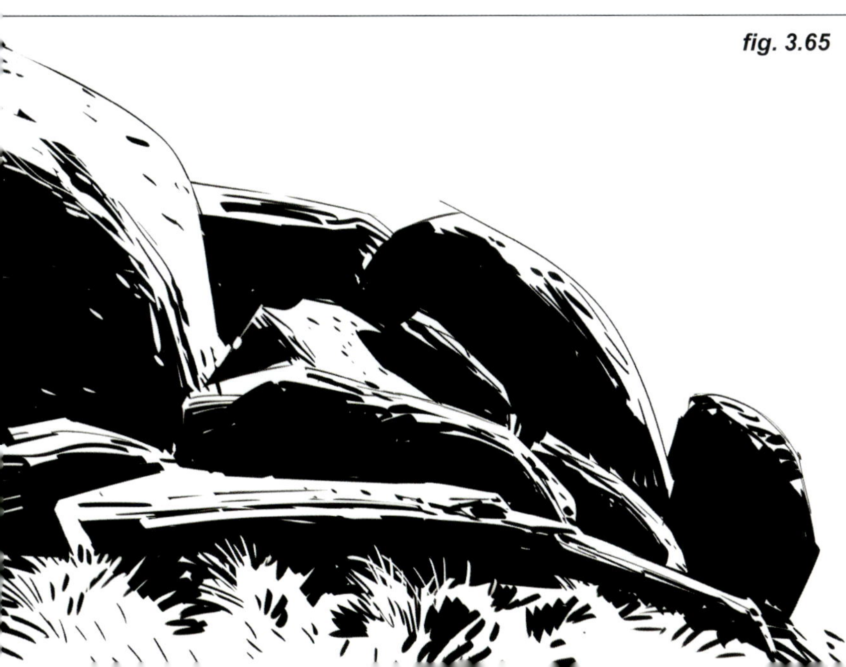

fig. 3.65

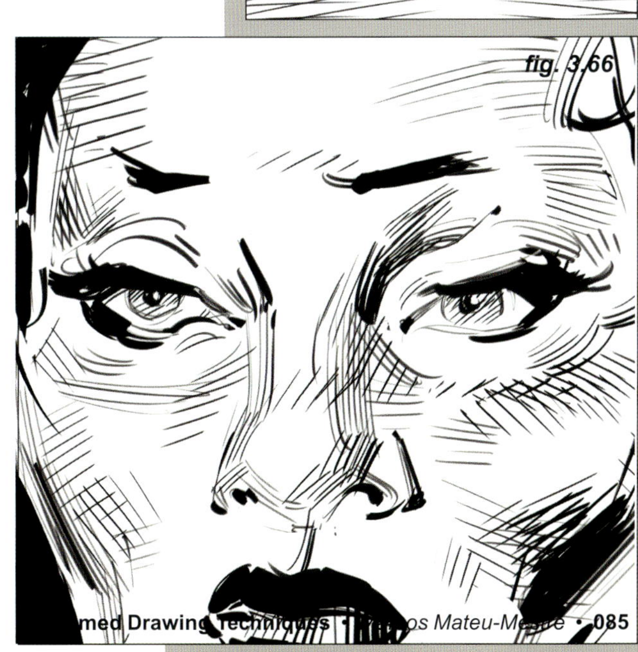

fig. 3.66

If we want our characters to live in a world we can perceive as believable, there will be many things around affecting them, the developing story, and all the emotionality these elements involve. Here are visual examples.

Figs. 3.67 and **3.68**: These are shown together for comparison. Weather conditions can get in the way of our otherwise usually clean, straightforward depiction of a location. When this happens, we need to have a few things in mind.

Fig. 3.67 shows a snow-filled landscape. If there is no snow falling at the time, you can afford to ink things a bit more realistically, with a bit more nuances. See, for example, how the tree foreground left is more detailed than the version in **Fig. 3.68**, where the same tree is more graphic, further simplified so that the falling snow on top can offer a clear, better read.

Also, the background trees were originally treated with both solid blacks and clear breathing areas to depict a more complex sense of atmosphere. In **Fig. 3.68**, they have now been simplified to a black mass for the same reason.

The snowflakes have been drawn as simple dots with a round brush, varying size and pressure, and then applied a slight diagonal motion blur (under the Photoshop "Filter" menu) for a more dynamic look.

On the next page, a simple swimming pool (**fig. 3.70**) takes on a different meaning the moment I add rain to it. A swimming pool is often associated with a nice, sunny day, and a bunch of kids in floaties running around while the grownups sip coca-colas. The idea of an abandoned (meaning empty, void of life) pool on a cold, rainy winter day, is not the usual image that comes to mind when someone pictures a pool, and therefore it adds a bit of drama to the situation because of the unusual depiction of such a location. It is the same reason why a murder scene with a body floating on a pool is especially disturbing

Rain is not the only important visual element in the panel. Notice the omnipresent effect the rain has on the ground surfaces, the pool water and the surrounding pavement, with a thousand little splashes caused by the pounding rain.

Fig. 3.69: The detail of the rendering includes the actual bounced-off splashes and the little ripples around them. The falling rain has been rendered on separate layers with parallel streaks hand drawn and stretched (Edit/Transform menu, see page 076), and then different degrees of opacity applied to each one of the rain layers for depth.

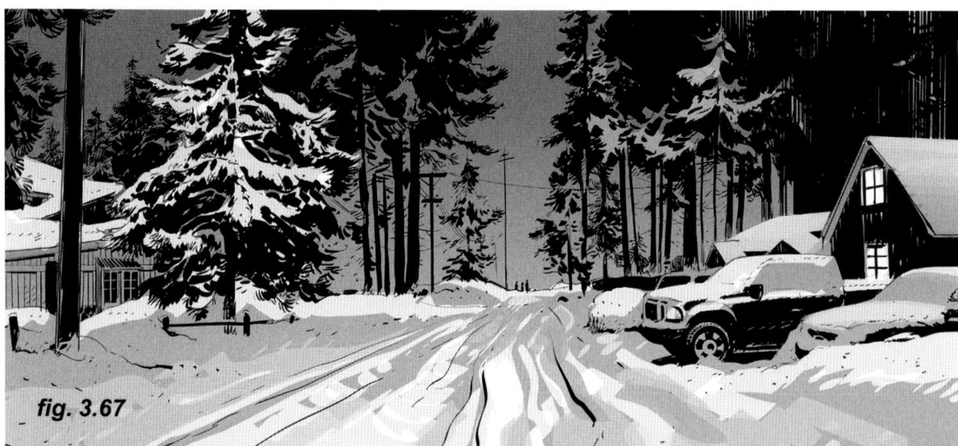

fig. 3.67

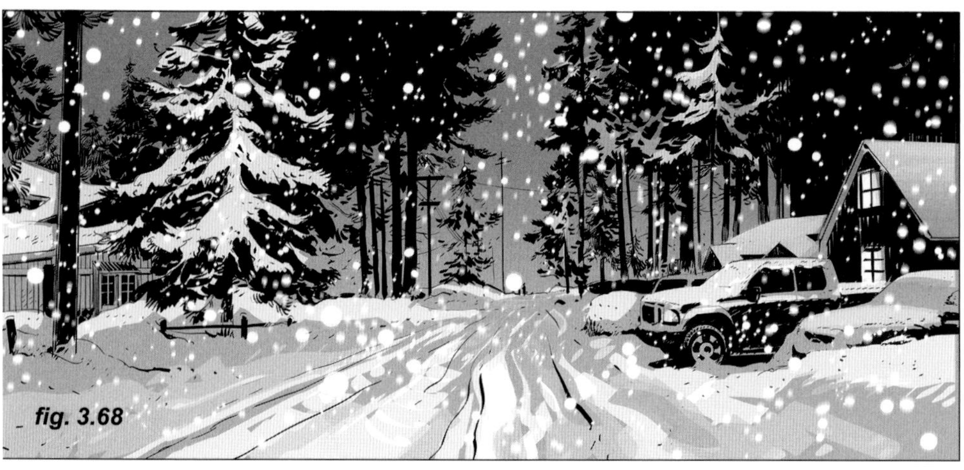

fig. 3.68

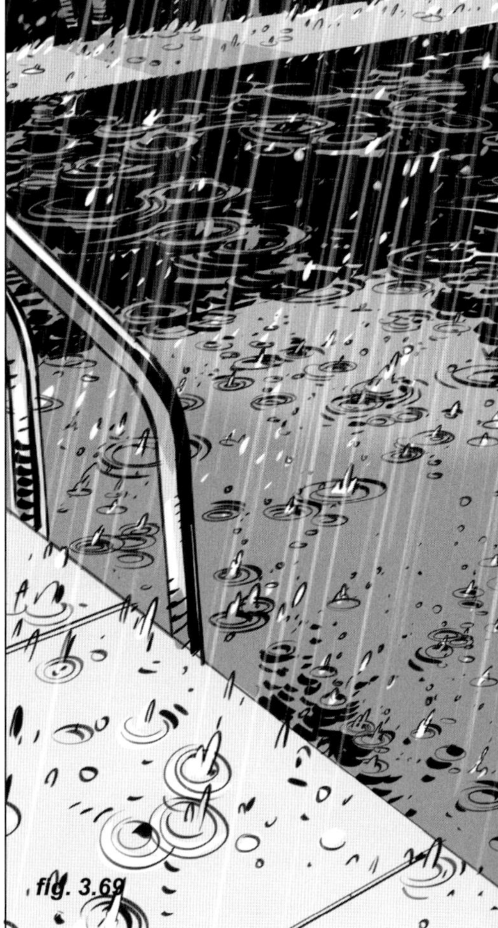

fig. 3.69

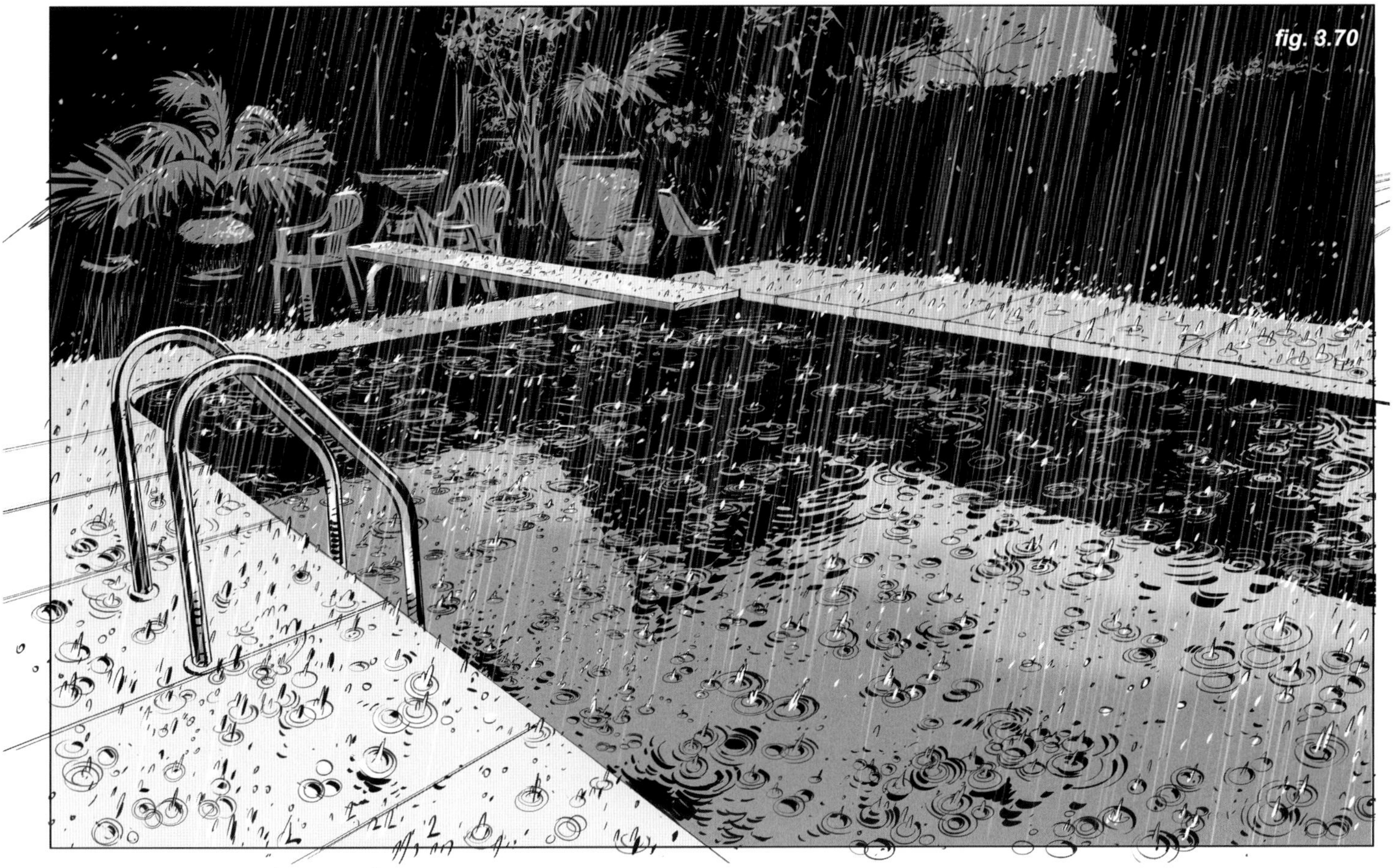

fig. 3.70

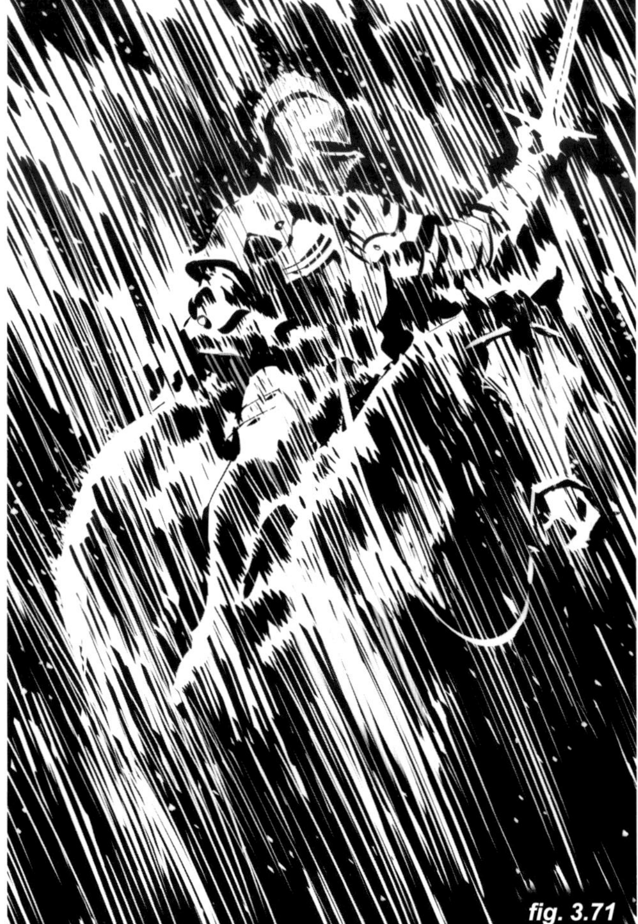
fig. 3.71

Fig. 3.71: In the pool shot, I superimposed rain as “lines on top,” while the set, the pool, is the “positive,” or camera’s main focus.

On the other hand, in the knight’s shot, the rain becomes the “positive” (main focus) and the character the “negative,” seen through the rain and defined by it. Here I make sure the main features that define my character will be clearly established (helmet, shoulders, arm and sword, and the horse’s head and top of its back). Once thse have been clearly established, then the rest of the elements can be left more ambiguous.

Fig. 3.72: An example of how horizontals (the waves) depicts a sense of calm.

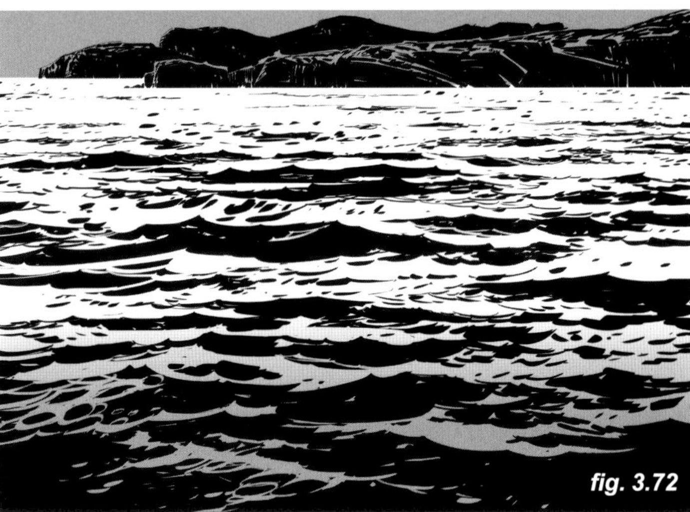
fig. 3.72

Sometimes the biggest challenge of rendering architectural spaces in our line of work is to make sure that the important technical aspects perfectly conform to the more organic elements in the story, such as human characters, animals, vegetation, weather, etc.

When it comes to drawing an image where architectural elements are at the essence, create a sketch first—an idea on paper that suits your narrative/artistic needs—before putting things in their proper perspective. Include all elements (characters and location) without being too concerned about or constrained by the idea of technical-perspective accuracy and perfection to then develop a proper, technically approached, structure always based on this first compositional impact of our sketch. (For further examples, see pages 111, 134, or 163 of my book, *Framed Perspective Vol. 1*).

After establishing this, focus on a number of different ways to render such subjects.

The photograph of an actual location is included below to show my thought process and how to interpret reality into art.

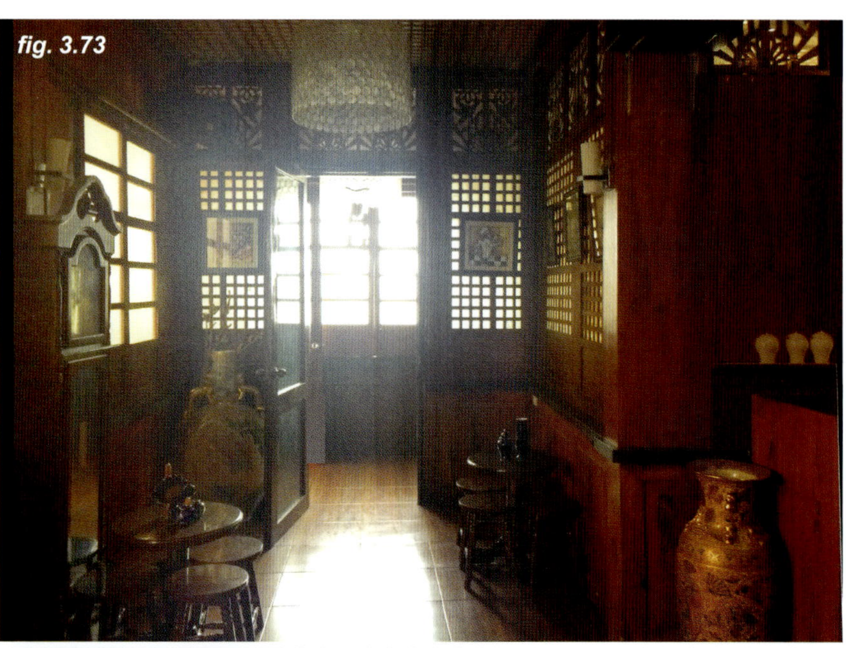

fig. 3.73

fig. 3.74

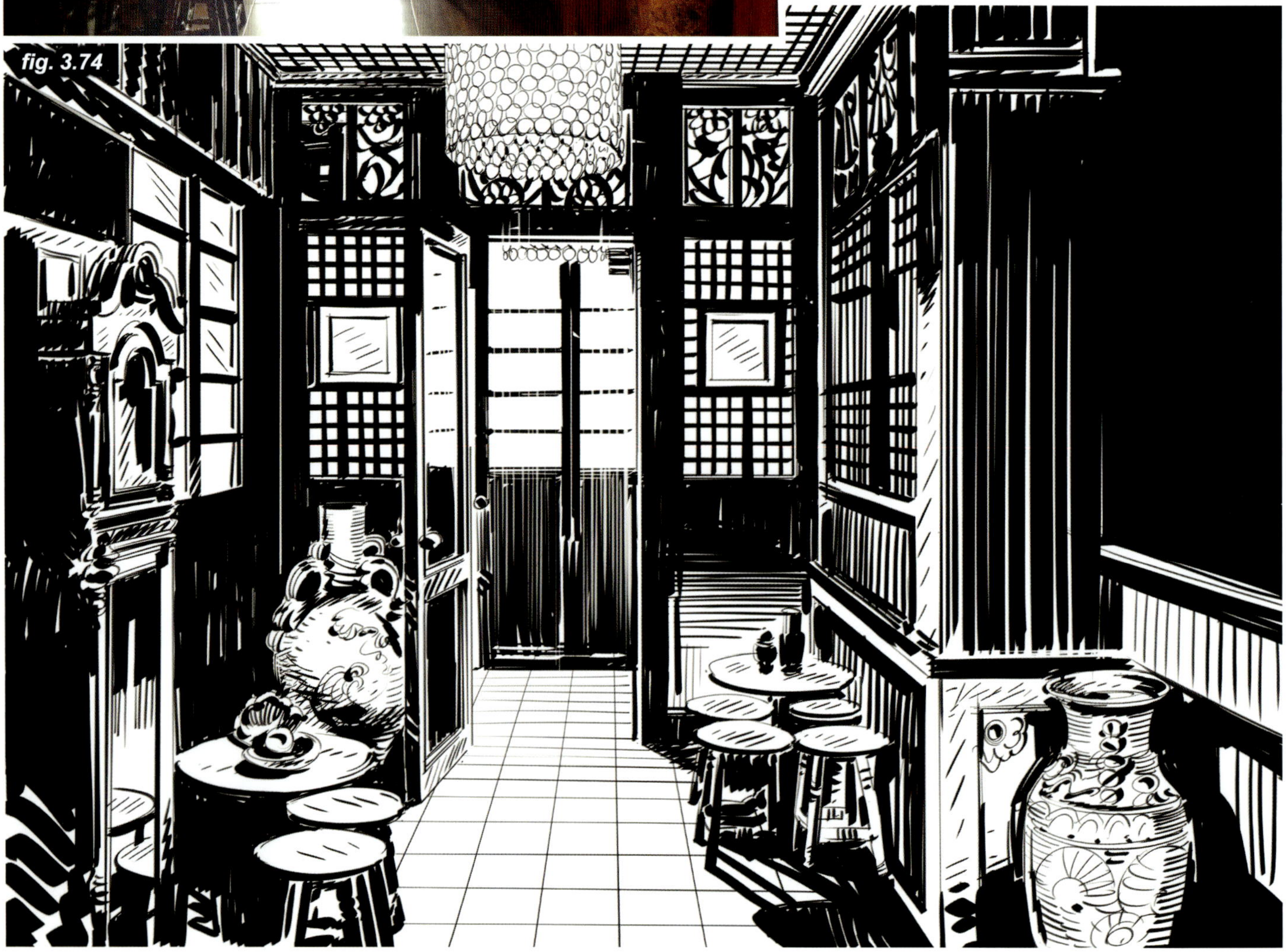

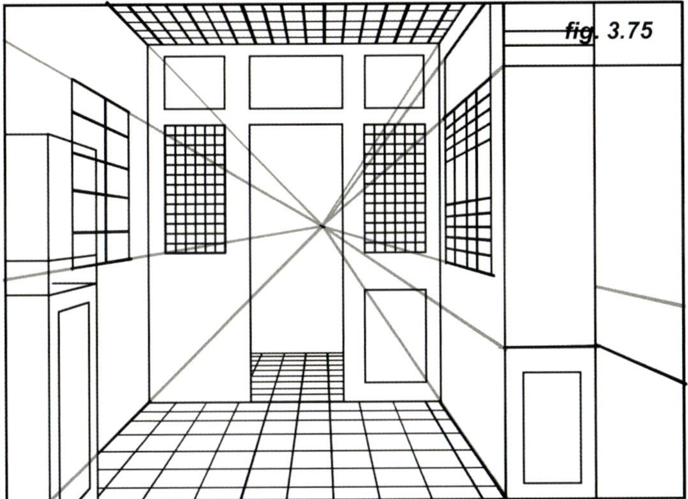
fig. 3.75

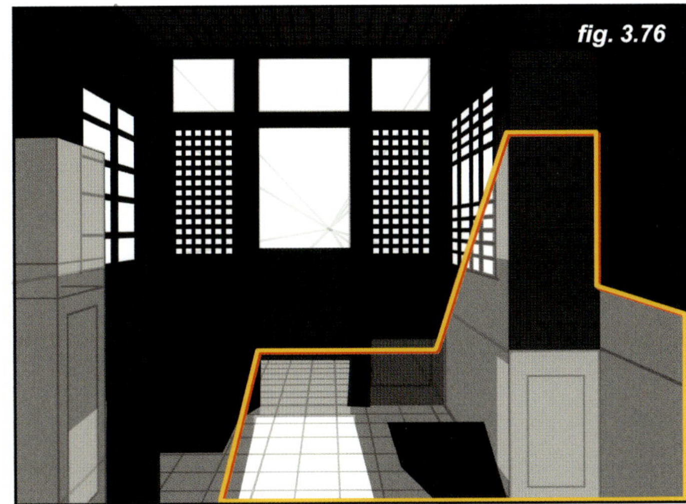
fig. 3.76

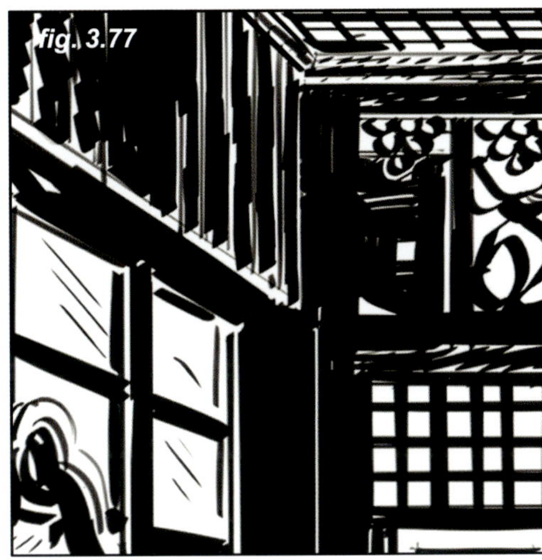
fig. 3.77

fig. 3.78

Dark interiors are a very interesting challenge for which we have to use any advantage or resource to depict depth and shape. They need serious ink work, with bold, big areas of black. If approached with extreme simplicity (of pure blacks), it might feel cold, a bit clinical. By highlighting little details here and there (not much, just enough) "emerging" out of the dark, this normally will give these areas a sense of life, a bit of vibration to them that I always recommend.

Figs. 3.73 and **3.74**: In this case, for example, despite most of the scene being so dark that it could pretty much translate directly into solid black, we will have to primarily rely on the sense of depth, space and perspective clearly established by the wooden grids on the doors, windows, and ceiling surrounding the room.

Figs. 3.75 and **3.76** are preliminary studies that establish the schematics of how both the perspective and the light play in this space.

It is important to perform these sorts of studies before getting into the final artwork. Although it is always a good idea to put these down on paper, with experience, you may eventually get to the point where these goals will mostly be thought out in your head.

Regardless, you always need a plan, and this plan might need a few tries so that you learn how to simplify, especially between the bulk areas of light and dark.

Observe and compare **Figs. 3.73** and **3.76**. See how mainly the lighter, more detailed areas exist within the area marked in orange. These areas still need to have a dark tone to them, but since they are lighter, you can use this opportunity to emphasize the direction of the surfaces and planes involved by the use of line direction (**fig. 3.78**). See also **fig. 1.12** on page 019.

The sets of parallel planes defining parallels have mainly been drawn in two ways: the shorter ones are pure freehand, and the longer ones were drawn like in example **Fig. 3.18** and **3.19** (page 076), where I drew a set of short parallels that I later selected and transformed/stretched. So, while they look straight and even, they still have a degree of irregularity in them that makes them look freehand drawn and organic.

Fig. 3.77 shows how even in the darkest areas, and within the solid black inks these require, you can still find subtle ways to let the drawing breathe a bit by leaving small blank spaces here and there that also help define shape and direction.

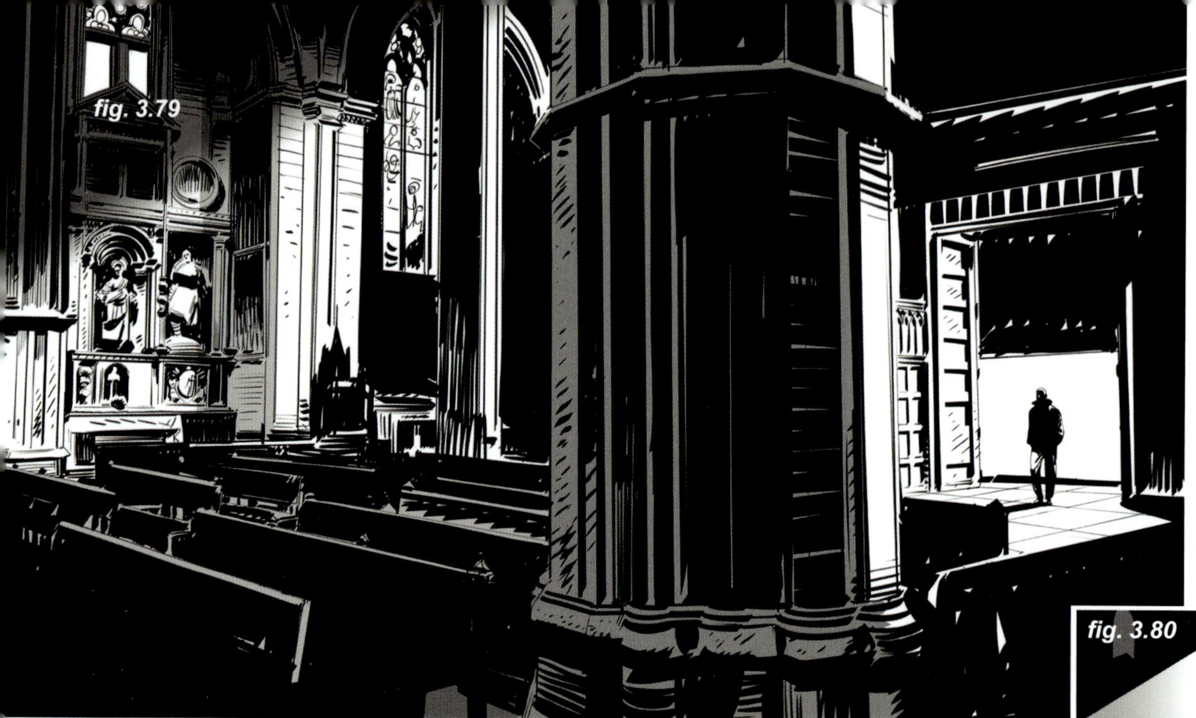

Fig. 3.79: One more example of how the masses of light and dark can be distributed and simplified (see **Fig. 3.80**) so that the point of a single human silhouette inside the context of a very elaborate architecture stands clear as a narrative point.

fig. 3.80

See that the examples in these pages introduce the element of a gray tone to find the middle ground between the extreme black and white.

Fig. 3.82: The way I work these grays is by doing so underneath the INK layer, which I turn from "Normal" to "Multiply," converting it into transparent so all opaque whites (if any) go away and only the actual blacks remain.

After that, create a new ("TONAL") layer underneath the "INK" one (**fig. 3.83**) and work the gray tones accordingly to the needs of the panel (lighter gray tones can be achieved by the use of lighter grays, or by the use of black with different percentages of opacity here in the red frame). Such grays will now show through the top "INK" level and become part of the final image.

Fig. 3.81 shows a quick and solid black-and-white render of a house. See that even in these harsh shadows the brushwork always allow for a bit of breathing, which indicates some reflected light. The way these shadows go around the building's corners emphasizes the three-dimensional aspect of it without much need of actual contour lines to define corners and such.

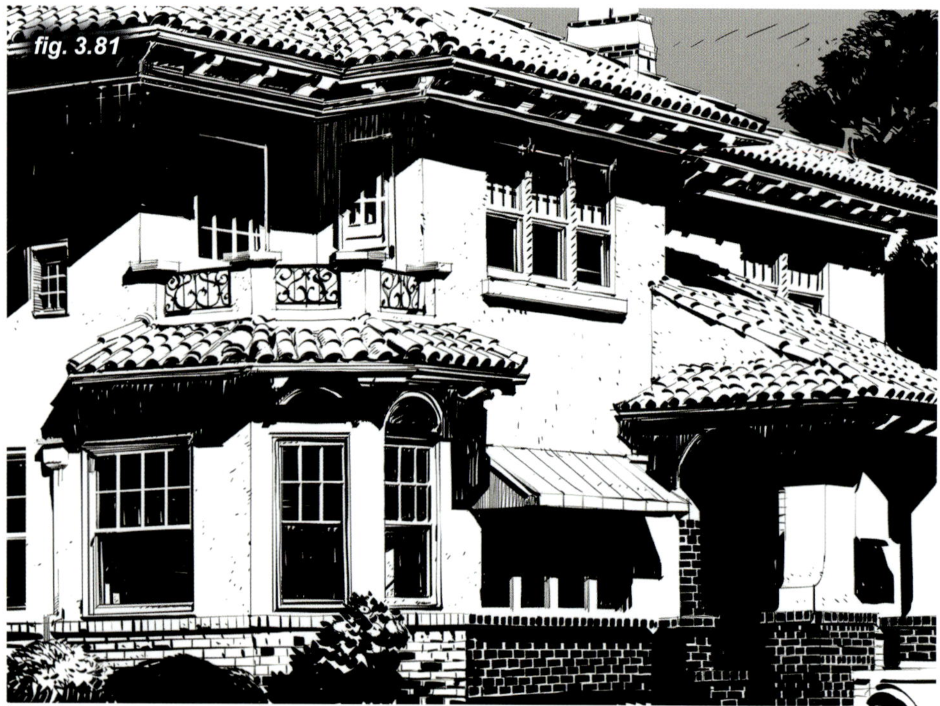

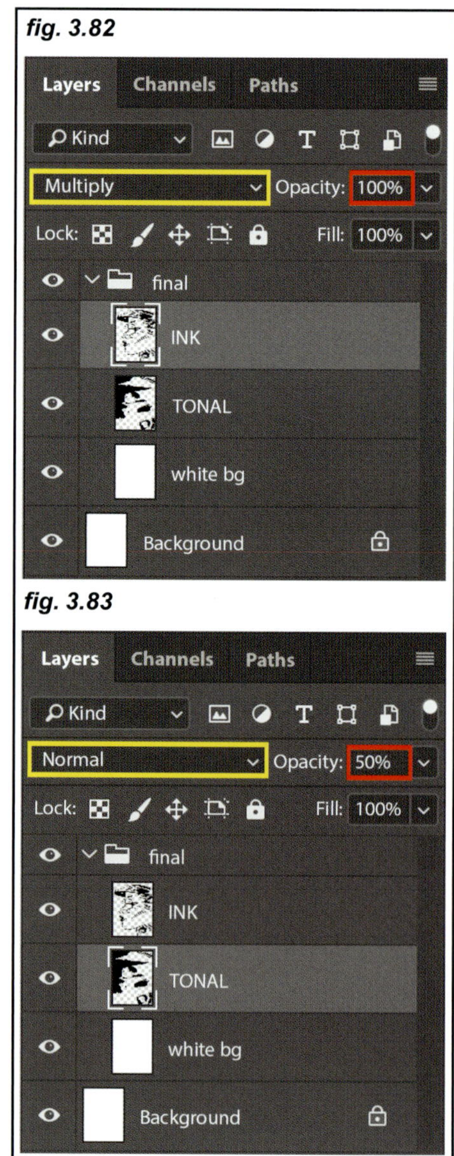

Fig. 3.84 shows how to use parallels in the shadows, emphasizing a sense of clean, classic architecture and again allowing for a sense of reflected light.

For the many straight lines that will appear in these type of drawings you can either freehand them or draw them by pointing the initial spot at one end of the line, then press/hold the "shift" key with the other hand, take the pen to the precise spot on the tablet's surface where you want the straight line to finish and press with the tip of the pen right there. The straight line between the two dots will draw itself automatically.

Fig. 3.85: In this case the whole shaded area was selected at once with the Polygonal Lasso tool (**fig. 3.86**) and then a gradation of grays (**fig. 3.87**) (lighter at the top, darker at the bottom) was created within the selected area. A darker tone at the foreground bottom creates the illusion of atmosphere toward the distance, hence enhancing a sense of space and perspective.

fig. 3.85

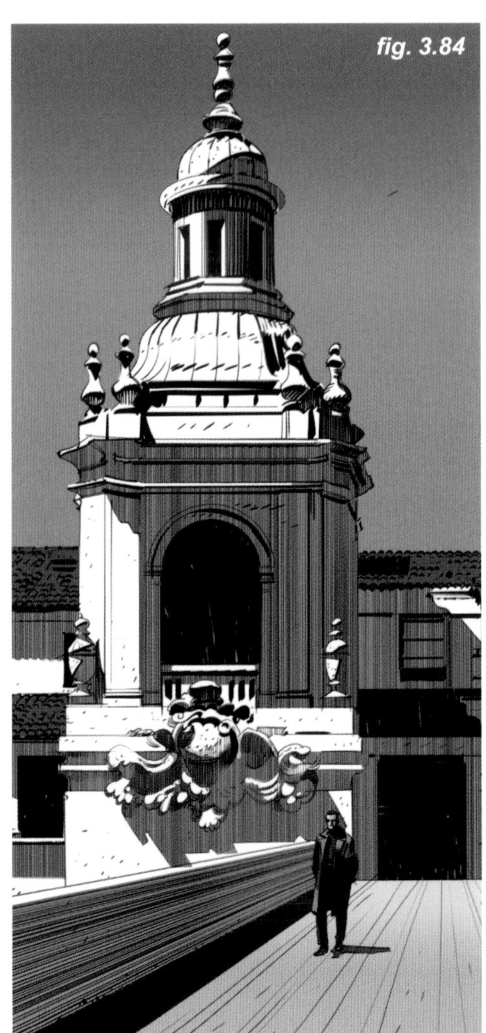

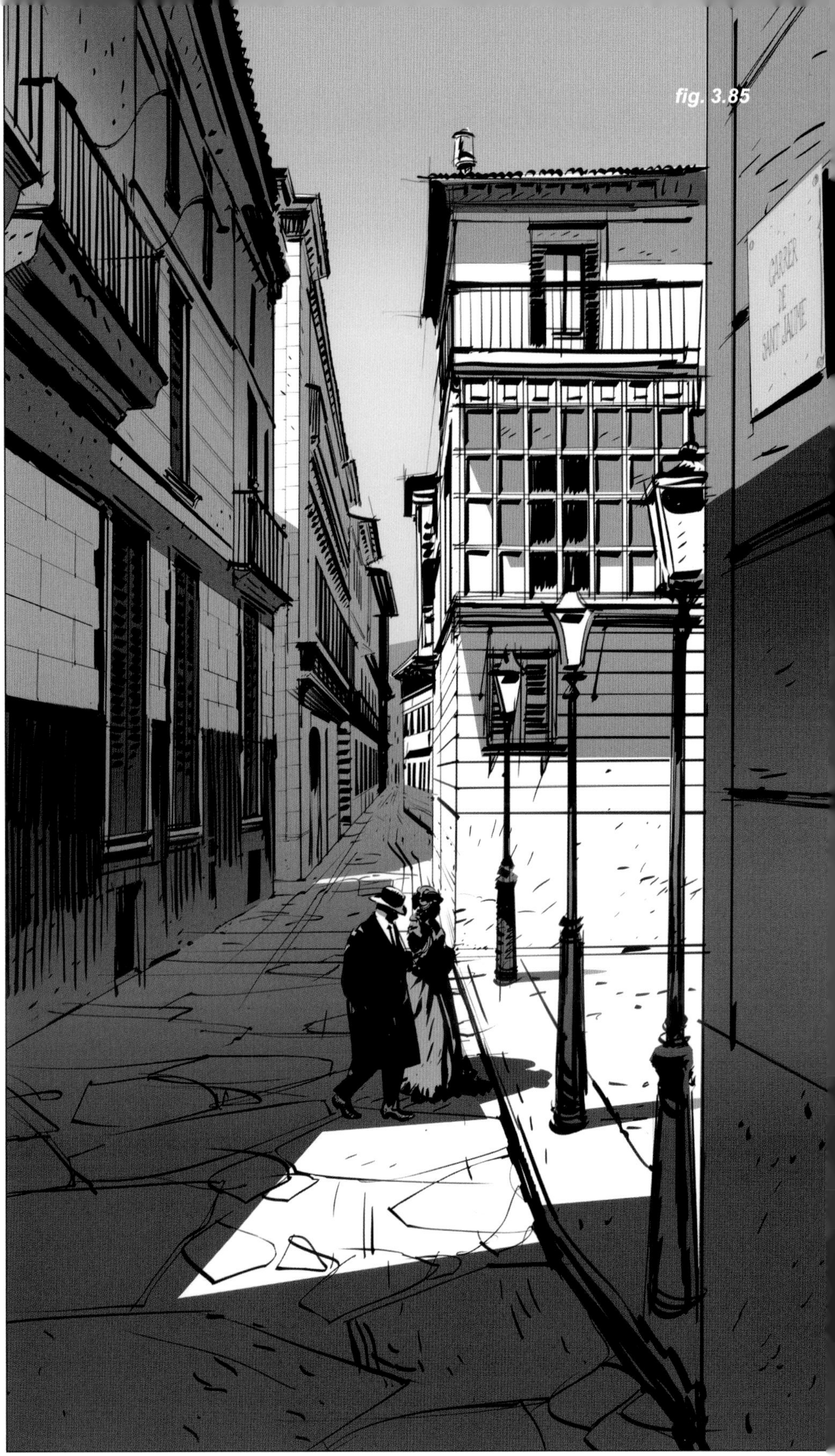

fig. 3.84

fig. 3.86

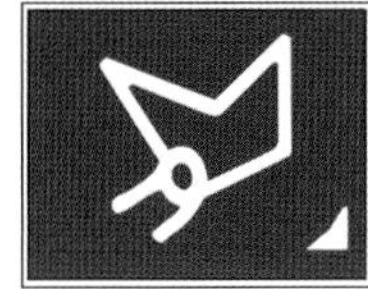

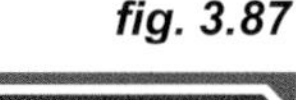

fig. 3.87

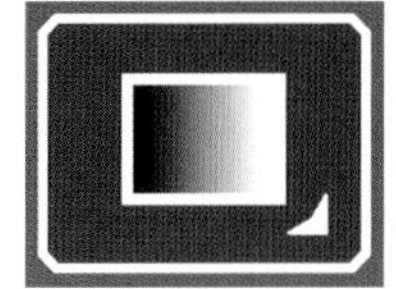

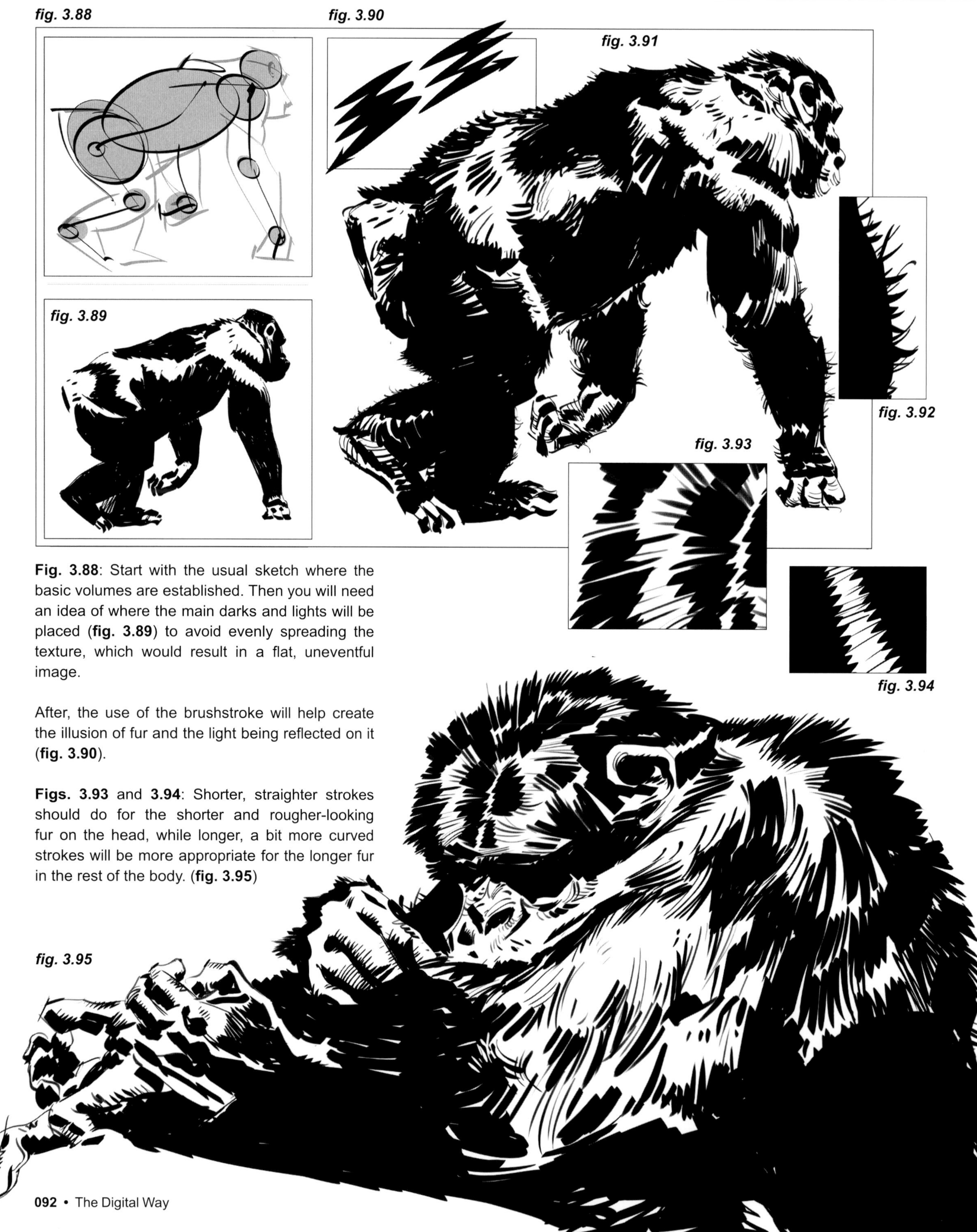

fig. 3.88 *fig. 3.89* *fig. 3.90* *fig. 3.91* *fig. 3.92* *fig. 3.93* *fig. 3.94* *fig. 3.95*

Fig. 3.88: Start with the usual sketch where the basic volumes are established. Then you will need an idea of where the main darks and lights will be placed (**fig. 3.89**) to avoid evenly spreading the texture, which would result in a flat, uneventful image.

After, the use of the brushstroke will help create the illusion of fur and the light being reflected on it (**fig. 3.90**).

Figs. 3.93 and **3.94**: Shorter, straighter strokes should do for the shorter and rougher-looking fur on the head, while longer, a bit more curved strokes will be more appropriate for the longer fur in the rest of the body. (**fig. 3.95**)

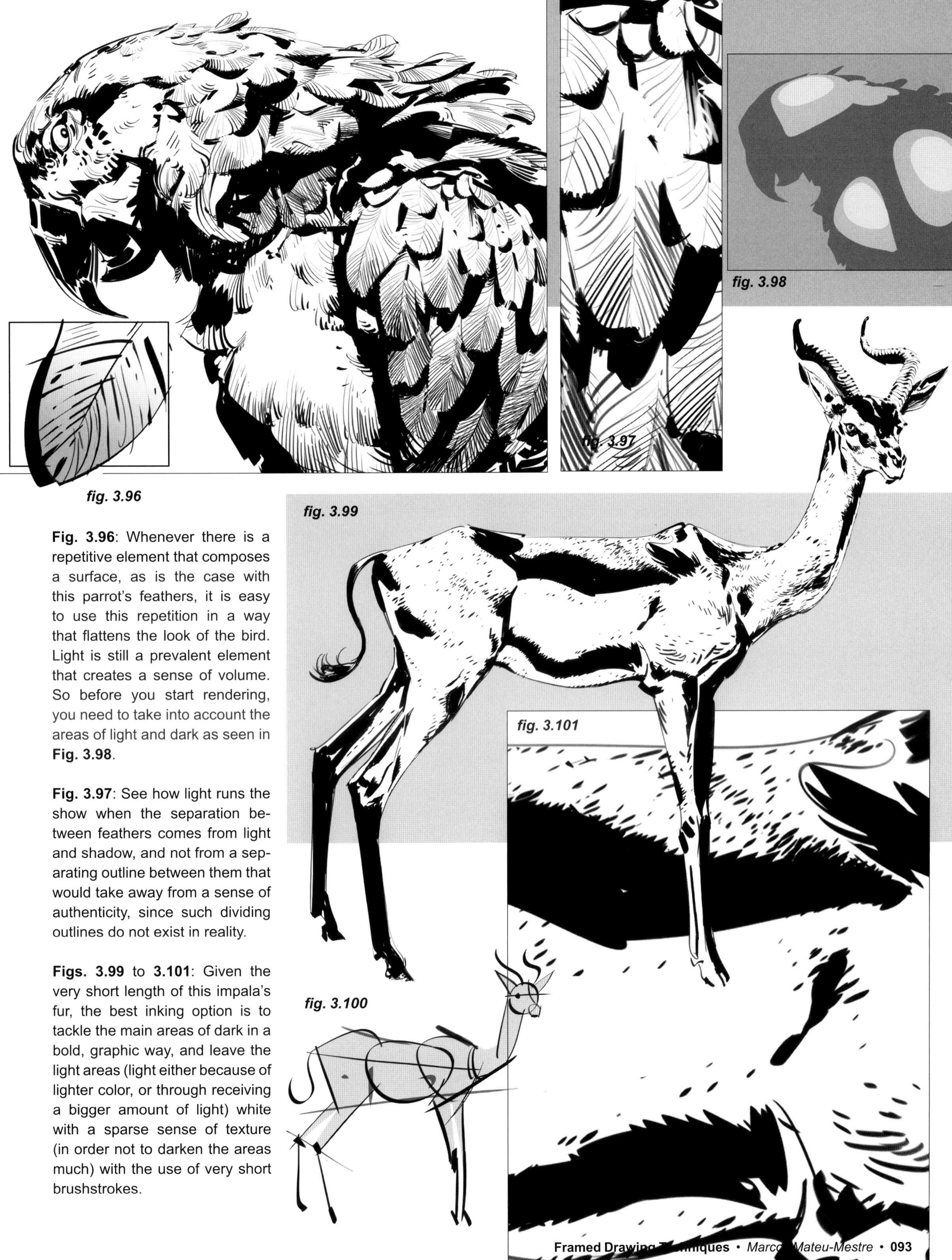

fig. 3.96

fig. 3.97

fig. 3.98

fig. 3.99

fig. 3.100

fig. 3.101

Fig. 3.96: Whenever there is a repetitive element that composes a surface, as is the case with this parrot's feathers, it is easy to use this repetition in a way that flattens the look of the bird. Light is still a prevalent element that creates a sense of volume. So before you start rendering, you need to take into account the areas of light and dark as seen in **Fig. 3.98**.

Fig. 3.97: See how light runs the show when the separation between feathers comes from light and shadow, and not from a separating outline between them that would take away from a sense of authenticity, since such dividing outlines do not exist in reality.

Figs. 3.99 to **3.101**: Given the very short length of this impala's fur, the best inking option is to tackle the main areas of dark in a bold, graphic way, and leave the light areas (light either because of lighter color, or through receiving a bigger amount of light) white with a sparse sense of texture (in order not to darken the areas much) with the use of very short brushstrokes.

Horses appear often in films, graphic novels, and illustrations, so it is useful to learn to draw them.

Before rendering your first steps, there will need to be an understanding of the parts that compose the horse (here shown as volumetric ovals and spheres) from a specific point of view, its general sense of movement, and a notion of its anatomy (**figs. 3.102**, **3.103** and **3.104**).

Studying live horses and photographs and video of horses is essential to understand and integrate this beautiful animal into part of your visual language. It is crucial to get the flow of a horse's dynamics before even depicting its accurate proportions.

Once you have achieved a level of experience, the final ink rendering will support and reflect the anatomy of the horse and the tension or calm expressed by it as you see where both light and shadows fall.

One way to achieve this is to chisel this shadow with bold ink statements and then connect these and the lit areas with a midtone created by crosshatching lines (**fig. 3.110** detail next page, top).

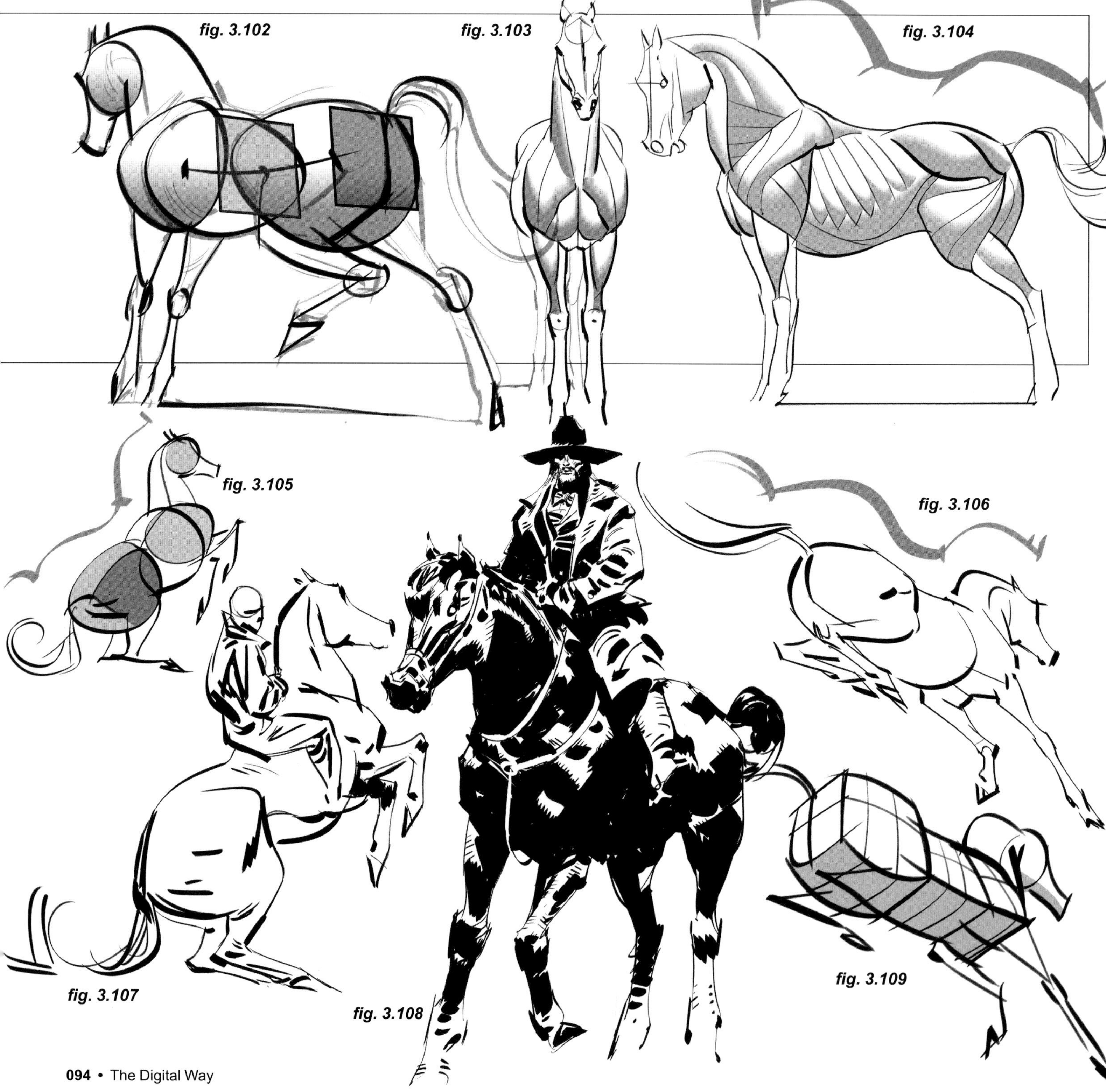

fig. 3.102

fig. 3.103

fig. 3.104

fig. 3.105

fig. 3.106

fig. 3.107

fig. 3.108

fig. 3.109

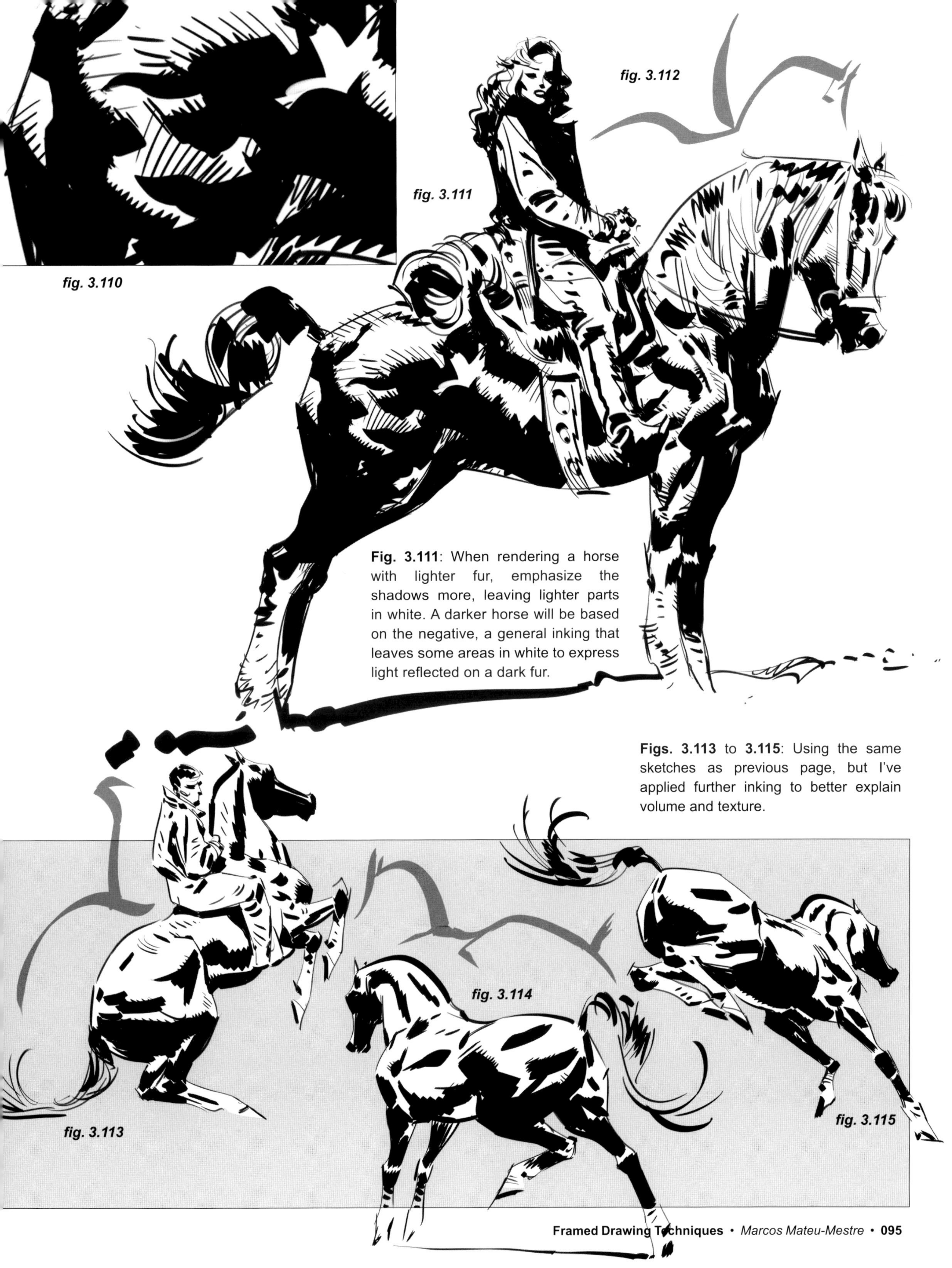

fig. 3.110

fig. 3.111

fig. 3.112

Fig. 3.111: When rendering a horse with lighter fur, emphasize the shadows more, leaving lighter parts in white. A darker horse will be based on the negative, a general inking that leaves some areas in white to express light reflected on a dark fur.

Figs. 3.113 to **3.115**: Using the same sketches as previous page, but I've applied further inking to better explain volume and texture.

fig. 3.113

fig. 3.114

fig. 3.115

Characters—whether human, animal, a distinctive location, or otherwise—are usually the center of the story, and because of this, they require special attention when being visually integrated into the story and its artwork.

Although the amount of subtleties when it comes to gesture and expression will directly take us into the world of acting, the execution techniques here will essentially be the same as with any other subject, also counting on how light, shadow, camera angle, and composition will give us the description of how shape, dynamics, and volume work.

Let's look at a few examples, starting with a couple of the most recognizable elements in a character: the head and face.

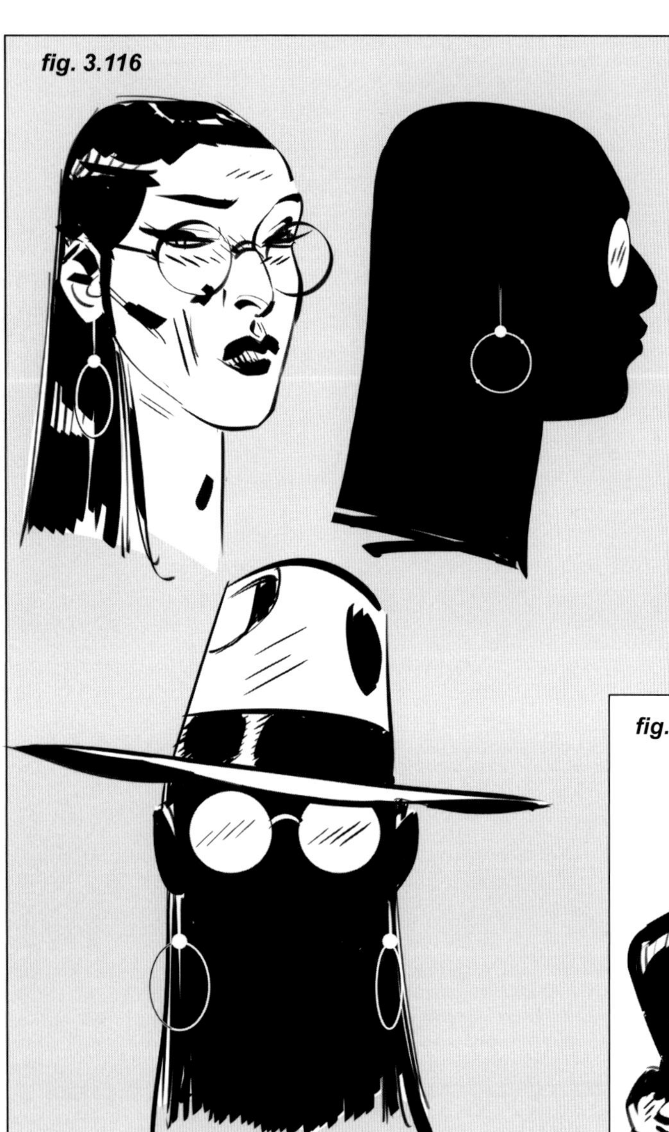

fig. 3.116

fig. 3.117

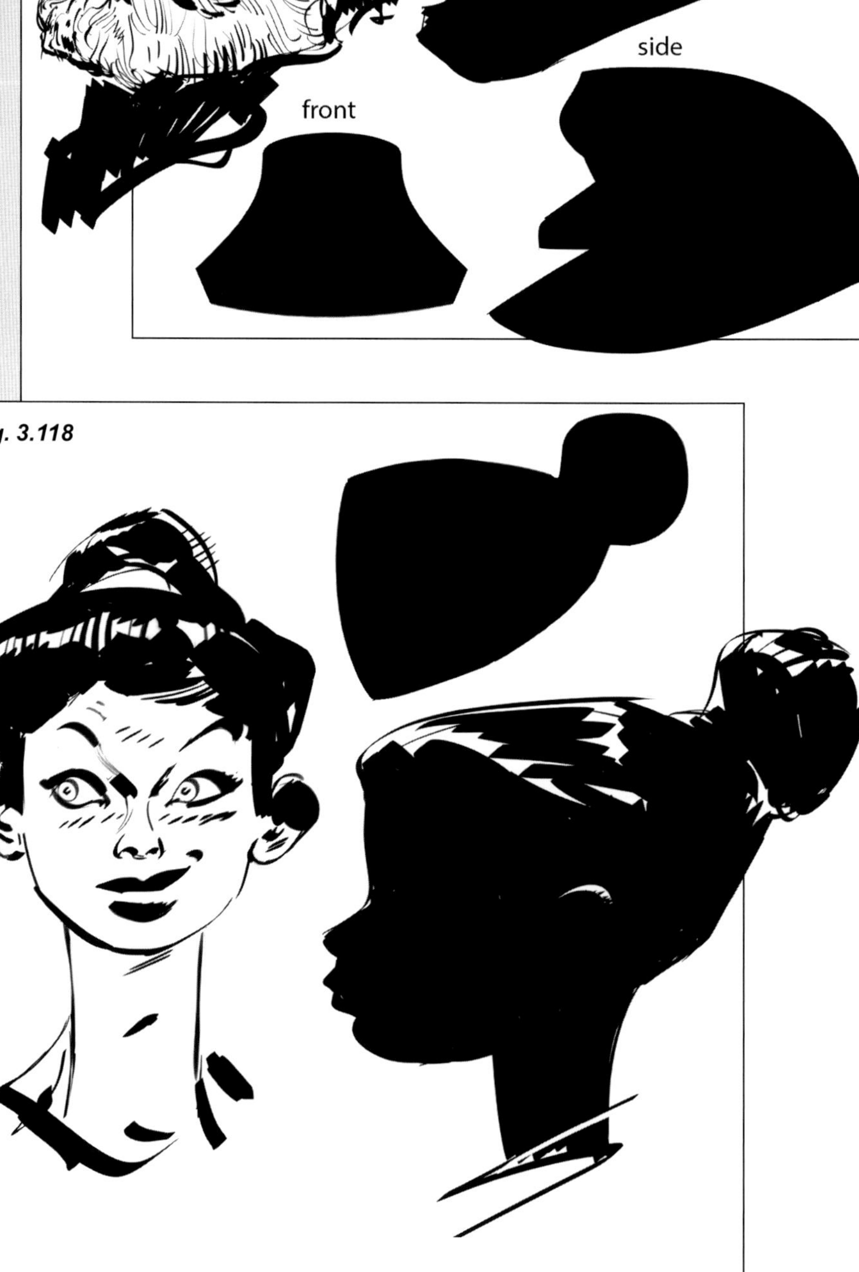

fig. 3.118

Figs. 3.116, **3.117**, and **3.118** show how to create a character's head based on essential shapes and silhouettes while keeping them consistent from every angle, to always make the character readable and recognizable. The last thing you need in a story is to lose the flow of it by creating any confusion.

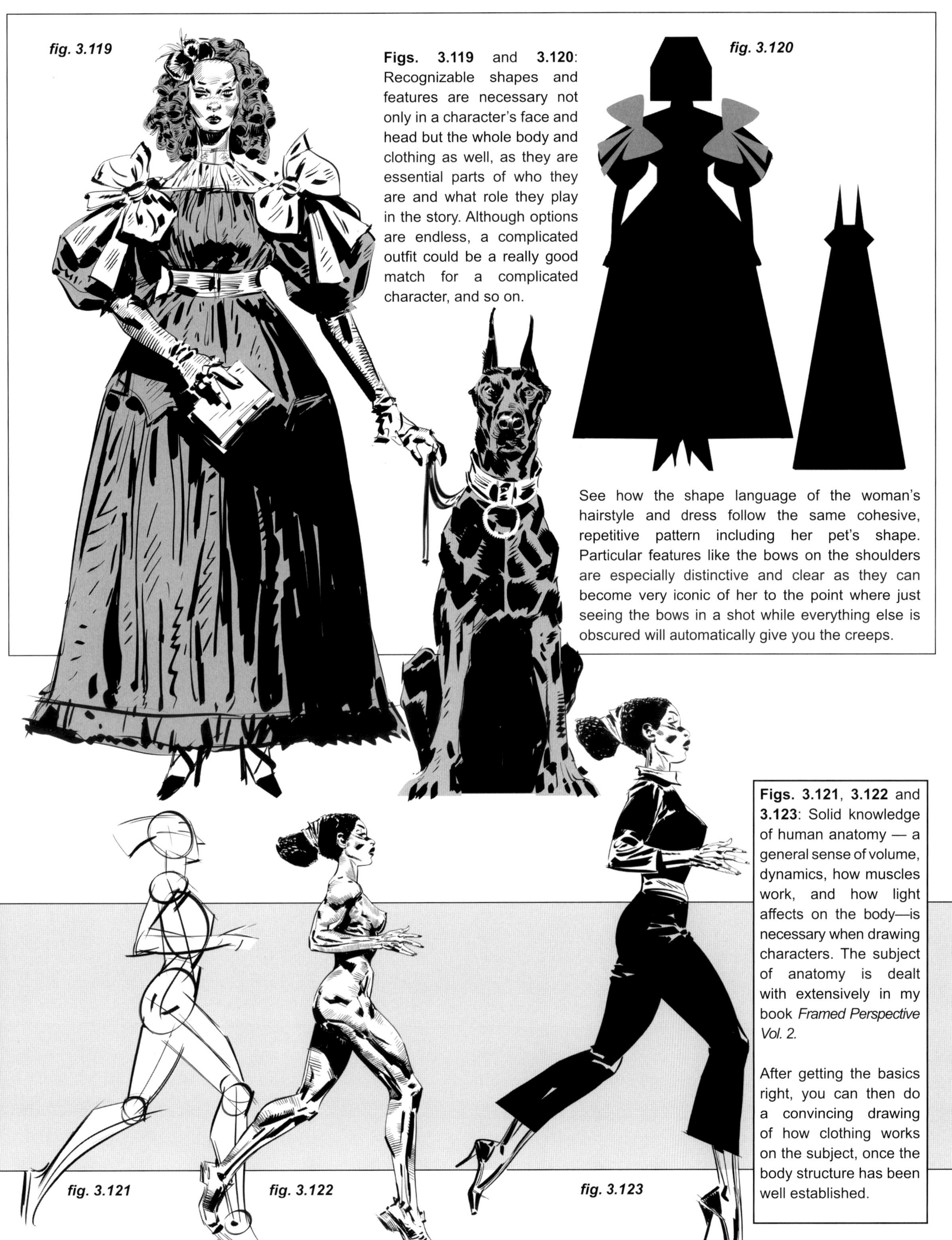

fig. 3.119

Figs. 3.119 and **3.120**: Recognizable shapes and features are necessary not only in a character's face and head but the whole body and clothing as well, as they are essential parts of who they are and what role they play in the story. Although options are endless, a complicated outfit could be a really good match for a complicated character, and so on.

fig. 3.120

See how the shape language of the woman's hairstyle and dress follow the same cohesive, repetitive pattern including her pet's shape. Particular features like the bows on the shoulders are especially distinctive and clear as they can become very iconic of her to the point where just seeing the bows in a shot while everything else is obscured will automatically give you the creeps.

Figs. 3.121, **3.122** and **3.123**: Solid knowledge of human anatomy — a general sense of volume, dynamics, how muscles work, and how light affects on the body—is necessary when drawing characters. The subject of anatomy is dealt with extensively in my book *Framed Perspective Vol. 2.*

After getting the basics right, you can then do a convincing drawing of how clothing works on the subject, once the body structure has been well established.

fig. 3.121

fig. 3.122

fig. 3.123

Figs. 3.124 to **3.128**: The eyes are windows to the soul of a character, and through them alone you should be able to see emotions. When inking a character's eyes, work them as a volumetric body, with hills and valleys that get hit by light and project shadows. Don't just use contour outlines. Lines (thinner or thicker) should overall be descriptive of how the light source falls on that area.

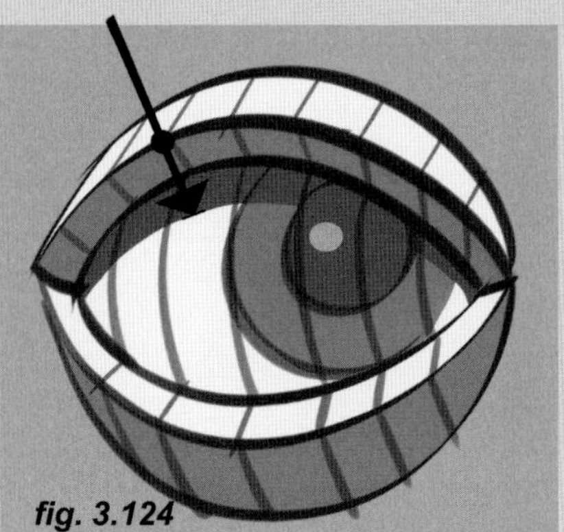

fig. 3.124

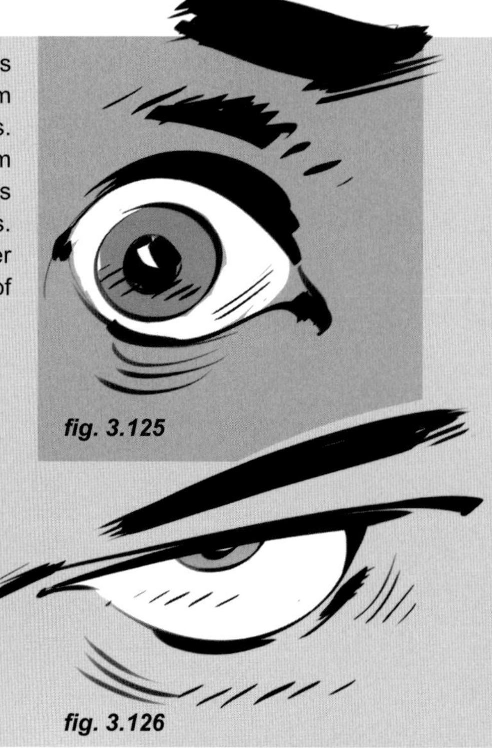

fig. 3.125

fig. 3.126

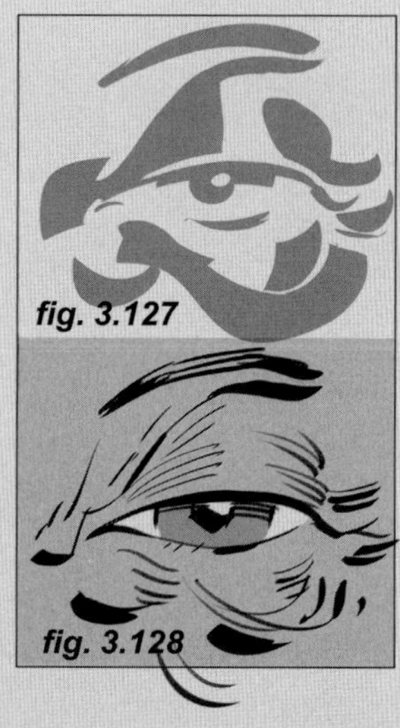

fig. 3.127

fig. 3.128

Figs. 3.127 and **3.128**: Group line work according to a preconceived plan that describes volume through lighting.

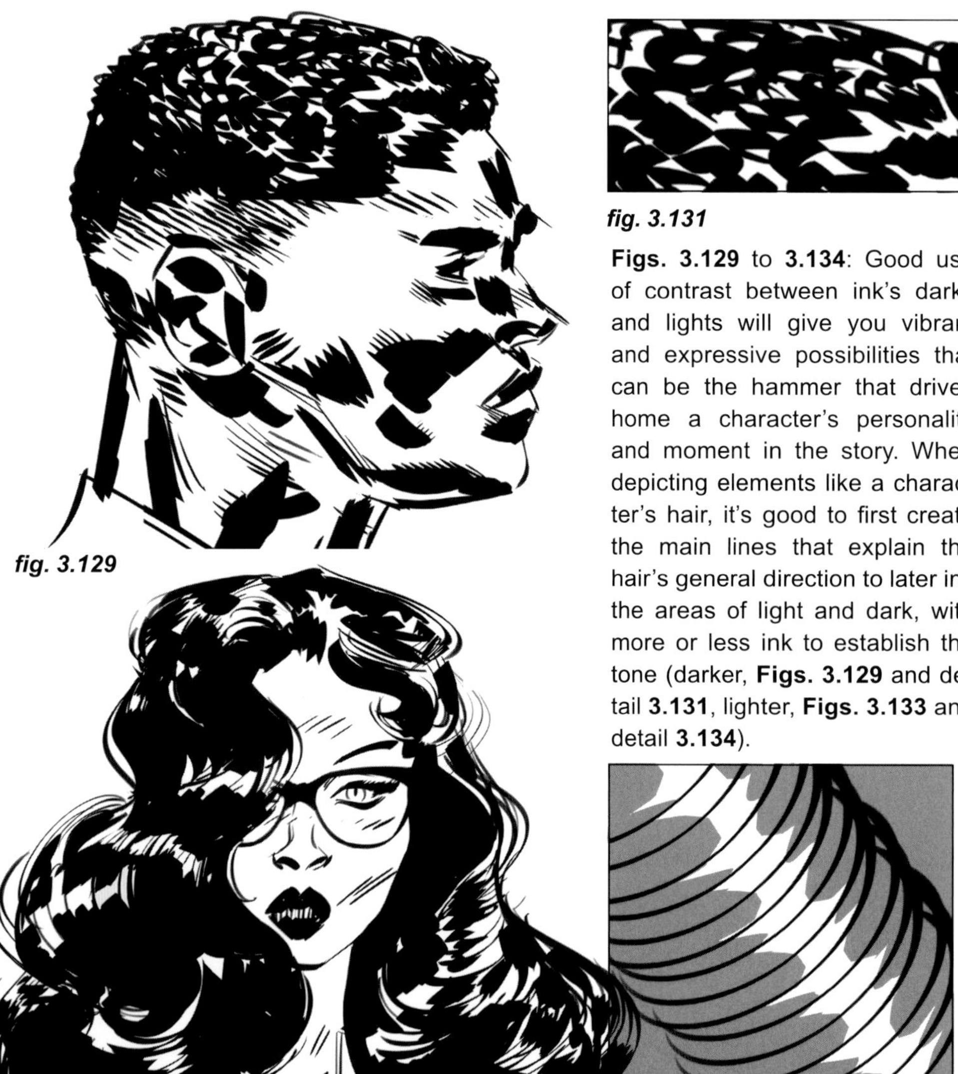

fig. 3.129

fig. 3.131

fig. 3.130

fig. 3.132

Figs. 3.129 to **3.134**: Good use of contrast between ink's darks and lights will give you vibrant and expressive possibilities that can be the hammer that drives home a character's personality and moment in the story. When depicting elements like a character's hair, it's good to first create the main lines that explain the hair's general direction to later ink the areas of light and dark, with more or less ink to establish the tone (darker, **Figs. 3.129** and detail **3.131**, lighter, **Figs. 3.133** and detail **3.134**).

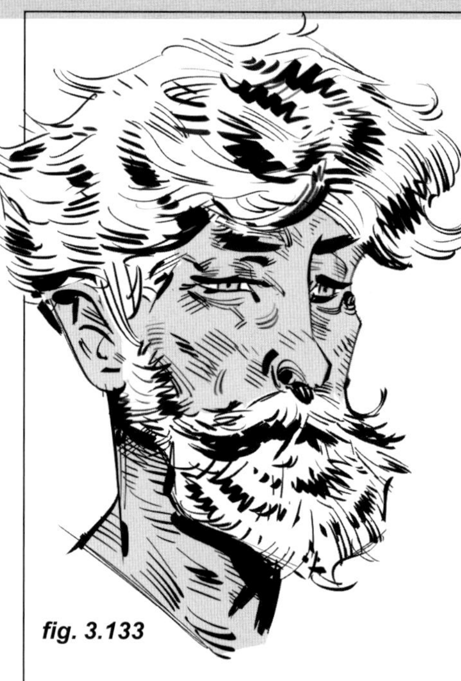

fig. 3.133

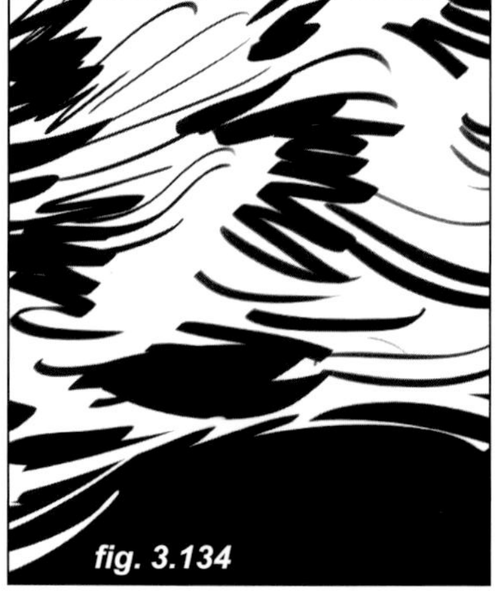

fig. 3.134

A very useful device is to integrate characters within the lighting of the scene, and use this to reinforce the visual narrative of the moment. Characters do not need to be shown 100 percent in every shot. As I've also mentioned in *Framed Ink*, suggesting can be way more powerful than showing. Revealing some details can be much better than showing all your cards at the get-go. Also, by integrating characters in an environment effectively, the resulting image usually feels more credible and realistic.

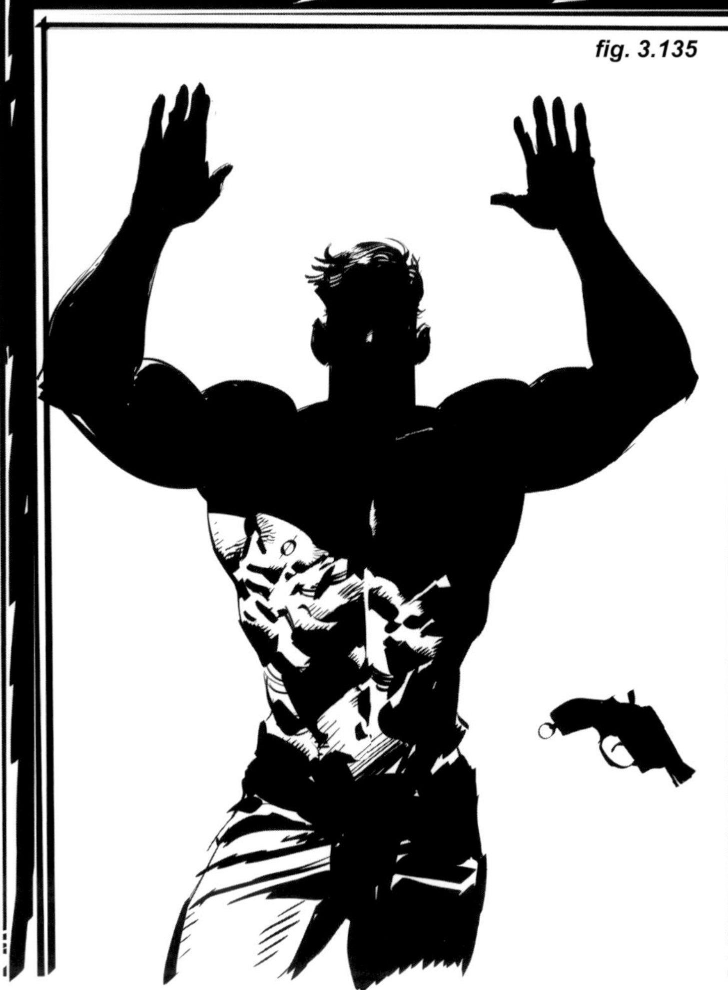

fig. 3.135

fig. 3.136

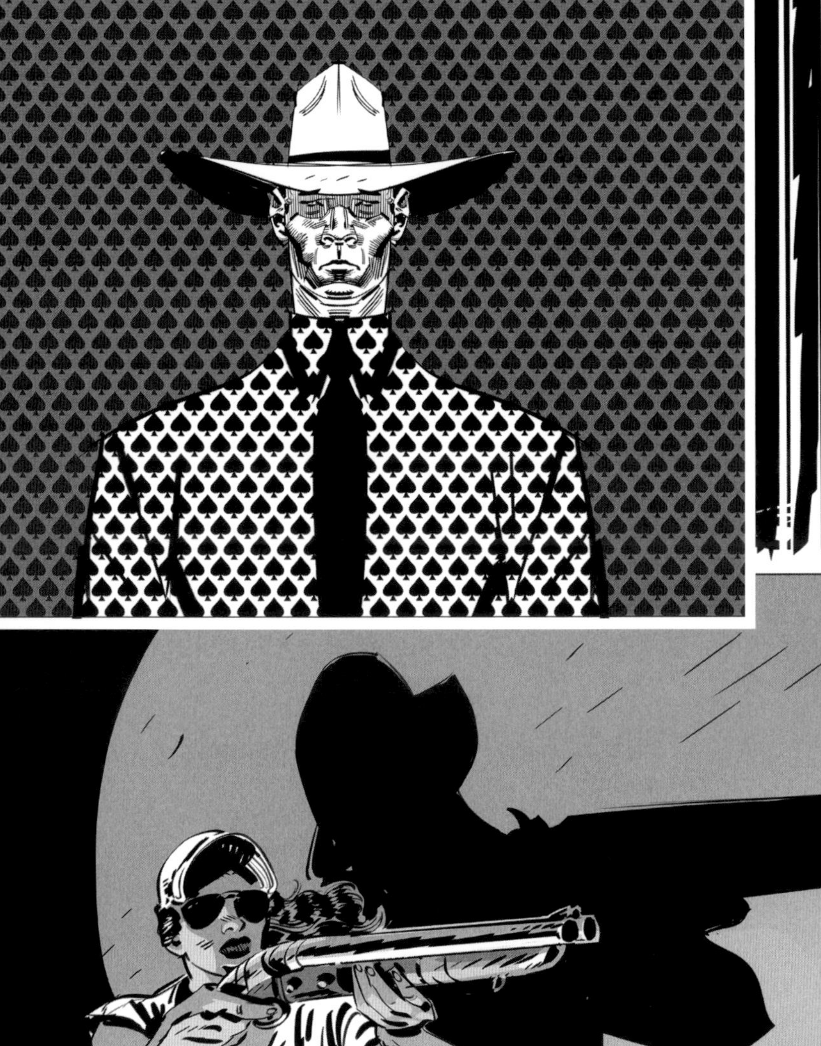

fig. 3.137

Fig. 3.135: The man approaching with his hands up from behind the doorway might have a second concealed weapon. The fact that he is possibly playing a hidden card can be emphasized by visually concealing his face in the shadows. Or maybe this lighting device offers a chance to go from here to the next panel where he has stepped into the light, revealing his previously concealed (and important to the story) identity.

Fig. 3.136: Introducing a character with some striking visual component, for example, a guy whose shirt blends in with the background's wallpaper (here very stylized) will make him more distinctive and memorable.

Fig. 3.137: Projecting a character's shadow on the wall behind while she/he is performing a powerful action can emphasize this action even further by visually doubling it.

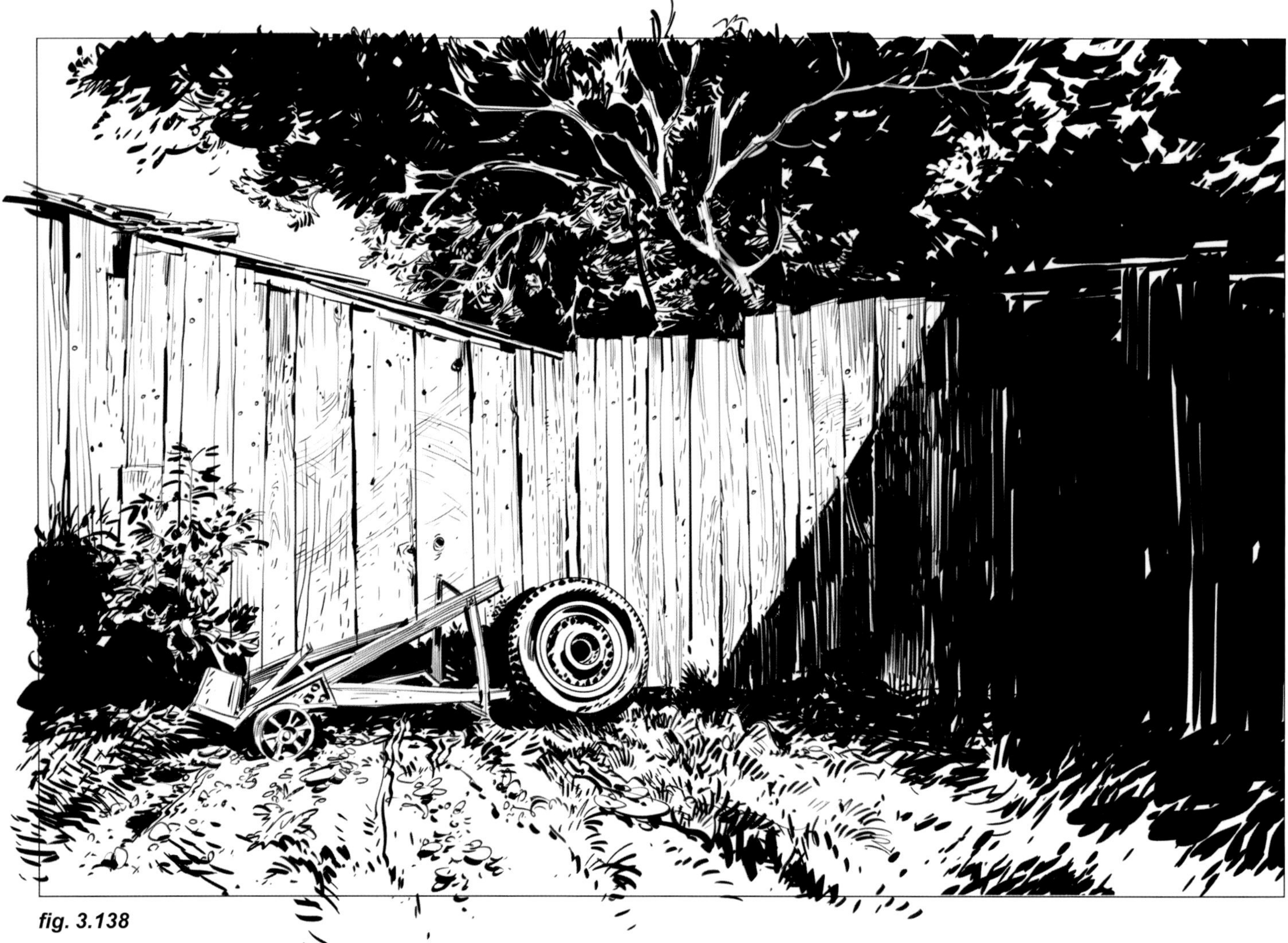

fig. 3.138

Next let's play with elements that will help us establish a solid sense of space, depth, and perspective. This includes blocking the basic shapes of the lights and shadows (or blacks and whites) and using specific types of brush and their resulting brush marks (what I tend to call "calligraphy').

First, analyze this drawing of a fenced backyard (**fig. 3.138**) and all elements within it.

Use of reference, either live or photographic (**fig. 3.139**), is common in our trade. It is important though to take these only as a base for your personal interpretation.

The visual world you create can sometimes reflect magic and fantasy, but it always is a poetic version of the reality around us. By poetic I mean a stylized version of reality that makes our worlds dynamic, alive, and dramatic while credible; emphasizes, frames, and points a special light at the things that turn that potentially ordinary and mundane scene into a piece of storytelling. This could be something that explains to the audience what they need to know or be aware of, and will do it in a way that will strengthen the narrative, the vibe, the poetry as I like to think of it (whether we are talking about a romantic moment or a rough, gruesome medieval battle).

In essence, when looking at a scene like this (**fig. 3.138**), we shouldn't just see grass, a fence, a tree, a cart, and a tire. We should be seeing, depending on the needs of the story, a childhood memory, a rendezvous place with a fellow spy that will reveal to us a crucial secret, or the place where we last saw our car keys, keys that we desperately need to drive away from a serial killer as fast as possible.

Fig. 3.139: Before I get into a formal analysis of how the panel was drawn, let's look into how the image in the photo reference was modified and worked into a more potentially meaningful drawing.

Using the merciless contrast between black and white and pushing the light and the texture on the fence, and the darks on the trees at the other side, now the fence becomes visually stronger than in the photograph.

fig. 3.139

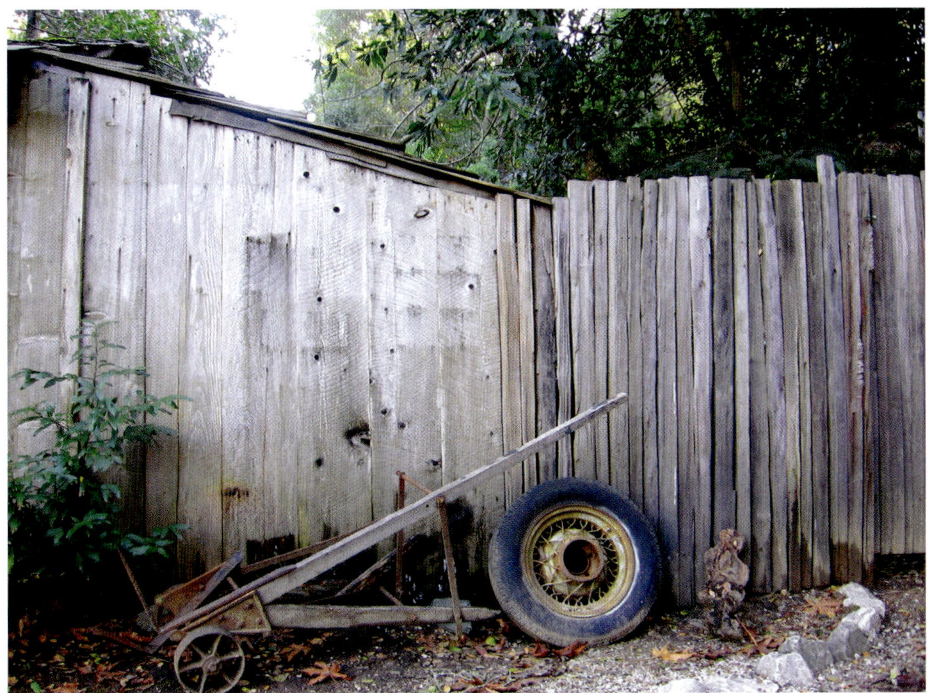

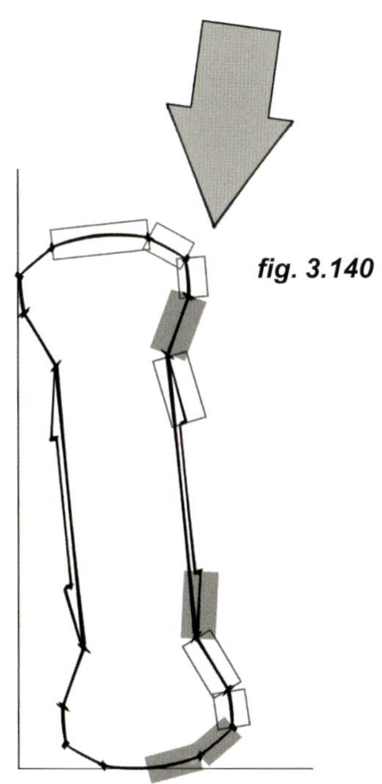

fig. 3.140

Also by further opening the frame at the bottom of the image and enhancing the sense of perspective by the use of converging lines with the grass patterns, a feeling of a dead end (always an unpleasant one, or at least one that makes us question things) becomes stronger. This sense of a dead end is further emphasized by the stronger contrasts on the fence.

In addition, by opening the frame more at the top to reveal the presence of the tree, a potentially meaningful landmark, has now more of an impact. (See all these elements taking up a bigger personality.) Then opening the scene more to the right, this allowed me to include a shadowed area that becomes one of mystery to be filled in by the audience's fantasy and imagination.

After these adjustments, the image I started with all of a sudden became meaningful and complex in a way that offers many possibilities as a set where an emotional story happens. As far as actual inking techniques, I'll start with the tire resting up against the fence.

Fig. 3.140 shows a side section of it that is important because it shows the different plains of which it is composed. The gray arrow above indicates the direction of the light source. Putting it all together you see that the areas framed by the white rectangles are exposed to the light, while the areas framed by the gray ones are in shadow.

Once you understand this simple fact, you will have a sense of structure that gives you a system, a way to organize the areas that you will leave blank and the areas that you will need to ink.

That doesn't mean that you have to simplify the inking to its minimum expression and make the final image look like **Fig. 3.141**, obviously you can choose to do something more organic in the lines of **fig. 3.142**. At this point it is all a matter of personal style and taste, but at least you have knowledge of how that particular body is constructed and how light works on it.

fig. 3.141

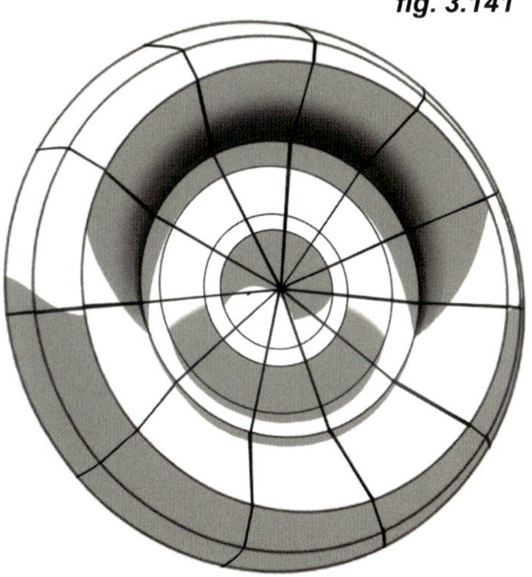

fig. 3.142

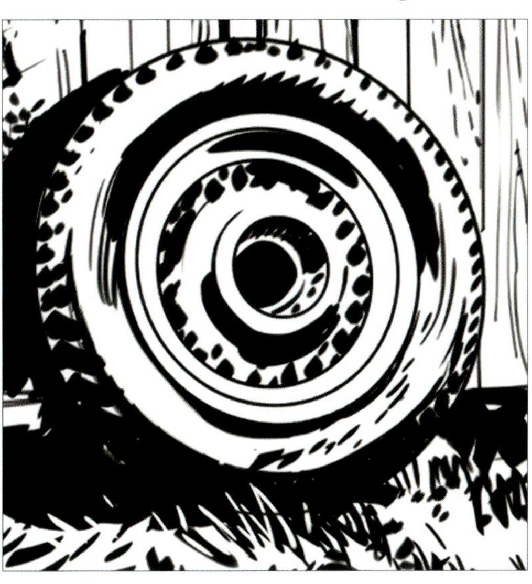

fig. 3.143

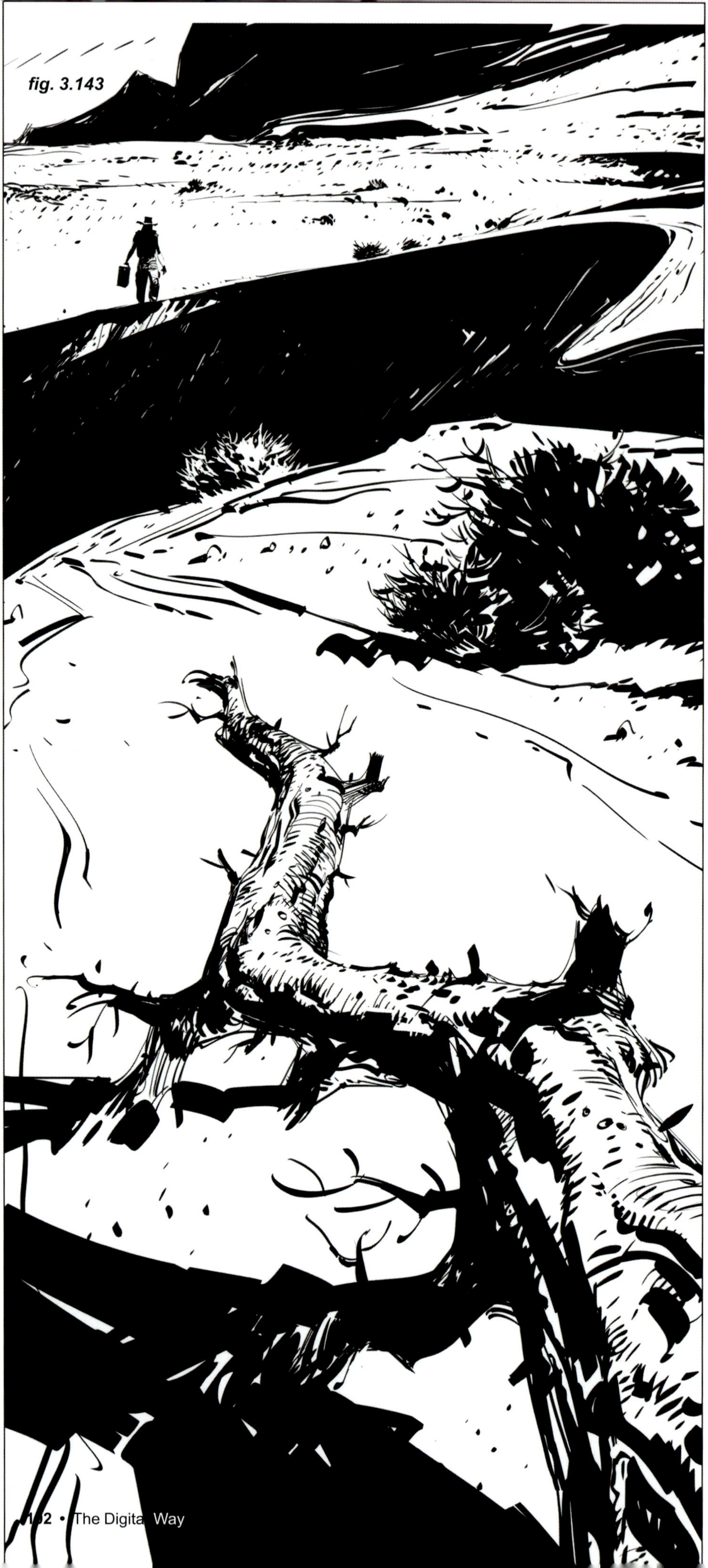

Fig. 3.143: Here's another case of how you can transform a seemingly plain reality (**fig. 3.144**) into something more dramatic. The reference is an interesting, extreme landscape where one can tell many things can happen.

Fig. 3.145: Although there is a distant character in the photo already, it is not very obvious. You might have to look for the figure, so I brought it closer to the camera.

I edited down the number of bushes in the shot to a minimum, just enough to emphasize a 1, 2, 3 sense of depth in the foreground first (all circled in red), and then the rest as dots in the far distance to help create the dry texture and atmosphere (area in yellow).

The character is framed by the black sand dunes' shadow that the person stands on, in the top third of the drawing, plus the overexposed, bleached-out white background.

The converging lines on the foreground sand together with the now magnified trunk (in green) seem to point at the character, so that she or he becomes a better focus of attention.

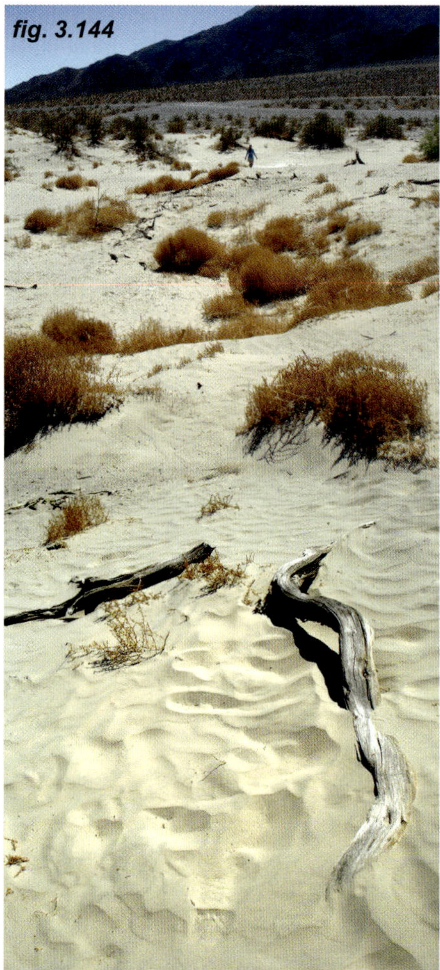

fig. 3.144

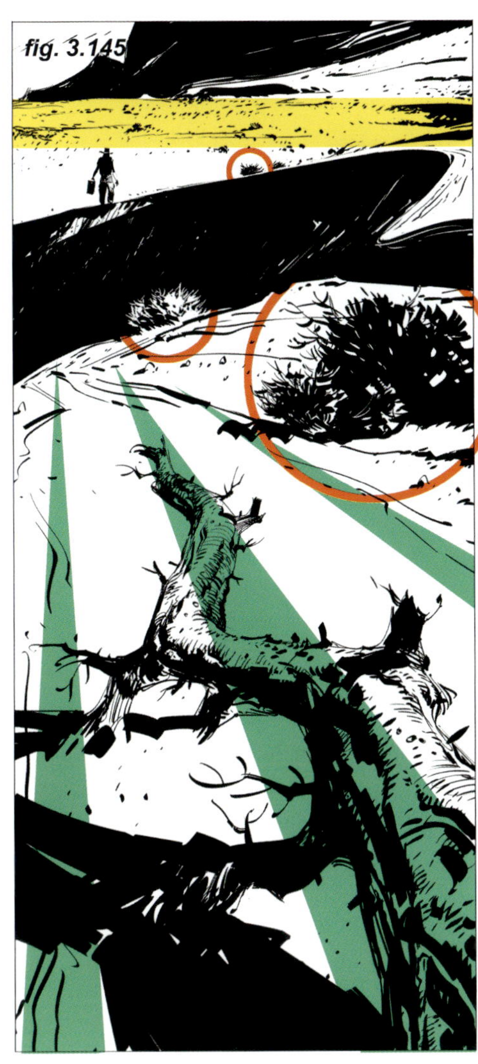
fig. 3.145

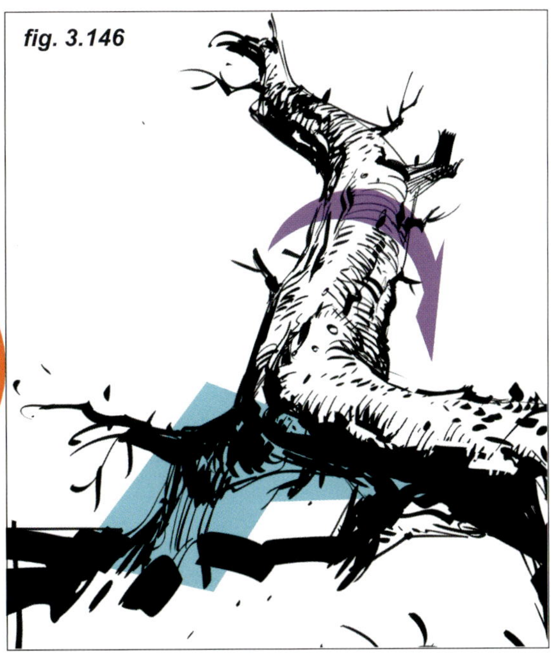
fig. 3.146

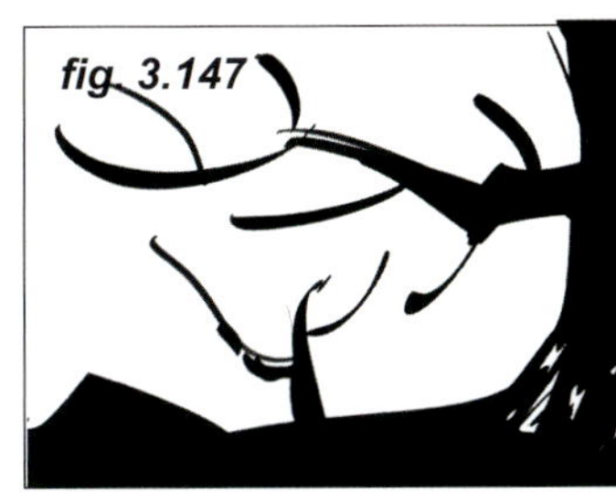
fig. 3.147

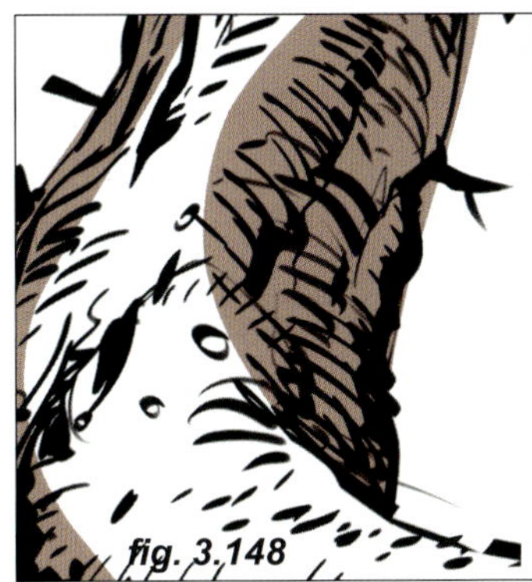
fig. 3.148

Fig. 3.146: After treating the shadowed areas of the trunk with almost solid blacks (always allowing for a bit of reflected light there in blue for a sense of atmosphere and realism) I will treat the lit side with some thin brushwork on both sides of the cylinder a trunk usually is, leave the center of it white, and suggest the reflected sunlight in that area.

Fig. 3.147 shows that smaller branches have been added to our version of the trunk to make it clear that this indeed is a trunk. In the original photograph the branch could have easily been mistaken for a snake.

Fig. 3.148: This detail of the trunk shows how its texture has been worked out to show volume through a number of irregularities that concentrate mostly on the sides (in brown) leaving a brighter center to imply its volume and roundness.

fig. 3.149

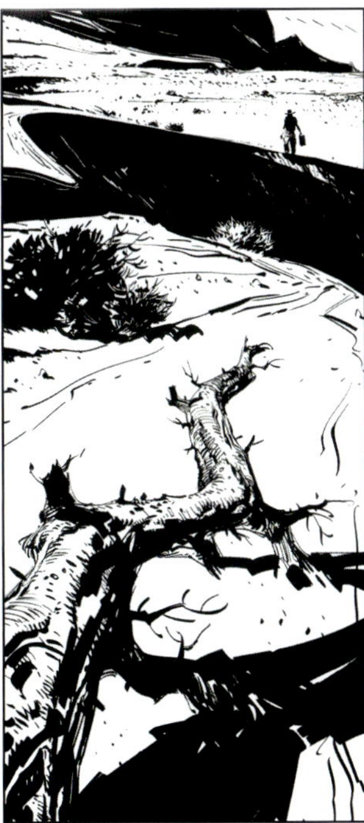

fig. 3.150

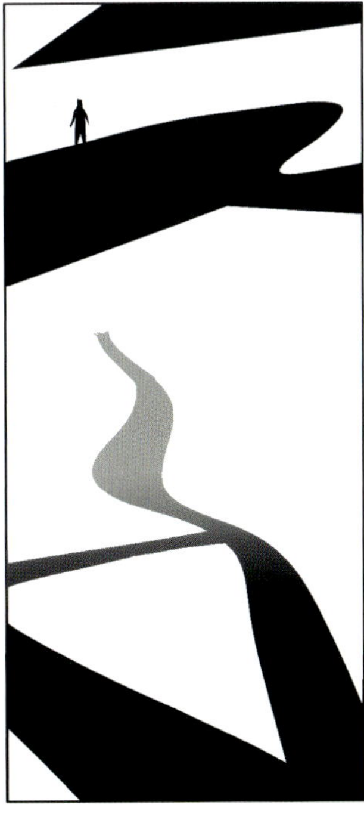

Fig. 3.149: A drawing must withstand the "flopping" test. In the old days this test implied the use of a mirror, or turning the artwork upside down for a fresh new look on it to see if there were any obvious mistakes (composition, balance, proportions, rendering, line direction, etc.). Now with Photoshop or similar software, just go to "Edit/Transform" menu and then "Flip Horizontal."

What this provides is a totally different, surprising point of view on your work, where, again, any mistakes that your brain got so used to during the process of creation that you accepted as good and normal, will suddenly pop out screaming and demanding a rework.

Fig. 3.150: A schematic of the drawing's basic dynamic lines explains the essentials of the composition and overall flow of shapes. On these bare bones I built further layers of complexity. Observe how the farther end of the trunk in gray represents the thinner, less dense lines in the final drawing that together with the solid black of the character makes him more visible in the scene.

fig. 3.151

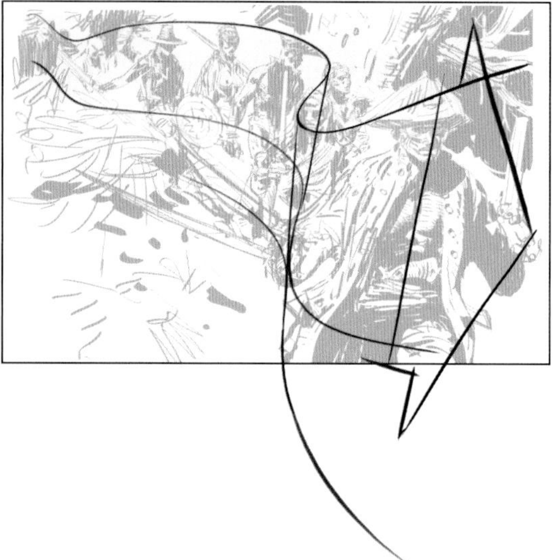

Fig. 3.151: Achieving a proper sense of space, depth, and perspective is essential when it comes to putting all the pieces together in a single dynamic flow. A visual path (here indicated by the arrow) has been designed to make sense of the whole line of characters as they walk through the jungle, and the overall sense of dynamics and perspective has been based on their proportionally reduced size in the shot as we go farther into the distance.

fig. 3.152

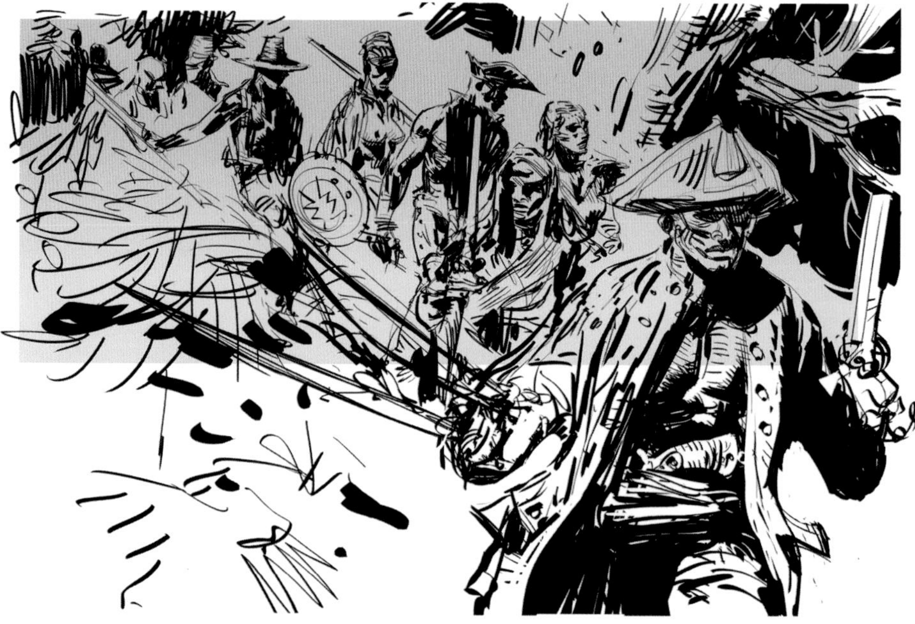

Fig. 3.152: With this structure in mind, a basic sketch was further rendered. Having previously established such structure allows us to get into a certain sense of detail knowing that these details will play well into the overall "music" of the narrative moment. (Sometimes I like to think of the similarities between what we do visually with music, as they both play within a sense of flow and rhythm, with structure supporting the delivery of an emotional message).

fig. 3.153

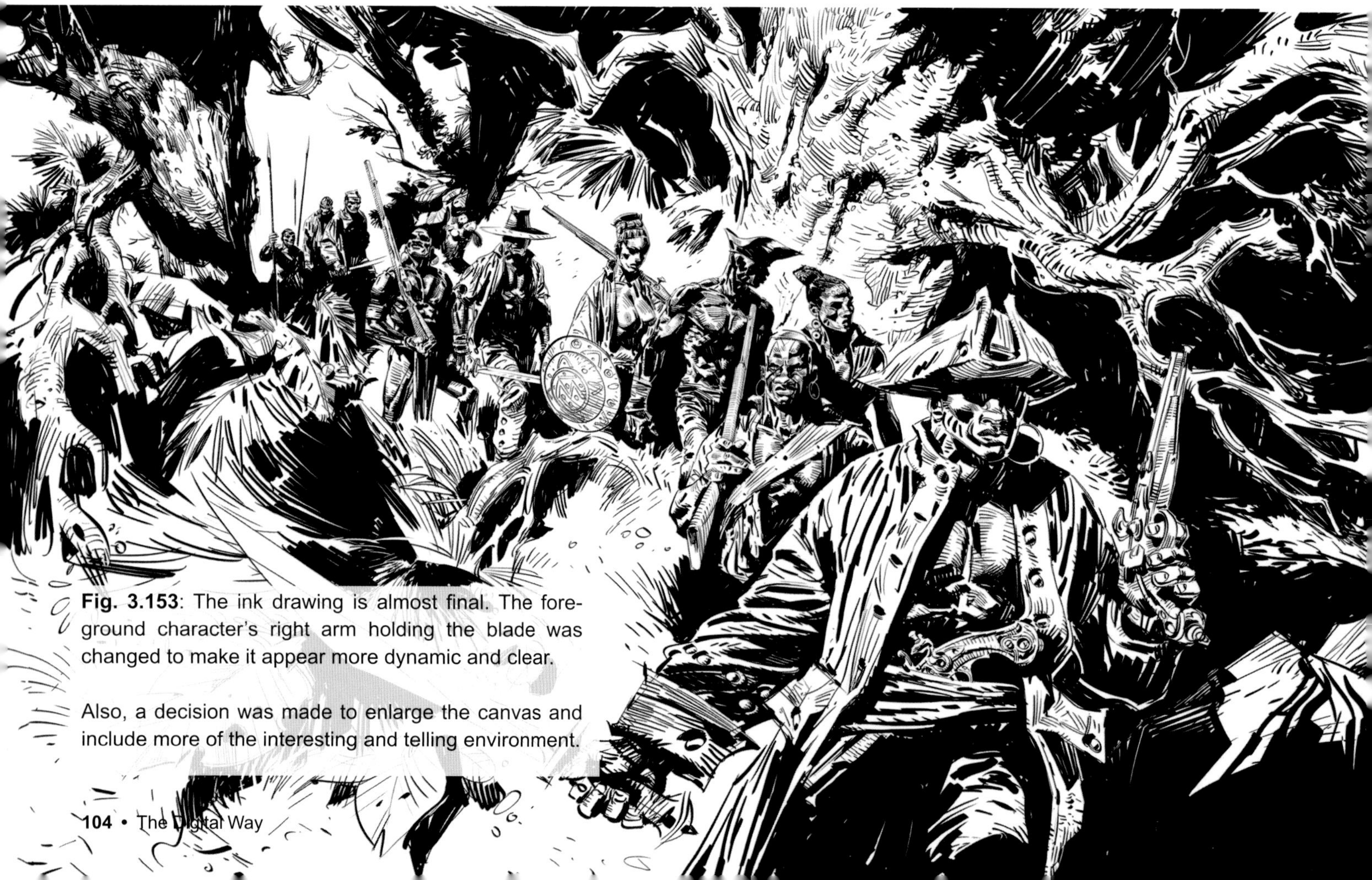

Fig. 3.153: The ink drawing is almost final. The foreground character's right arm holding the blade was changed to make it appear more dynamic and clear.

Also, a decision was made to enlarge the canvas and include more of the interesting and telling environment.

Fig. 3.154: In this first color pass, a general sense of temperature was established, warmer in the foreground and a little cooler in the background, helping emphasize a sense of distance. All further color development was rooted in this first quick layer.

fig. 3.154

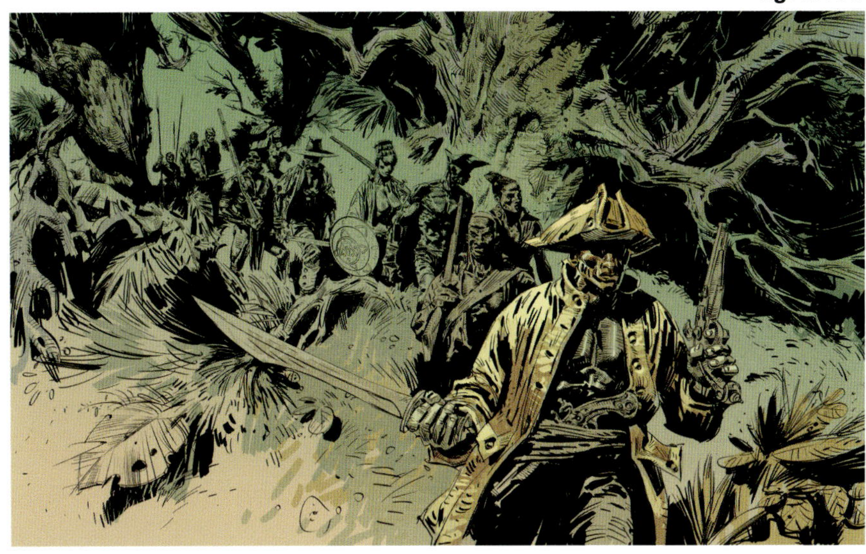

Fig. 3.155-3.157: Inking and rendering details in their original black-and-white version. Although color had been in mind since the first sketching steps for this piece (and aside from exceptions where color is supposed to be the star), I always try to make the drawing work in black and white first, as much as possible, before coloring.

The final, fully rendered illustration is on the next spread.

fig. 3.155

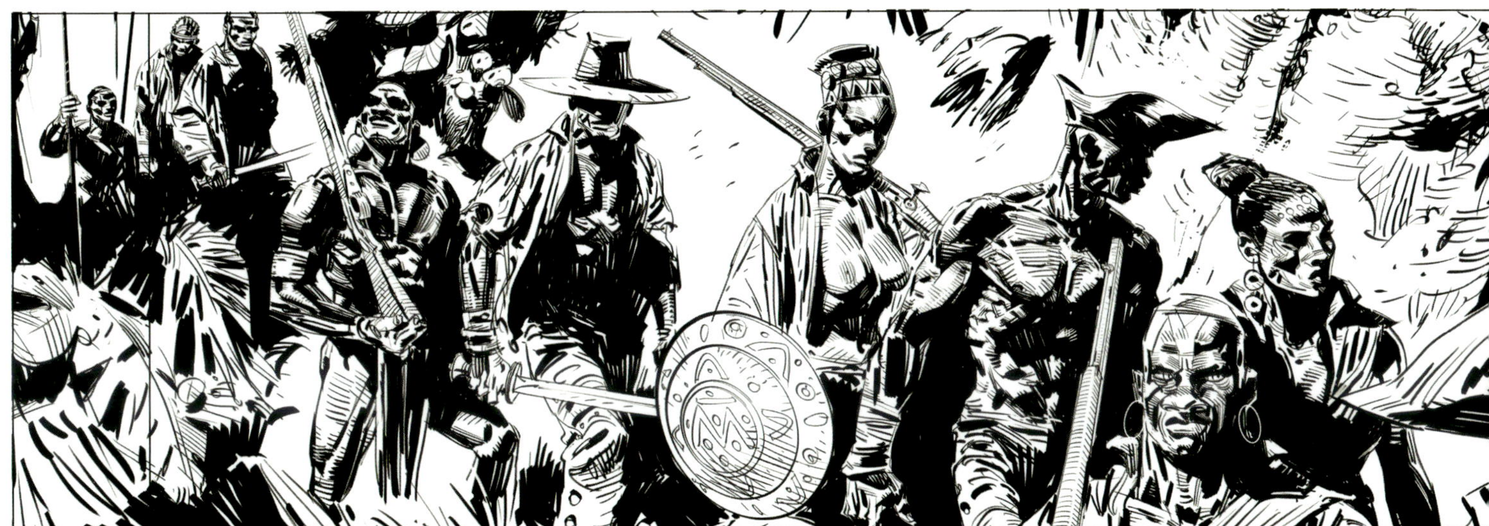

fig. 3.156

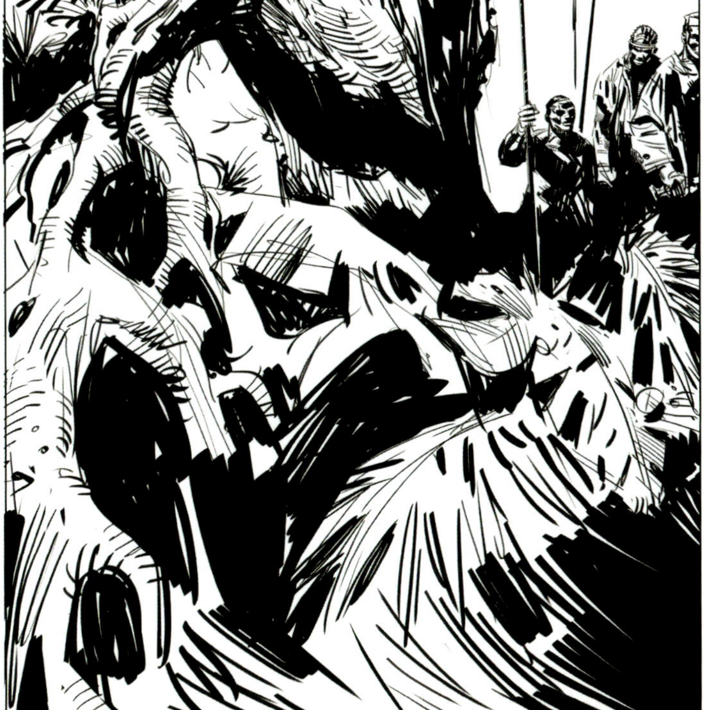

fig. 3.157

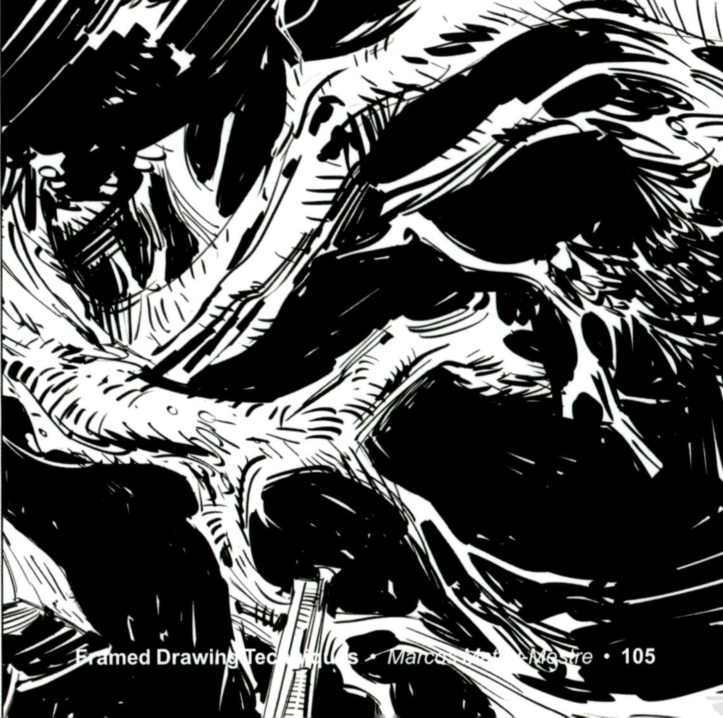

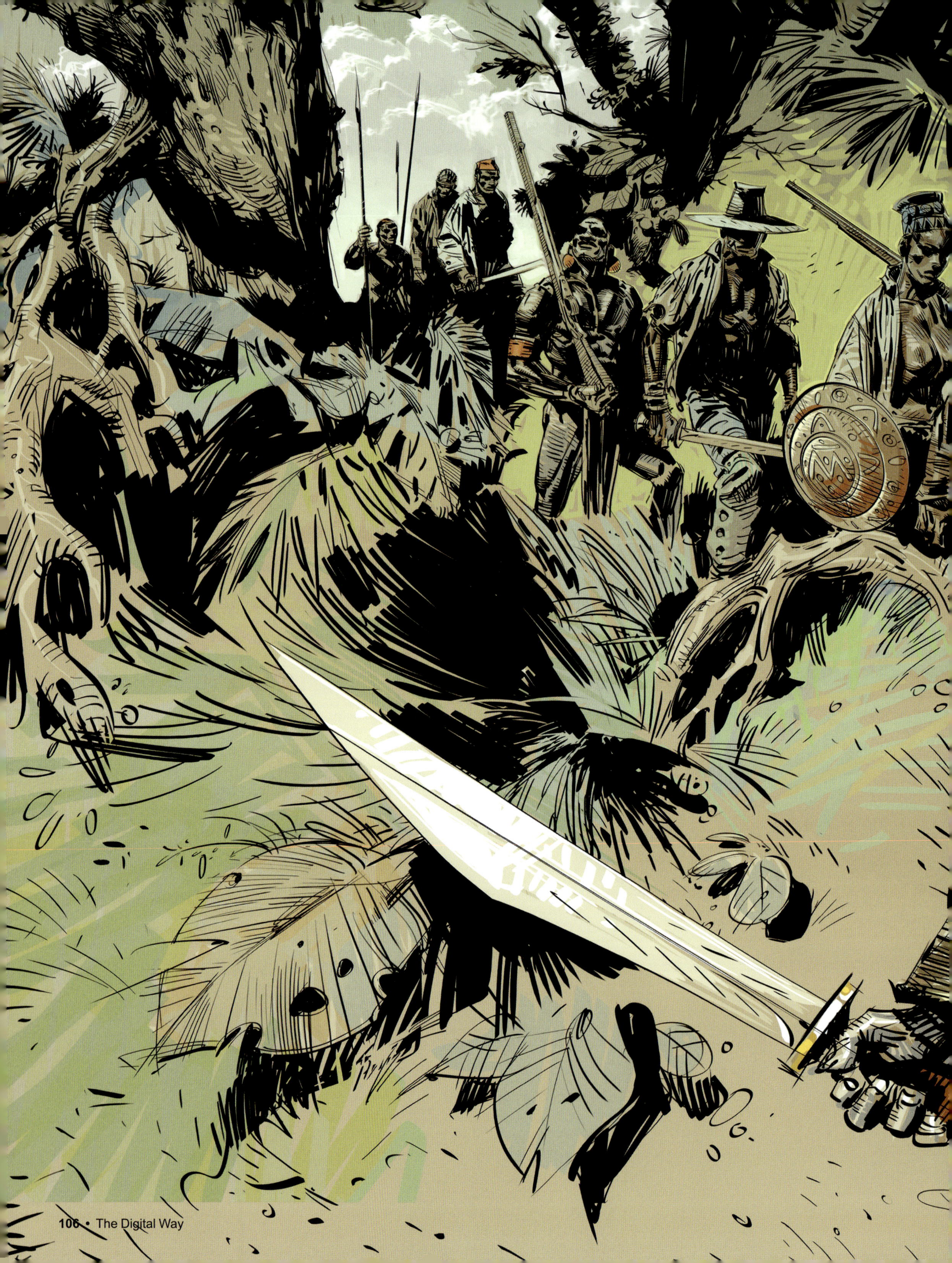

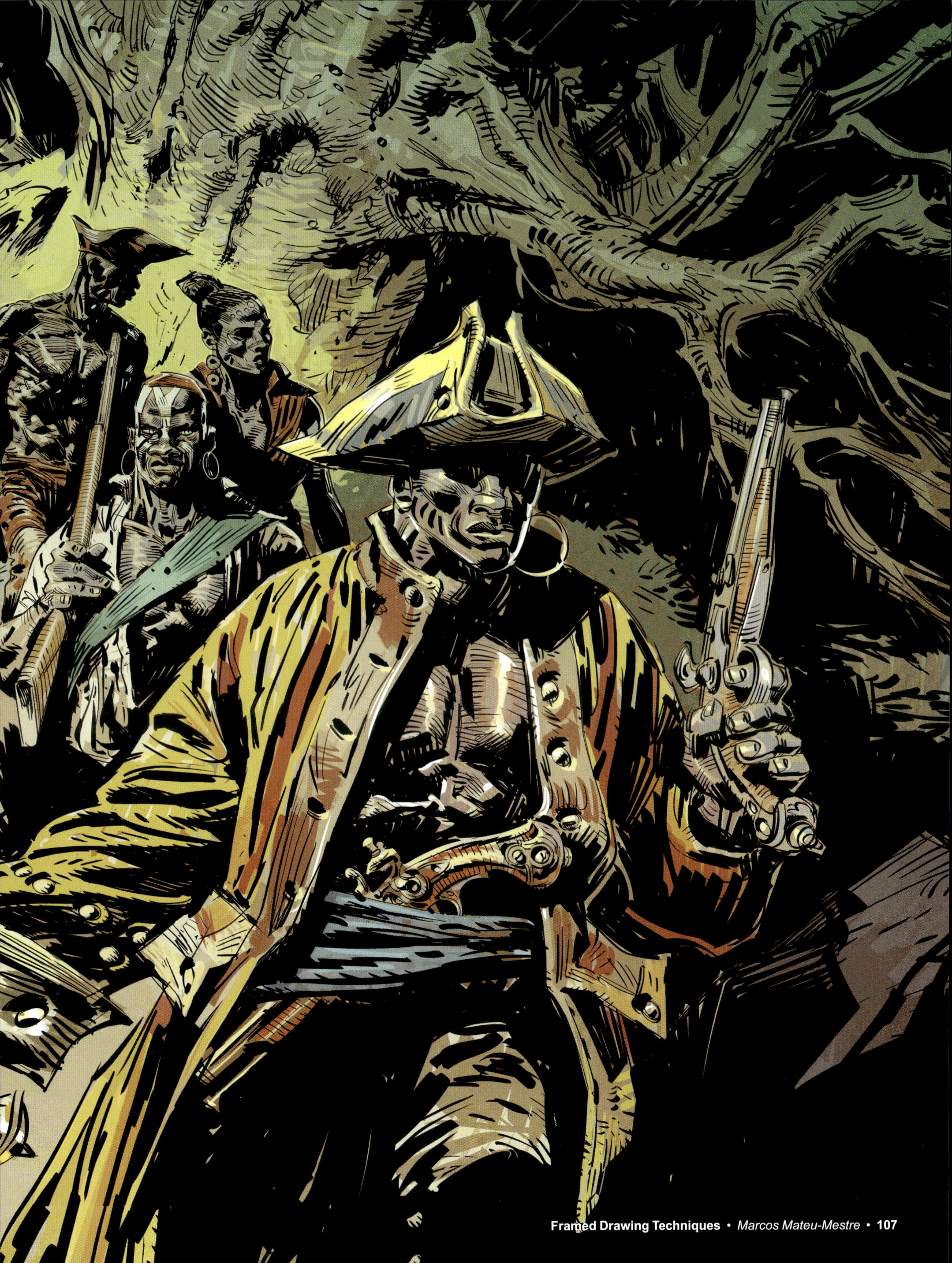

4

THE GRAY SCALE

In this gradation-based technique, you will have to play by blending in different shades or tones as seamlessly as possible. For this you obviously have the actual gradient tool in your software, but this is something you will use only as support to the main, more painterly freehand style–based gradation work.

If you use your brushes at a 100 percent of their opacity, all you will achieve will be a number of well-defined areas (**fig. 4.1**) that from a distance and in continuity will somehow convey the impression of a smooth gradation, but it won't hold on a closer view. So how do you achieve this smooth, blended-in look?

A way to do this is by bringing down the level or percentage of opacity of the brush you are using, so that at the moment of painting it will make the shade a bit paler (depending on percentage) than the one actually selected in your palette. This way you can either paint paler or go for the full tone depending on how much you insist on the same spot with the same brush. The more you paint over the same area the darker it will appear; the less you stick to the same area, the lighter it will show, independently of the amount of pressure you apply on the brush. In this example (**fig. 4.2**), the brush was set up at 60 percent of its potential maximum opacity.

Here, all shades (1, 2, 3, and 4) have been painted with the same brush, percentage of opacity, and shade of gray. The reason why 4 is the darkest and 1 is the lightest is because 1 was painted with a single pass or layer, 2 got treated a bit more as well as 3, and in 4 I made as many passes as necessary in order to obtain the black tone I originally selected from the palette. (See the separate layers in **Fig. 4.3**).

fig. 4.1

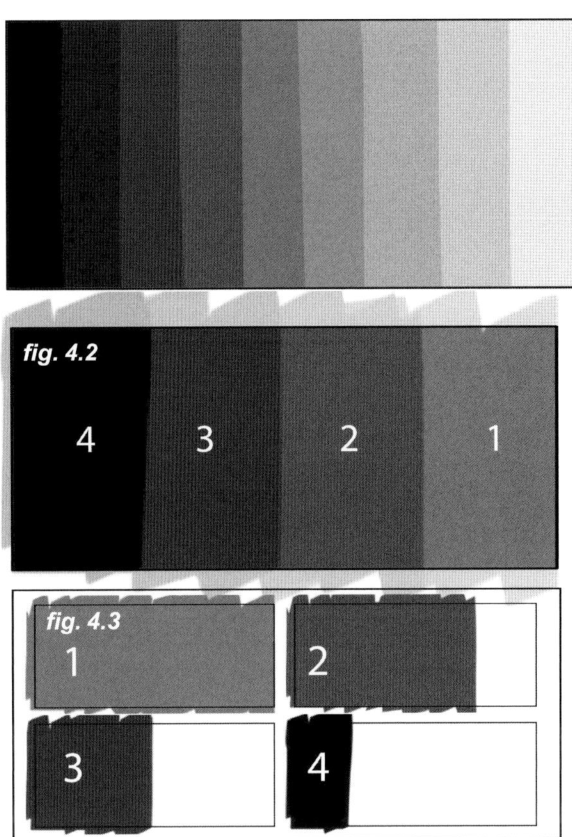

fig. 4.2

fig. 4.3

It is now time to pay attention to the eyedropper tool (**fig. 4.4**) and the following steps:

- Area 1: Select pure black as the color and set the brush at 70 percent opacity (for the sake of this example), and with this setup paint Area 1. Given the reduced opacity the result is a shade of gray (not black anymore) that will be called Gray A.

- Area 2: Now click with the eyedropper tool on top of Area 1's gray A so that you load the brush with it (brush still set at 70 percent opacity). With this paint Area 2 starting right where you left it with Area 1 (not overlapping it). Again given the reduced brush's opacity the shades of gray keep getting proportionally lighter. This is called new gray Gray B.

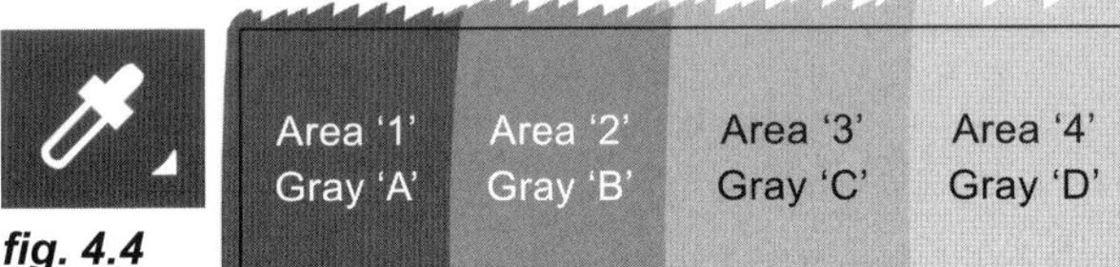

fig. 4.4

fig. 4.5

Now pick Gray B and keep repeating these steps (brush at 70 percent all the time!) all the way to the end.

Fig. 4.6: For this new exercise, paint Area 11 with black at 70 percent (obtaining Gray AA). Now pick Gray AA with the eye-drop tool, paint all over Area 11 again and extend the paint one more square to include Area 22.

Using the same Gray AA again and always with the brush at 70 percent, I start painting again from the beginning (fully including Area 11) and extending the paint all the way to include Area 33.

Each time, the new layers will be resulting in progressively lighter grays because of the reduced opacity of the consecutive brush passes, obtaining a new type of gradation.

fig. 4.6

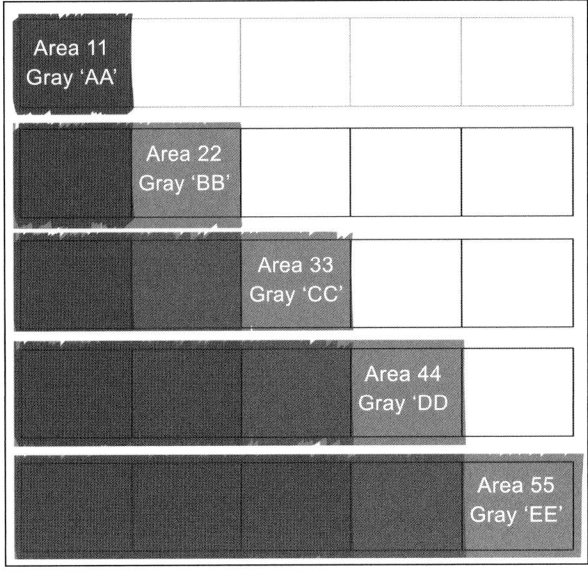

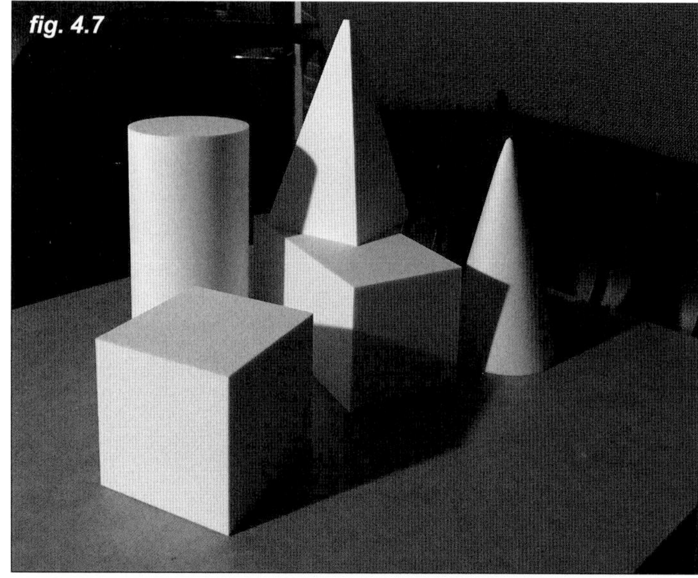
fig. 4.7

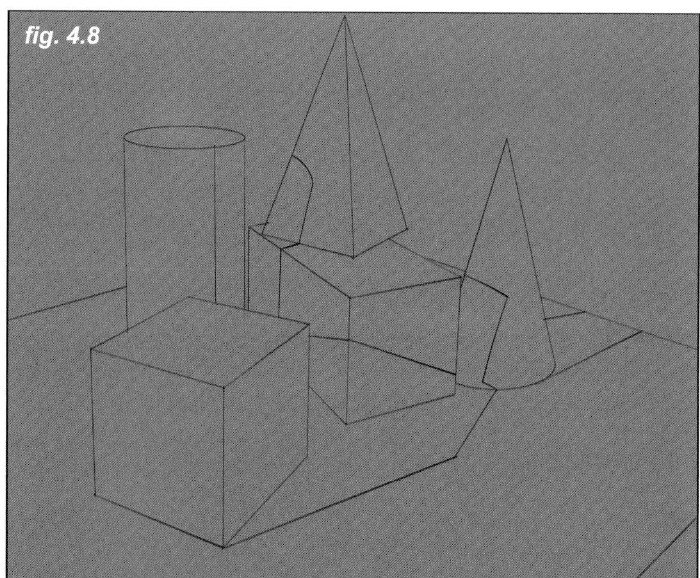
fig. 4.8

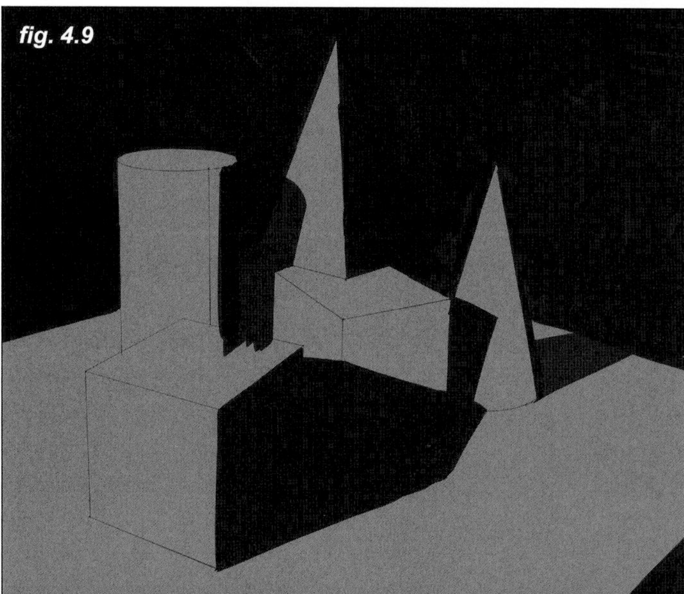
fig. 4.9

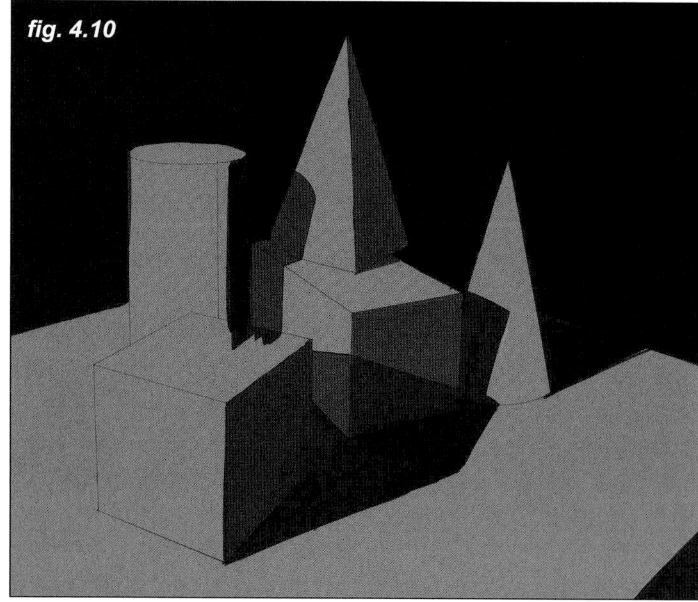
fig. 4.10

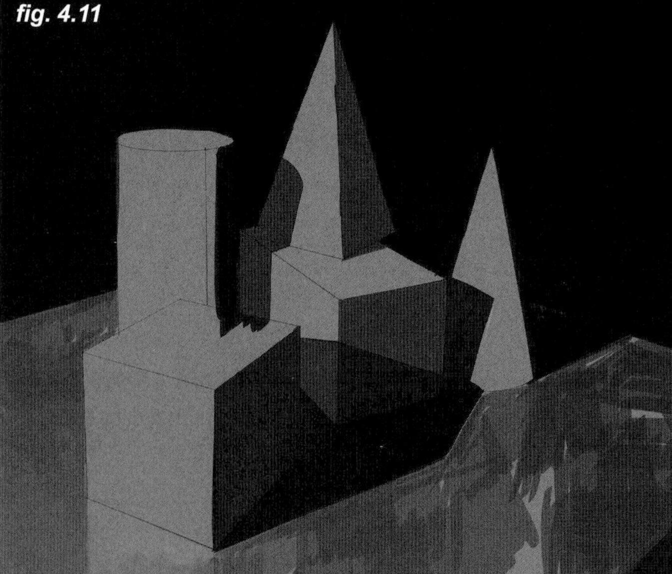
fig. 4.11

Step-by-step example based on **Fig. 4.7** photo reference.

Fig. 4.8–4.11: I start with a line drawing depicting both body contours and shadow/line separations on a midtone gray. On my first pass, I establish the main dark area. Next, I bring up the reflected lights within the shadows. Then I add some of the darker midtone on the table surface, emphasizing the reflection of the lighter sides of the polyhedrons.

Fig. 4.12: Next, I define lighter- and middle-tone areas, further working the table surface with mid-opacity brushwork and mild blurring of some of its areas with the blurring Gaussian and Motion filters.

Fig. 4.13: The specific areas on the cone and cylinder where light gradates into shadow have been polished up by overlapping a "white to gray" gradation (with the Gradient tool) on an overlay (separate layer), which gets rid of some of the too obvious brushstrokes.

Fig. 4.15: Final result: As explained in the previous pages, the brush has been always kept at a percentage of its opacity, never solid, for a more painterly effect.

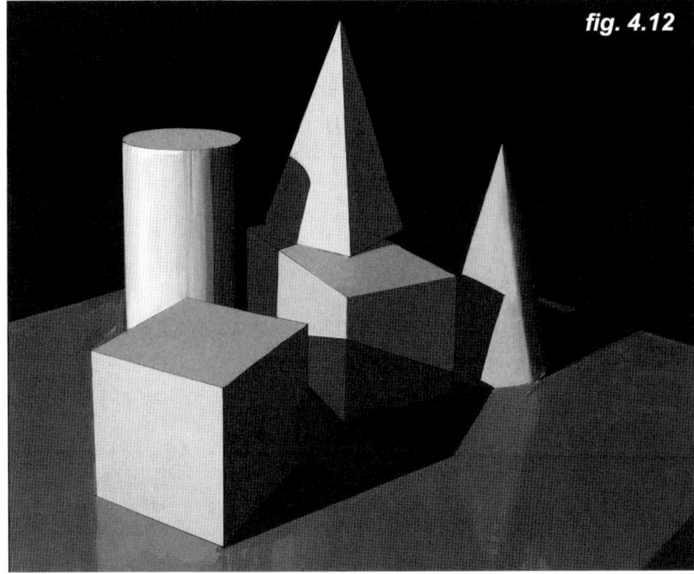

fig. 4.12

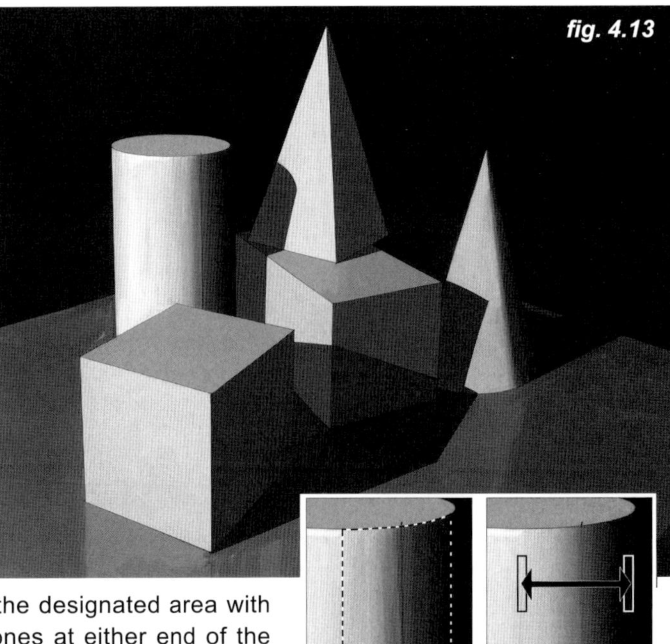

fig. 4.13

fig. 4.14

Figs. 4.13 and **4.14**: To overlap the smooth gradation, I select the designated area with a combination of the Marquee and Lasso tools, pick the two tones at either end of the area (beginning and end of the desired gradation), and then apply the gradation within this selection. After that, this gradation layer's opacity was brought down to a 65 percent so that some of the brushwork can still be seen, for a better match with the rest of the painting's work.

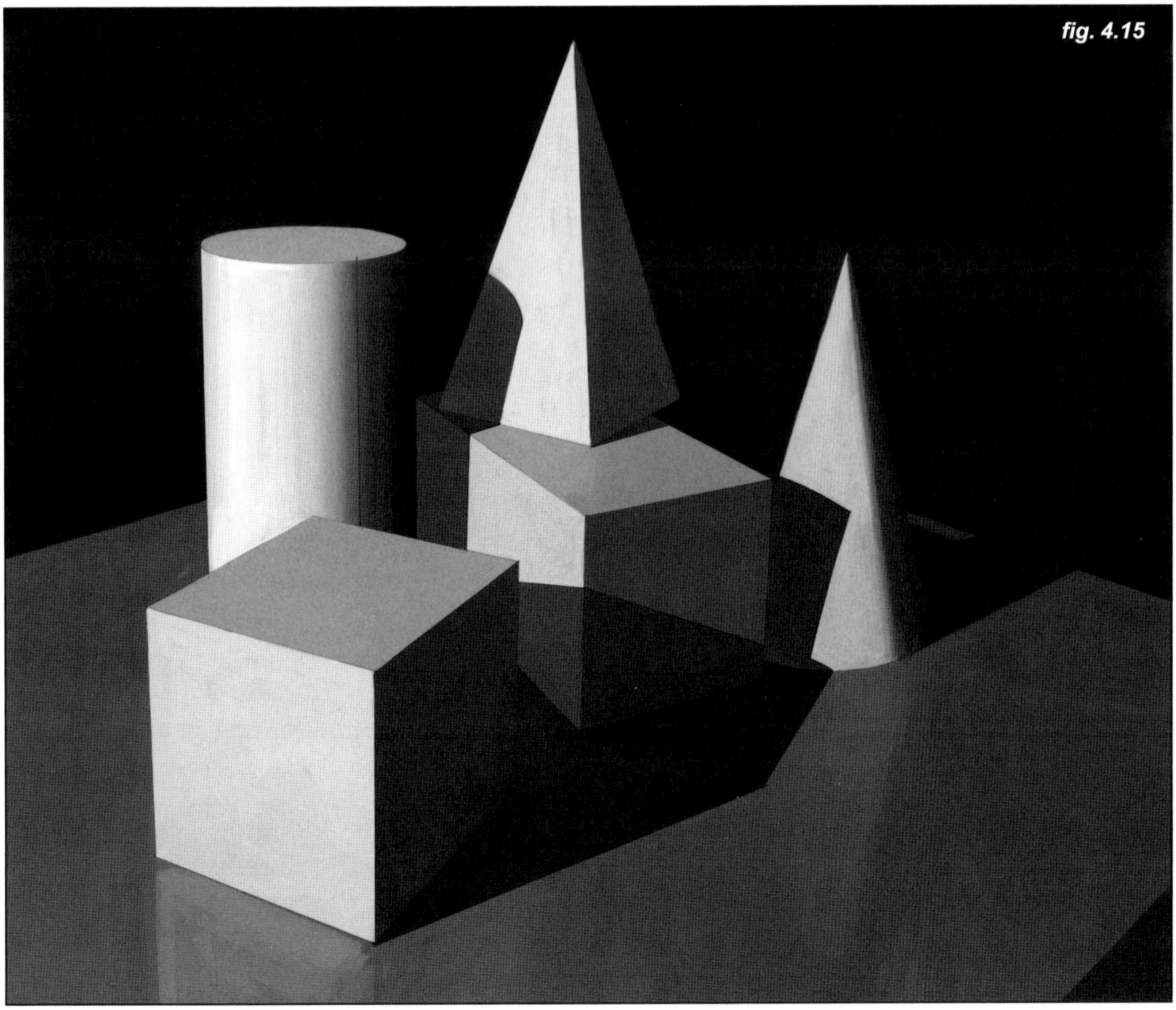

fig. 4.15

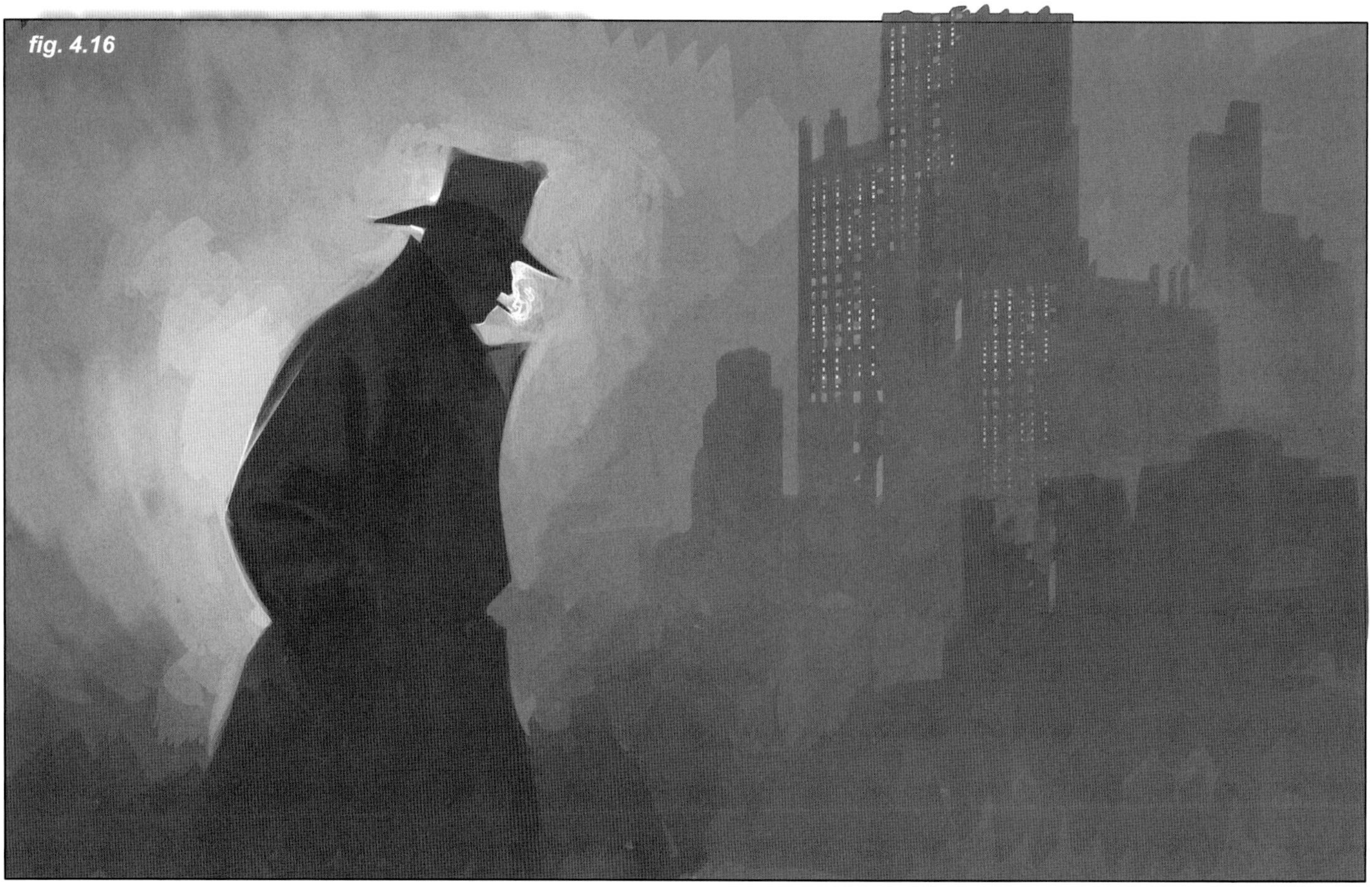

fig. 4.16

Fig. 4.16: This drawing shows a range of "levels of sharpness" that help focus attention on the important things of the shot (the top half of the character with sharper, more contrasted shapes) while blending in atmospheric areas that support the character by describing the world he lives in.

Similar effects can also be achieved in black and white (plus a shade or two of flat grays) when ink is our "weapon of choice." In such case the execution would rely more on a sense of abstraction of light and shape (see pages 078–079), but the use of a full gray scale will always allow you to be more realistic and descriptive within a sense of abstraction. You have a choice of depicting reality as it looks vs. reality as it feels. A pure representation of physical items without an emotional point of view can be worthless.

Fig. 4.17: The first thing to do is have a clear idea of the atmosphere you need for the shot and put it down in a very simple, basic way that anyone can look at and get it.

Figs. 4.18 and **4.19**: Once you have that on your first pass, commit to the idea. You can also blend in some areas a bit if the brushstrokes there are too obvious by selecting the desired area/s, then copy/paste them so they become an additional, separate layer. Blur them a bit with the use of Gaussian or Motion Blur (in the Filters menu), and then slightly erase the edges of this new layer a bit with a reduced opacity eraser tool so that no hard edges are seen.

fig. 4.17

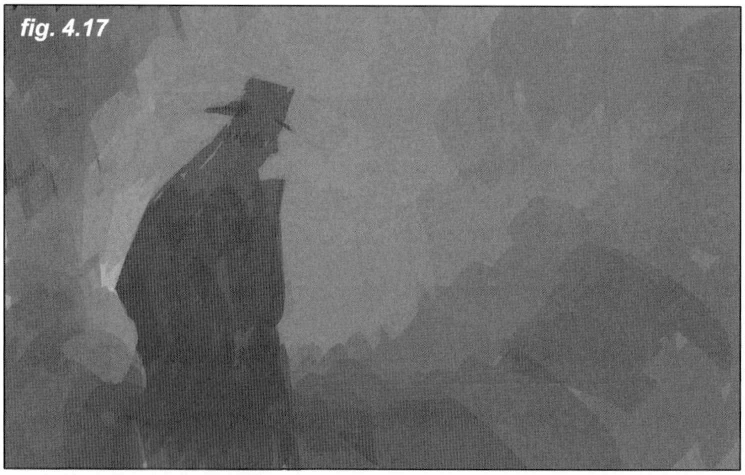

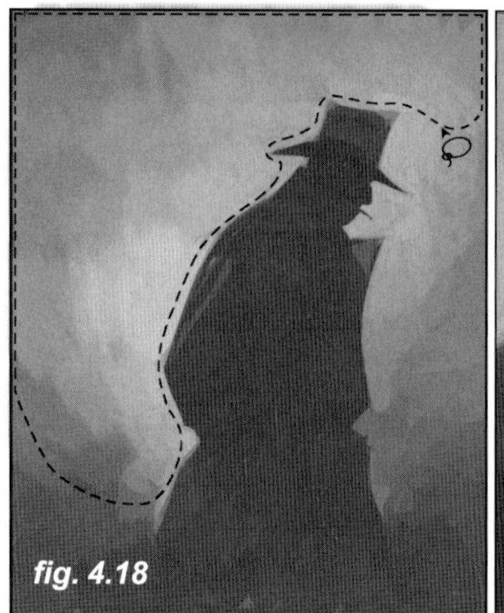
fig. 4.18

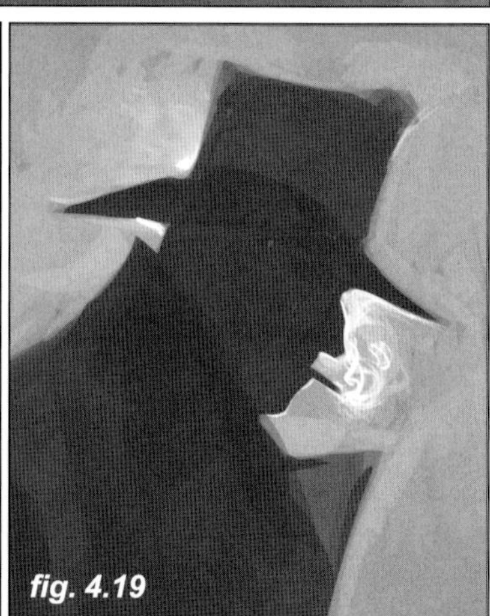
fig. 4.19

Figs. 4.20 to **4.21**: A step-by-step view of the background building's rendering: Use a loose brush on it so that it better integrates with the freehand and atmospheric feel of the overall image, while trying to anchor its architectural sense by using tools like the Rectangular Marquee (**fig. 4.22**) to make sure that the vertical rows of windows are solid and aren't distracting by looking too organic or out of balance.

You can then render the brighter lights that define each window as more freehand and energetic horizontal brushstrokes, while the overall verticals are solid (**fig. 4.21**), so that the balance between architectural and freestyle is established.

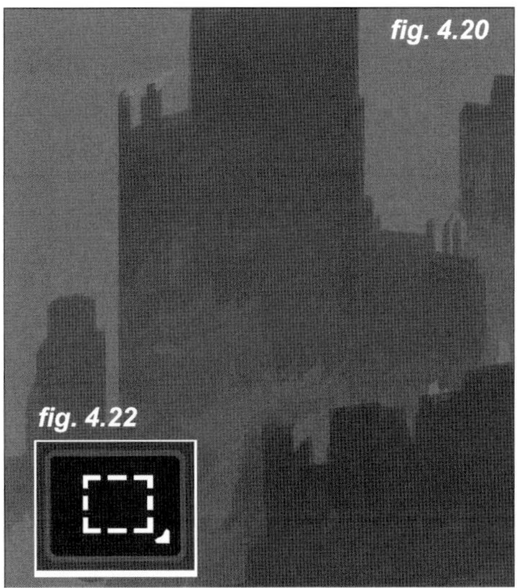

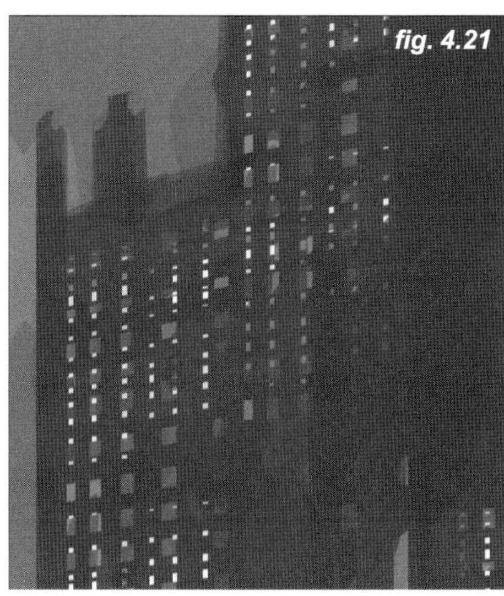

Fig. 4.23: To create the vibrant glow of the city lights, you can slightly move, diminish, or enlarge the rectangular marquee selections for second and even third brushstroke passes at different intensities and opacities of white. This way, the bright glow of the lights is not just a single steady item but has a vibration to it, suggesting a flicker.

All of this work has been executed with a brush at 70 percent of its opacity so that, as talked about on page 109, you can accumulate layers to progressively achieve bolder statements with a touch of irregularity, which makes everything more lively and vibrant.

At the very end, some windows have been knocked down a bit with the use of the Eraser tool to emphasize the different brightness of different windows (**fig. 4.25**, in the white frames).

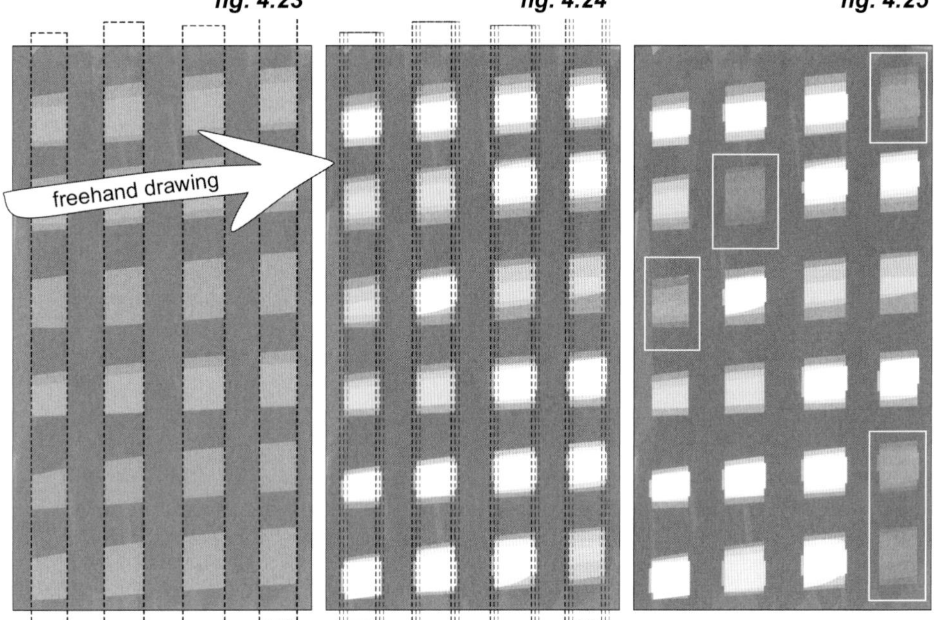

Figs. 4.26 and **4.27**: Two steps of a rain scene show the difference between this rendering and the one in **Fig. 3.71**, page 087.

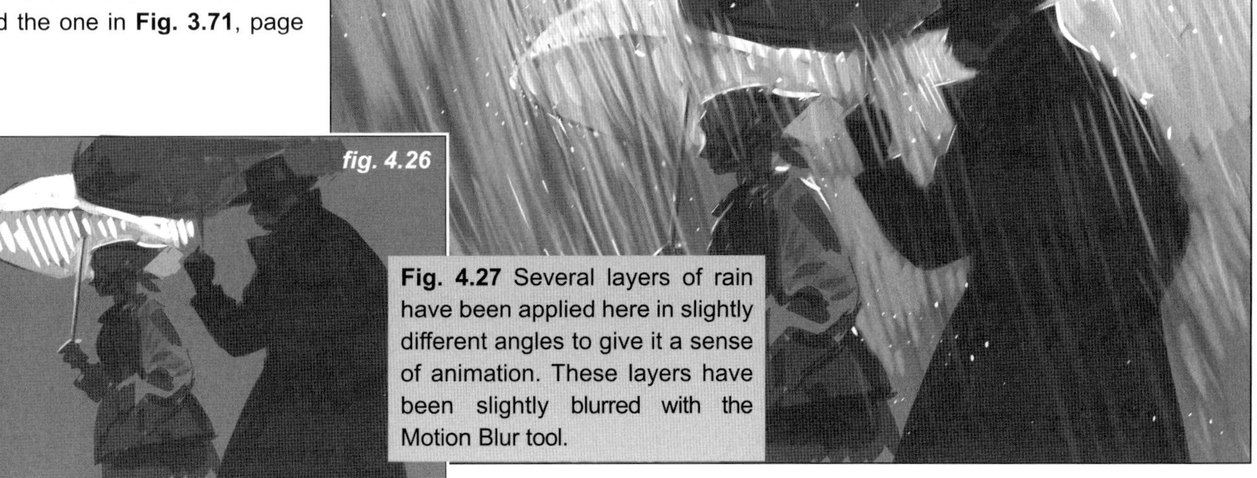

Fig. 4.27 Several layers of rain have been applied here in slightly different angles to give it a sense of animation. These layers have been slightly blurred with the Motion Blur tool.

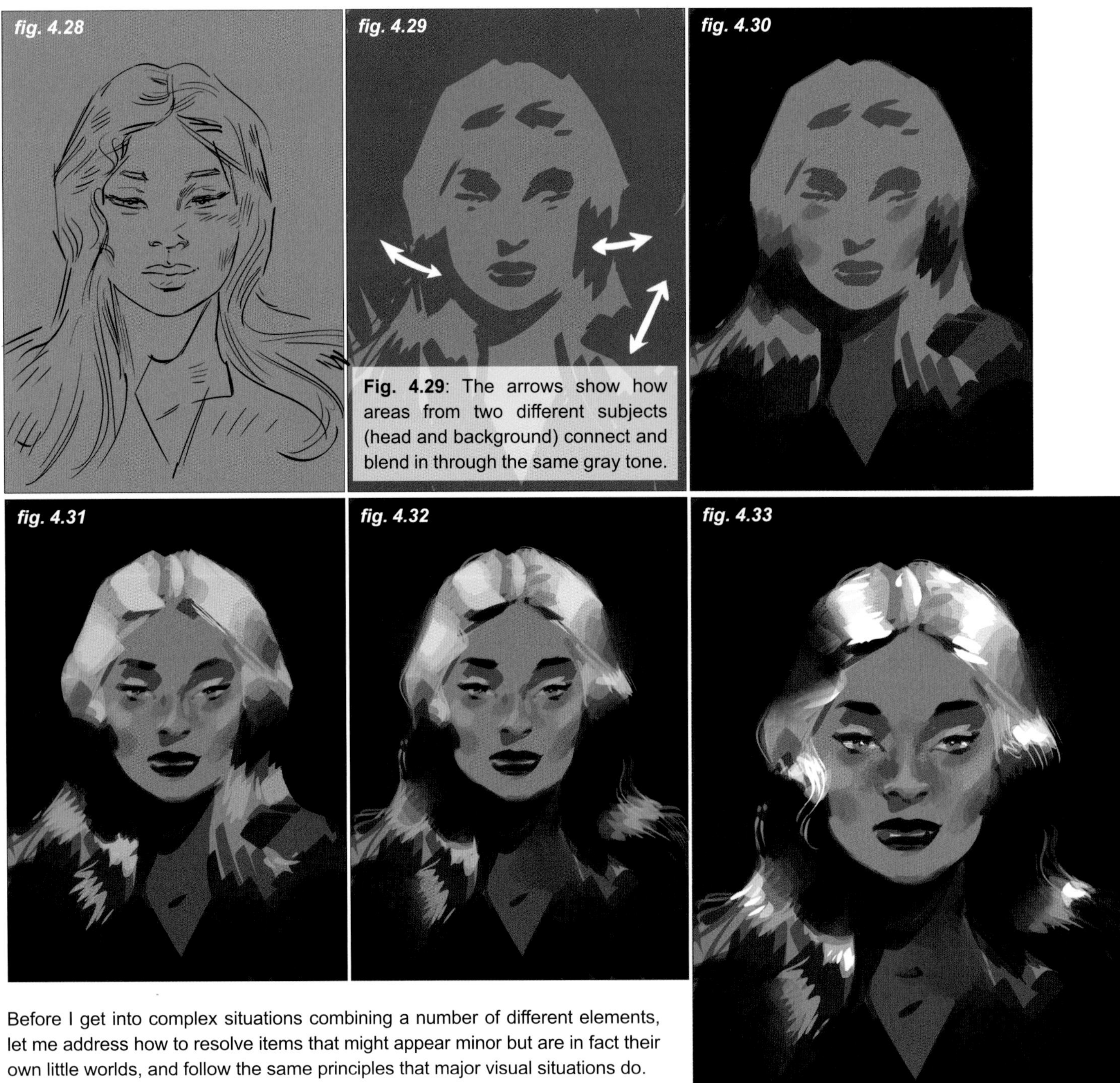

Fig. 4.29: The arrows show how areas from two different subjects (head and background) connect and blend in through the same gray tone.

Before I get into complex situations combining a number of different elements, let me address how to resolve items that might appear minor but are in fact their own little worlds, and follow the same principles that major visual situations do.

Whenever you use a gray scale, focus on getting the broad sense of "light and volume" right so that the result is a credible image. Further details can be applied where necessary to explain what the scene and the moment are about, leaving more unresolved areas to be addressed later, as you will see in different examples.

Figs. 4.28 to **4.39** show how to build from a mid-gray tone by emphasizing the darker areas and finally punching out the brighter accents in a way that the character and background feel part of the same world rather than a collage of separate pieces.

To darken certain areas, select the desired area, copy/paste this selection so it becomes an additional layer. Turning this new layer transparent by switching it into "Multiply," automatically darkens the area (more or less, depending on its opacity).

Finally, slightly go along the edge of the selection with a mid-opacity eraser brush to soften its sharp, distracting edge.

fig. 4.34

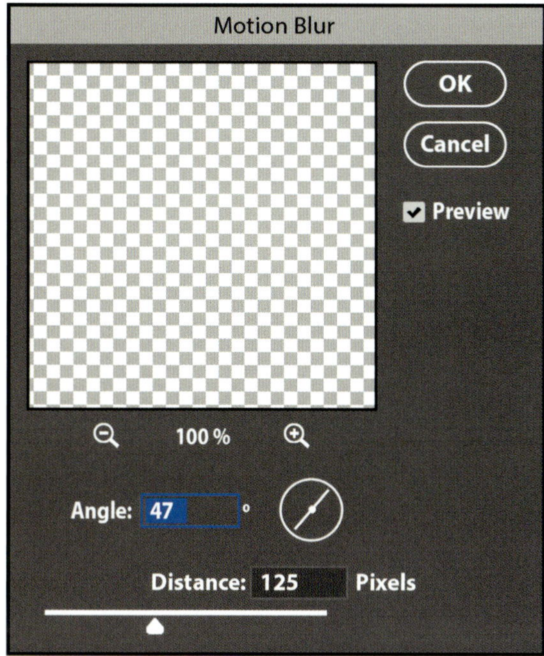

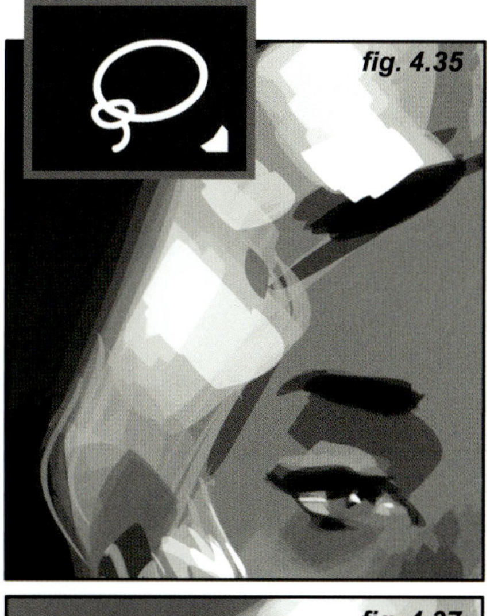

fig. 4.35

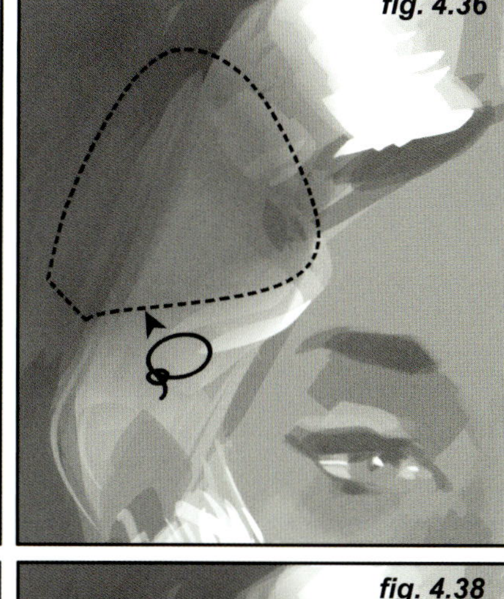

fig. 4.36

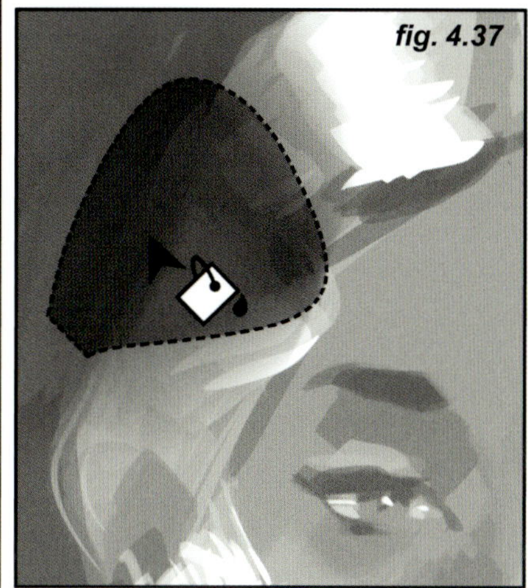

fig. 4.37

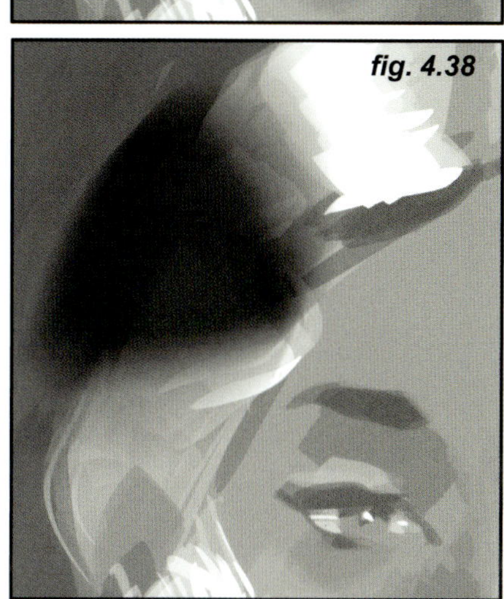

fig. 4.38

Fig. 4.35: This bright patch of hair in the center was brought down a bit tonally so that it wouldn't draw too much attention.

Rather than going at it with more brushwork the following was done: a new layer was created on top, given a "Multiply" quality out of the Layers menu to make it transparent, at an opacity of only 45 percent so you can still see the underlying brushwork and texture.

Fig. 4.36: Then, on this transparent layer, the area to be darkened was selected, extending it into the dark background behind the model so that both areas would blend together. This way, she doesn't feel like a light cardboard cutout on top of a dark background.

Fig. 4.37: The selected area was filled in with a mid-gray value with the Paint Bucket tool.

Fig. 4.38: The area was then deselected so that the edges of the shade of gray it contained could be blurred (using the Motion Blur effect in the Blur menu). In this case, the Blur tool was applied with an angle of 47 degrees and a distance of 125 Pixels (see **Fig. 4.34**).

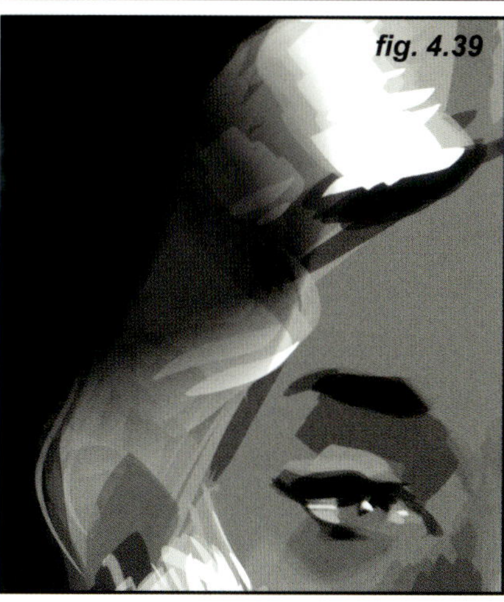

fig. 4.39

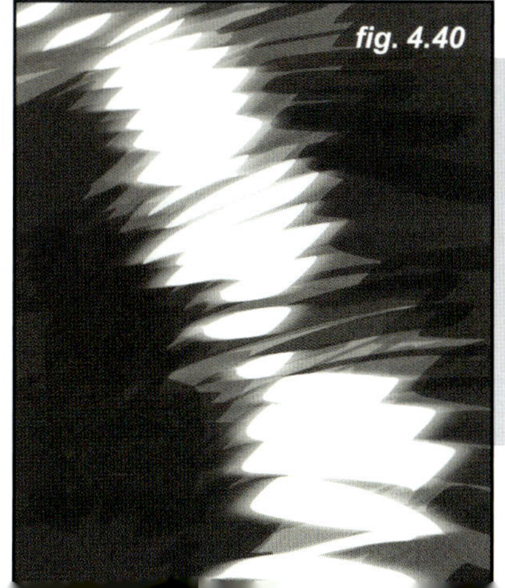

fig. 4.40

A similar effect was used in **Fig. 4.40** to achieve the silky subtlety of this lock of wavy hair.

In this case it is about the shiny reflection that was worked in with a slanted 100 percent opaque brush (see pages 074–075) on a layer also 100 percent opaque, with a quick zigzag motion imitating the hair's direction. (Refer to pages 076–077, where the direction of the stroke helps define surface planes, etc.)

After that, a Motion Blur effect was applied to create this glare/glow effect that drives this gold-like appearance home.

A BACKLIT LANDSCAPE

Let's see now how to apply all these principles to an actual location painting.

Fig. 4.41 is our reference image.

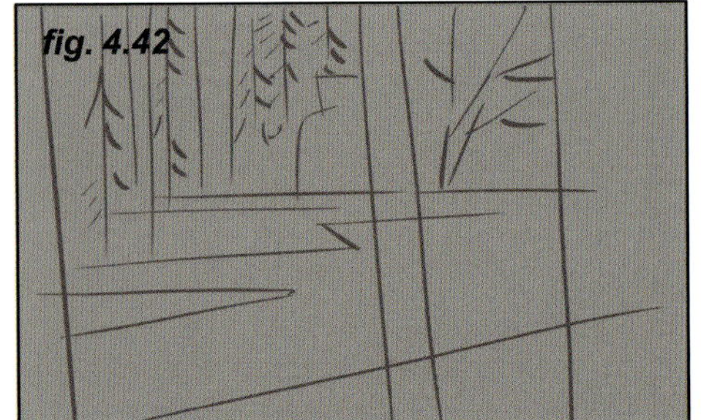
fig. 4.42

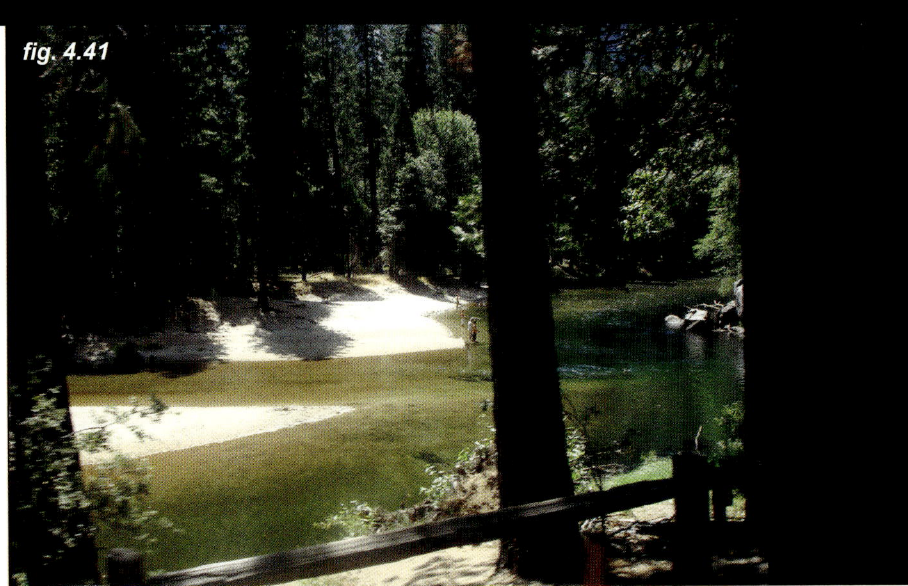
fig. 4.41

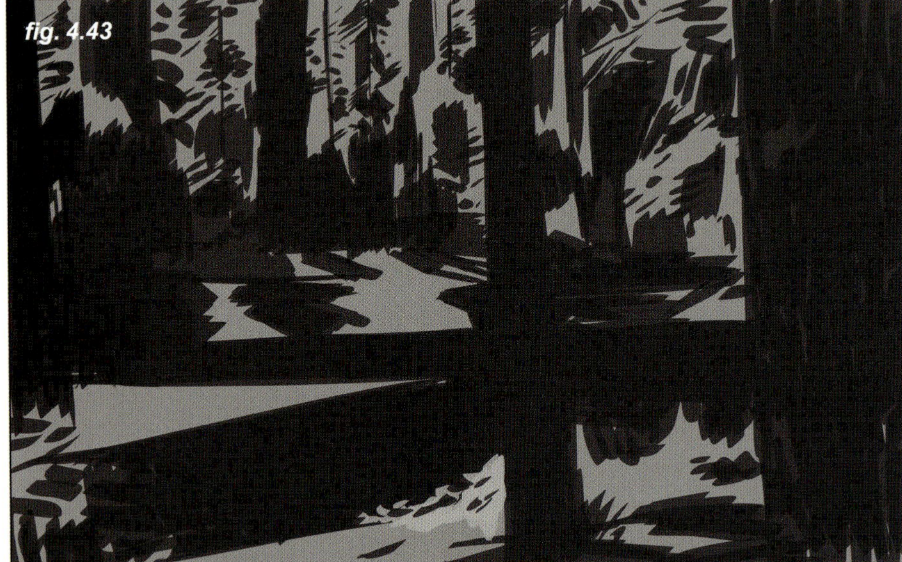
fig. 4.43

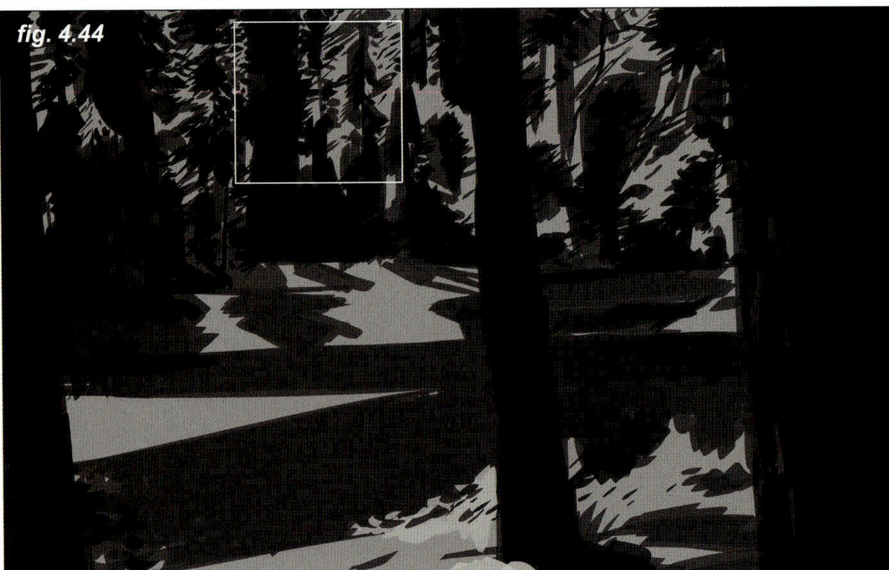
fig. 4.44

Fig. 4.42 (step 1): Start with a midtone on your canvas. It is advisable to draw a brief line sketch establishing the situation of the main landmarks and areas of light and dark, not any detail. Do not overdo it, you don't want to get stuck in "branches and leafs" details yet, just indicate dynamics and direction.

Fig. 4.43 (step 2): Look at the reference with squinted eyes (see Chapter 11, "Notes on freehand drawing and sketching" in *Framed Perspective Volume 1*) and do a quick first pass of how the main areas of light and shadow as well as the main shapes work.

Fig. 4.44 (step 3): On your second pass, accentuate the darker areas and some specific shapes (branches etc.), adding some depth and complexity to the scene. (See detail in **Fig. 4.45**.)

Fig. 4.46 (step 4): Now, further rendering is done, including abstract leafs and midtones. (See detail **Fig. 4.47**).

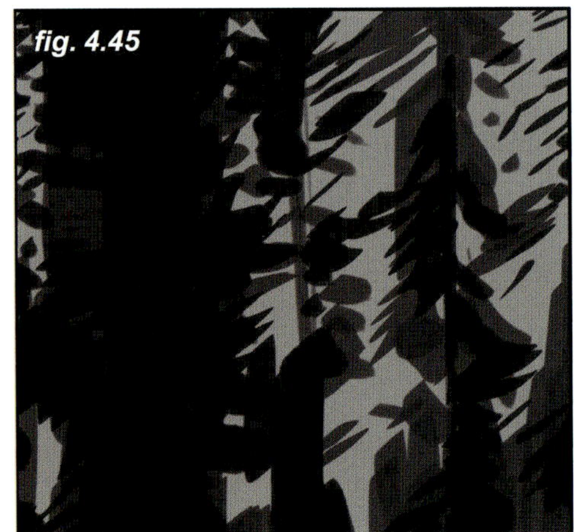
fig. 4.45

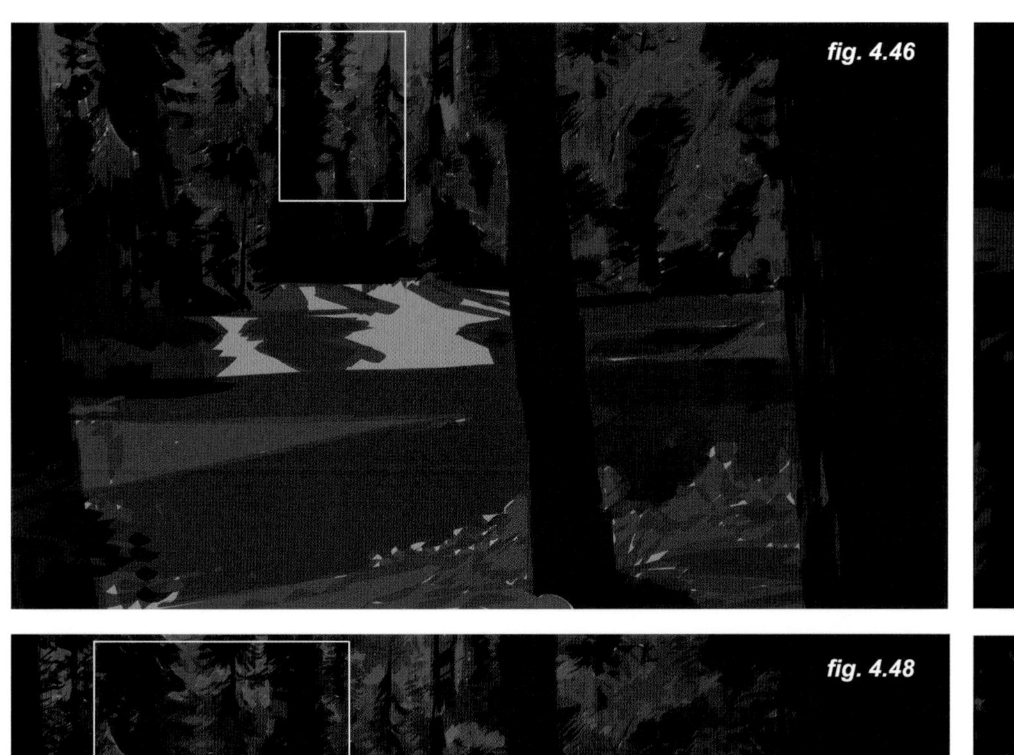
fig. 4.46

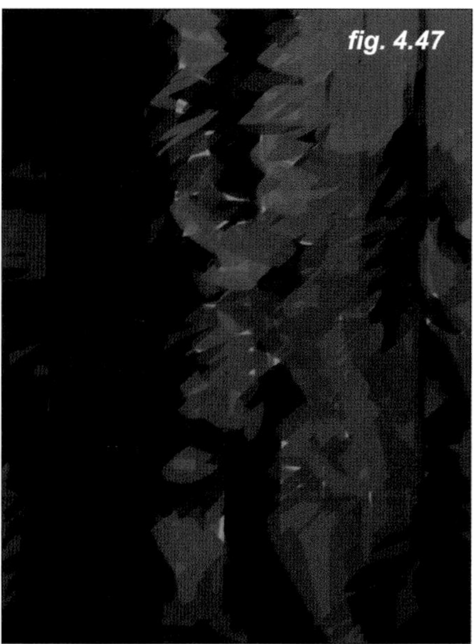
fig. 4.47

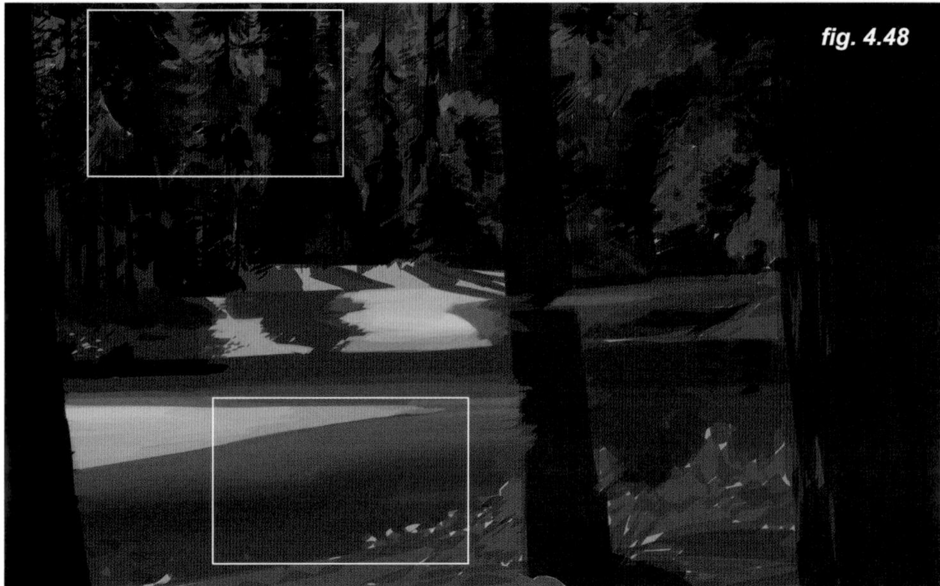
fig. 4.48

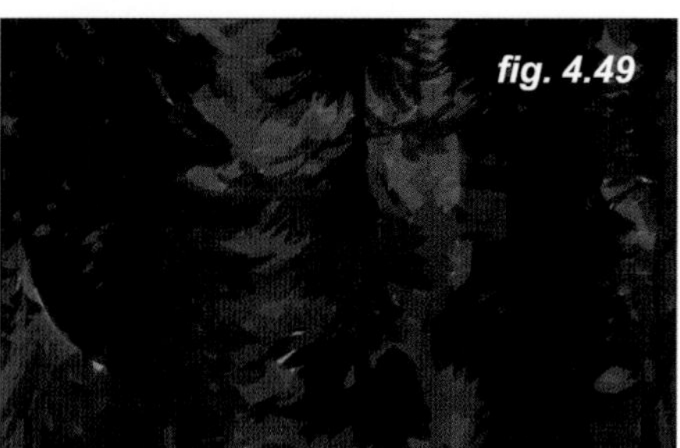
fig. 4.49

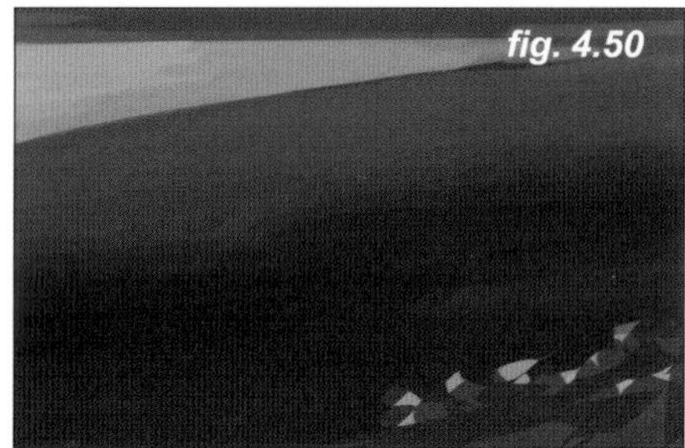
fig. 4.50

Fig. 4.48 (step 5): Time to start defining a sense of branches, even though vaguely, with the ones most visible in the reference model. Take into account you don't need to draw every single branch as it appears in reality. Just define the most obvious one so they read properly at a first or second glance. This will give viewers the information they need to realize they are looking at a dense forest (**figs. 4.49** and **4.50**). After that, their brains will automatically fill in the blanks and make the whole area feel full, give the impression of a forest, without you having to do all the work. In fact, drawing too much of it would be just distracting. What we draw on paper is not reality but an expression of it. We don't have "trees" on paper; we have lines and areas of ink representing shapes, lights and darks, not a reality but an abstract expression of it.

Fig. 4.50 shows the first steps of establishing the main tonal areas of the river's water, on which you will later develop further details.

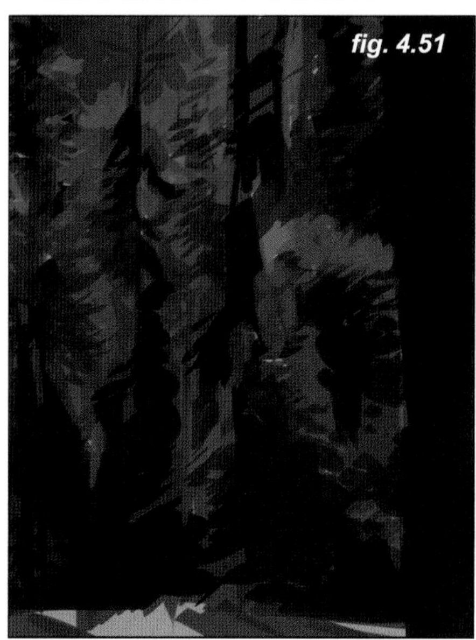
fig. 4.51

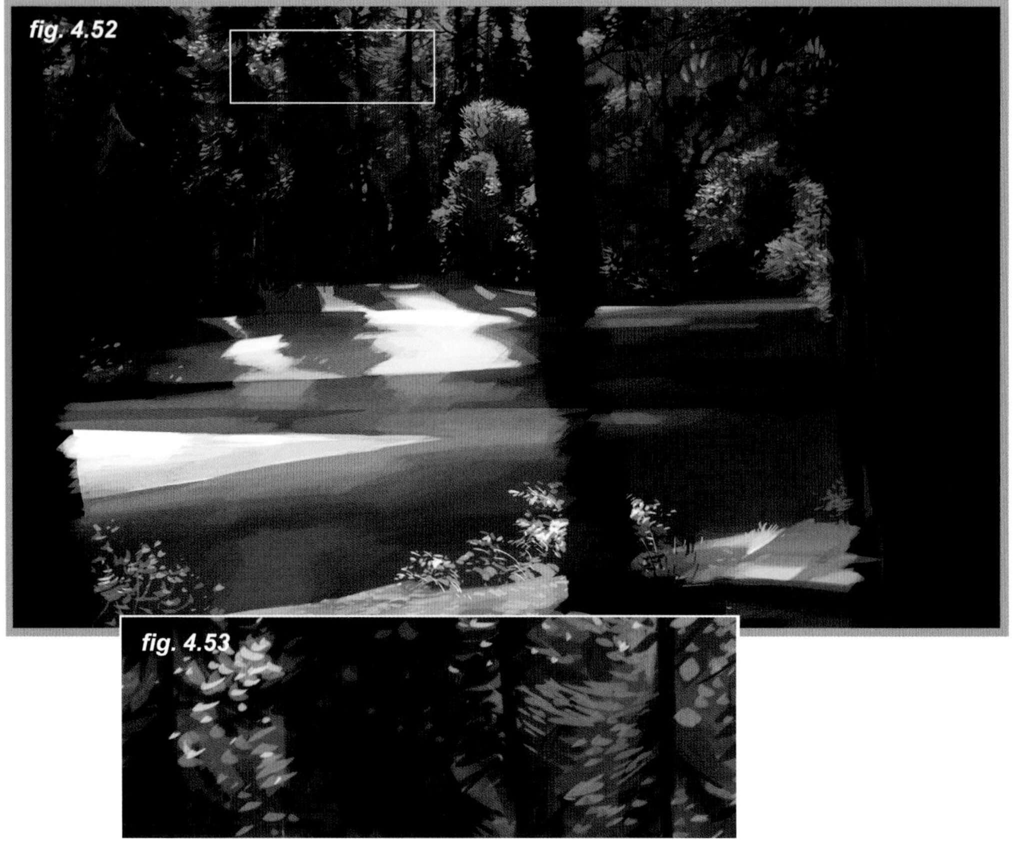

Figs. 4.52 and **4.53**: Now, bring up the lighter-toned leaves, the ones that reflect the sunlight most, from "almost" white (since pure white would make leaves in the distance appear to be close to us, breaking the sense of depth and perspective) to mid and lighter grays. This lighter tone work will also help define the shape of some key branches even further, so that viewers get the idea of a forest at a quick glance/read.

Keep in mind to always try to group things as much as possible. This also applies to masses of foliage and other specific item areas.

Also the value of the sand (lighter) and tonal subtleties, such as within the trees' shadows on the sand (center left of image) where the lower part has been brightened up, add to the atmosphere.

Remember, the sharper contrasts and more extreme values (black, white) are usually in the foreground and mid grays mostly stay in the more atmospheric background.

Fig. 4.54: The finished piece.

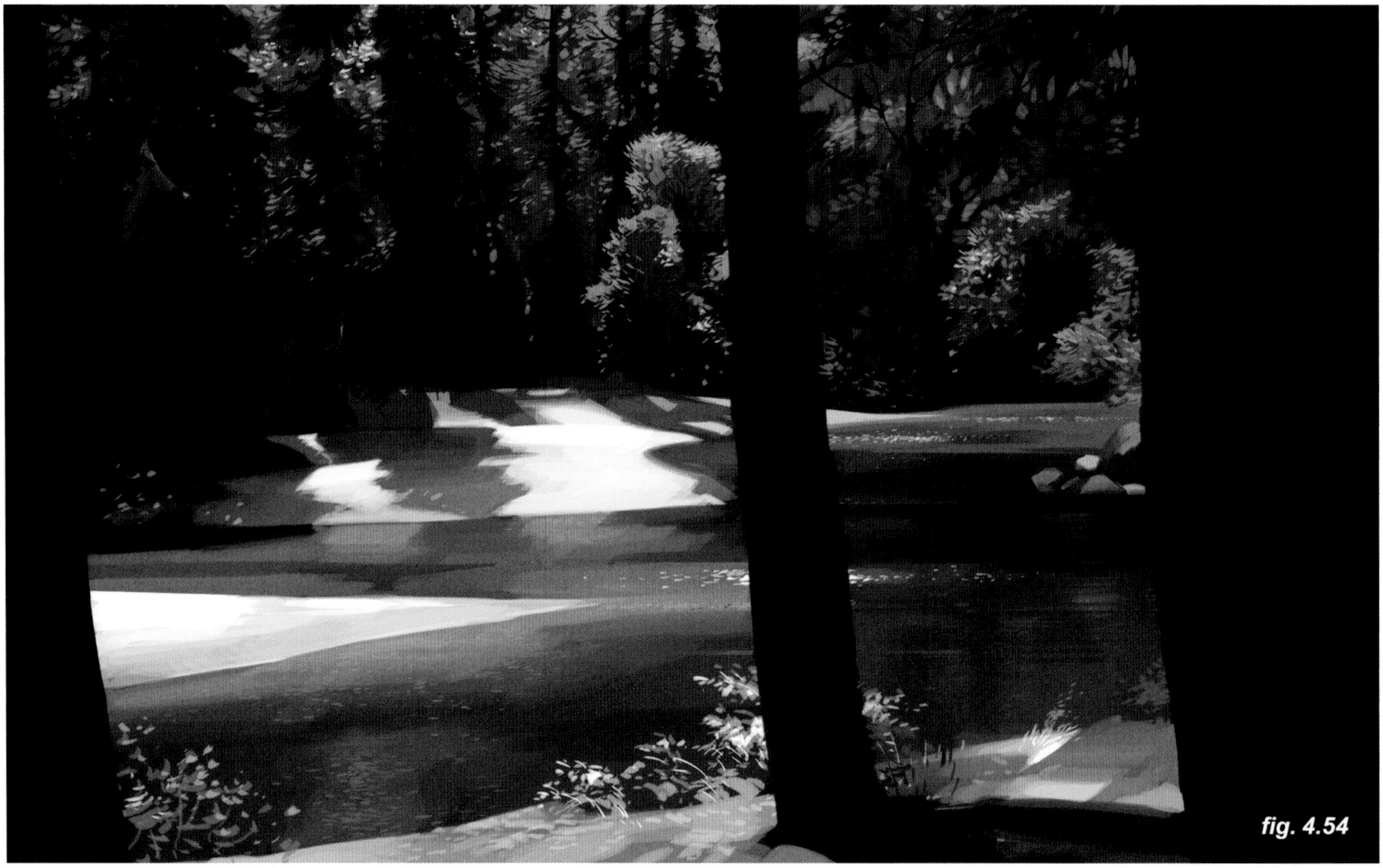

fig. 4.54

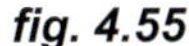

fig. 4.55

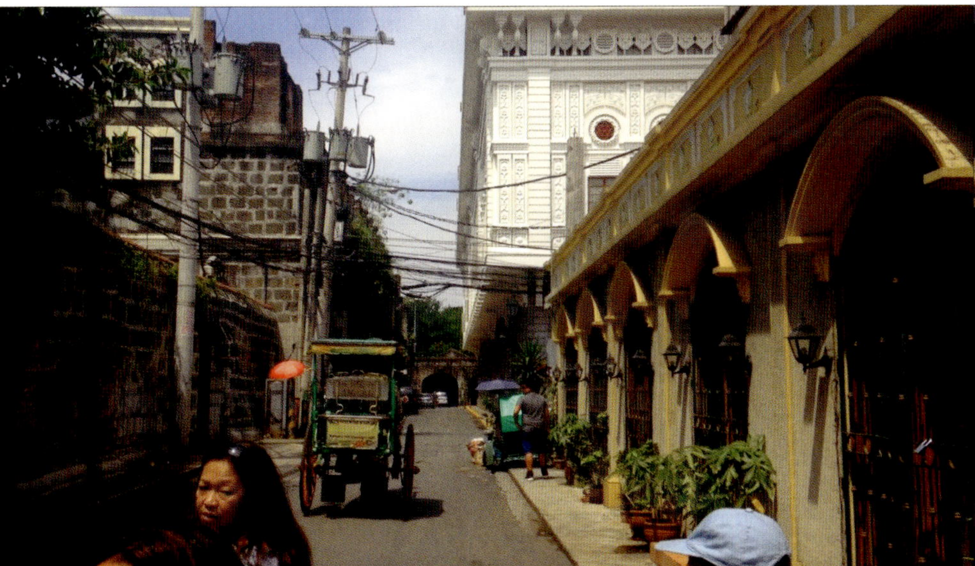

fig. 4.56

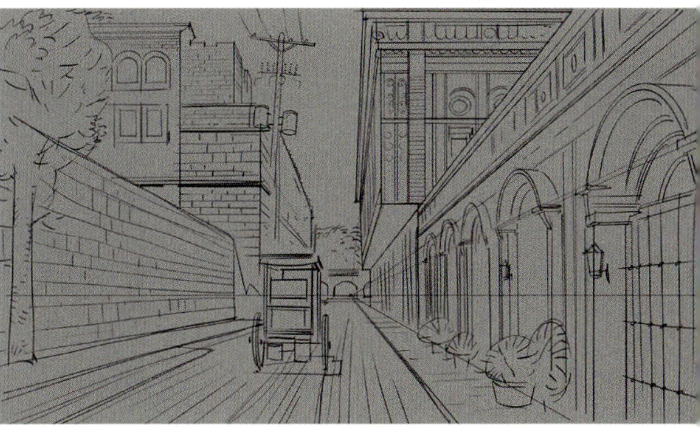

Fig. 4.56: As usual, I start with a drawing on a mid-gray background as a primer. Always keep tone and drawing in separate layers in case you need to modify one or the other. When it comes to architecture, a solid understanding of perspective is a must.

Fig. 4.57: After this, squint your eyes and tackle the main areas of light, dark, and mid grays to establish a base. I usually recommend staying within a range of grays at this point; as mentioned before, I tend to keep the extreme lights and darks for the end. This way I start by getting a sense of air and atmosphere to then later throw a one-two punch with the major accents at the end.

So far this image has been worked out with basically the grays only.

fig. 4.57

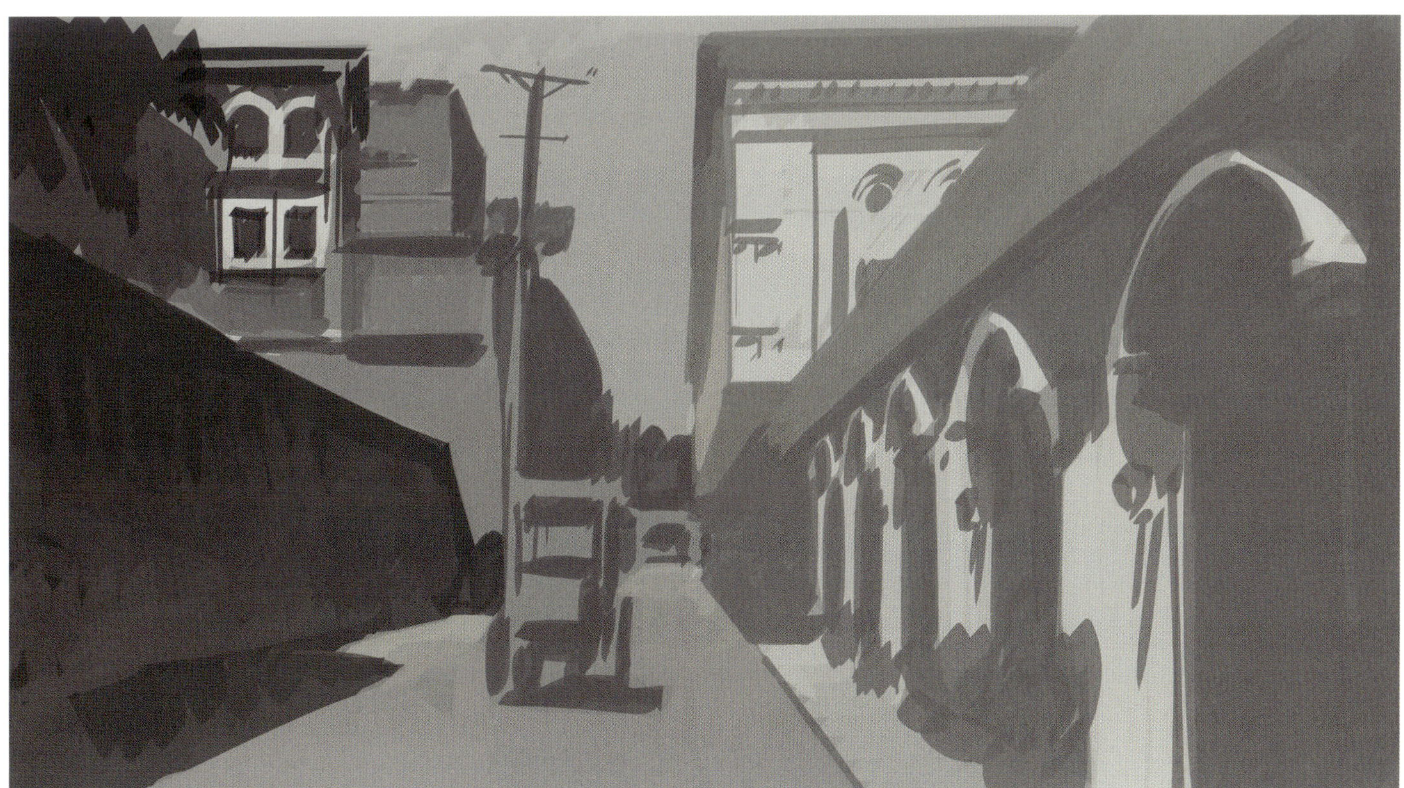

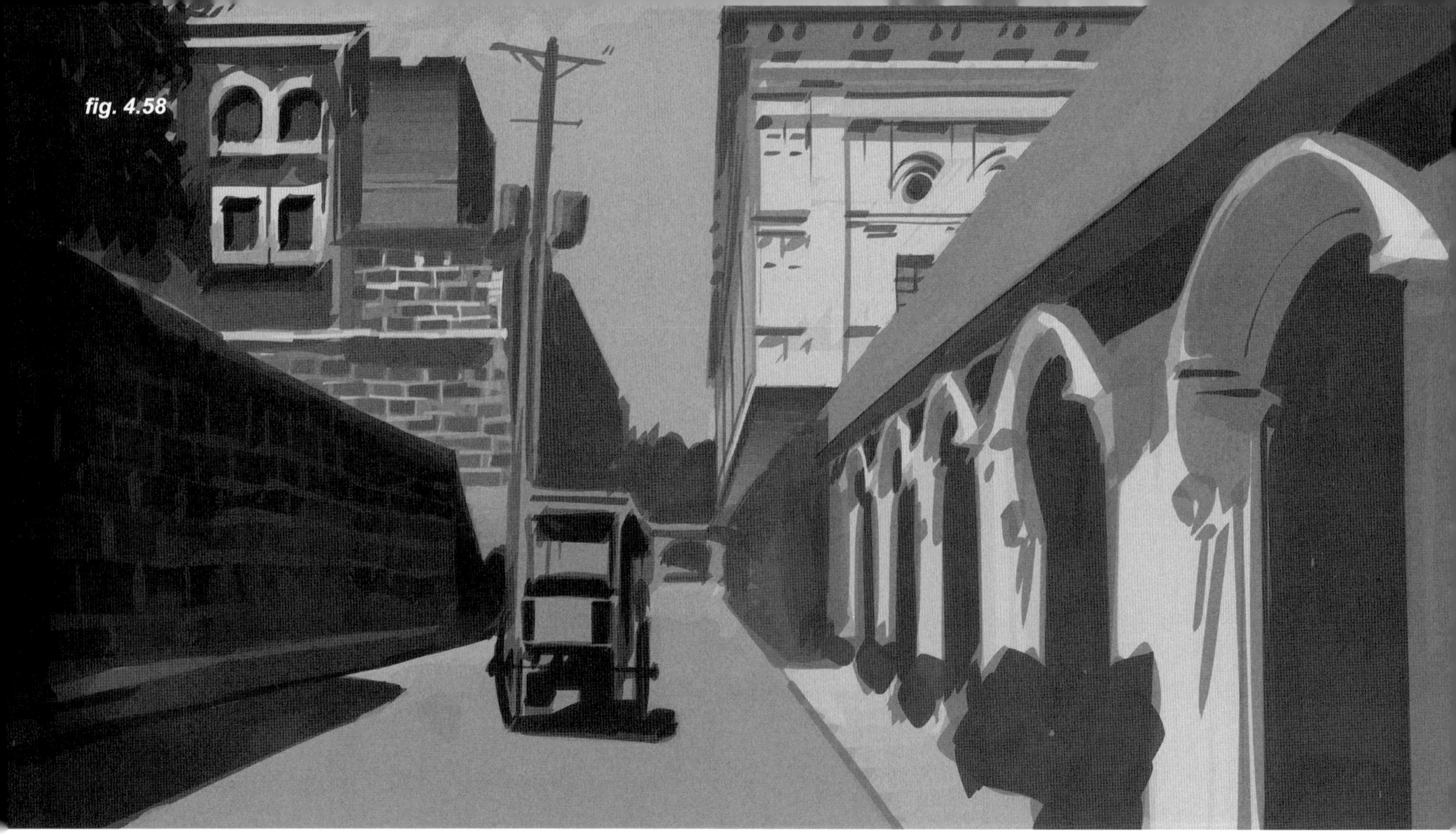

fig. 4.58

Fig. 4.58: See how the first significant accent of darker grays has just been added in the portals (arches) to the right and with some brick texture on the wall to the left. To paint the latest image the usual round brush has been compressed (see **Fig. 4.59** and pages 074–075) so that it became a thick vertical. With it, a simple and brief horizontal stroke will suffice for each brick.

Fig. 4.59: Here some of the first real darks are introduced, as well as some detail in the foreground (see the top above the arches) and the tree to the left. Notice how they blend in: the intent is to communicate a vibrant sense of realism not through detail but through believable and balanced lighting. See *Framed Ink* Chapter 2, Drawing and composing a single image basics.

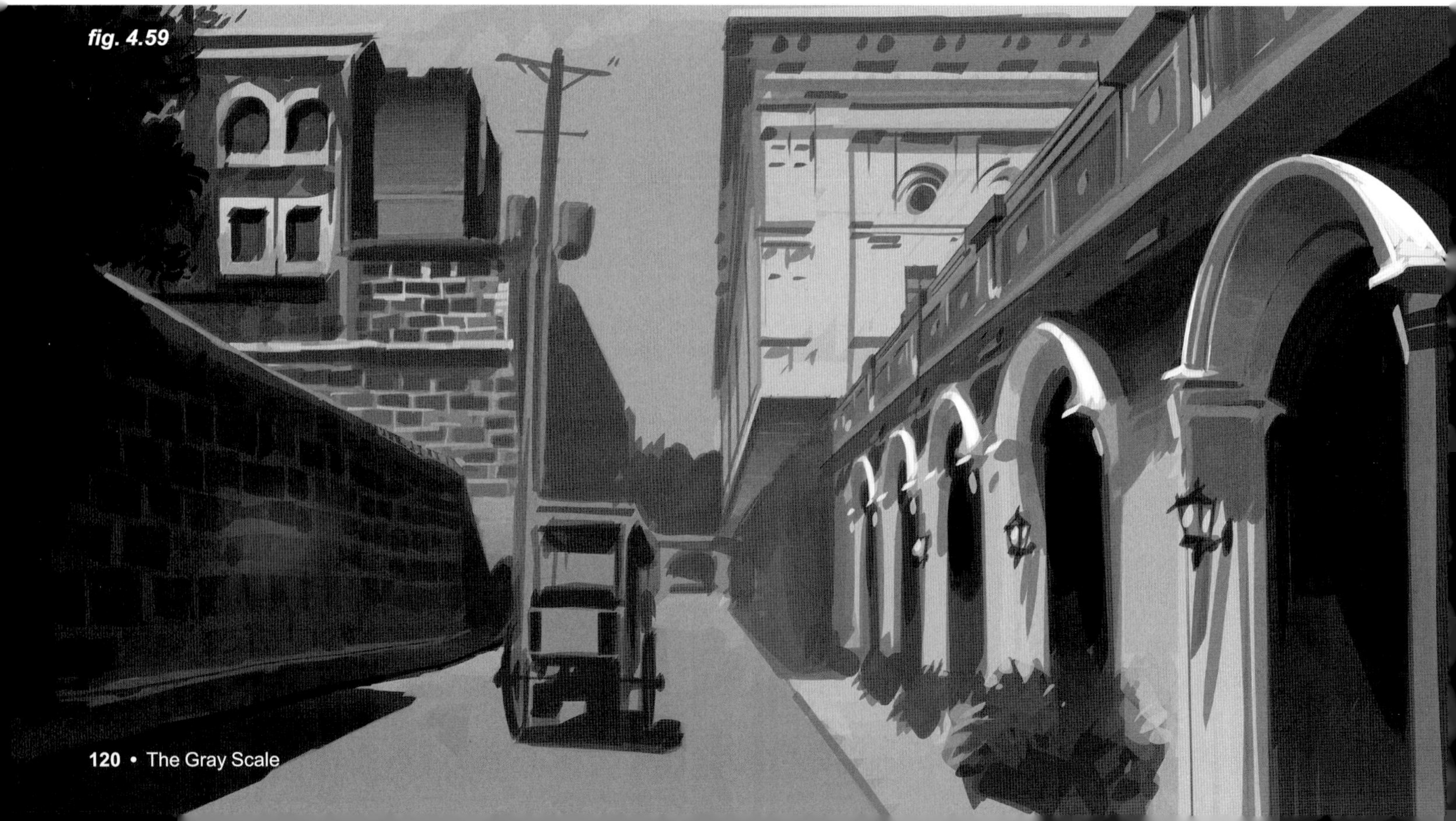

fig. 4.59

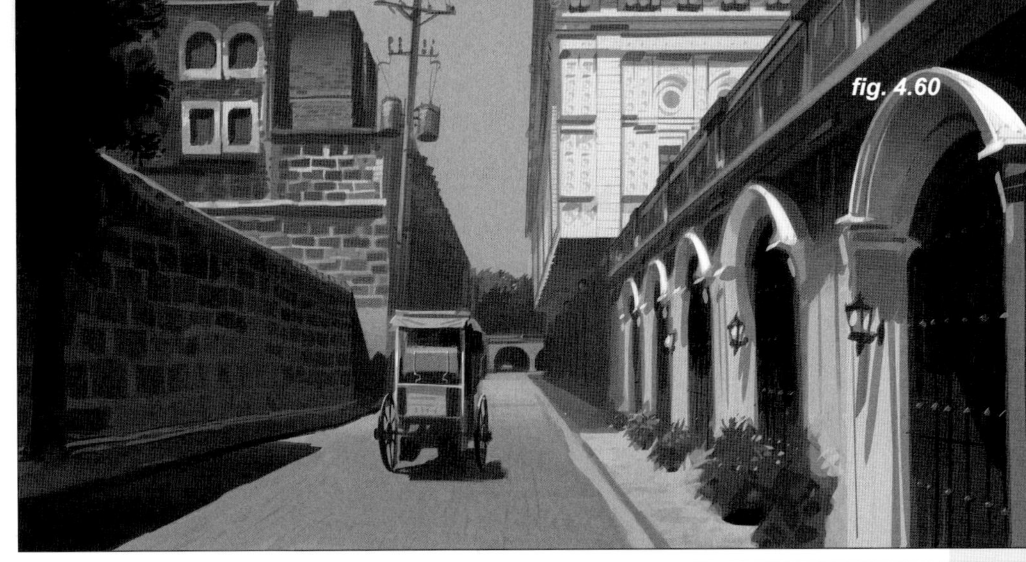
fig. 4.60

Fig. 4.60: I made sure at this point that the major planes are separated for depth. For example, the foreground building to the right is dark up against the lighter, (as an overall block) tall building behind it.

Keep adding detail, some loose and smaller (for distance) bricks at the top of the dark building on the left, next to the power lines, as well as the facade of the white building to the right (in a very subtle, atmospheric way).

Fig. 4.64: At this point some final general adjustments have been made to accentuate depth. The building with the arches has been darkened a bit, especially at the top by selecting its facade, created a new layer above it, throwing in a gray to white gradation (gray at the top), and then turning the layer on "Multiply" (transparent). (See **Fig. 4.63**)

Behind all this, the lighter parts of the back cream-colored building have been selected, a new layer created, and these selections filled in with white. After that, the opacity of this layer was reduced a lot, so that the details are still visible but the overall feel is much brighter.

Fig. 4.64: As a final detail, the wheels of the calesa (cart) have been more tightly defined. I wanted to make sure that, given its foreshortened point of view, it still reads fast as this type of old vehicle.

Fig. 4.65: A final overall contrast push was given using minor adjustments through the menu Image/Adjustments/ Levels.

fig. 4.61

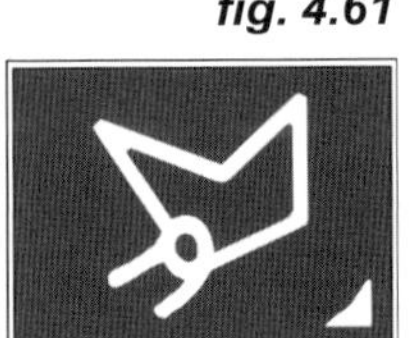

fig. 4.62

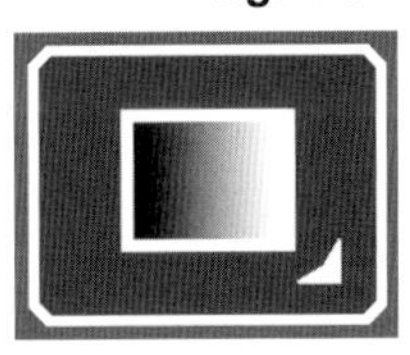

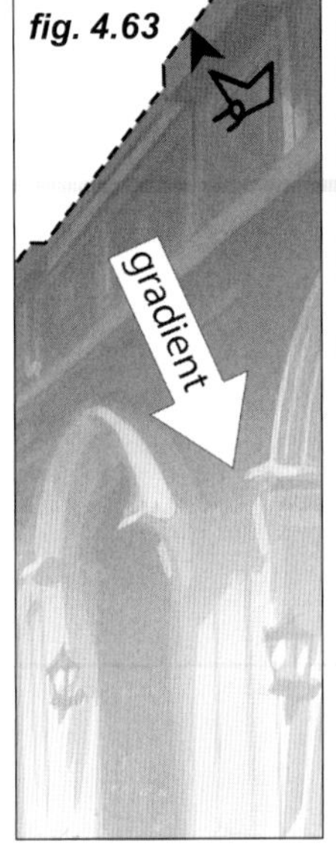

fig. 4.63

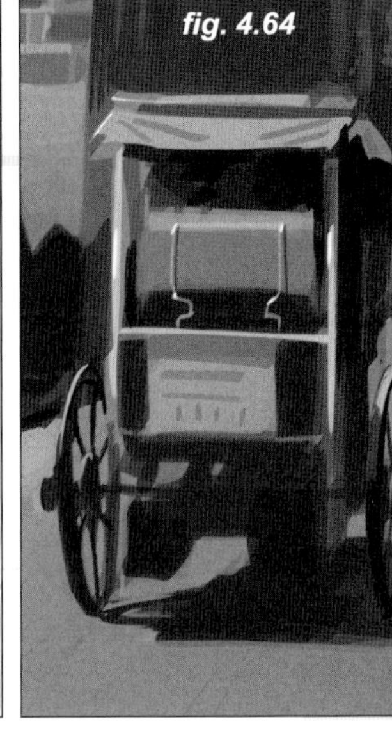
fig. 4.64

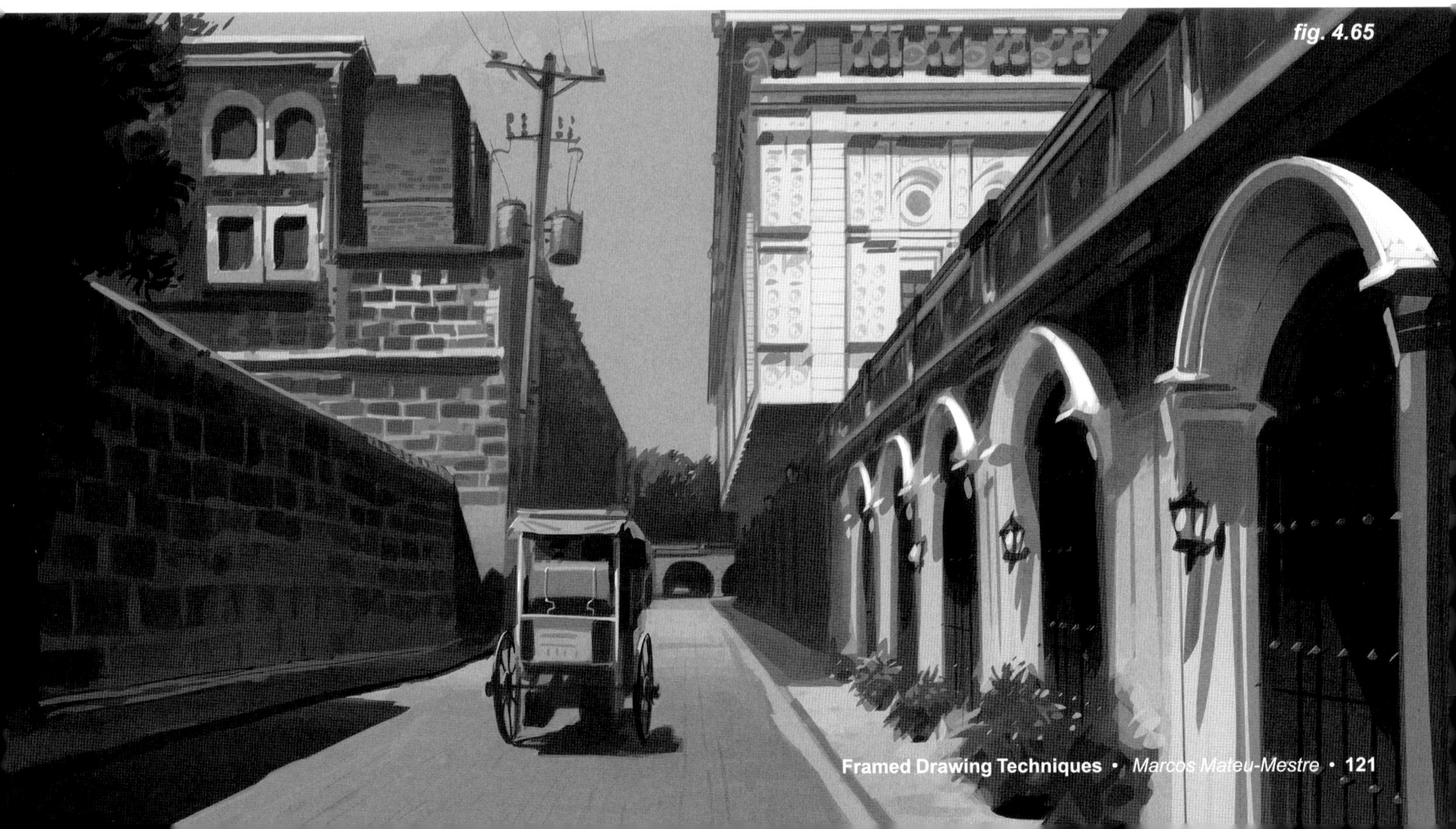

fig. 4.65

Once you know what your goals are and the steps you need to take to achieve them, then there is the how to do it. Two things are especially important: to free your mind and to always have an overall understanding of the job you are working on, so that everything fits into place to tell the bigger picture or story, and does so nicely.

Ultimately, the goal is to deliver a piece that conveys an overall single concept. You are not working on a collection of brushstrokes that mean nothing; it's about the general message and the tone of the energy it delivers. Every element (brushstroke, line, contrast, etc.) needs to fit in so as to deliver a cohesive work, which needs to be appropriate for the moment in the story.

Once you have this in mind, try to put all this down "on paper" in the most appealing, visually attractive way you can. And for this, working with a free, relaxed mind will play a major role.

I always recommend to draw and paint with no attachment: like you can throw away the piece if you don't like what you see. And in the case of digital work, approach as if you could digitally erase a brushstroke or an entire section of the painting if the results are not up to expectations, because you actually can.

Remember to always keep your excitement going. If what you do works, great; if it doesn't, you are learning from your challenges and your mistakes. It really is a win-win situation for us.

When we see the work of an artist that we applaud, one of the things that we feel is admiration at the amount of experience that person has. Well, here is your chance to build your own experience, always having in mind that results can eventually only get better and faster.

As artists, we need to look forward to our future, in both the drawing we are currently doing and our artistic future in general. As long as we are getting closer to what we want, let's just try to enjoy our way and remember that speed comes with knowledge, and knowledge comes with time.

In time you want to have a body of work that represents who you are, because doing things that have meaning to you is the only real shot you have at doing things that will have meaning for others.

Although we live in a social environment that praises the achievement for the achievement, try to do things that have a meaning for you. You want to be able to look back in time and realize that the value of your work is not only about what you have done or how much of it, but how solid and meaningful your whole experience has been. In time you want to have a body of work that represents who you are, because doing things that have meaning to you is the only real shot you have at doing things that will have meaning for others.

In *Framed Ink* I had written that we cannot give what we do not have: I can only give someone 10 dollars if I have 10 dollars. We are in the business of making people vibrate with the results of our efforts. If your experience as an artist is intense with all its positives as well as negatives, that's healthy and you'll be able to communicate them through your art.

So let's be honest and do the things we believe in, otherwise we'll just follow trends and fashions and will not lead in any way, just following what the market puts in front of us as a trendy carrot.

Let's also be the general on our own battlefield by having a global idea of where our work as a whole is at any given time.

Some painters paint with long handle brushes so they don't get caught up in details that would not necessarily progress their global work. The value of a detail within a drawing or painting is only equal to its contribution to the greater scheme.

I've personally seen highly skilled artwork from a technical point of view where everything was very well thought out and accurately responding to some technical concept, yet left me emotionally cold; no excitement was involved in it.

Whenever we try to shock an audience it is because the narrative moment requires it. So we need to know the actual importance and meaning of each section of our art piece within the whole narrative, and its life will come from how it informs and enriches our final goal, not as an independent entity within an ocean of information for the sake of information.

So I suggest exercises to control the temptation of magnifying details that are not that crucial after all, exercises that lead us to pay attention to the whole "battlefield" so that it makes global sense.

The exercises on the following pages refer to a dynamic workflow coming from having a to-do list in our mind that prioritizes working the image as a whole. They start with abstract shapes that respond to your narrative needs while having a constant overall view on your work, being able to pull out and see how everything feels and what kind of primal emotional response your image inspires at any given time, and how you can connect all these concepts with a good, appealing flow. (See my book *Framed Ink* for a more in depth approach to lighting and composition.)

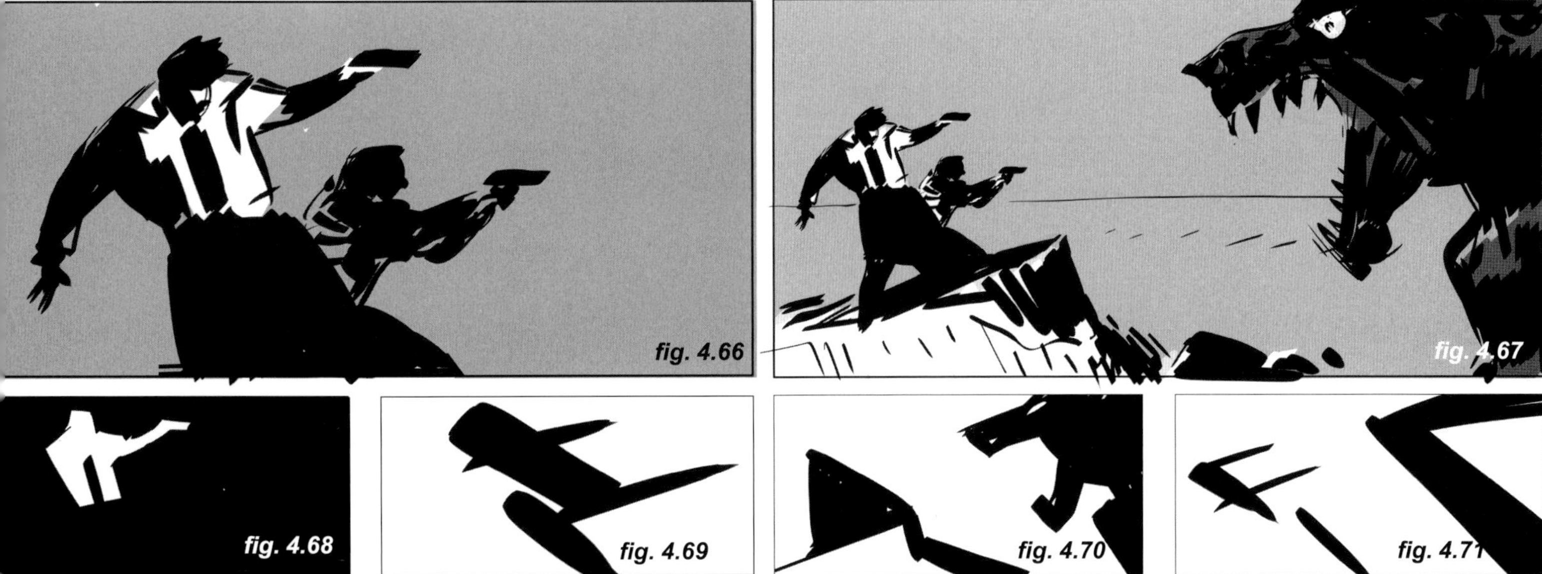

fig. 4.66 fig. 4.67 fig. 4.68 fig. 4.69 fig. 4.70 fig. 4.71

In order to achieve a graceful and meaningful rhythm in your panels, aim to base them on very simple, visually striking and interesting dynamic lines. Each drawing here comes with two additional thumbnails: the first follows how the lighting works; the second, how the dynamic lines of action/tension work. Let's see some examples.

Figs. 4.66 and **4.67**: The big amount of real estate that these two characters occupy within the shot makes it feel like they have more control of the moment. The lighting (**fig. 4.68**) indicates that the white shirt on the foreground character helps give him more prominence, establishing an order of importance so I don't end up with a flat image.

Figs. 4.70 and **4.71**: By opening the frame, I reveal the fellow they are defending themselves from. The two armed men used to be in control, right? Not anymore. The big dark mass on the right comes in at a dynamic diagonal, visually cornering the two guys.

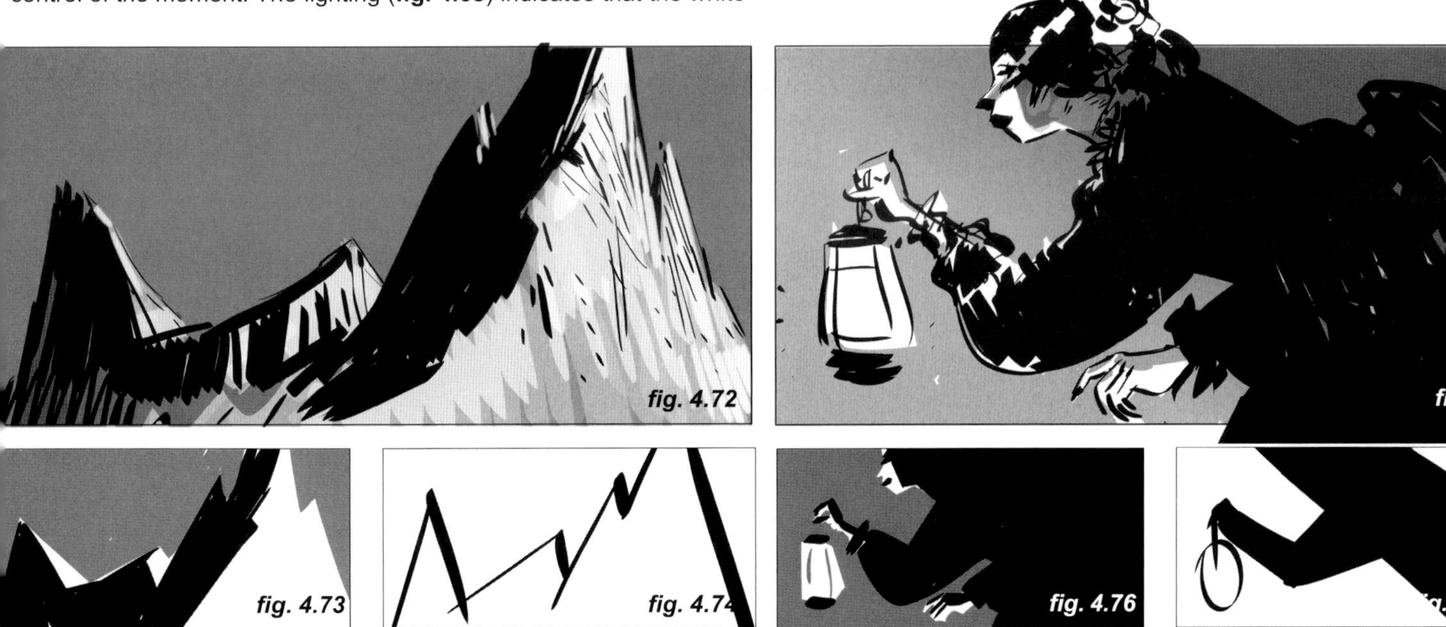

fig. 4.72 fig. 4.73 fig. 4.74 fig. 4.75 fig. 4.76 fig. 4.77

Figs. 4.72, **4.73** and **4.74**: This mountainous shot above creates a spiky, very uneven overall line that crosses the frame from left to right. This, plus the strong contrast between the lit and shadow sides of the spikes make for a tense situation, alerting us that whatever is coming next is no good.

Figs. 4.76 and **4.77**: The intensity of this shot comes from different sides. First, we are very close to the person searching for something in the dark. This allows us to read every minor detail of her expression. The shot is also composed in a diagonal shape, giving an unsettling sense of unbalance.

Finally, the high tonal contrast of the shot, someone in the dark wearing a black dress and with an oil lamp as the only light source, certainly adds to the mystery.

These are examples of ways you should think/approach a raw, dynamic-flowing composition, from lighting and shape point of view. This thinking should definitely affect the way you address a grayscale tone from the base for a narrative shot.

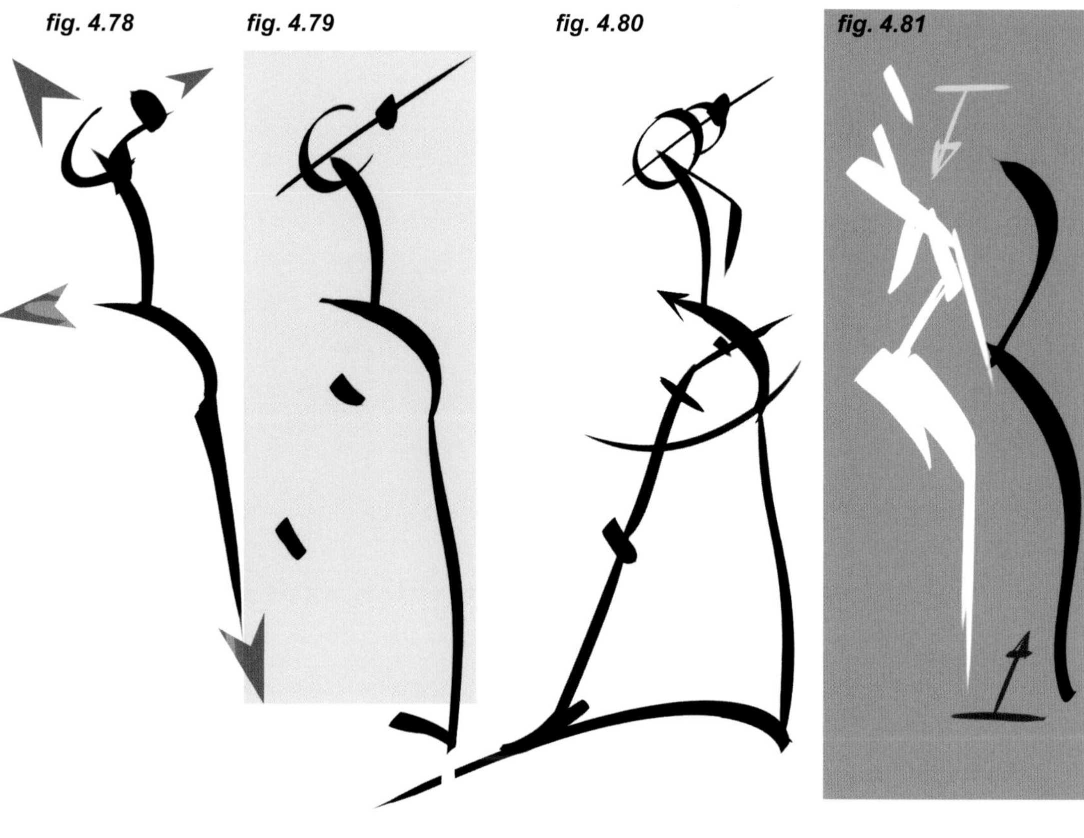

fig. 4.78 *fig. 4.79* *fig. 4.80* *fig. 4.81*

A strong sense of dynamics and proportions will be of the essence before you start an anatomy piece.

First sketch these (**figs. 4.78** to **4.81**) either on what will be the final drawing surface, as a separate sketch, or just make them clear in your head for an understanding of the essentials, while warming up your wrist and hand for the task ahead. You can choose to exaggerate shapes a bit—you are not drawing reality, reality belongs in the physical world—we are drawing a representation, and a version of reality, so pushing shapes a bit will certainly help bring things to life.

(**fig. 4.81**) In this case, even the rim light helps define a sense of movement, so use this to your advantage too.

Figs. 4.82 to **4.84**:
Following previously shared techniques (pages 110–111, as an example), I will visually sculpt this image by creating a midtone first, then working the darker tones by layers and punching the lights at the end.

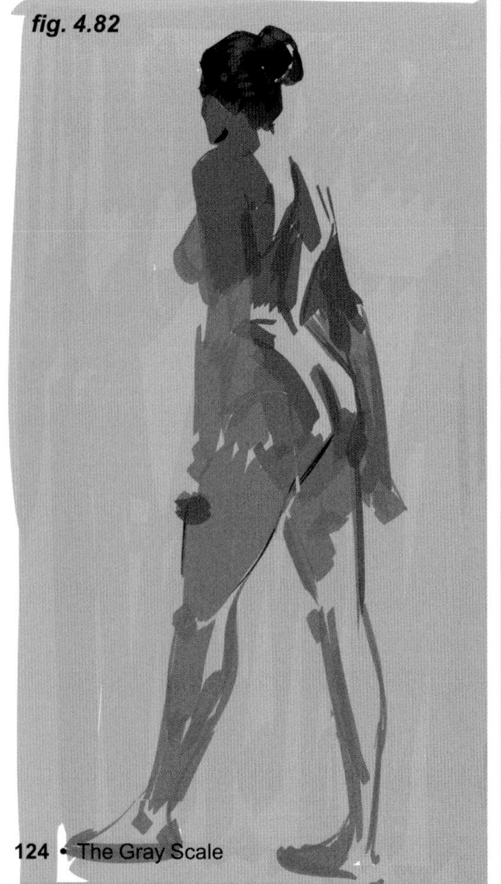

fig. 4.82

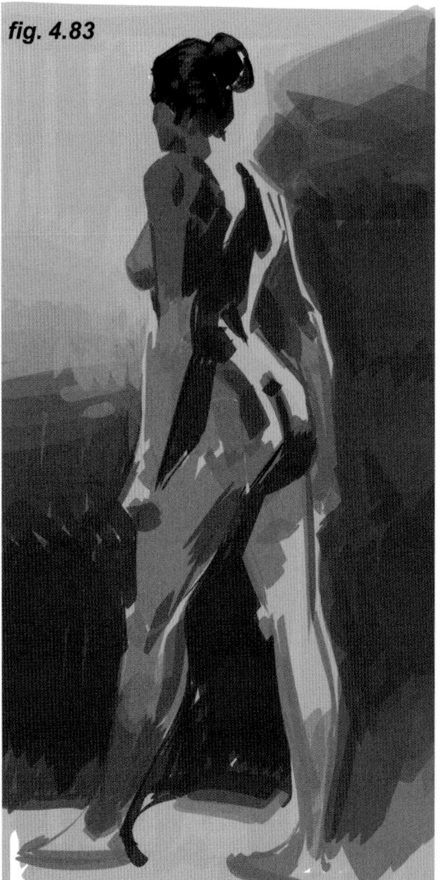

fig. 4.83

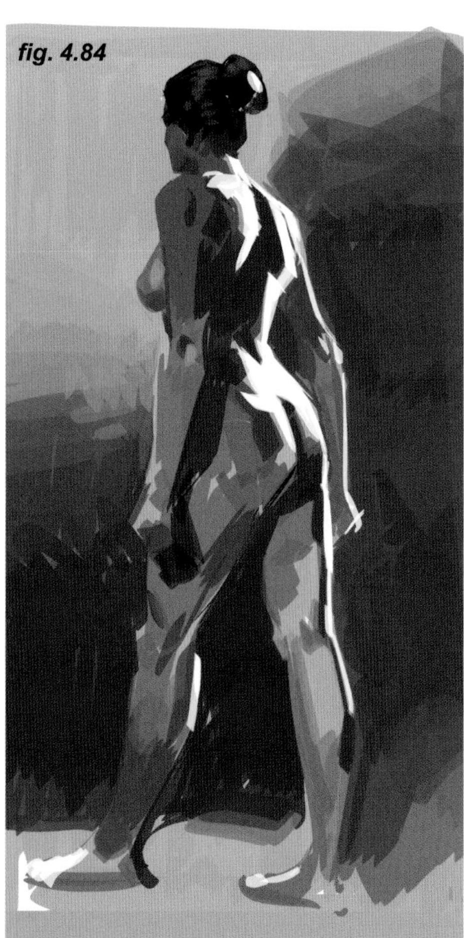

fig. 4.84

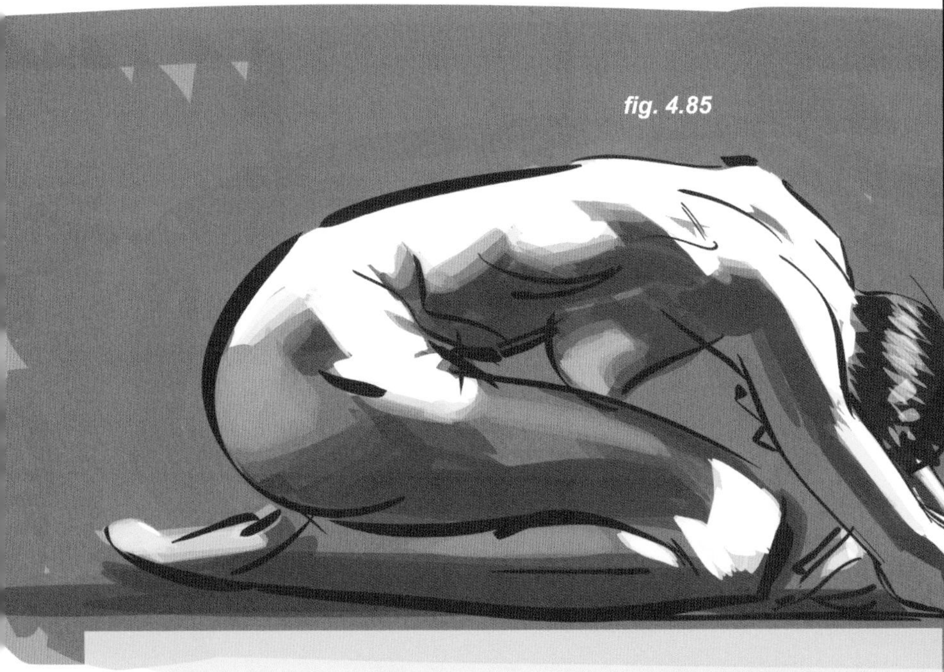

fig. 4.85

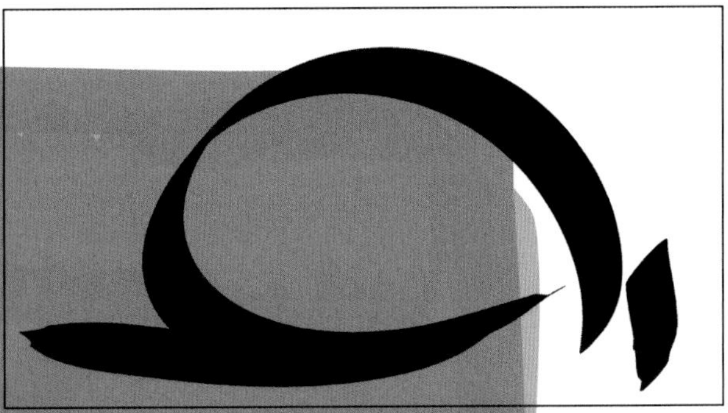

fig. 4.86

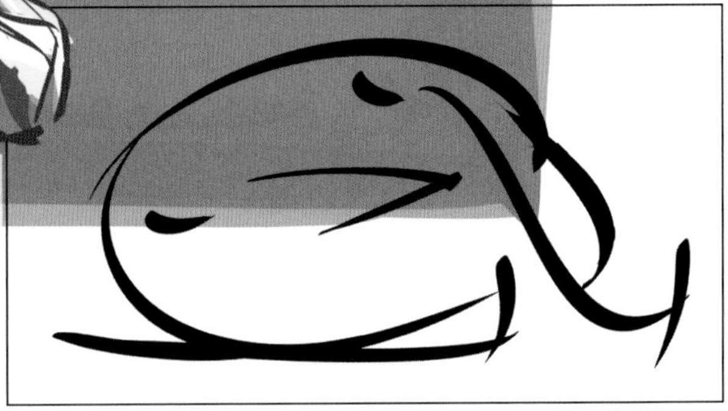

fig. 4.87

Figs. 4.85 to **4.90**: The subject we are drawing or painting (landscape, person, animal, interior, etc.) is our excuse to picture the energy we need to represent the narrative moment: electric, peaceful, soothing, mysterious. And it is this sort of energy that we will establish, first through the use of shape, light, dynamics, etc., the combination and contrast of all these elements, how we stretch them, squeeze them, align them, throw them out of balance (unsettling), put together (claustrophobic), spread them apart (isolation), and emphasize diagonals (action), horizontals (calm), verticals (balance), circles (soft), squares (strong), angles (sharp). All these will put together the emotion we are trying to convey.

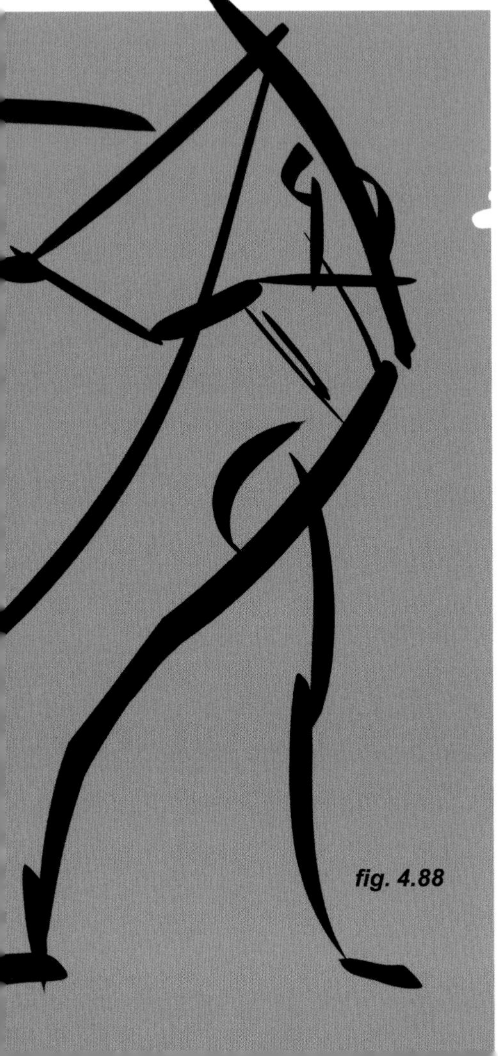

fig. 4.88

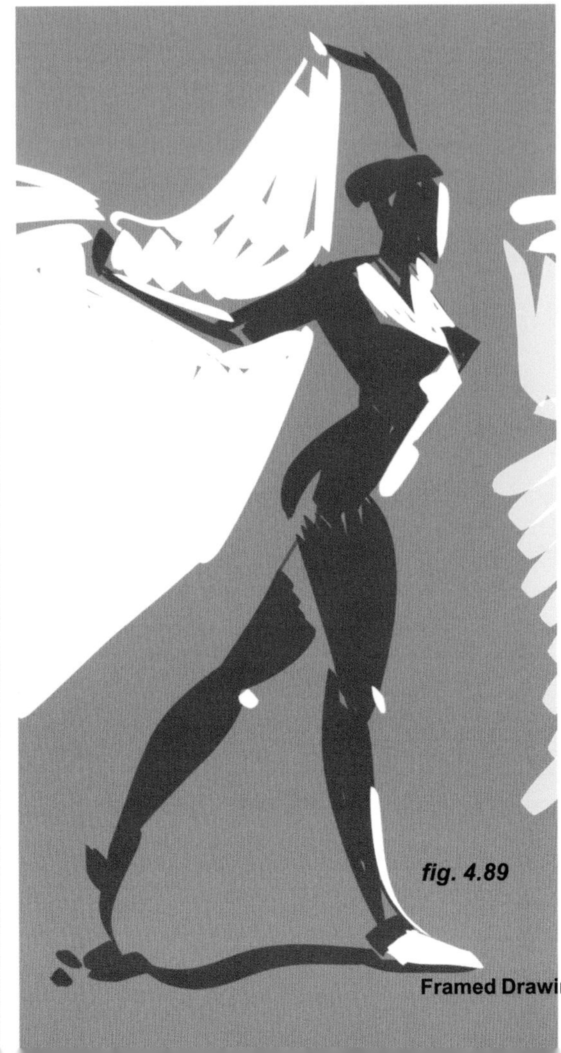

fig. 4.89

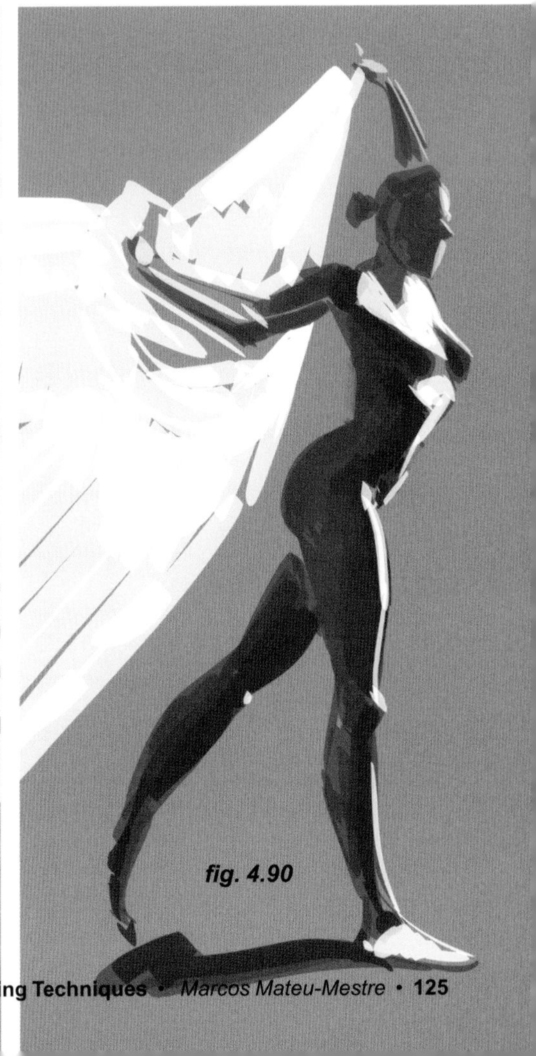

fig. 4.90

A quick, gray gradation painting (including the extremes of black and white) is a great way to visualize the artistic direction of a shot, depending on its narrative intention.

Fig. 4.91: Here is an example of a pure black-and-white sketch and its conversion into different story-point options through different technical and artistic solutions.

Fig. 4.92: In this shot a strong visual link has been established between the police team and the city below them. The city has become its own character through its under lit strong statement, which turns the location into an equally important player within the action.

Fig. 4.93: The emphasis here is on the firepower display of the cops, a sense of vibrant action, rather than the one of mission or purpose illustrated in the previous shot.

Fig. 4.94: Here the dry and dusty backdrop tells of a more difficult environment, like a wild animal lurking in the shadows waiting for the prey to get any closer. Also, due to the fact that there is more light in general, there is the opportunity to play with characters' expressions, reactions, and dialogue.

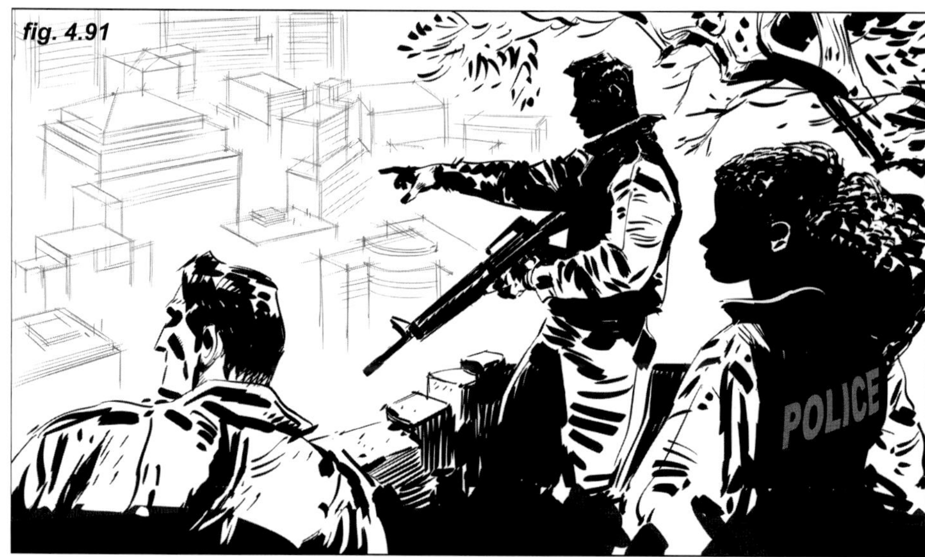

fig. 4.91

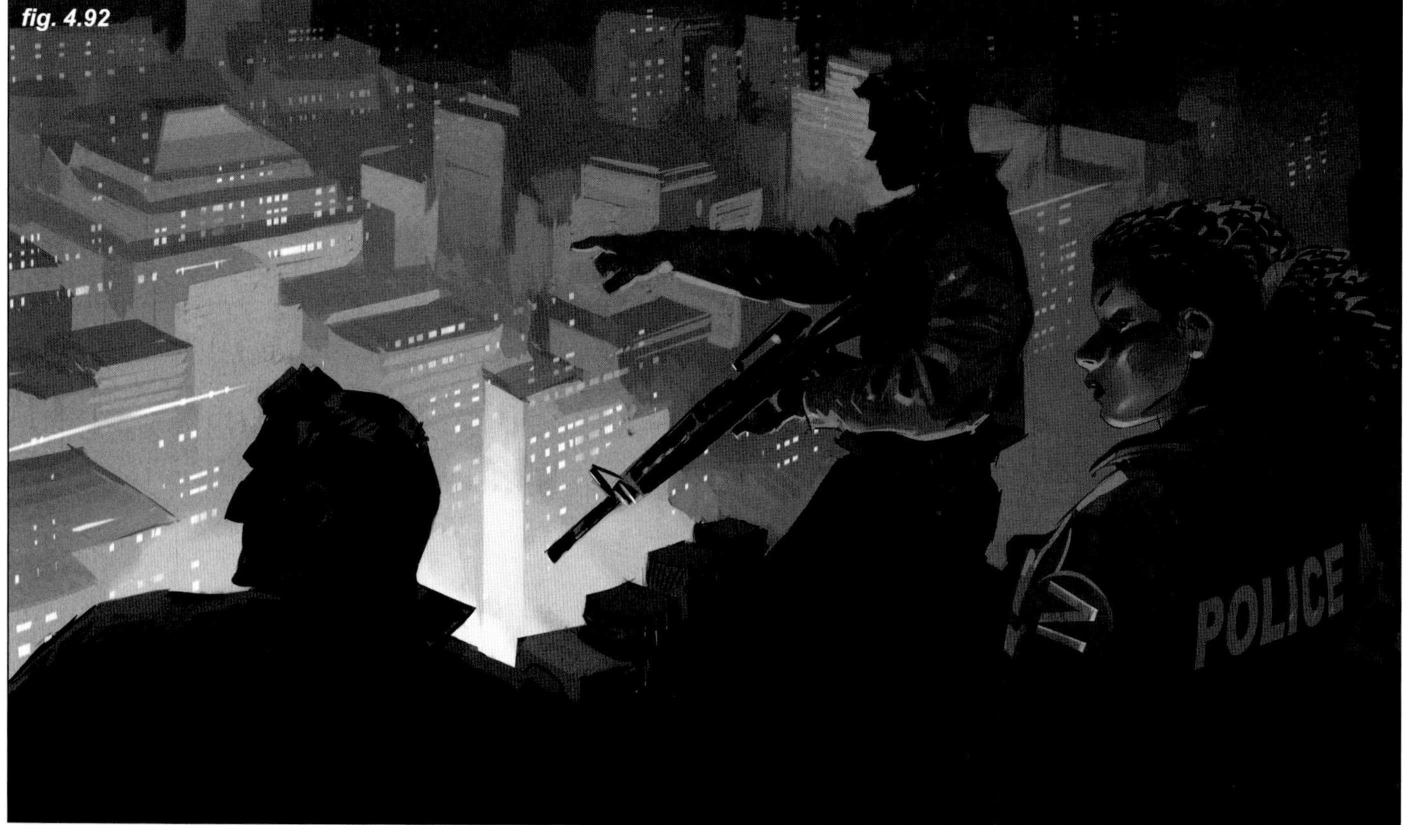

fig. 4.92

fig. 4.93

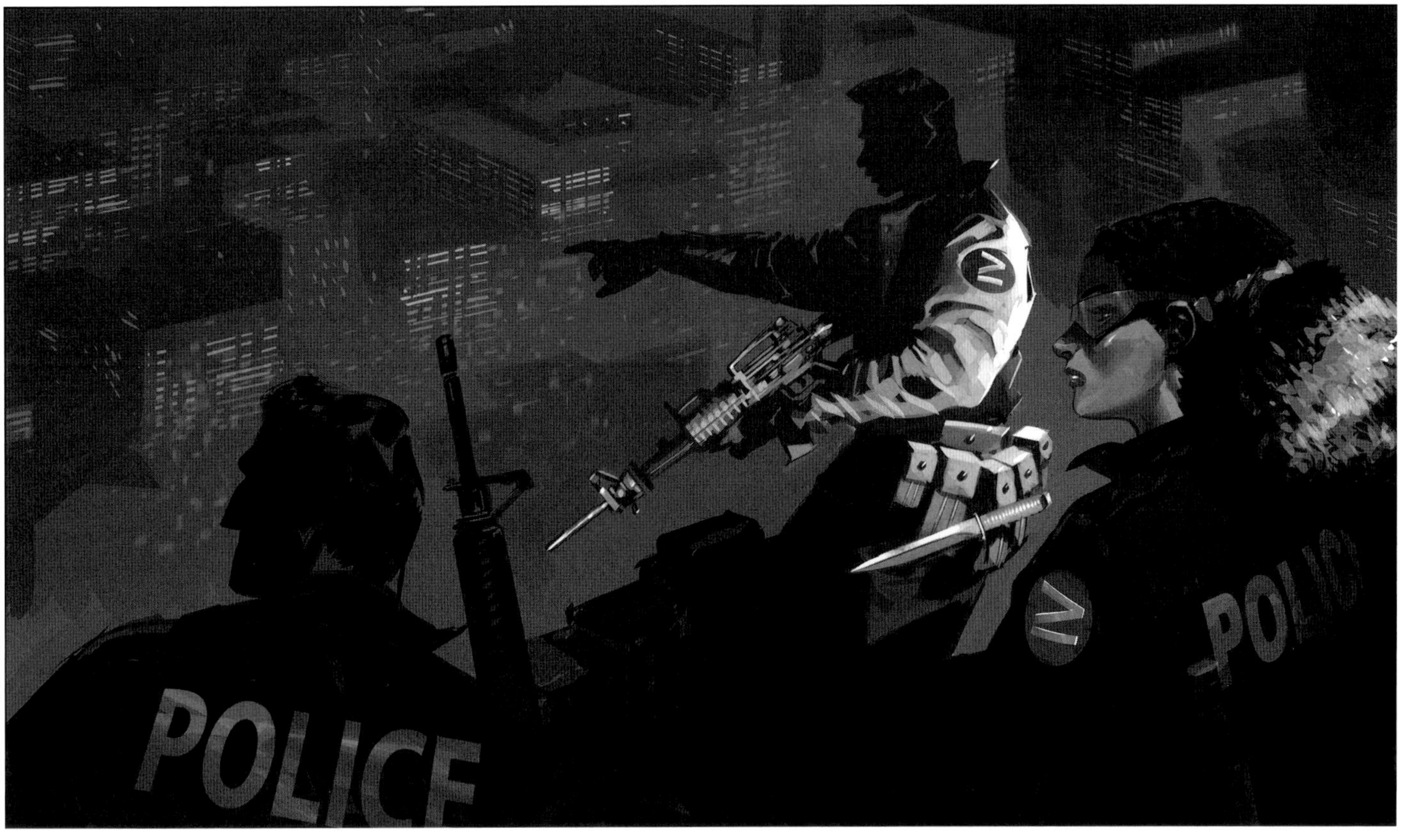

fig. 4.94

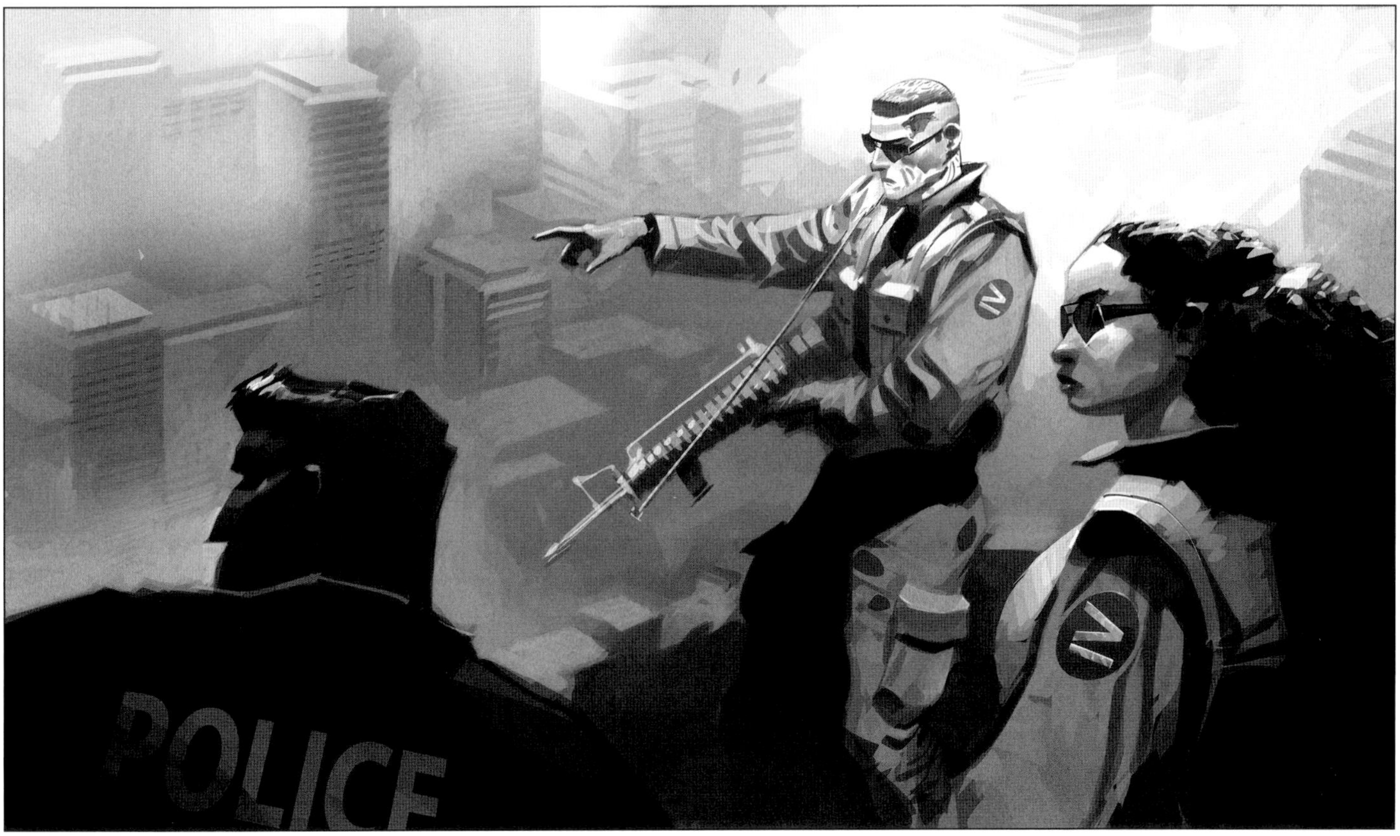

So after all that's been said and the practical examples displayed, here are a few things that you can do to employ these concepts. These are reference-based exercises that will give you a better, practical understanding of how all these techniques can help you better tell moments and stories visually.

SECTION 1

Take color photographs of interesting landscapes preferably with a variety of tonal values in them. Also capture street scenes with buildings, characters, and vehicles, and on different days and weather and lighting conditions, but always from the same angle.

Do black-and-white drawings based on these photographs using different techniques and tools: pen, graphite, and ink (digital, or traditional brush and ink). For this, squint your eyes to see only the bold, visually graphic statements the image offers.

Keep trying to simplify your visual statements.

See how each technique can bring up different visual takes on the same scene:

- the detail of the pen
- the subtle gradations and reflected lights of the graphite
- the vigorous brushstroke and boldness of the brushes' (digital or traditional) black and white

SECTION 2

Now scan and digitally desaturate these reference photographs 100 percent into black and white and then gradually push the contrast of these so that you have three options:

- a full-range grayscale tone
- an almost black-and-white image with a reduced numbers of gray values
- a pure black-and-white image without midtones

Analyze these new photo versions and compare them with the drawings you have previously done. Think about what you are satisfied with and what you now think could have been done better in terms of synthesizing the image.

Draw them again after this analysis, and see how and where they have now improved.

SECTION 3

Choose a few photographs or stills that feel like something you would see in a movie or in a graphic novel, an interesting composition with characters and a compelling environment.

Now choose an element of the photograph you want to stand out, an element of your choice that you want to make the shot, the "story" about: a person, a car, a building, how crowded the street is, how empty it is. Make your next drawing about that (through the use of lighting, framing devices, contrast, cropping in or widening out the frame, etc.) and try to emphasize the feeling that this storytelling element provides.

Once you have made the different story points in different drawings, write down on separate pieces of paper the emotion or point you were trying to convey on each image.

Show the drawings and the pieces of paper (with the concept written on them) to a friend and ask him/her if they can match the image with the concept. This way you'll see if you nailed the exercise or if you need to do it again, now with the experience you have under your belt.

SECTION 4

Next, go ahead and do the opposite: create similar emotions with very different visual elements. Express joy, for example, with a circus scene using the dynamic responses and expressions of the kids in the audience, and then do it with penguins in the arctic by showing how a penguin dad and mom care for their baby underneath a beautiful blue sky. Again, write down on paper a number of different emotions and ask a friend to match your drawing with the right emotion.

The possibilities are endless so get pen and paper and use them to your advantage. All these prove that it's not about the physical elements we have, but how we combine them, show them, and play with them.

Always use your techniques proficiently and make sure you don't lose track of what you want to tell while also making a drawing with strong visual/artistic values.

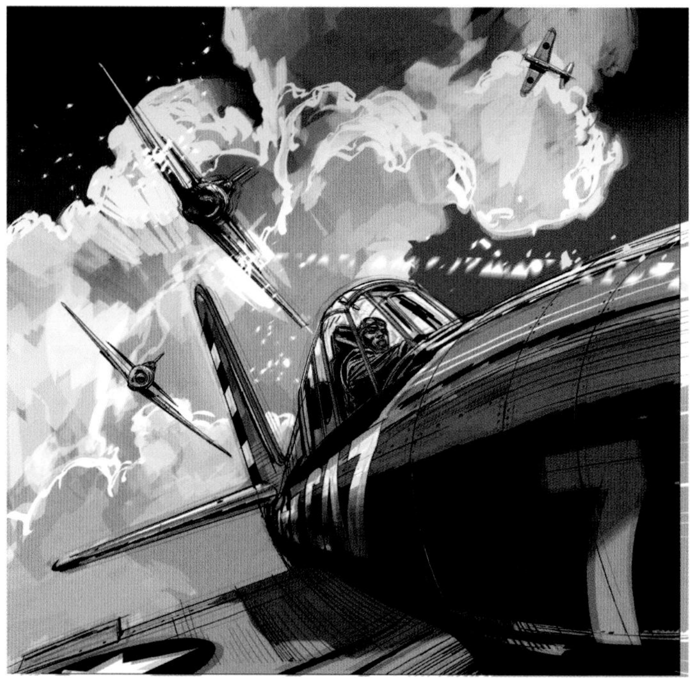

OUR DAILY JOURNEY INTO TERRA INCOGNITA

Alright then, I am closing "the store" for today.

Remember, before starting any piece of artwork, take a moment or two (or three) to think about and understand what that bit of story is. You can write down on paper what it is about, the one or two main things that you are trying to communicate with each shot, and why is it necessary. Is it about anger, love, mystery, doubt, confidence? Is it a necessary pause, is it a bit of important information, is it telling us something new about the characters, the time period in which their story happens? Does it add to the romance, or the tension of the moment?

Once you are clear about this, then organize the visual ingredients of your scene (characters, landscape elements, a balcony, a castle, an airplane interior, the time of day, weather, a lighting situation) in a cinematic way through the use of a camera angle or lens, or lighting and editing— what you want to show as well as what you want to leave out of the shot, etc.—so that you make sure the panel tells that thing you need to tell.

Enjoy what you are doing because the frustration of something not working out well for you today will put a big smile on your face the day it does, no matter how long it takes.

And remember, the physical support that allows us to put all these visualized narrative ideas on paper is the knowledge of the drawing techniques, some of which we have seen and talked about in this book.

Selecting the one you want to work with for a specific job or story is very important, as this will enhance certain narrative aspects that will wrap your work in the appropriate visual language.

Using a pen can, for example, bring up the intricate detail of a story that happens in say the 17th century. The subtleties of a graphite pencil could show delicacy in a romantic or emotional story, or bring in the mystery of a spy adventure, or talk about the life of an artist with all its nuances. The bold use of blacks can perfectly cater to a horror or an action story. Keep in mind most techniques can deliver for most types of stories if you manage to take all the juice you can out of them for the purpose you need.

The same way a live-action cinematographer will choose a specific type of film, or just go digital, or use natural or artificial light, color or black and white, we do have an array of possibilities in front of us.

Regardless, the whole process is always very challenging, giving us the opportunity to discover new things every day and be a better artistic version of ourselves as time goes by.

Guaranteed we won't learn everything or find all the solutions in a single moment—that doesn't happen (not to me, at least)—and we all have different ways, paths, and speeds at which we learn things, so enjoy what you are doing because the frustration of something not working out well for you today will put a big smile on your face the day it does, no matter how long it takes. And once you get a solid understanding of something in your daily journey of discovery, find the next opportunity to get out of your comfort zone and venture into new horizons, again.

Always keep your eyes open to the world around you, how things look, how things feel. Also pay attention to all artwork, movies, illustrations, graphic novels, sketches, etc. available through either books, films, or definitely online. The digital world now gives us casual, everyday access to so much of what is being produced daily by so many amazing artists at so many different corners of the globe.

At the same time, do not be overwhelmed by all this, make sure you are selective, keep track of the works and people who somehow speak to you. Chances are you will see some of your thoughts reflected in the work of quite a few artists who apply what you understand are correct artistic solutions to specific artistic problems. And this, together with your thinking, hard work, practice, and experimentation will help you develop your own personal voice and vision one step at a time.

Thanks for giving me the opportunity to share these ideas with you. My hope is that this work and examples will help clarify a number of things and also motivate you to take your own paths of exploration and to solidify your ideas.

Visually telling stories is a fascinating journey of discovery, and it's always a great feeling when the breeze starts pushing your sail toward the horizon. It doesn't get a lot better than that.

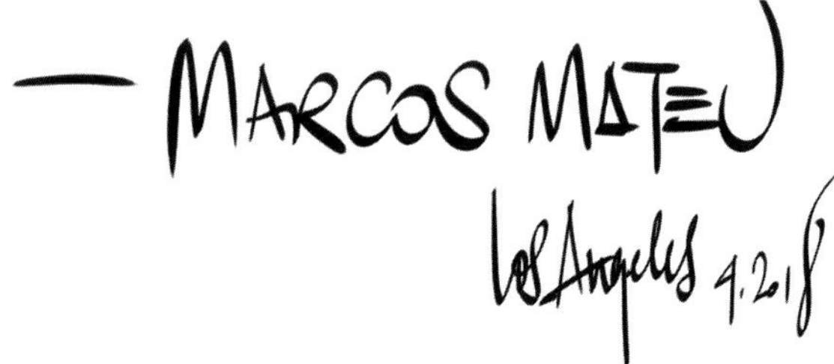

INTERVIEW WITH THE AUTHOR

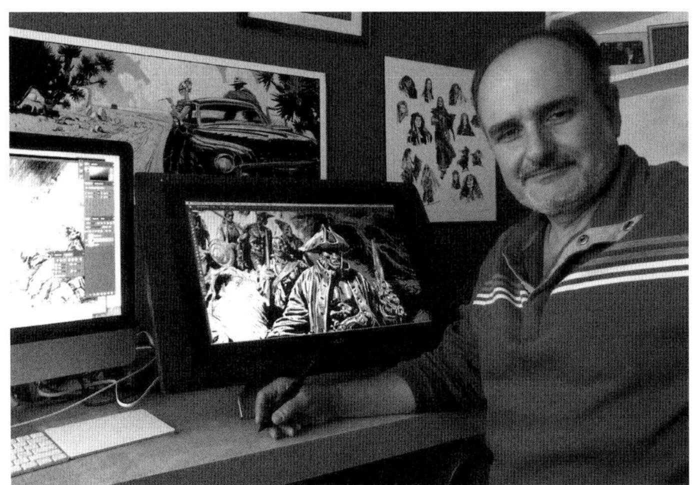

"I got to the best places in my life usually after hitting rock bottom first, because a true reaction is then needed. Same with art: the more we get ourselves into trouble, the more we grow."

Marcos Mateu-Mestre is a visual concept, traditional animation layout, and graphic novel artist with almost three decades years of experience in feature animation. Some of his film credits include ***Balto***, ***The Prince of Egypt***, ***Asterix and the Vikings***, ***Surf's Up***, and ***How to Train your Dragon 2***. His work in film, primarily for DreamWorks Animation and Sony Pictures Animation, has focused on the design and cinematic aspects of frame composition, lighting, and visual continuity—experience he shared in his international best-seller, *Framed Ink: Drawing and Composition for Visual Storytellers*. In addition to his work in film, for more than a decade, he has taught drawing, illustration, and visual storytelling techniques.

Editor Teena Apeles spoke to the Los Angeles–based artist to gain more insight into his artistic process and where he gets his inspiration.

The level of workmanship in your drawings is awe-inspiring, a level so many people work toward, which can be a very tiring and intense process. What would you say to aspiring artists as they go through this process?

Sometimes we, as artists, are going to get into frustrating and even very frustrating situations trying to draw this and that, things we've only dared to look at from the outside before, assuming we would not be able to draw them well given their extreme complexity, extreme simplicity, or lack of apparent interest. But we need to get in there, even if we do not get very good results for a while. We might eventually get to master that, or maybe just get, for now, to a level good enough so that we can feel we managed to get onto the right path, with the opportunity to always revisit it later on and progress, one step at a time.

How have you dealt with obstacles to your growth?

For me, the more I get in trouble the better. I got to the best places in my life usually after hitting rock bottom first, because a true reaction is then needed. Same with art: The more we get ourselves into trouble, the more we grow. The more we can then look back and realize the importance of the path traveled, the overall progress. That means taking on challenges.

When working as an artist or designer, this means taking opportunities to step out of your comfort zone, to discover the appeal and the beauty you didn't see at a first glance in a project and then learn how to approach it in a way that will turn it into something valuable and exciting. For example, it might be easy to make a battle scene look visually interesting, but can I make the image of a fork on a table look equally meaningful and engaging?

I've always been an admirer of many fantastic, talented artists who I know got there despite adverse circumstances, sometimes with families or social environments that did not care much or understand what art was about. Yet, regardless, they became references I learned so much from. While others didn't have to struggle against something to somehow become a better artist every day, maybe they were born in places where artistic expression was accepted as a legitimate way of understanding life. I am among them; it was my luck of the draw.

With so many influences, it can be difficult to distinguish one's style, voice, from others. What do you tell your students about this?

To be aware of what their take on things is, their point of view on things as a result of their own experiences as opposed to imitating someone else's. Copying other artists happens when one is enamored with the way somebody else represents things on paper, with the appearance of it. It is an exercise of pure admiration for other people's understanding of things, missing the point of expressing one's own perspective.

I read an interview with a number of graphic novel artists many years ago. They were all asked at some point, "Who are your favorite peers?" All of them answered with the names of several talented artists many of us have learned so much from. Only one of the interviewees had a unique response: "Any artist I can look at his [or her] work and immediately say, 'I know who did this.'"

Back in the day I thought, *"How about someone whose work is immediately recognizable yet not very good?"* Over time, I adjusted my position on this. Sure, solid talent and technique are essential to a valuable body of work, but so is having one's own voice, a special idea and interpretation of things.

I believe we all received (and consciously or unconsciously keep receiving) inspiration, influence, and knowledge from other artists we admire. It is not only legit and common, but also unavoidable to look for all the help one can find, especially at the early stages of the artistic experience. Though this help should only *inform* our understanding of things, never *take over*.

Who are some of your influences?

My first encounter with comics was through the Spanish version of *The Adventures of Tintin* comic in the mid '60s, when I was about four or five years old. Hergé (Georges Remi) was the master who taught so many of us about pacing and atmosphere: their importance and significance within a story, how every moment and situation has a place, and how nothing can replace a good sense of suspense, mystery, and intrigue, as well as making things believable through the support of good visual references.

I also remember from that time the stories of Ric Hochet by Tibet (Gilbert Gascard), especially *Mystère à Porquerolles*, which felt very close to home as the captivating action was taking place on a Mediterranean island while I was growing up just a few miles away in Mallorca. Not to mention *Colonel Clifton* by Raymond Macherot, with that opening scene with a view of the Houses of Parliament in the middle of a quiet (somehow eerie) and rainy night in London right before a big diamond gets stolen. These things stay with you for life. I still think these stories are amazing today at age 55. Imagine being five, newly arrived on the planet, and getting the first glimpses of all the possibilities still ahead.

My second big moment of discovery was the day when my parents came back home with a copy of the Spanish magazine *Trinca* in the very early '70s. For years I had been doing nothing but drawing but didn't know exactly what to do with my artistic passion so that I could integrate it into my life in a permanent way. That question was quickly resolved the second my eyes saw a page of *Mathai-Dor* by Master Victor De La Fuente. No more questions after that, I can tell you. Comics were the answer—telling character stories through sequential drawings.

And then just a few pages later, *El Cid*, by the other Master, Antonio Hernandez Palacios, a man who didn't just draw gorgeous comics—it was way more than that—he was bringing history and its epic characters into your hands, live.

Not a bad five minutes.

After that it was all constant inspiration from seeing the work of some of the best artists in my opinion to ever live (those were two fantastic decades indeed): Jesus Blasco Monterde (who taught me a lot in a few visits to his Barcelona studio), Hugo Pratt, Alberto Breccia, Frank Frazetta, Jean Giraud, José Luis Salinas, Arturo Del Castillo, Milton Caniff, Frank Robbins, Sergio Toppi, and so many more. As artists, we can never thank these people enough for the legacy they left behind.

Can you pinpoint what it was about these artists' works that drew you to them?

We always admire our idols for a number of reasons. For me, this admiration is because of their skill, mastery, and technical abilities, but also due to something more personal: recognition of their work's capacity to resolve specific visual challenges that I also always considered an important issue and a priority. This shared point of view creates a personal bond between this artist's work and myself the moment I say, "This person pays attention to the same things I consider important in a drawing and resolves issues in a way that I agree with."

These important things can include the actual use of a type of line, the representation of textures in objects, the capacity to express volume, the emotions on characters' faces, body posture language, convincing lighting, a sense of rendering; essentially they are the visual solutions I was looking for at the beginning of my life as an artist and had difficulty finding. And these talented people were offering me direction the same way an art school teacher would in a classroom or studio.

Do you see the impact they have on your own work?

It is only natural that influences will always be visible in an artist's work. Beyond the people that painted those incredible animal and hunter silhouettes on the caves of Lascaux, Altamira, Kondoa Irangi, or the Canyonlands to name a few, I would say not many people have been really free of influences after that. Regardless, as long as influences are only used as a starting point or part of a base to something else that one will eventually own and on which to build a personal voice and body of work, then their use has a solid validity to it.

We will, from time to time, have the very unusual, and therefore very celebrated, game changers—people with a vision and understanding of things that even while dealing with the same elements most people play with, will look at them, rearrange, and resolve them in ways that represent a major departure from pretty much anything done before: the Picassos, Monets, Leonardos, Velazquezs, Mozarts, Hypatias, Marie Curies, and Einsteins.

Do you encourage your drawing students to experiment in other mediums?

I've had pupils that were always looking for additional points of view. Some pupils took oil painting classes, some would attend photography courses after hours to learn how to look through different lenses to have firsthand experience of how that would impact an image and how to apply that to the stories they wanted to tell. This approach will definitely make us better when it comes to finding paths and solutions, making the look of our work richer, more complete and sophisticated. As long as we manage to communicate what we need to communicate, we can either use these techniques individually or combined.

What attracts you to someone's work, for instance when you're choosing something to enjoy in your free time?

Needless to say, I am for great characters and stories. At the same time, personally, even when someone recommends a graphic novel to me on the basis of the story alone, if I can't connect with its visuals at a first pass, it will be very difficult for me to take the next step and start reading it.

When I say, "connect with its visuals," I don't mean just a number of pretty pictures to look at. They might be, but I'm talking more about something I could find engaging, expressive, and appealing at one level or another—something that I find telling about the characters and the story at a first glance, something that resonates as the type of atmosphere and pacing I think would match the kind of tale I'm about to read. And this could be realistic, stylized, extremely stylized, abstract, childlike, with an energetic brushstroke, or maybe a very soothing one, but always with a lot of character, the "right" character, and certainly with a good level of technique. Then I'm all in.

What challenges do you face now after all these years as an artist, outside of the professional sphere?

Art seems to have a basic dual aspect to it, with its intense flow of energy on one side and the actual discipline of drawing, physical representation of this energy on paper, on the other: all the enthusiasm and intensity of the early process, to eventually trying to tie everything down with as solid of a technique as possible.

The search for a balance between these two elements, raw energy vs. technique, can be an interesting process. I'll say in my case, I first had to realize I had an issue with it before working toward a solution. It happened years ago after running into drawings I had done much earlier, which seemed to have a freer quality than my "better technically resolved" latest. I then realized that being so focused on technique, I had gone past quite a few stops in this pursuit, to the point that it was definitely affecting the communicative aspect of my artwork.

That's when the conscious search for this forgotten freedom and looseness started, while believing that all I had done, worked for, and progressed toward in terms of technical knowledge would still be there even if I momentarily let go of it while pursuing more expressive ways I had departed from in the past.

Has developing technology helped you on this front?

Freeing one's mind has become a bit easier in the last decades with the rise of digital technologies, as they facilitate the process of editing the things we are not happy with in a drawing or a painting, in a fast and clean way. One has to worry less about the possibility of error, which considerably frees the mind and helps it better explore this ideal balance between expressivity and technique.

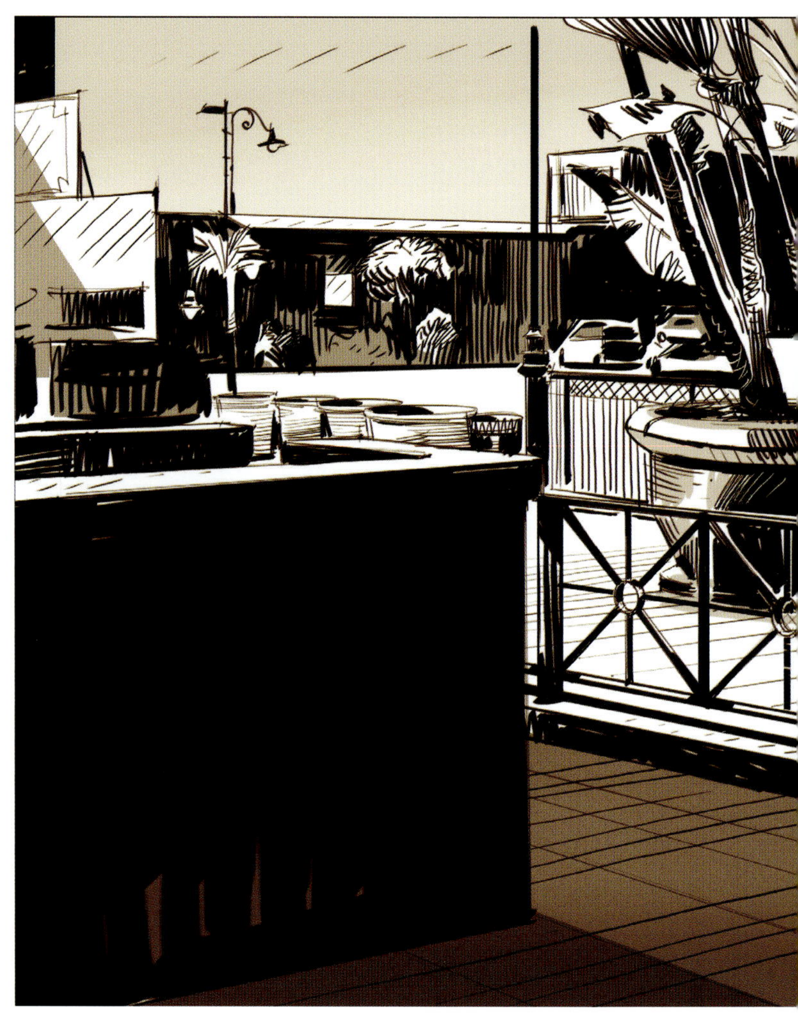

What we now call "traditional" used to be the only means available to produce artwork, both fine art and commercial. On the commercial side, since its final destination was to be printed or used in the process of making a movie, for example, rather than be shown as an original, whenever an illustration, comics page, panel, or even section of a panel was not 100 percent satisfactory to its author, he or she usually would edit the original by cutting off and replacing the undesired part, or even cover such problematic area with Wite-Out and then rework on top of it.

Now, when working commercially (for printing, film industry, etc.), it's great to have all these tools, old and modern, available. Nowadays any art produced by graphite, ball pen, marker, etc., can be scanned and easily edited, if that's our choice, with the use of the appropriate software. What was literal cut-and-paste or Wite-Out in the past has now become digitized.

Now that you have four books in the* Framed *book series, what can fans expect from you next?

I'm always thinking of something new. I have to tell you, producing these books is a real challenge to me, and a great experience. Up to a degree, I have to adapt things like my drawing style to the subject and spirit of each one of them. For example, in *Framed Ink* I could go at the artwork more loosely since it was all about the energy of the shot, and how to convey this to the viewer.

For my two *Framed Perspective* books I had to control my style a bit more, be a little tighter, a bit more formal somehow, simply because it had to match the main subject of these two volumes: technical perspective. So I couldn't really go as loose with my characters as I did in *Framed Ink*, nor have a level of disassociation between characters and environments. I mean perspective can be approached loosely as well, of course, but not so much in an instructional book, where you are trying to establish clear technical principles for people to have as a solid guide.

What I'm saying is that besides enjoying the actual process of making these books, there is also an exciting sense of challenge for me that turned each book into an actual artistic adventure, a learning experience, and a part of my growth and process.

Whatever is next—and there will be next—will also be a product of this passion and will, in a way and within logical parameters, reshape my approach to drawing and make each drawing I do feel like my first. I'm certainly not into driving on automatic pilot.

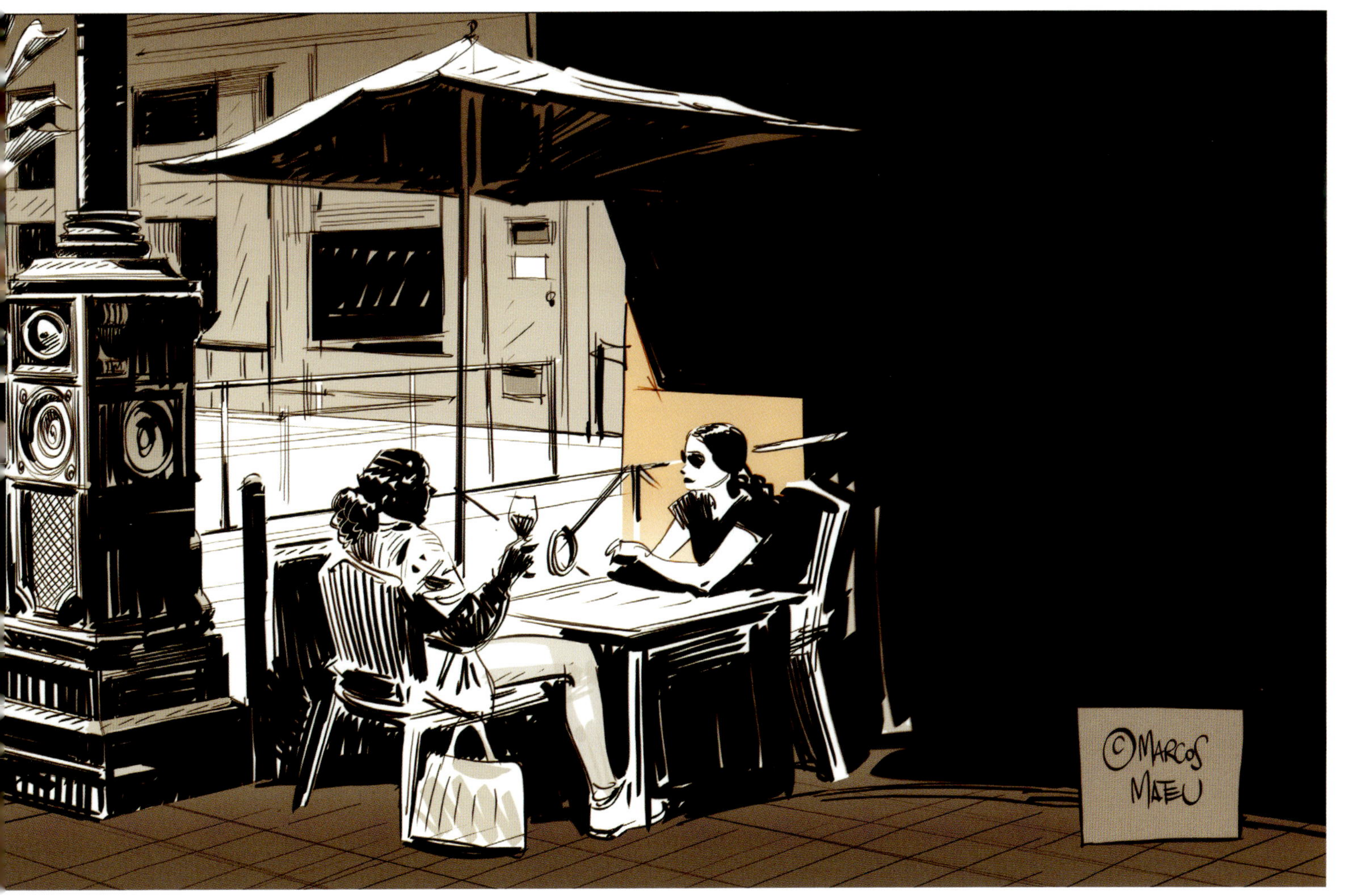

INDEX

R

S

T

V

W

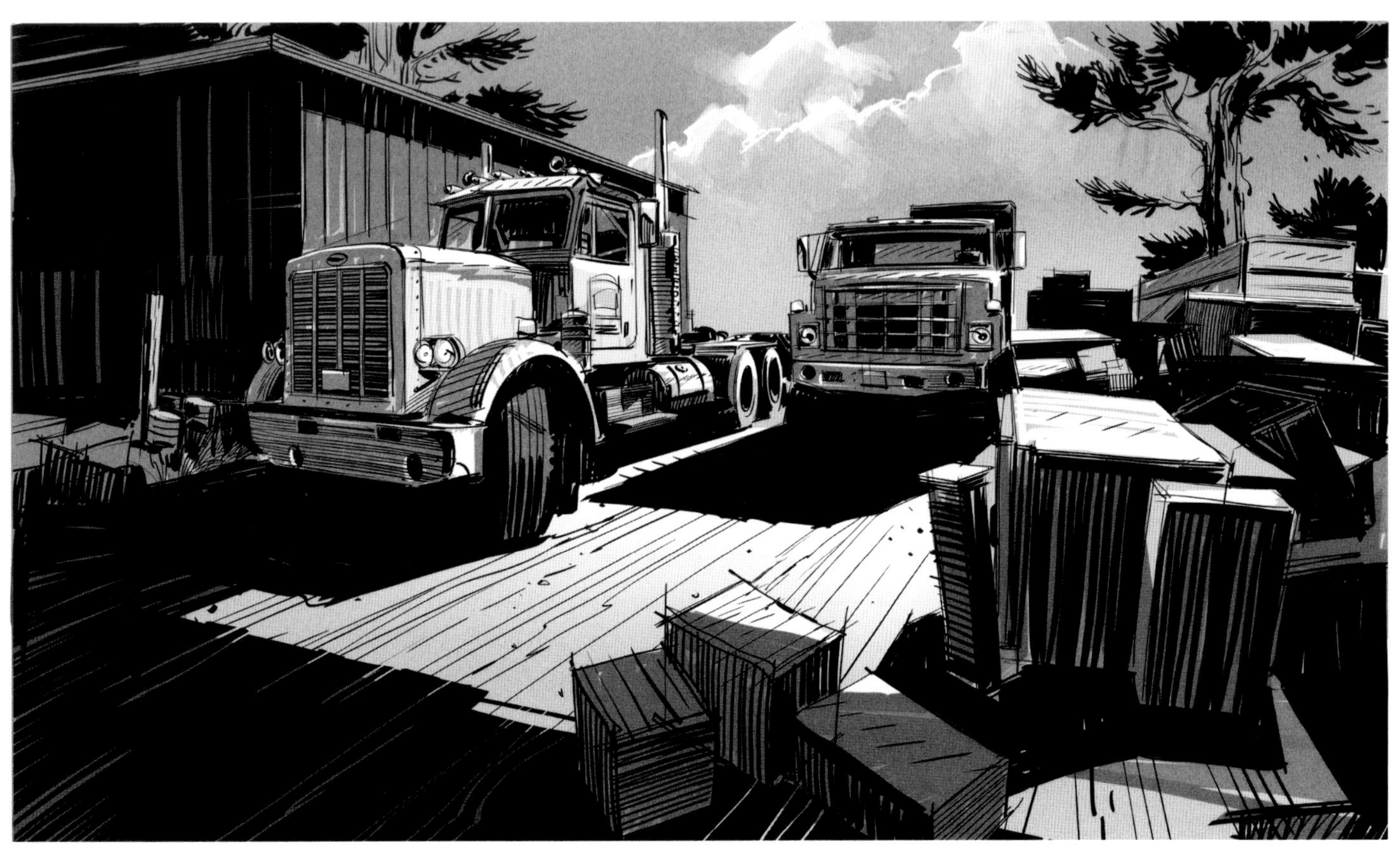

ALSO FROM MARCOS MATEU-MESTRE

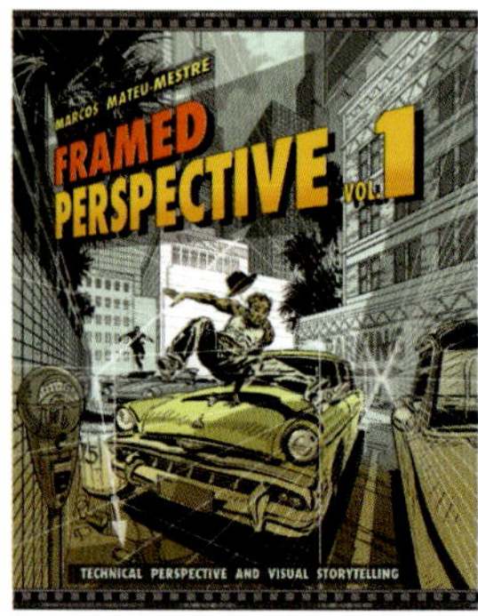

Paperback: 978-162465030-7

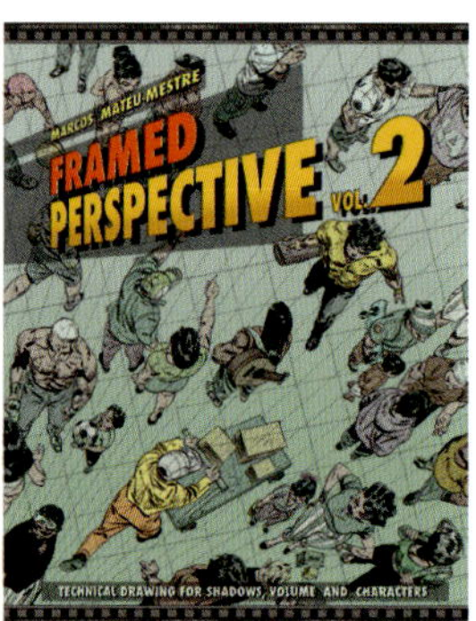

Paperback: 978-162465032-1

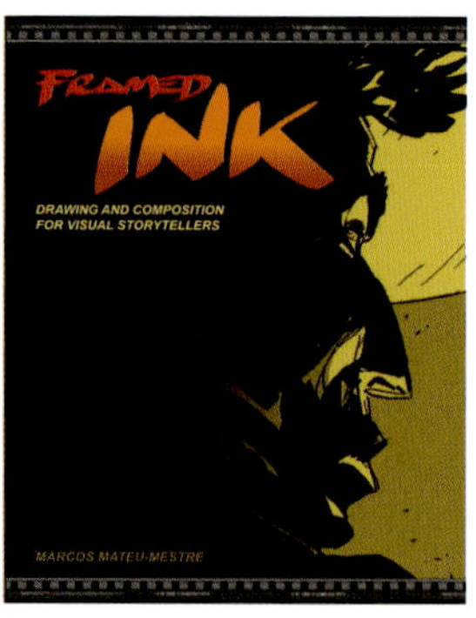

Paperback: 978-193349295-7

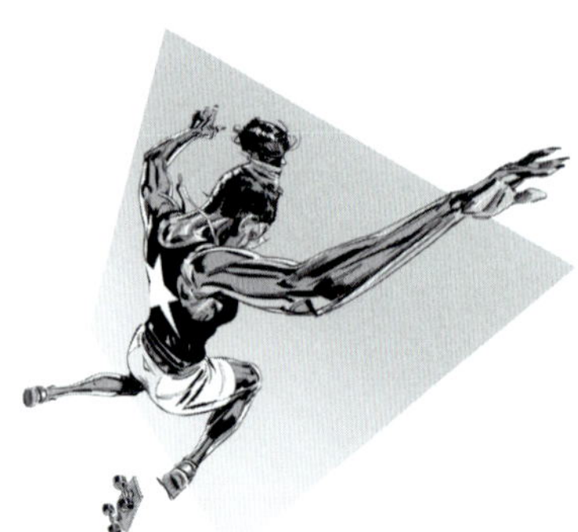

OTHER TITLES BY DESIGN STUDIO PRESS

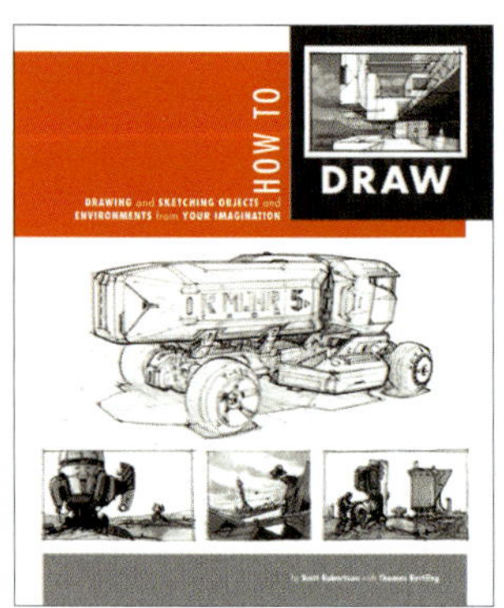

Paperback ISBN: 978-193349273-5
Hardcover ISBN: 978-193349275-9

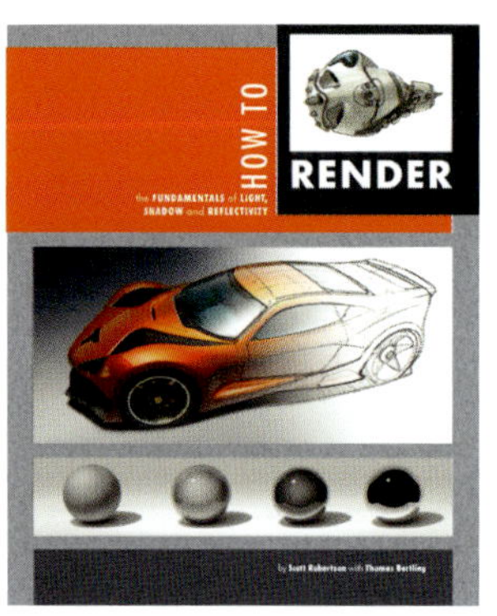

Paperback ISBN: 978-193349296-4
Hardcover ISBN: 978-193349283-4

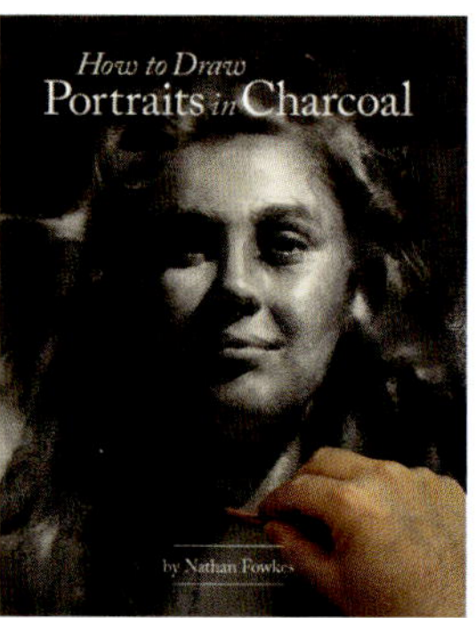

Paperback: 978-162465031-4

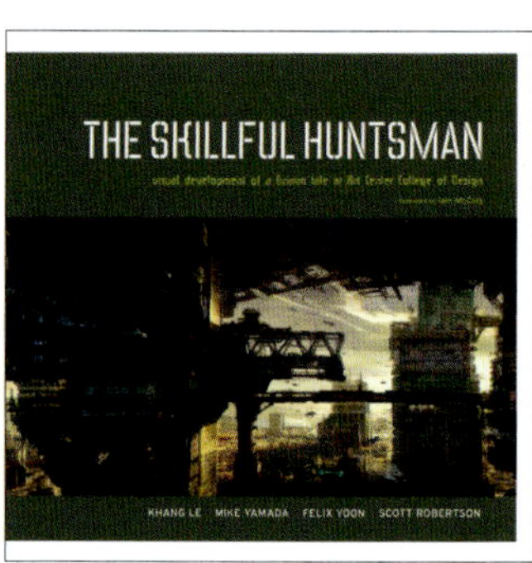

Paperback: 978-097266764-7

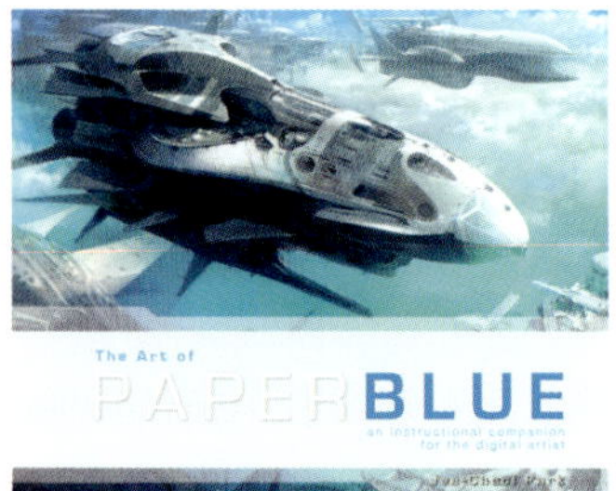

Paperback ISBN: 978-162465014-7

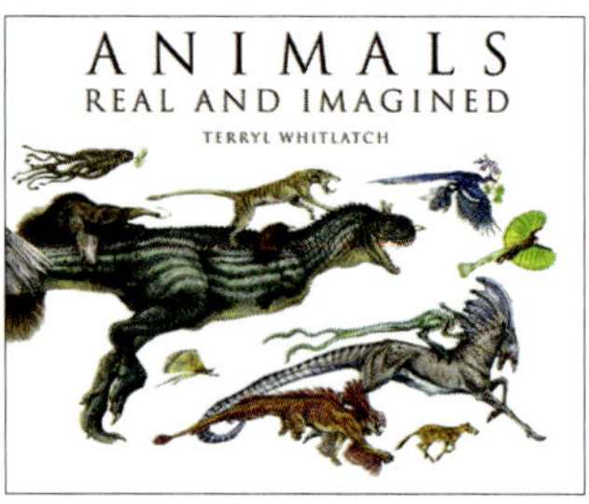

Paperback ISBN: 978-193349292-6
Hardcover ISBN: 978-193349291-9

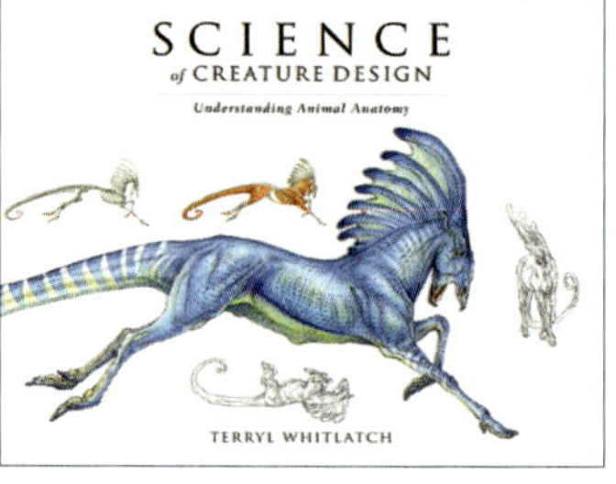

Paperback ISBN: 978-193349256-8
Hardcover ISBN: 978-162465029-1

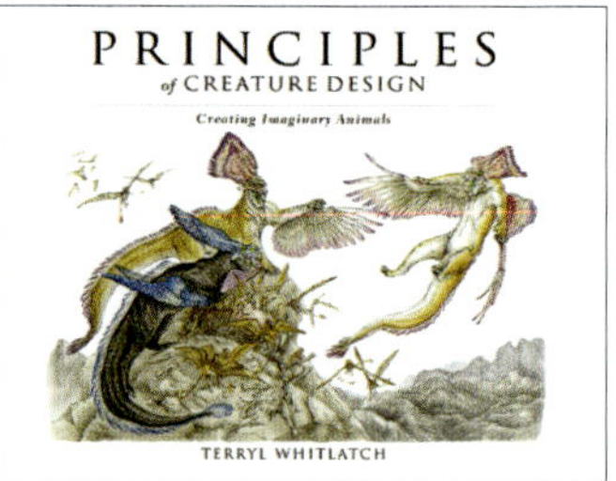

Paperback ISBN: 978-162465021-5
Hardcover ISBN: 978-162465028-4

To order additional copies of this book, and to view other books we offer, please visit:

www.designstudiopress.com

For volume purchases and resale inquiries, please email: info@designstudiopress.com

tel: 310.836.3116

To be notified of new releases, special discounts, and events, please sign up for our mailing list on our website. Like our Facebook page and follow us on Twitter:

facebook.com/designstudiopress
twitter.com/DStudioPress

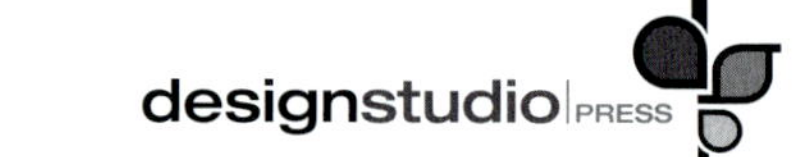